CW01584043

THE DNA OF MARKETING

Ira S. Kalb

THE DNA OF MARKETING
Copyright©2005 by Ira S. Kalb
©2005 by DNA Press, LLC. All rights reserved.

All rights reserved under International and Pan-American Copyright conventions. No part of this book may be reproduced or transmitted in any form or by any means, electronic or mechanical, including photocopying, recording, or any information storage and retrieval system, without permission in writing to DNA Press at the address posted at www.dnapress.com. Published in the United States by DNA Press, LLC.

For information regarding permission write to: DNA Press, LLC, P.O.Box 572, Eagleville, PA 19408, USA or contact: editors@dnapress.com.

ISBN 0-9748765-3-4

Printed in the United States of America on acid free paper.
First Edition

Library of Congress Cataloging-in-Publication DataKalb, Ira S. The DNA of marketing / by Ira S. Kalb.— 1st ed. p. cm. ISBN 0-9748765-3-4 (alk. paper)
1. Marketing. 2. High technology—Marketing. 3. Biotechnologyindustries—Marketing. I. Title. HF5415.K256 2004 658.8—dc22

2004028454

DNA Press, LLC
PO Box 572
Eagleville, PA 19408 USA
www.dnapress.com
editors@dnapress.com

Executive Editor: Alexander Kuklin
Art Direction and Production: Studio N Vision (www.studionvision.com)
Cover Art : Sudio N Vision (www.studionvision.com)

This book is dedicated to all those brilliant people working in the life sciences who understand how to develop lifesaving products, but have trouble marketing and selling them.

ABOUT THE AUTHOR

Ira S. Kalb is President of *Kalb & Associates*, a consulting and training firm that specializes in marketing, sales, management and business systems, *K&A Press*, a publishing firm that publishes books and articles written by *Kalb & Associates* consultants, and *Out-of-this-World Marketing*, a firm that creates marketing materials that effectively sell. He also teaches courses in marketing, international management, business systems and sales for major universities around the world as well as a variety of other organizations and private corporations.

Prior to founding *Kalb & Associates*, he served nine years as Vice-President of Marketing and President of *Compal Computer Systems*, a California corporation 25% owned by *Xerox* that specialized in developing, marketing and installing micro-computer systems and software for businesses. Before joining *Compal*, Mr. Kalb spent six years as a staff and senior consultant with such top firms as *Accenture* and *Economics Research Associates*. This experience has given him an in-depth background in systems, management, and feasibility consulting as well as a staff perspective of a variety of companies in many different industries.

He has written, as well as been featured and quoted in, numerous published articles, and is considered one of the pioneers of the multi-billion dollar microcomputer industry. He has appeared on award-winning TV programs, such as the *NBC* news program *Third Thursday*. He is also the author of the following books available from K&A Press: *Nuts & Bolts Marketing*, *The Fundamentals of High-tech Marketing: What Marketers Need to Know*, *Selling High-tech Products and Services*, *Structuring Your Business For Success*, *Marketing Your Legal Services*, *Zero Budget Marketing*, *Creating Your Own Marketing Makes Good $ & Sense*, and *e-Marketing: What went wrong... How to do it Right*.

Ira has invented many original marketing concepts that clients and students are employing with great success in the marketplace including the Universal Marketing Structure™, Universal Business Structure™, Universal Sales Structure™, Universal Web Structure™, Moving Buying Window™, Sales Army™, Corporate Image Protection System™, and Lock and Key Positioning™. He has also created award-winning ads, brochures, and other marketing communications for clients.

Mr. Kalb holds a Masters degree in Business Administration and a Bachelor of Science degree in Bio-Engineering Systems from UCLA, where he graduated with honors. He was elected President of the UCLA Graduate School of Management Students Association for the 1972 academic year. During that year, he received the American Marketing Association's award as Outstanding Marketing Student. He was elected President of the American Marketing Association in Southern California for the 1995/96 year, and he has served on the Board of Directors of the Jazz Bakery, one of the world's premiere entertainment venuses.

During high school and college, he partially supported himself by playing saxophone and other woodwind instruments in various musical groups. Along with physical fitness, music and art continue to be his major hobbies, with many of his original paintings adorning the walls of his home and office.

These creative abilities together with Ira's unique combination of experience in line management, staff consulting, and teaching provide him with a rare multi-dimensional perspective of business that he shares with his clients, students, and readers of his books.

TABLE OF CONTENTS

PREFACE

"Why the DNA of Marketing?"

WHY WRITE THIS BOOK?

I have always had a special affinity for, and interest in, science. Upon graduating with a degree in Bio-engineering from UCLA, this bond grew even stronger. After graduating, however, interests and opportunities took me in the direction of business with a special focus on marketing.

Throughout my career, I have marveled at the fact that scientists and engineers who have invented many life-saving products do a very poor job of marketing those products. In fact, too many brilliant inventions never even make it to the marketplace.

Since my expertise is in marketing goods and services others find difficult marketing, I thought I might help those in technical fields by writing this book.

GOOD MARKETING IS IN SHORT SUPPLY

There is very little good marketing being practiced — especially in the life-science, high-technology, biotechnology fields. Typically, most companies start with a product or service idea that is the brainchild of a company inventor. Too often, nobody has bothered to even determine if there is a market for this product or service. Moreover, unless pushed by a "*street-smart*" venture capitalist or business advisor, the decision-makers in the company frequently overlook the importance of marketing. If marketing is considered at all, many essential marketing ingredients are overlooked. Usually, only the more familiar marketing functions of sales and advertising are employed. And because of the absence of a marketing information system using proper market research, the advertising often misses the mark. It usually suffers from appealing to company insiders rather than prospective buyers. In fact, if you look at most life science ads, brochures, Web sites and other communications, it is a miracle that any sales are generated at all. Rather than blame their poor marketing efforts, those who don't understand marketing use the failure of their marketing communications as evidence that marketing doesn't work or matter. This becomes a self-fulfilling prophecy that either hinders sales, or even worse, causes the company to fail.

INEFFECTIVE MARKETING HURTS EVERYONE

All you have to do is pick up any newspaper or magazine, listen to the radio, or watch television, and you will unfortunately see too much ineffective marketing. This hurts everyone — especially when the examples of marketing don't tell the truth or don't properly communicate the intended message. Because of abusers, many equate marketing with lying or stretching the truth. This, of course, hurts all those who do tell the truth in their marketing programs. It also wastes the resources of the companies that are not doing proper marketing. That is, bad marketing just doesn't work over the long run. Confusing or insincere messages don't sell products and services. Whatever is spent on them is wasted money. Moreover, the opportunities to sell more products, boost the firm's Corporate Image, and to create more happy customers who will, in turn, help to increase sales via positive word-of-mouth advertising are lost forever.

It's a fact that everyone ends up paying for a company's marketing inefficiencies. Customers pay higher prices and receive less-desirable products. The company pays in the form of reduced revenue and profits. Employee's pay via reduced compensation and opportunities for advancement, and sometimes they pay by becoming victims of layoffs. Vendors pay by receiving smaller and fewer orders. Government pays by collecting less taxes on reduced profits. Stockholders and owners pay in the form of lower dividends and reduced stock prices. And society pays by having fewer available job opportunities, fewer corporate donors, fewer employed workers who buy products from other businesses, and fewer companies helping to shoulder growing tax burdens. Good marketing, on the other hand, pays for itself many times over by reversing the scenario described above.

I'M ON A MISSION

Since 1972, I have seen so many high-technology companies with brilliant people and inventions fail miserably in the marketplace. Why? Most believed the old cliché that all they had to do is "build a better mousetrap and people would line up to buy it." While they were brilliant in technical areas, they had a low marketing IQ. They did not realize that, to be successful in business, you have to find the buyers of those "mousetraps." You have to determine what they need, develop products to meet their needs, let them know you exist and what you can do for them that your competitors cannot, and make it convenient for them to find, buy and use your products.

The tragedy of the companies described above is that they had almost everything they needed to make themselves and the world better off. What was missing was one ingredient — Marketing expertise.

Properly marketing the products that we need and want makes all of our lives better. It frees us from repetitive and laborious tasks, gives us medical breakthroughs to eradicate disabling diseases and correct physical impairments, improves our educational opportunities, enables us to better communicate with each other around the globe, allows us to travel to far off places in short time spans at affordable prices, and it provides us with new avenues of affordable entertainment. By writing this book, I hope to do my part, however small, to help my readers to successfully market life-improving products and services and, at the same time, strengthen the economy and provide more opportunities for all of us.

NOT MANY PLACES TO REALLY LEARN MARKETING

One of the problems is that it is hard to find a place to learn practical and useful marketing. Anyone who has had the good fortune of receiving a business education from our school systems and universities knows that too many of them don't really teach you what you need to know. For example, even though knowing how to sell is a skill that is essential for success in virtually every walk of life, many universities have decided that teaching *Sales* is not an activity in which lofty educational institutions should be engaged. The ones that do offer sales courses typically make them electives rather than requirements. As a result, too many graduates never learn how to sell themselves, and they have difficulty finding good jobs, getting good promotions, and attracting customers. Even those who major in marketing at the university (I'm speaking from experience as a marketing student and part-time professor) are often led down theoretical paths by inward-thinking professors who use out-of-date textbooks that still teach them that there are only *4 Ps of Marketing*. In the past, once in the job market, a young graduate could learn focused brand-marketing by taking a job with *Procter & Gamble* or high-tech sales by going to work for *IBM*. In recent years, however, certain missteps made by these truly great companies suggest that there is a *new world order in marketing* and that their training programs need to be adjusted accordingly. Competent courses and seminars in marketing do exist, but there are far too few of them, and they are therefore difficult to find. The best (and worst) place to learn is on the job, but that's expensive for everyone, and requires many years of learning by the *making-expensive-mistakes* method. The other problem with this method is that it often promotes and institutionalizes bad habits. The goal of this text is to give readers the fundamental concepts and techniques they need to avoid making expensive mistakes and developing costly bad habits on the job.

POPULAR DEMAND

Many of my clients and students from the technology and life science industries suggested I write this book. They wanted me to go into more depth than I was able to in my client reports and course lectures. They also assured me that many would buy the advice I had to sell. While I hope they are right, I know that one of the worst mistakes marketers can make is to *fall in love* with their own ideas and to lose objectivity. Moreover, as you will learn in this book, often the best products don't survive unless they are properly marketed.

TARGET AUDIENCES

I am optimistic and confident about who can benefit from reading this book. Everyone can. **Students** of marketing can benefit by learning the basic fundamentals and structures, which do not change over time. **Professors** can benefit by giving their students fundamentals and structures that are absent from marketing textbooks on the market. **Marketing professionals** can benefit by both deepening and broadening their understanding of the basic fabric of marketing. They learned from the same books and professors from which I learned, and given the poor track record of marketing campaigns (Phillip Kotler, the author of the most widely-used college texts on marketing has admitted the failure rate is up to 80 percent), they need the fundamentals and structures presented in this book. **Business owners** can benefit from having a better understanding of marketing since the lack of proper marketing is given as one of the primary reasons why most new businesses fail. **Scientists, engineers, musicians** and **artists** can benefit since the most universal reason why many people in these groups are not more successful is that they don't know how to market themselves.

MOVING FORWARD

Now that you know some of my reasons for writing this book, I hope you will find it informative, interesting, and contributory to your success. If you do find it helpful, or if you have suggestions for improvement, I hope you will let me know. All products, no matter how good they are, can be improved. I want to continually improve this one, and your input is invaluable to that process. Thanks for acquiring this book.

Chapter 1

Introduction

It is perhaps the most important, interesting, and misunderstood of all business activities.

WHAT IS MARKETING?

A good place to start a book on Marketing is with a definition of the term — especially since most people associate marketing with advertising or sales. Marketing is *the process by which products (goods and services) are developed and brought to market.* The word "process" means that marketing is continuous and ongoing. While "products" usually refer to both goods and services, they also include ideas, concepts, and other elements that can benefit from being marketed. The word "market" (also known as marketplace) refers to the place where these products are sold. This "place" can be *geographical* such as California, the Northeast, the USA, or the developed world; based on *customer-type* as exemplified by the markets for women, runners, doctors, teenagers, DNA researchers, senior citizens; *product-based* such as the market for computers, automobiles, and legal services; *life-style-based* such as the utilitarian, health, or upscale markets; *socioeconomic* such as the upper, middle, and working class markets; or based on a variety of other grouping criteria. A pictorial description of this process is shown in *Figure 1-1*.

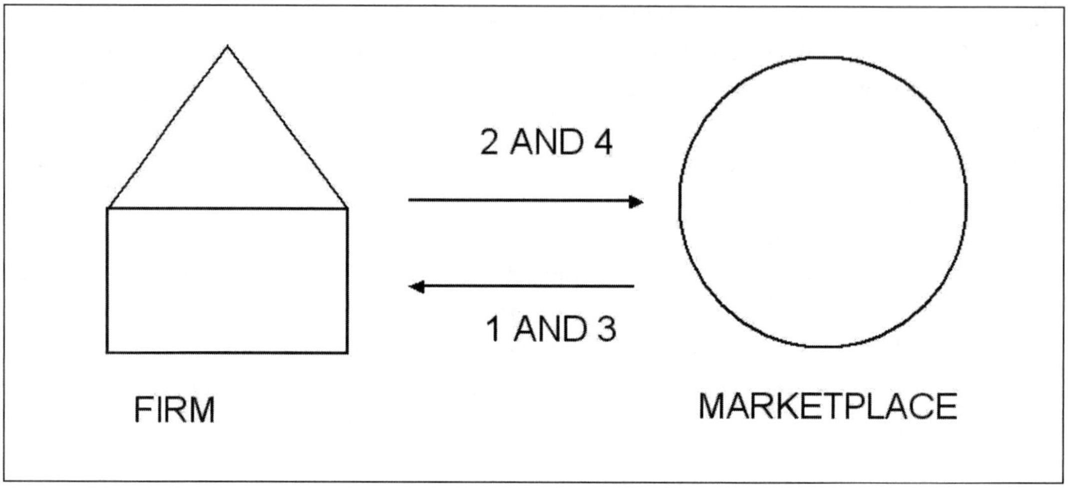

Figure 1-1. The Marketing Process.

1. The firm obtains Information from the market place as to what identified market targets want.
2. The firm creates a marketing plan to achieve company goals. Goals are achieved by giving target markets what they want. To do this, the firm develops marketing strategies to satisfy target market needs and wants - that is the Marketing Mix [Positioning, Product, Place (Distribution), Pricing, and Promotion that will optimally satisfy them].
3. The marketplace gives feedback to the firm on the Positioning, Product, Pricing, Distribution, and Promotion.
4. The firm alters its strategies in light of this feedback. It receives the Product and/or any of the strategies to better satisfy market targets.
5. The above steps are an iterative process, which is repeated until such time as the firm is successfully satisfying customers and products (the market targets).

HOW DOES MARKETING FIT IN THE OVERALL BUSINESS?

When done properly, this process starts in the formative stages of a company's development. Before deciding on the company's raison d'être — or its reason for existing, the market should be investigated to determine the kinds of products (goods and services) that prospective customers, or *market targets*, want. Based on the *Marketing Research* collected, the company's structure, fabric, culture, personnel, and products should be designed or selected to best meet the needs of potential customers. In marketing terminology, companies that follow this market orientation are called *market-driven* or *customer-driven*. In contrast, those companies that organize and develop around a product idea without formal regard for the wants and needs of the marketplace are typically called *product-driven*. That is, a product is developed as the brainchild of some inventor or founder without benefit of the knowledge that there are a sufficient number of people in the marketplace who want to buy it. While many product-driven companies have been successful, they have typically achieved their success with superior technology and in an environment that has little competition — that is, where the customer needs the product but has few alternative places to buy it. They often have considerable difficulty adjusting to the pressures brought by changes in the market environment, such as the entry of formidable competitors.

In addition to *Marketing Research*, the *Marketing process* incorporates a number of other elements. As with the *Periodic Table*, which represents all of the known elements in the universe, or DNA, which represents the building blocks of life, marketing is based on seven basic elements known as the *seven fundamental building blocks of Marketing*. Years ago, there were only four building blocks, known as the *Four P's of Marketing*. Unfortunately, most marketing texts and courses still teach these *Four P's*. Since we want to be more successful and complete, we recognize seven in this book.

THE DNA OF MARKETING

Although each of the *seven fundamental building blocks of marketing* will be discussed in more detail in subsequent chapters of this book, it is useful to introduce them here so you understand how they fit together as you advance through this book.

Corporate Image

Because every company and individual has one, a good one can greatly help to market the company's products, and a bad one can be devastating to the success of the company, corporate image is probably the most logical building block with which to start. Simply stated *Corporate Image* is the *image of the organization* in the minds of its publics. Publics include all the groups with which the organization interacts in its normal course of doing business including customers, prospects, employees (past, present, and future) vendors, stockholders, directors on the board, media, Government, and the local community.

Positioning

Once the image of the organization is defined, it is important to begin the marketing of the company's products with positioning. *Positioning* is the *image of the product*. A more technical definition is *identifying a market segment with an unfilled need and filling that need with a product image*. The reason why *positioning should come first* in the marketing of the firm's products is that once the image of the product is defined, it is much easier to define the *product*, determine the *price*, find the best *place* to sell the product, and determine the best ways to *promote*, or communicate, all of the above to the target audience.

Corporate Image and Positioning

Many people confuse the *corporate image*, or the image of the company, with *positioning*, or the image of the product. This is natural because most companies derive at least part of their image from their products and vice versa. Competent marketers, however, know the importance of keeping these two building blocks separate. By keeping them separate, they can put them together when it is to their advantage. They also know when it is to their advantage to keep them apart. Quite simply, you put them together when they benefit each other without any known risk. You should separate them under the following conditions: (1) the organization or the product has a bad image (example: *ValueJet* airlines); (2) the product is risky and could cause damage to the entire company and its other products (example: Suzuki Samurai); (3) the company is too closely identified with one type of product (examples: *IBM* selling copy machines or *Xerox* selling computers); and (4) incompatible market segments and product images (examples: *Toyota*, *Honda*, and *Nissan* selling their luxury models under the brand names *Lexus*, *Acura*, and *Infiniti*).

Product

Product refers to the goods and services developed to satisfy the unfilled needs or your market targets and achieve the goals of your *marketing plan*. As mentioned earlier, *product* in this context could be a good, service, or idea. When it is offered to the market it should be *complete*. That is, a complete product has parents, or a *corporate image*, a *position*, a *price*, a *place* from which it can be bought, and it is *promoted* so that market targets know that it exists, why it is unique, what it costs, and where they can buy it. It should also have a *marketing information system* mechanism by which its success can be measured.

Price

Price is simply the amount of money for which buyers are willing to pay and sellers are willing to sell the product to achieve the goals of their marketing plan. It should be set at a level that market targets are willing to pay at the same time that it covers your firm's costs, and provides a sufficient profit incentive to prompt continued production.

Place

Place, or *Distribution*, aims to make it convenient for market targets to find, buy and use your product and achieve the goals of your marketing plan. It also serves to provide adequate incentives for everyone in the distribution chain to push the product through distribution channels to the end buyer.

Promotion

Promotion communicates the *benefits* of the *complete* product to prompt a buying action and achieve the goals of the marketing plan. Because promotion is used to communicate all the other building blocks, it should be done *last* after positioning, product, price, place, corporate image, and marketing information strategies are put in place.

Marketing Information System

The *Marketing Information System* is developed to *collect*, *analyze*, *report*, and *take action* on critical market information in order to give market targets what they want and to insure customer satisfaction. It also organizes and governs the methods of monitoring, collecting and reporting information to insure that the *marketing process* continues to work according to plan and at optimum effectiveness.

Integrating the Seven Building Blocks to Form a Coordinated Strategy Mix

Marketing is the process by which products and services are developed and brought to market. The process starts by doing *market research* and finding needs in the marketplace that are not being satisfied. These unsatisfied needs are also called *market niches*. They represent *spaces* or *holes* in the market that are opportunities for companies or organizations to fill. Successful companies uniquely *position* themselves to penetrate these open windows of opportunity by developing *products* and other marketing strategies to satisfy the unfulfilled needs identified. Once developed, the products are *priced* to fit the budgets of market targets, cover costs, make a reasonable profit, provide adequate margins for distributors, and be compatible with the position selected. They are *placed*, or distributed, in the marketplace through channels that are convenient and economical for buyers to find, buy and use. Once all of the above strategies are in place, the products are *promoted* to inform prospects about the unique benefits and features, availability, and places where they can buy them with the objective of prompting a buying action. A *marketing information system* is developed to collect, analyze, report and take action on market information in order to improve performance and achieve market plan goals, give market targets what they want, and maximize customer satisfaction.

BEYOND THE SEVEN BUILDING BLOCKS

To continue with the explanation of the *marketing process*, it is important to note that there is a lot more to Marketing in an organization than the *seven fundamental building blocks*. The *Marketing Plan* outlines the marketing goals and the strategies to achieve them. The *Marketing Cycle* determines the sequence and timing of the Marketing process. The *Marketing Organization* delineates the authority and responsibility of each person involved in the process. And, the *Universal Marketing Structure*™ provides the structural framework for creating successful marketing materials, ads, Web sites, and commercials. All of these will be considered in more detail in subsequent sections of this book.

To promote a more intuitive understanding, you might consider marketing as *a process that incorporates all of the activities required to successfully sell your products and enhance your corporate image*. That is, if done properly, marketing should do as much as possible to *pre-sell* your products so that either (1) prospects will order them directly or (2) if a sales person is required to sell them, the sales person's job will be made as easy as possible.

In his book *Marketing High Technology*, another view of marketing is provided by William H. Davidow. Mr. Davidow says the following:

> *"Marketing is civilized warfare... Your competitor's job is to capture business and then defend that new perimeter. So is yours... Now, a lot of marketing is creative. It's strategic. Cerebral. But eventually you make a move — and then the fighting begins".*[1]

IT IS ESSENTIAL FOR SUCCESS

In the short run, success can be achieved with luck. Over time, good marketing is a necessary ingredient for success in virtually any endeavor. This has been proven over and over. In addition to offering a great product, *Albert Einstein*, the *Beatles*, and *Abraham Lincoln* were assisted greatly by effective marketing. In fact, there is a large body of empirical evidence to prove the statement that *great products poorly marketing are typically failures*, whereas *mediocre products properly marketed are often successes.* Specific examples are not provided here to avoid incurring the wrath of their companies. The reader should be able to easily recall many examples of both cases. The important point to remember is that it is a great myth to think that all you have to do is offer a superior product or service and people will *beat your door down* to buy it. A *better mousetrap* won't do it. You need good marketing.

HOW DOES MARKETING FIT INTO THE ORGANIZATION?

The Marketing division of any organization is vital because it brings in the money. Because of this, many chief executives of successful organizations have a strong marketing background. In fact, studies consistently show that the CEOs of roughly 31% of the *Fortune 1000* companies come from the ranks of marketing. This is especially significant since marketing is only one of the five classical functional areas of an organization (the other areas typically include *Finance*, *Engineering and R&D*, *Production*, and *Administration*). On a purely statistical basis only 20% (or one-fifth) of the chief executives should come from marketing. Since 31%, or nearly one-third do, marketing is obviously a very important function. Unfortunately, it is too often undervalued and misunderstood by technical and life science companies, who tend to be *inward-focused* and *product-driven*.

Within any particular organization, whether it is a small professional services firm or a Fortune 1000 company, many advance based on their ability to *bring in the business*. The core of most *Business Plans is the Marketing Plan*. And marketing is, or should be, the conduit through which information flows into and out of the company.

WHAT IS THE TYPICAL STRUCTURE OF A MARKETING ORGANIZATION?

Whether or not the Chief Executive has a marketing background, the top marketing executive should be the *Vice President of Marketing*, or *Chief Marketing Officer*. In the typical marketing organization, the next level is the *Director or Manager* level. On this level, are the Director of Marketing, Sales Manager or (although it should be noted in some organizations the chief sales executive is given the title of Vice President of Sales), the various Marketing Managers typically organized by function (Advertising, Distribution, Marketing Research, Marketing Support, Direct Marketing, Online Marketing, Service, etc.) or Product (Product line or Brand managers) or a combination of both. At the next level are Sales representatives, Marketing Support personnel, Service Technicians, etc. And, as with all organizations, there is an administrative and support staff which services all levels. This staff typically includes secretarial personal, graphic artists, administrative assistants, etc. *Figure 1-2* gives a graphic picture of the generic marketing organization and how it fits into the larger company.

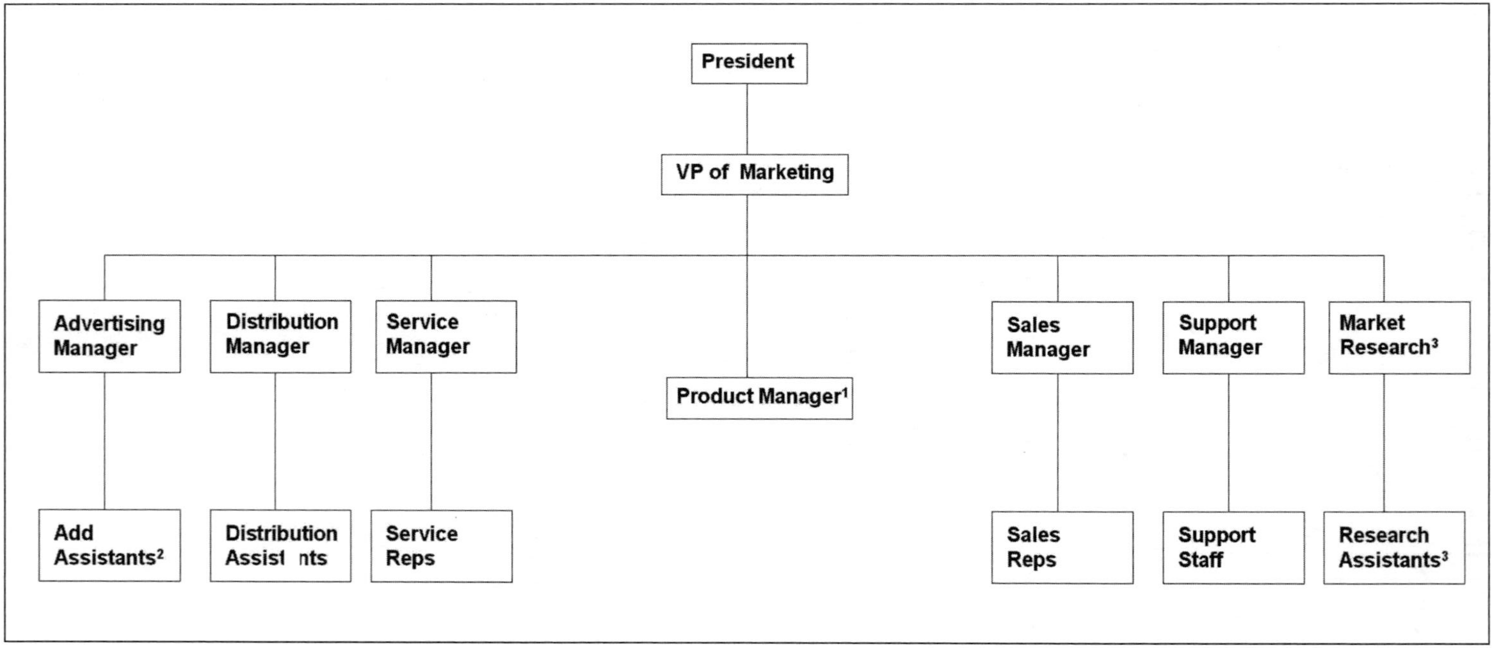

Figure 1-2. Generic marketing organization.

1. In some companies that are organized by product line, the Product Managers have their own advertising, distribution, market research, service, and support staffs, which report directly to them.
2. These often include copywriter, graphics personnel, photographers, and others involved in the advertising process.
3. While historically called market research, it has grown into marketing Information System Manager (which includes market research) in more advanced companies.

To better understand this marketing organization and the functions of a marketing manager, it is useful to know that all managers have four main functions to perform in an organization — *Planning*, *Organizing*, *Executing* (*including Leading*) and *Controlling*. *Planning* involves setting measurable goals and developing strategies to achieve them. *Organizing* refers to grouping resources (capital and human resources) into specialties, assigning authority and responsibility relationships, and delegating work in order to achieve the goals of the plan. *Executing* involves providing leadership and overseeing the day-to-day duties necessary to achieve the goals of the plan. *Controlling* refers to monitoring results, comparing them with the goals of the plan, analyzing and reporting any discrepancies, and taking corrective action to achieve better results in the future.

If properly organized, all marketing personnel have their responsibilities and authorities clearly delineated so that they know what is expected of them, who they report to, who reports to them, and what they need to do to rise to the next level in the organization. As you will learn later, the personnel in an organization are one of the most important *publics* your company and marketing department need to consider when designing and implementing marketing programs. Excellent companies understand this, and treat their people very well. They understand that marketing concepts have to be applied to current, past and prospective employees as well as customers and prospects.

MARKETING HIGH-TECHNOLOGY AND LIFE SCIENCES

Any up-to-date text on marketing needs to address the special problems associated with marketing technology and life-science products. While marketing fundamentals are marketing fundamentals — no matter what the product or service, those who have been marketing consumer products for years seem to have difficulty transitioning to marketing technology products, and Why? Perhaps they really don't truly understand all the fundamentals. In any case, it is important to understand that many of the techniques historically used to market commodity or consumer products do not work effectively when applied to technology products. On the other hand, understanding how to market technical products can actually help to market consumer products. To learn why, it is first necessary to understand more about what *high-tech* means.

What is High-tech?

The term *High-tech* is a shortened version of the words *High-Technology*. It originally referred to industries, companies, products, and services that have a high degree of technology associated with them. Some apply the term to technologies that change frequently. According to the U.S. *Bureau of Labor Statistics*, an industry is classified as *High-tech* if it has twice the technical personnel and R&D expenditures as the national averages for U.S. manufacturers.

Many believe that this measurement is inadequate because it does not consider indirect R&D inputs from products and devices, such as computers, used in the manufacture of the end products. It also doesn't consider foreign averages or inputs. In a world where manufacturing has become a global activity, comparison with only U.S. averages seems to be rather shortsighted. Furthermore, many technology and life-science companies don't do their own R&D but sell and service the products resulting from the R&D of others.

As a result of the media's fascination with the term, high-tech has evolved into a much broader meaning. It is now used in reference to styles of art, lettering, furniture, music, clothing, hair, and virtually anything that looks or sounds new, metallic, "*computerish*," or contemporary. In a recent newspaper ad, there was a reference to a *Men's Leather Full Feature Hi-Tech Tennis Shoe*. As Al Ries and Jack Trout say in their book Positioning: *The Battle for Your Mind*,

> *"Meanings are not in the words. They are in the people using the words. Like a sugar bowl that is empty until someone fills it with sugar, a word has no meaning until someone fills it with meaning."*[2]

The same is true with high-tech and the life sciences.

In the context of marketing, *this text will extend the "high-tech label" to any products or services that have significant "intangibles" associated with them*. The reason for this is that the marketing of intangible products involve much the same processes as the marketing of conventional technology or life-science products. To better comprehend this concept, it is useful to explain how *high-tech* marketing is different from the marketing of non-technical, or consumer products.

How is Marketing of Technology Different?

Because of the greater complexity of high-technology products, properly marketing them often requires a modified approach. Some of the differences are explained in the following sections.

Product Education is Required

Typical consumer products, such as soap, require little or no explanation before they are sold. Virtually every consumer understands what soap, cereal, wine, and toilet paper are. With high-tech products, the situation is quite different. Even if the prospect vaguely knows what a computer or satellite system can do, the marketing function of the business has to educate the prospect on the benefits and features of these products before the sale can be made.

Even though consumer products usually do not require education or significant explanation before a sale is made, product education can help to sell more of them. A classic example is

Arm & Hammer Baking Soda. As its name implies, this product was originally developed as an ingredient to be used in creating baked goods. The *Arm & Hammer Division of Church & Dwight Co., Inc.* learned of other beneficial uses from its customers. They discovered the product is also useful for deodorizing refrigerators and kitchens, acting as an antacid to combat heartburn or a sour stomach, and brightening and cleaning plaque from teeth. While there are most likely other uses, the firm's marketing department has promoted those listed above by describing them on the product's packaging and has developed a broader line of products specifically for different applications. The makers of soaps, foods, cleaners, and a variety of other consumer products have learned that consumer product education can be a useful and powerful marketing strategy. Therefore, the discipline of providing product education, which is essential for marketing high-tech products, can also benefit the marketing of consumer products.

Longer Sales Cycle and Shorter Product Cycle

Another important difference related to the complexities of high-tech products is that more explanation is necessary, and more follow up is required. Because of this, the marketing/sales cycle is much longer than with consumer products. This often requires the sales people in high-technology industries to develop personal relationships with their prospects.

Ironically, even though the *sales cycles* for high-tech products tend to be longer, the *Product Life Cycles* tend to be shorter. This means that high-tech sales people have to balance their relationship-building activities with the need to sell existing products. This places an additional burden on high-technology organizations. They have to convince prospects and customers to buy existing products now when most buyers know that they are likely to be replaced with newer, more advanced versions sooner rather than later. This is done be clearly explaining the time and money-saving benefits of buying now to the prospect. If prospects continue to wait, they will lose the immediate benefits that tend to greatly outweigh future price savings and improved features.

While not required of consumer products, the developing of personal relationships with customers and prospects can help to boost sales and create customer loyalty.

Higher Caliber and Better-Qualified Personnel

Greater product complexities and more knowledgeable customers also mean that high-tech marketing, sales, and support personal require a greater degree of knowledge, intelligence and sophistication than those involved in low-tech sales activities. Product knowledge is a prerequisite for success in sales, and with high-tech products, there is a lot more to know. Additionally, high-tech products change much more rapidly than other products. Sales people have to be able to learn new concepts, techniques and features to keep pace.

Perhaps it is obvious that consumer-product companies can also benefit from higher-qualified personnel. They present a better corporate image, they do better quality work and make fewer costly mistakes, they are able to learn and communicate additional uses of existing products, etc. What is apparently not so obvious is the cost justification of these higher-qualified personnel. That is, too many look at acquiring human resources as a cost rather than an investment. As a result they hire someone who is less expensive rather than someone who is better qualified. Instead of getting a bigger return on their slightly higher investment, they only incur greater costs — more mistakes, higher training costs, more unhappy customers, damage to the firm's Corporate Image. When all these costs are added up, they dwarf the savings of hiring the less expensive person.

State-of-the-Art Products

High-tech products often represent the latest technology. New technology requires greater education of the customer that, in turn, lengthens the sales cycle even more. Also, many prospects don't want to be the first to try new technology. They prefer to wait until other *guinea pigs* find and work out all the *bugs* for them.

Although many consumer products are not considered state-of-the art, they may be the result of state-of-the-art processes that improve the product. For example, pain relievers use state-of-the-art safety packaging to prohibit tampering. Some foods are being processed with new techniques that eliminate fats, caffeine, preservatives, and pesticides in their growing and processing. These new methods can be promoted as unique product benefits that distinguish the company's products from the competition.

Higher Degree of "Real" Product Uniqueness

While the inherent complexities of high-tech products tend to distinguish your products from those of competitors (and thereby minimize competitive pressures), prospects have a tendency to overlook these differences so as not to overburden their minds — i.e. a computer is a computer, a microprocessor chip is a microprocessor chip, a hip implant is a hip implant. Therefore, the marketing personnel have to be sure to explain and justify any differences and to emphasize the benefits of their product over their competitors'.

Since consumer products have a tendency to be very similar to those of competitors, marketing must introduce unique benefits to the product in order to distinguish it from the competition. If marketing is not successful in doing this, buyers may view company's products as *commodities* that are virtually indistinguishable from competitors. Without any unique advantages, the company is usually forced to compete on price — leaving itself vulnerable to competitors who can fight back with even lower prices. This often escalates into price wars where there are no winners.

Higher Price

The costs of making and selling high-tech products are often higher as a result of more costly materials, labor, and the need to amortize greater research and development (R&D) expenditures. As a result, the price tags of such products are often higher. The higher price serves to further lengthen the sales cycle and to make marketing and sales more difficult.

As discussed above, consumer products can typically command higher prices only if they offer unique advantages. Another reason for higher prices of consumer products might be shortages of such products. In such cases, the laws of supply and demand tend to drive the prices higher.

Promotion Has to Be Conducted at Higher Level

Since the products and problems are more complex, the average high-tech customer has a tendency to be more serious and sophisticated than the average soap buyer. As a result, promotion has to be conducted at a higher level. It has to be serious and non-insulting, non-high pressure and non-aggressive, and appeal to the prospect's intellect.

Consumer marketers can learn from the high-tech marketers need to communicate at a higher level. As consumers get more sophisticated, many of them feel insulted by marketing that insults or "talks down" to them. Many feel the days when consumers are motivated to buy by the power of *white tornadoes* or the *"squeezability" of toilet paper* are numbered. The best marketing is benefit-oriented and non-insulting as well as attention-grabbing and entertaining.

Service and Support are Very Important

A soap buyer does not require training, service or support. A buyer of high-tech products often does. The more technical the product, the more these services are required. Since service is an important concern of most high-tech buyers, Marketing has to do everything possible to insure that service is of the highest quality and to communicate this to the customer. It also has to make sure the company portrays the image of stability and strength so that prospects are assured that the company will remain in business to service their needs during the life of the product.

Consumer products companies have recently learned of the benefit of providing service and support to their customers. Department stores, such as *Nordstroms*, discount stores, such as *Wal-Mart*, and megastores, such as *Home Depot* have taught other retailers about the power of taking good care of customers. Many other consumer product companies have installed toll-free support lines to answer questions about product usage and to respond to complaints from customers. They have found that in addition to collecting some very valuable marketing information, they are able to develop a closer, more trusting relationship with customers. This translates into greater sales and free, positive word-of-mouth advertising.

As illustrated in the paragraphs above, marketing high-tech products requires some different approaches to marketing. However, consumer and industrial-product marketers can also benefit from learning high-tech approaches and techniques.

Why is Learning High-tech Marketing Particularly Important for everyone?

In addition to helping you to market virtually any type of product, learning high-tech marketing is important for many other reasons including the following:

- *High-technology accelerates economic growth.* Producing and marketing simple products such as rice and t-shirts do not require much skilled labor or large supplier chains. Their economic impact, therefore, tends to be quite limited. Such simple economies are characteristic of most third-world countries. The manufacture and marketing of high-tech products, on the other hand, creates a complex network of suppliers who, in turn, employ many people, use sophisticated plant and equipment, and increase demand for goods and services in the areas in which they are located.
- *High-technology attracts the most-talented people.* The greater levels of skill and knowledge required to produce and market high-tech products attract some of the best-educated and trained people from around the world.
- *High-technology improves efficiency and improves the quality of life.* By enhancing their capabilities, high-technology products are helping people to do more with less, allowing small companies to compete with big companies, giving individuals who don't have significant resources to better compete with those who do, enabling researchers to find the cure for dreaded diseases, and helping companies to produce products that save and enhance the quality of people's lives.

In spite of the ever-increasing importance of high-technology as described above, there is an alarming lack of good-quality high-tech marketing. William H. Davidow points out in his book *Marketing High Technology*,

> *"The Duties of Marketing are quite simple, yet few high-technology companies perform them. Why? Naiveté is one answer, but I suspect that in most cases the consequences of facing up to those responsibilities are so distasteful, companies refuse even to try."*[3]

Perhaps the real reason so few high-tech companies do marketing is that it is new to them. In the recent past, high-tech companies could compete and be successful merely on the basis of their technology. All they had to do is develop a new technology that filled a need in the marketplace, patent it, and they would own the market. Now, however, the market has become much more crowded. Upon seeing the success of a new technology, competitors are attracted to enter the market with similar products that are just different enough to avoid violating patents. Still others are entering without worrying about patent violations since they assume that most companies don't have the resources to defend all of their patent rights.

The result of this phenomenon is the diffusion of proprietary technology throughout entire industries and around the world. Products that were formerly exclusive, unique, or special are becoming more like commodities. This, in turn, has caused a situation in which companies are competing on the basis of costs rather than technology. This has moved many manufacturing operations *offshore* primarily to less-expensive locations. This movement has aggravated already suicidal price wars, made technological secrets susceptible to theft by foreign governments and companies, and has caused a movement of many high-tech jobs from domestic to foreign locations. At the risk of sounding too alarmist and oversimplifying the situation, these problems have caused a chain reaction that has served to further strain the economy and security of domestic interests at home and abroad. That's the *bad news*. The *good news* is that, there is a *way out*. The way out is not through exercising military or political muscle, finding less-expensive labor in other parts of the world, or erecting higher trade barriers. The way out is through practicing better marketing. When buyers around the world understand the advantages of your product, they will buy it. If your marketing does not give them good reasons to buy your product, they will buy from someone else who does. It is that simple.

This means that the lowest-priced option does not have to be the winning alternative. Companies, especially high-tech companies, can better compete on quality, product differentiation, service, and variables other than cost or price. In fact, price alone can be one of the weakest competitive positions because there is always someone who can come along and offer something similar at a lower price. The most successful companies in the world rarely offer the lowest-priced products. The difference is that they know how to do good marketing.

Improving the marketing in high-technology and consumer companies, therefore, becomes an important mission. It's in the interest of everyone in the domestic market and in all the countries of the world to be strong economically. Producers need consumers, and vice versa. And history has proven over and over again that conflicts and wars have little basis to start and continue when people are prosperous.

As you learn more and more about the power of *high-technology marketing* throughout this text and your career, you will understand how it can help you, your product, your company, your marketplace, and your country. The mission starts with you. Therefore, *you have to believe that you can make a difference.*

MAIN PURPOSES OF MARKETING

With the above look at marketing as a backdrop, it is useful to round out this introductory chapter with a list, in lay person's terms, of some of the main purposes of High-tech Marketing, most of which are applicable to all types of Marketing. They are to:

- Provide information to and collect information from the market.
- Create a buying action.
- Educate prospects, customers, and other publics.
- Create interest.
- Get the prospect's attention.
- Project a favorable image, personality, culture.
- Get publics to remember your company and products.
- Develop a positive relationship with prospects, customers, and members of other publics.
- Differentiate your product and company from the competition.
- Plant seeds. The more you plant, the more will blossom into sales.
- Communicate the benefits of your products and company.
- Make it convenient for market targets, to find, buy and use your products.
- Create and push for new ideas, products, and services.
- Get the product in the hands of customers in the most effective ways.
- Give customers what they want — good value.
- Create customer satisfaction and loyalty.

While all of the above are very important, the last one — *creating customer satisfaction* — is the ultimate goal of the marketing function.

Don't forget this ultimate goal. Those who do tend to chase after the money end up losing the customers. More often than not, they get lost on the road to success, and find themselves failing. Those who do focus on customer satisfaction and understand the other main purposes of marketing tend to *stay on track* even after they hit the inevitable bumps they find along the difficult road to success. Moreover, they tend to make the largest profits.

[1]William R. Davidow, *Marketing High Technology: An Insider's View.*

[2]Al Ries and Jack Trout, *Positioning: The Battle for Your Mind*, pg. 201.

[3]William R. Davidow, *Marketing High Technology: An Insider's View.*

TIPS and Exercises

1. Read as much as you can — collecting successes and failures, noticing patterns, and filing them for future reference.
2. Ask yourself why one marketing campaign worked and another didn't.

Chapter 2

The Marketing Cycle

"Marketing is a continuous process that follows a definite cycle."

WHAT IS THE MARKETING CYCLE?

The *Marketing Cycle* is basically the sequence of *marketing activities delineated in the Marketing Plan*. Each step of the Plan should be executed in the proper sequence so that it can serve as a recipe for successful marketing. Given this sequence, it is also important to emphasize that Marketing is an *iterative* process whereby any number of steps may need to be revised due to new information, collected by a *Marketing Information System*, which requires changes to be made for the plan to succeed.

The Marketing Cycle sequence of the Marketing Plan steps typically includes the following:

- Recognizing and identifying *market needs*.
- Focusing on the *needs that are compatible* with your organization's strengths.
- Determining the *market potential* of product(s) that fill those needs.
- Estimating the organization's likely *penetration* of this market potential.
- Setting *measurable* market-plan goals based on market penetration estimates.
- Developing *marketing strategies* to achieve plan goals.
- Developing *budgets*, *forecasts*, *organizational assignments*, and *schedules* to support execution of the strategies.
- *Executing the marketing strategies* within the framework of the marketing plan and supporting budgets, assignments, and schedules.
- Developing a *Marketing Information System* to collect, analyze and report information, measure performance against goals, and to take corrective action to improve performance.
- Revise strategies, goals and plans as necessary.

Unfortunately, too many companies don't develop a *Market Plan* or follow the sequence of activities in the *Marketing Cycle*. They typically develop a product that is the brainchild of a brilliant inventor without much regard to satisfying a need in the market place. Once developed, the company tries to find customers for the product. While this can work, it often does not.

The companies that are successful over the long run are marketing oriented or *market driven*. That is, they look at the needs of the marketplace first. If the size of the market (or the number of potential buyers) is sufficiently large to warrant the investment required to develop and market a product to satisfy those needs, they proceed with a full-blown Marketing and Product Development Plan. The first step in this process is to recognize a need in the marketplace.

RECOGNIZING A MARKET NEED

While recognizing a market need sounds as if it is a passive activity, it shouldn't be. Formal systems should be established to generate and screen new product ideas that stem from needs identified in the marketplace. These systems are best strung together into one unified *New Product Development System*. This system is critical to the longevity of all companies, but is especially important to technology companies that depend on innovation to survive and be successful.

NEW PRODUCT DEVELOPMENT SYSTEM

A graphic representation of a *New Product Development System* is provided in *Figure 2-1*. As shown in the figure, this system is designed to identify as many good ideas as possible and progressively screen them so that only those with the highest likelihood of success will be developed into products. This system has several distinct stages including: *Needs Identification and Idea Generation*, *Initial Screening*, *Secondary Screening*, *Selection of Ideas for Prototype Development*, *Testing of Prototypes*, and *Selection of Products for Commercial Development and Marketing*.

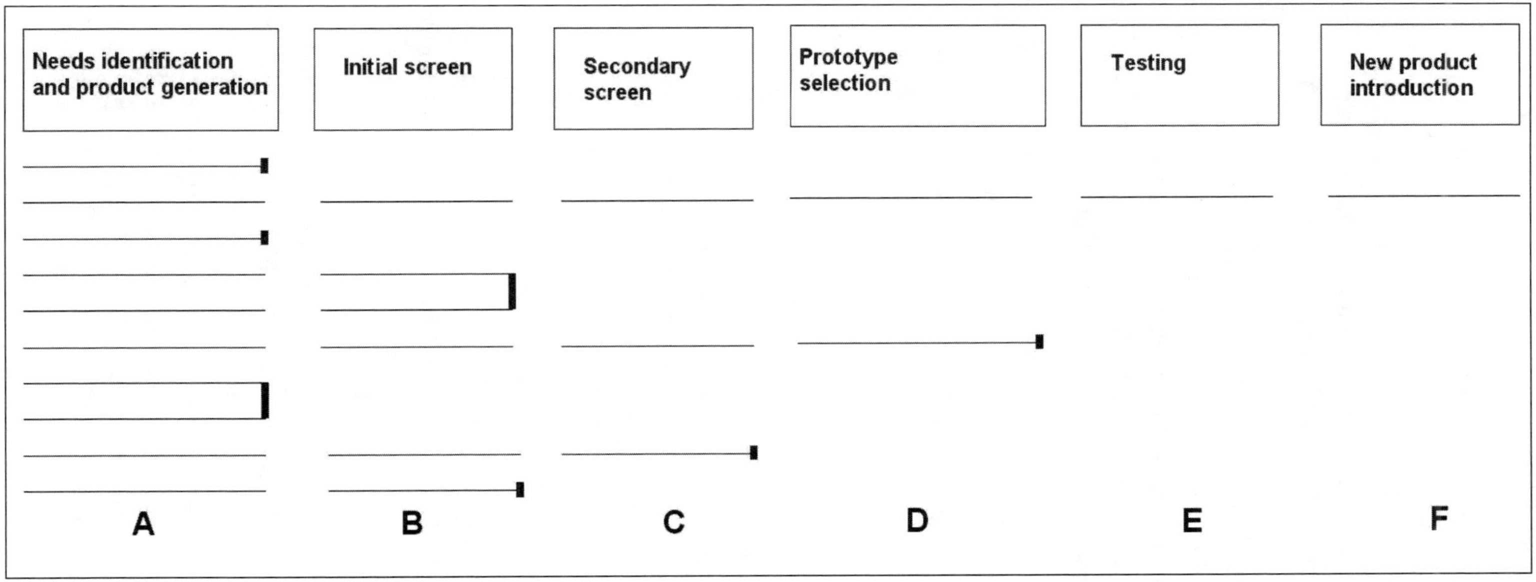

Figure 2-1. New product development system.

A. Many Ideas are generated from different sources during this phase.
B. Those Ideas, which fit within the goals of the company plans pass through.
C. The new product development committee evaluates and selects the most promising ideas for prototype development.
D. The prototypes are evaluated for product and financial feasibility as well as market viability.
E. Those prototypes, which pass feasibility tests, are market tested.
F. Those prototypes, which pass the market tests, are turned over to normal marketing channels to be introduced as new products. Based on marketplace feedback collected by the Marketing Information System, improvements are continually made.

Why aren't all good ideas developed into products? The reason is that no company, however large or successful, has the resources to properly develop and market all the ideas that it identifies as good. Even *IBM* and *Microsoft*, with their vast resources, are seldom the first to commercially produce a product that is based on a technology that they pioneer in their laboratories. The reason is that they understand that while the costs to develop a product can be very high, such product development costs are typically small when compared to the costs to properly market the product. That's why *IBM* waited several years before introducing a personal computer and why *Microsoft* waited for *Apple* to prove the commercial viability of a graphical user interface (GUI) before introducing its Windows operating system. They left the pioneering to such companies as *Compal*, *Commodore*, *Vector Graphic*, *Altos*, *Radio Shack*, and *Apple*. *Apple* is the only one left standing with a very small market share.

Intel Corporation chairman, Gordon Moore, once described the process of developing a new product or technology as “swallowing like an elephant and defecating like a canary.”

How does a *New Product Development system* work to the benefit of the company? The following sections will answer this question. The first stage is identifying market needs and generating new product ideas.

Needs Identification and Idea Generation

Although it is useful to be aware that most ideas will be screened out or shelved for later consideration, the best new product development systems are designed to generate as many good ideas as possible. The reason is that it's better to spend a little extra time screening ideas than it is to eliminate possible “winners” at the outset without giving them a proper evaluation. There are many good sources for ideas. The following are some of them.

Internally-Generated Ideas

As part of their orientation to the company, employees should be trained and encouraged to look for market needs and new product ideas. In addition to serving the purpose of generating new ideas, it is likely to make them more responsive to customer's suggestions and complaints and to make them feel more a part of the company.

Market Information Form. There should be a formal mechanism for recording and reporting New Product Ideas or Market Needs. This can be accomplished by (1) giving a pad of preprinted *Market Information Forms* (see *Figure 2-2*) to all those who have contact with the marketplace and (2) placing copies of these forms at various employee meeting places around the company. In addition to prompting important information, these forms should have space for "free-form" comments and should have directions as to where they should be sent after completion (usually someone in Marketing who collects them for the Vice President of

No. 419

DNA of Marketing • Market Information Form

Specializing in High-technology Markleting • Sales • Systems Consulting and Training

INSTRUCTIONS — PLEASE READ FIRST. Continued success of our company requires the ongoing assistance of everyone in our organization (the company's "eyes and ears") to provide marketplace information on a timely basis. Whenever you are able to collect such information please complete this form and send it to the marketing department. Bonuses will be awarded to the top submissions, and performance reviews will reflect your efforts. Thank you.

Type of Information — ☐ New product ideas ☐ Competition ☐ Compliment ☐ Complaint ☐ Strategy feedback ☐ Other________

Source of Information

Name		Date
Position		Phone – –
Company		Fax – –
Street		P.O. Box
City	State	Zip –

Employee Reporting

Name	Position	Department	Phone Extension

Market Information (Please write on back or attach a separate sheet if necessary.)

The following signature releases the company from any obligations or liabilities associated with using the above information for its marketing or other purposes.

Signature	Title	Date

Form No. K&A 081492 • Last Revision 9/30/92

Please send to Marketing Department when completed.

Figure 2-2

Marketing or the head of the New Product Committee). Those personnel who have the most contact with customers and prospects (Reception, Sales, Support, Customer Service, Accounts Receivable, and Accounts Payable) should be given pads of such forms to keep at their desks or to take into the field. If possible, incentives should be built into the system that give employees a bonus of some kind for identifying an important need or suggesting an idea that is developed into a product. *American Airlines* instituted a program in January of 1987 to award employees for ideas on how the company could cut costs, make more money, and improve quality of service. In the first year of the program, the company paid employees $6 million in either cash or goods for ideas that raised additional revenue or cut costs totaling $27 million[1] — yielding a return on investment of 450%!

Suggestion System. The suggestion box has been around the workplace for quite a long time. However, it has been used too infrequently by businesses in the United States. In Japan the average employee submits 25 suggestions per year to top management. In the U.S., the figure is 0.14 suggestions per year.[2] In cases where suggestion systems are used, however, the results can be quite impressive. There are roughly 200,000 companies that employ 50 or more people in the United States. Of these, only about 6,000 are believed to operate suggestion systems. Approximately 1000 — mostly the larger corporations — belong to the *National Suggestion Systems Group*, which estimates that its member organizations saved $2.3 billion in 1990 by implementing 328,000 employee suggestions, for an average savings of $7,012 per suggestion. As a reward for submitting their suggestions, employees received an average of $491 in cash or merchandise — yielding a return on investment exceeding 1428%![3]

Customers and Prospects

While many *internally-generated* ideas originally come from customers, they are typically channeled through company employees. The *marketing department* should also develop additional mechanisms for soliciting ideas directly from customers, thereby avoiding possible employee or management biases. In addition to its inherent value, this information will help to corroborate the information that is often filtered by employees.

One common mechanism is the *questionnaire*. Often times, questionnaires appear with warranty cards since customers are accustomed to answering questions when filling out warranty registrations for products that they've just purchased. Even better, is a follow-up e-mail, phone interview, or form sent to customers after they have had the opportunity to use the product for a while. Through this approach, the company can impress the customers with its concern about their satisfaction at the same time it obtains valuable market information. Necessary questions should include: *Are you satisfied with the product?*; *What features, if any, would you like to see added in the future?*; and *What features, if any, do you consider unimportant or unnecessary?* There should always be a more open-ended question such as:

Do you have any other suggestions that you feel would improve our product or service?

Since most people do not like filling out questionnaires, the number of questions should be kept to a minimum. Also, consideration should be given to giving respondents a nominal incentive for returning the questionnaires or responding to e-mails. The best incentives are useful, inexpensive, and contribute to the marketing of your company and products. Popular examples include pens, coffee mugs, calendars, and t-shirts with the company and product name, logo, slogan, and contact information on them.

Many times, customers will offer suggestions even when not solicited. The problem is that many company personnel look at these suggestions as annoying complaints or interruptions of their work, and they don't note them down or report them to any of the company decision makers. Marketing-oriented companies, however, have mechanisms for noting them and reporting them to the proper personnel within the company. They understand that the best information often comes directly from customers and prospects, who after all, are the marketplace. According to the *Wall Street Journal on Marketing*, a book which excerpts articles from the paper's weekly marketing column,

> *"Proctor & Gamble learned of faulty bottle caps from telephone complaints, and since Polaroid just last week went out of business and it dates the book. Surprisingly only a minority of calls are complaints. P&G classifies one third of its calls as such; Clairol, 15 percent, and GE, 8 percent."*[4]

Companies have discovered that one of the best ways of getting customer suggestions over the phone is to install a toll-free phone number, publicize it on all marketing literature and product labels, and make sure that enough lines and personnel are in place to handle the call volume. The goodwill of a toll-free number can be destroyed, however, if the caller has to wait for a long time to talk with a human voice. In recent years, Web sites, e-mails and Weblogs are also proving to be an effective channel for collecting ideas if Web URLs, e-mail addresses, and Weblog links are also listed on all marketing literature.

Whatever channel is utilized, customers should be encouraged, not discouraged, to give their opinions even if they are complaints that employees don't like to hear. Complaints should be looked upon as opportunities to turn negatives into positives. If not handled properly, they can negatively effect the company's image and sales. Also, complaints reflect market needs and ideas because they give the company a direct indication of how the market feels about their products and services. In addition to being properly handled, they should be written down and formally passed to the appropriate department in the company for proper resolution. Collecting this information is particularly critical to high-technology companies that have the on-going problem of reconciling *short product cycles with longer sales cycles*.

Frequent Requests

Requests, complaints, and other ideas that are frequently repeated should be given particular attention since they are typically a good indicator of a market need. While this statement seems so obvious, it is presented here because a significant number of product-driven companies ignore such requests whether they are frequent or not. Their approach is so self-directed that such information is often viewed as an annoyance. If it doesn't fit in with their charted course, they ignore it rather than consider changing direction. Also, employees and managers in most companies tend to filter the information, or tell their bosses what they like to hear — especially when these bosses tend to "kill the messenger" when they do not like the message.

When considering frequent suggestions, however, it's important to determine whether these suggestions apply to all market targets or if they apply to only a specific vocal group. The reason is that it might be a disastrous mistake to make company-wide decisions based on the needs of a small local group when those needs, if they can be economically addressed at all, are best handled with local solutions. This determination is best made during the *screening phase* of new product development.

Compatible Market Niches • Complementary Products

Many good ideas are generated by looking for market needs not currently satisfied, but within the scope of the company's business. In technology companies, product upgrades, training, support, service, supplies, and accessories are good examples of complementary products to fill compatible needs. That is, if a company is already offering a product, it may receive calls for support and assistance. Support can easily be turned into a product. All the company has do is to make it clear to customers at the time of sale that support is included in the price during the first 90 days after the sale. Subsequently, the customers may purchase a *support contract* that entitles them to support during the contract period. The same is true for hardware maintenance and other services such as *delivery*, *installation*, *training*, *supplies*, *accessories*, *rush orders*, and *extended warranties*.

Products that can be made with little or no additional investment

Quite often, new product ideas are created with the same tools and skills used to make existing products. For example, they can be by-products that are automatically created by the manufacturing process of existing products. These by-products might fill an important need in other markets. Many times, all that has to be done is to find these markets. The garage sale is a good example of this. What is one person's junk is another's antique. Scrap metal, paper, and other by-products of the manufacturing or assembly process can be sold to companies that specialize in recycling them. Rather than throwing away parts that go into products that are obsolete, they can be listed in a spares catalogue and sold to customers for repair and replacement, or they can be sold to special distributors who specialize in used or no-longer-manufactured products. Many list these parts and products on their Web site, or use *eBay* for this purpose.

Small companies or individuals with good ideas

Since small companies are typically the innovators in many industries, they often develop new and unique products. Looking at what they develop may kindle new ideas, complementary products, or joint-venture possibilities. A good example of this is a company that set up a small business to refill toner cartridges for laser printers and copy machines. This company responded to a need in the marketplace for less expensive cartridges and those who are interested in recycling. Prior to its inception, users of laser printers would routinely discard cartridges once the toner was depleted, and buy new ones at a premium price. The company figured out an economical way of collecting these cartridges, refilling them with toner, and reselling them for a healthy profit and at half the price of new cartridges. A larger supplies firm, who was losing some cartridge business to this new upstart, thought this company had a good idea and purchased it to the advantage of both parties.

Good Accidents

In research laboratories of companies, many products are developed by accident. *Procter & Gamble* was trying to make a special type of soap. It dumped what seemed to be "failed attempt" in the Ohio River. Someone noticed that the soap floated, and thus was born *Ivory Soap — the soap that floats* — an important benefit to those who take baths. A scientist at *3M* was working on producing a new adhesive. By accident, he dropped a "failed effort" on a piece of paper, and noticed he could pick up the paper and stick it back down without tearing the paper. Upon test marketing the product, called *Post-It* notes, the company knew it had a winner. To date, it is one of *3M's* most successful products.

Competition

Every company should regularly review the products of its competition. Often times, the competition develops innovative products. These products either lead to new ideas or present competitive problems that need to be addressed by the company to maintain its market share.

Industry Journals and Local Newspapers

All marketing and product-development personnel should regularly read industry journals for new product ideas. Such ideas could come from competitive products, articles by industry experts, or quotes from academics. The local paper is important because it acts as a barometer of the ideas that are shaping the thoughts of local customers and prospects. The founder of *FedEx* got the idea for the company from reading *Inc. Magazine*.

From a wide variety of sources

There are many other sources of new product ideas. Your company should actively look for market needs and solicit new product ideas from as many sources as is feasible. This involves identifying sources and encouraging them to recognize market needs and submit their suggestions and ideas to the proper personnel in your company.

Once submitted, new product ideas should be subject to various screens and tests to determine those that should be released as new products.

Initial Screen

The ideas that are outlined on *suggestion*, *Market Information*, or new product idea forms should be reviewed by someone, usually in Marketing, who has the ability to recognize good ideas from bad and who knows whether or not ideas are compatible with the company's overall business and marketing plans. Those ideas deemed worthy are briefly summarized in a *New Product Idea Report*. This Report should be submitted to a *New Product Committee*.

SECONDARY SCREEN

The *New Product Committee*, which is typically comprised of senior executives from Marketing, Engineering/R&D, and Finance, meets periodically to review the ideas summarized in the *New Product Idea Report*. They quickly eliminate the weaker ideas and concentrate on those that they feel has the most potential. After due consideration, they select those which they feel should be evaluated further. They agree to have their staffs analyze them in more detail and to report the findings at a subsequent meeting. This more detailed analysis will involve *"penciling out"* the selected ideas as to their marketing, engineering, and financial viability. This means estimating the costs in both dollars and people-power to finance, manufacture and market the products.

SELECTION OF PROTOTYPES

At the evaluation meeting, the various members of the committee present the results of their detailed analyses. The product ideas that show promise for satisfying your company's return on investment criteria are selected for the next step — *building a prototype*. The Engineering/R&D representative proceeds to develop the prototype, while the Financial member of the committee figures out the best way to finance the development, and the Marketing representative begins to outline a plan for testing the market viability of the product.

TESTING

While the R&D people build and test the product, the Marketing people check and double check the market place to make sure that the product satisfies the needs originally identified and that a sufficient number of customers and prospects will buy it when it is available. They do this by engaging in such activities as *interviewing* people, conducting *surveys* and *focus groups*, and testing various promotional approaches to the marketplace. In many cases, companies should make sure that any pre-introduction interviews or contacts with the marketplace are conducted in the strictest confidence. They don't want to "tip off" competitors any sooner than necessary. In addition to engaging legal assistance to protect the product with patents and trademarks, this usually involves making sure that all interviewees sign nondisclosure and confidentiality agreements.

Once new product candidates pass these preliminary tests, many companies will actually *test market* them in a limited geographical area to measure the actual reaction of market targets. Small cities or towns that are considered "typical" or "characteristic" of the general market are chosen for this purpose. For pharmaceutical and other products that are subject to government regulation, agencies such as the FDA may require testing and proof of concept that can take up to seven years before the product is approved for release.

NEW PRODUCT INTRODUCTION

Products that pass the scrutiny of the testing phase are introduced as new products. By this time, *marketing plans* including *strategies* and a *marketing information system* should be put in place to properly launch and monitor the success of the product. More about these will be discussed in subsequent chapters.

SHELVED FOR FUTURE

It should be mentioned that all *good* ideas that are rejected along the way should be kept on file for future review and re-evaluation. This is particularly true for those ideas that were rejected because market and financial conditions were not right at the time of the initial evaluation. Many companies have introduced products derived from "moth-balled" ideas that were subsequently reevaluated when market conditions changed. For example, in 1981, *Zenith* decided to resurrect its *"flat tension mask"* screen — an idea that had been rejected and shelved in the 1940's because the available technology could not produce it at a price the market could afford. *Zenith* is betting that the development of this technology will protect the company from the fate of the 15 other U.S. makers of color TV Sets who have all left the market in the last decade as a result of cutthroat competition from the Far East and Europe.

A WORD ABOUT SERVICES

It may appear to some that the *New Product Development System* discussed above applies only to companies who manufacture tangible goods. While this is perhaps the appearance, it is not true. Service companies go through basically the same process in generating and screening ideas. There may not be any physical prototype built, but there is typically a company brochure, presentation booklet, video, or some other physical representation of the service that is used to turn the "intangible" service into a "tangible" product in the minds of prospects and clients. These tangible representations of new services to be offered can be produced in prototypical form and tested in similar ways to any physical product. The key marketing challenge of service businesses is to make the services offered appear to be tangible in the minds of prospects and customers. Often, successful service companies do this by creating a physical product which represents the service — for example a diploma for an educational service, a leather bound extended warranty contract, a professionally-produced consulting report, a detailed legal report of work completed on the client's behalf, or some other physical representation of the service. It's interesting to note that a successful marketing strategy for many physical products is to do the reverse — add intangibles such as sex appeal, status, or anxiety avoidance.

THE SWOT MODEL

SWOT is an acronym for *Strengths*, *Weaknesses*, *Opportunities* and *Threats*. The *New Product Development System* discussed above should automatically incorporate the *SWOT* model. That is, it should only consider *Opportunities*, or new product ideas, that are compatible with your company's *Strengths*. Strengths typically refer to a company's expertise, experience, unique advantage, and know-how. At the same time, it should avoid products that involve *Weaknesses*. The opposite of strengths, weaknesses usually refer to a company's *lack* of expertise, experience, advantage, or know-how. When evaluating opportunities, it should also avoid those that pose serious *Threats* to the company. Threats, also known as limiting factors, typically refer to those dangers, both obvious and hidden, that are likely to drain company resources. They often include "cutthroat" competition, government regulations, obsolescence, unavailable distribution, hostile legal environments, unfamiliar markets, new territories, alien cultures, lack of expertise in a given product line or market, and limited resources.

DETERMINING THE MARKET POTENTIAL

Once *opportunities* are evaluated in terms of *strengths*, *weaknesses*, and *threats*, the *Market Potential* for each is estimated. Market Potential is the *total market for the product in a specific area*, called the *Market Territory*. It is usually expressed in terms of units and dollars and is the product of the following.

Market Potential Units = Number of potential buyers x Number of units they are likely to buy over your market planning period (usually one year).

Market Potential Dollars = Market potential units x Estimated Price per unit of product (usually a weighted average price of all products in your product line).

The Market Potential is determined after asking the following questions:

- Who are the market targets (customers, prospects, and suspects)?
- Where are they located?
- How many of them are in the market territory?
- Which, and how much, product do they really need or want?
- How many are they likely to buy?
- How frequently are they likely to buy?
- When are they likely to buy (seasonality)?

The Market Potential that results from these questions is reviewed and revised as necessary during the various phases of *New Product Development* and *Introduction*. The final number is then formally put into the Marketing Plan.

It is unlikely that a company will ever achieve the numbers represented by the Market Potential — unless, of course, this potential has been vastly underestimated. The reason for this is that every company is constrained by several *limiting factors* (also referred to as *threats* in the previous section) that are likely to prevent them from realizing their entire potential. Some of the most common of these are described below.

Competition

All companies and products have competition. Even if there is no product quite like the product being marketed, there are always alternatives including the alternative of not buying. For example, a prospect could always use a typewriter and a manual accounting system as an alternative to a computer; public transportation or a bicycle as an alternative to a car; a telex, overnight mail, or e-mail instead of a fax; and so forth.

Limited Company Resources

No matter how large, no company has all the resources to completely cover an entire marketplace. It takes a lot of time and marketing dollars to find prospects and let them know that your company and products exist. Since some people don't have access to standard communications media, there is no way to reach them. Many who do may not speak the same language or may not read or view the media in which your ads are placed that day. Moreover, it takes a tremendous amount of time, manpower and dollars to find, hire, train, and support sales personnel to sell the product in the various territories of the market — especially if the market is international.

Government regulations

Governments may have anti-monopolistic rules and regulations that prevent one company from dominating an entire market. They may also put environmental restraints, tariffs, or other regulations on companies that interfere with their ability to realize their full market potential.

Technological changes

In many high-tech markets, technologies are changing so rapidly that some products are rendered obsolete before they have realized their estimated market potential.

Limited Distribution

Many parts of the market territory may not have easy access to sales outlets, outside sales reps selling the product, or the Internet. This is particularly true of territories outside the bigger cities. As a result of this difficult access, many potential customers, who would otherwise buy the product if access were easier, will choose other more easily accessible alternatives.

MARKET PENETRATION OR GOAL

Based on these limiting factors, the company should determine how much of the Market Potential it expects to "penetrate" or sell. The resultant figure is usually expressed as a percentage of the total potential, in units, or dollars and is called *Market Penetration*. It becomes the goal of the Marketing Plan. Another commonly-used term for *market penetration goal* is *market share goal.*

If Data is Readily Available

While the market potential and expected market penetration are sometimes very difficult to estimate, every attempt should be made to do so. If nothing else, the company will collect valuable information about the marketplace and the competition by going through the exercise. There are many good data sources provided by the *Department of Commerce*, *Hoovers*, *Dun & Bradstreet*, industry associations, industry publications, the *Census Bureau*, and the research departments of local newspapers, and most of these are found in public or university libraries or on the *Internet*.

If Required Data is Too Difficult to Obtain

In those cases where it is too difficult to obtain data, it is useful to work backwards. For example, the company can assume a very conservative penetration, say 1%, and look at the *return on investment* needed to achieve that level of penetration. It can also look at *"worst case"* and *"optimistic"* scenarios and the numbers that would result. Another way to do it is to look at the figures required to *"break-even"* — that is, where the revenues and costs are in balance and no losses are incurred — and to assess the effort required, given the number of people available to do the work, to achieve these numbers.

Whatever methods are used, the important point to remember is a *market penetration* figure should be derived because this will become the *goal* against which success is measured. This *goal* will also serve as the essential starting point from which all plans of action and budgets will be derived and a target at which all company personnel can aim and focus their efforts. Obviously, the more reliable and verifiable the data, the more likely company personnel will hit their targets. However, even if not verifiable, logically constructed numbers are better than no numbers at all. In addition to the importance of these numbers to a workable internal plan, they are also important to attracting outside financing sources. Venture capitalists, banks, and other sources of financing and assistance will want to see that the management of the company has at least gone through the exercise of thinking through the problems and "penciling out" the goals the company expects to achieve.

MARKETING STRATEGIES

The next step in the Marketing Cycle is to develop *Marketing Strategies* to achieve the goal or goals identified in the Market Plan. As will be discussed in detail later, the Marketing Strategies are constructed from the *7 Building Blocks of Marketing*. These building blocks, in turn, relate to the following questions:

1. What is the company's *Corporate Image* in the marketplace?
2. What *Positions* (images) do company products occupy in the minds of market targets, or buyers?
3. What benefits do company *Products provide to buyers*?
4. What *Prices* are buyers willing to pay for company products (and will the company make money at these prices)?

5. Where and how should company products be *Placed*, or *distributed, in the marketplace* to make it convenient for targets to find, buy and use the product?
6. What are the most efficient and effective ways to *Promote*, or communicate, the benefits of company products to prompt market targets to take buying actions?
7. What *Marketing Information System* mechanisms should be built into the *product* and its *promotional* activities to collect critical information about the marketplace and to measure the success of the company's marketing strategies?

Because 5 of these building blocks begin with the letter "P," they are often called the *5 P's of Marketing*. Actually, many books on marketing refer to the 4 Ps of Marketing. These books are either outdated or sacrifice reality for tradition since they leave out one of the most important P's — *Positioning*.

Since all company resources are limited, the *optimal mix of strategies*, called the *Marketing Mix*, needs to be developed. As with any recipe, the *Marketing Mix* should contain the right amount of each of the marketing variables, or building blocks, (Corporate Image, 5Ps, and the Marketing Information System) in order for the final result to turn out as planned. From this Mix, forecasts, budgets, programs, organizational assignments, and timetables are developed to determine how human and financial resources will be most efficiently allocated to properly execute the above strategies.

MARKET INFORMATION SYSTEM

While many companies don't even have one, a *Marketing Information System* should be developed and installed to…

- Collect information from the marketplace to determine what market targets need.
- Measure the effectiveness of strategies and the viability of goals.
- Effectively report deviations from plan goals.
- Evaluate or analyze reported results.
- Change strategies if goals are not achieved.
- Adjust goals if changing strategies doesn't work.
- Change the entire plan if necessary.

In developing such a system, the following questions should be answered:

- Where does the information come from? (phone calls, presentations, sales, orders/invoices, letters, media, customer/prospect comments, reports, etc.).
- How is the information collected?
- How is it reported?
- To whom is it reported?
- How is it analyzed? By whom?
- How will proper action be taken? By whom?

To insure the integrity of the system, it is important to…

- Listen to facts.
- Determine which facts are relevant.
- Think at all times.
- Not assume a result and make data fit this result.
- Not use a statistically *insignificant* number of examples to generalize a whole case.

Because of the importance of the *Marketing Information System* to your success, it will be considered in much greater detail in a subsequent Chapter. For now, the only other point to be considered is its use in eliminating old or obsolete products.

Eliminate Old/Obsolete Products

While the *New Product Development System* helps the company introduce new products to the marketplace, the *Marketing Information System* is used to evaluate and eliminate old or obsolete products.

Product Life Cycle

Firstly, one should realize that every product has a *life cycle*, and that due to rapid changes in technology and competition, high-tech products typically have shorter cycles. As shown in *Figure 2-3*, a typical product life cycle has four phases that economists and marketers have modeled after the human life cycle. These phases are: *introduction*, *growth*, *maturity*, and *decline*.

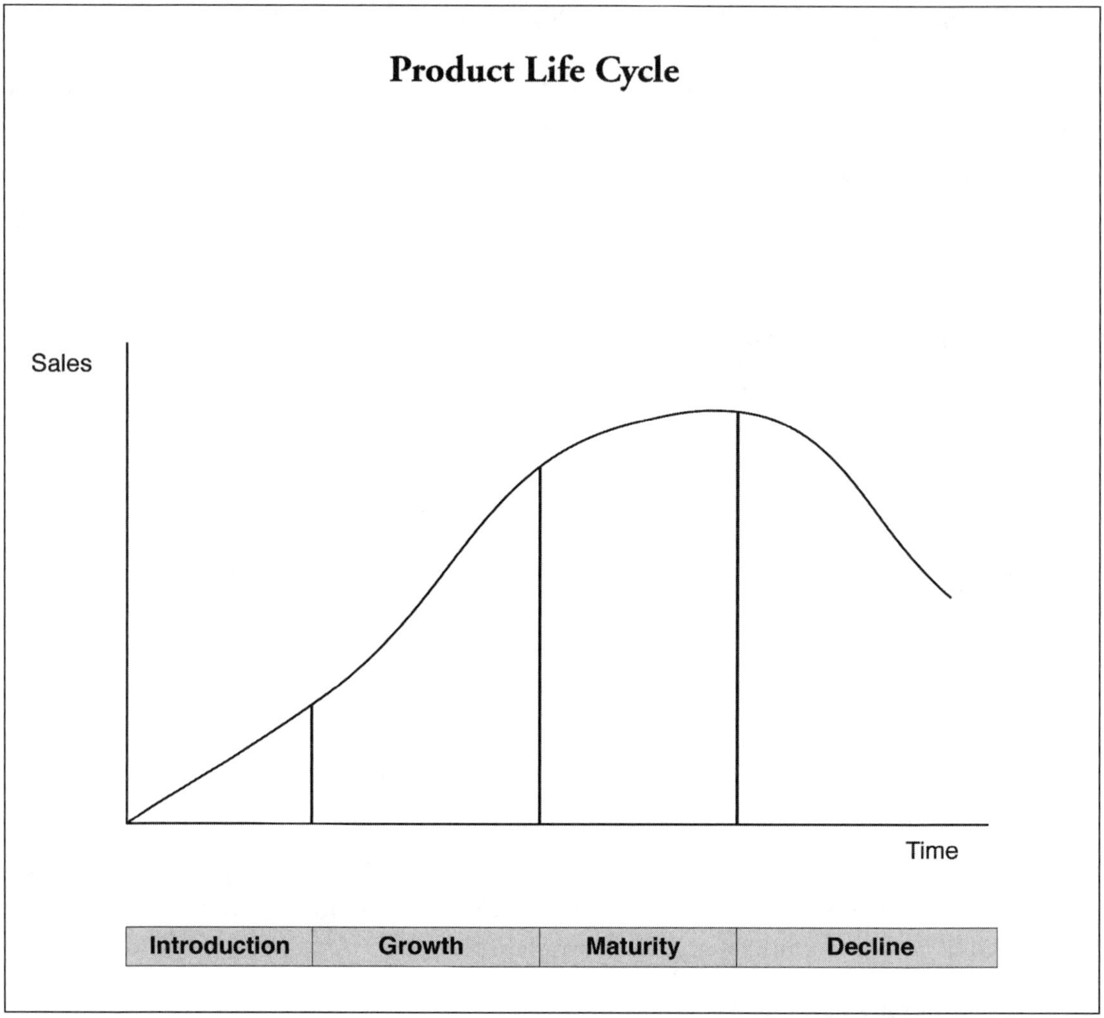

Figure 2-3. With good marketing, the company can prolong the growth and maturity phases and avoid the decline phase. For example, products such as Coca Cola are still dominating in world sales without any sign of decline.

Return on Investment

How do you know when a product should be eliminated from the company's product line? The answer is conceptually simple — you look at the product's return on investment, or ROI. That is, when the return realized from selling the product is no longer worth the continued investment to keep it in the product line. With high-technology products, the *obsolescence factor* also has to be considered. In other words, has the product been replaced by something better?

Opportunity Costs

When retrieving and evaluating the information from the Marketing Information System, it is important that marketing costs and opportunity costs are considered. Marketing costs, of course, are the costs to continue to market the product (position, promote, distribute, price, and upgrade the product). Opportunity costs are the costs of not investing in other opportunities that might produce a higher return.

The 80/20 Rule

The 80/20 rule is often useful in evaluating the worth of products in the product line. This rule says that 20% of the products in the product line produce 80% of the revenues or profits. While it sounds unbelievable, it's often true. What do you do when you discover the products in your line follow this rule? The first action you take is to perform market research to find out why. If the answer is that you haven't been devoting sufficient marketing resources to these products, you should intensify your marketing efforts. If the answer is that you are doing all you can, but it is still not selling well, then you should consider dropping the product from the line. If you don't consider dropping poor performing products, your company might be wasting resources on such products needlessly. More importantly, you may be losing revenues that could be generated by more promising opportunities.

Goodwill Products

Sometimes it is necessary to keep an old or obsolete product in the line for reasons of customer *goodwill*. That is, a lot of customers are using the product, and they want to continue to find parts, support and service. They might get mad if you eliminate the product. The costs of upsetting and losing them should be considered in your ROI calculation. One way to eliminate such costs is to offer them assistance in finding old parts to keep their older products up and running. Another way to avoid upsetting customers is to offer upgrades or trade-ins toward a new model. Most automobile dealers do this, and some computer dealers and manufacturers do as well.

Examples

Coca-Cola met with considerable customer resistance when they tried to change the formula of their popular drink. Two-hundred thousand taste tests indicated that a sweeter formula would be more popular with those in *Coke's* prime target market. However, taste tests did not prove to be as important to customers as their emotional attachment to the *all-American* traditional drink. *Coca-Cola* had become a trusted member of many households. Changing the formula was akin to removing *an old friend* or disrupting the *comfort zone* of buyers. Of course, customer reaction prompted *Coca-Cola* to re-introduce the old formula under the name *Coca-Cola Classic*.

Ford has experienced the same situation with the *Mustang*. Up until the end of 1993, the company treated the *Mustang* as an *orphan product* by avoiding modernizing the plant where it is manufactured and by neglecting to put significant marketing resources into promoting it. This neglect occurred even though *Mustang* was consistently the runaway sales leader in its class — outselling the *Chevrolet Camaro* and *Pontiac Firebird* combined and leading such imports as the *Nissan 300ZX* and the *Honda Prelude*.

Microsoft experienced similar customer resistance when they introduced *Microsoft Word 6.0* for *Macintosh computers*. *Word 5.1* was a very efficient and useful program. When *6.0* was introduced, it was found by many to be a "memory hog," slow, and cumbersome to use. Additionally, it changed many of the commands required to perform certain functions. As a result many users revolted — deciding to continue using *version 5.1*. They were not ready to upgrade even though, the new version introduced many new features. *Microsoft* responded by having a special *5.1 toolbar option* in subsequent versions.

The key to these stories is that customers will let you know if you try to *eliminate old products before their time*.

While the decision to eliminate old products from the product line should be based on return on investment, the ROI calculation should factor in all relevant information including the costs of customer resistance, the impact on corporate image, and the relationship of the product to others in the line.

THE MARKETING PLAN

With the overview of the various steps in the *Marketing Plan* provided by this discussion of the *Marketing Cycle*, it is useful to look at an outline of what should be in a *Marketing plan*. This outline is provided below.

TYPICAL OUTLINE

1. **Introduction:** Brief description of the need for the company and its products.
2. **Executive Summary:** Summarizes the main points of the entire plan for venture capitalists, bankers, other key financial sources, and stakeholders. This should be as brief and to the point as possible. The word *Summary* should be taken quite seriously.
3. **Background of company.**
    - **Mission:** Brief restatement of the company's mission to satisfy the need in the Introduction. What is it organized to do? Who are the market targets? What makes the company unique?
    - **History:** Brief history (If it is a new company, give background and experience of key executives).
4. **General description of product line.**
5. **Definition of the Marketplace and the Market Potential.**
    - **Target Market:** Definition of market and identification of market targets.
    - **Market Potential:** Size of market in terms of number of buyers, units, and dollars.
    - **Market Potential Adjustments:** Adjustments to the market potential should be made to reflect (1) growth or decline rates of the marketplace, (2) your plan to take business, or market share, from competitors, and (3) your plan to enter other markets.
6. **Limiting factors.**
    - Competition's expected share of the market.
    - Coverage of marketplace possible with available human resources.
    - Coverage possible with available financial resources.
    - Other limiting factors such as production capacity, distribution obstacles, lack of experience, etc.

Note: After talking about these limiting factors, this section should end on a positive note with your plan to counteract, neutralize, or compensate for them.

7. **Expected penetration.** This expected penetration or anticipated share of the market should then become the primary goal of the plan.

8. **Marketing Strategies to achieve penetration goals** (*Marketing Mix* based on the combination of the 7 Building Blocks).

9. **Translation of the Strategies into Budgets, Programs, Peoplepower, and Timetables.** This should contain just the right amount of detail — *detailed enough* to convince investors and stakeholders and provide a blueprint for company insiders to follow, *but not too detailed* to restrict the flexibility and creativity necessary to operate the business. The key bullet points are discussed here and the details are often put in an Appendix.

10. **Sales Forecast** (Units and/or $).

11. **Futures.** An optimistic view of the future to which the company can look forward.

Purposes of the Marketing Plan

This *Marketing Plan* will serve two primary purposes — (1) as the *blueprint* for the company to follow in marketing its products and services for at least one year, and (2) as a *selling document* to attract investors, financing from banks, key employees, and other necessary publics. Beyond the first year, or more frequently if necessary, the *Plan* should be revised to reflect updated information about the marketplace and the company's performance that will be measured and analyzed by the Marketing *Information System*.

Because of their importance to the successful execution of the Marketing Plan, each of the variables of the Marketing Mix – the *Seven Building Blocks* will be discussed in detail in the following Chapters.

[1] Robert E. Dallos, "Winning Friends in High Places," *Los Angeles Times*, July 31, 1988 pg. 6.

[2] Bob Baker, "Employees Suggestions Take on Weight in Lean Times," *Los Angeles Times*, September 15, 1991 pg. D-1.

[3] Cheryll Aimée Barron, "Getting Serious About Service," *New York Times Magazine — The Business World*, Part 2, June 11, 1989 pg. 52.

[4] Alsop and Abrams (Editors), *Wall Street Journal On Marketing*, 1986, pg. 147.

TIPS and Exercises

1. Do a SWOT Analysis of yourself and/or your company.
2. Identify opportunities in the marketplace that match your strengths.
3. Take at least one opportunity and collect information on the market potential of that opportunity — focusing on the unfilled need that this opportunity will fill.
4. Identify the limiting factors that will prohibit you from getting the entire potential.
5. Try to quantify the market potential and limiting factors as much as possible, or at least take them into account.
6. Using the above data, determine your measurable goal in selling the product(s).
7. Outline your strategy for achieving that goal.
8. Put all of the above together in the form of a Marketing Plan.
9. Put systems in place to collect new product ideas (suggestion boxes, market information forms, etc.) and encourage all who are involved in your organization to contribute ideas.

Chapter 3

The Marketing Mix

"With the proper mix, you'll get the right result every time..."

WHAT IS THE MARKETING MIX?

The *Marketing Mix is the combination of integrated marketing strategies employed to achieve the goals of your Marketing Plan.* It is the combination of, and interaction between, the 7 *Building Blocks* that include the *5Ps* (*Positioning*, *Product*, *Price*, *Place*, and *Promotion*), *Corporate Image* (which some marketers at *Procter & Gamble* are now calling the sixth P — *Projection*), and the *Marketing Information System* mixed together into coordinated strategies to achieve the company's marketing objectives.

CAKE ANALOGY

The marketing mix is analogous to the process of baking a cake from a mix of ingredients. That is, once the ingredients are mixed together and heat is added, the resultant cake can no longer be broken down into its original constituent ingredients. The same is true of the marketing mix. Once the building blocks, or marketing variables, are put together into integrated strategies, it is virtually impossible to separate, or change, them without affecting all the others.

UNDERSTANDING THE INTERDEPENDENCE OF MIXED VARIABLES

Many who practice marketing actually don't understand this integrated nature of marketing variables. For example, many marketers respond to competition by lowering prices without thinking through the affect this will have on their other marketing strategies. In many cases, lowering prices will affect the product's Positioning as well as the perceived value of the Product and the Corporate Image of the company. It is also likely to affect the Distribution channels and the way the product is Promoted. A couple of actual examples should help to clarify this concept.

HOW CHANGING ONE INGREDIENT WILL AFFECT OTHERS

In the 1970's, the "alligator shirt" from *Izod Lacoste* occupied an exclusive and upscale *position* in minds of its market targets. It became a *status symbol*. At that time, the company's parent company, *General Mills*, thinking it would capitalize on this trend, flooded the market with product by expanding distribution beyond exclusive channels. Because the shirt became commonplace, it lost its *position*. It was no longer exclusive, and upscale buyers did not want to be associated with the other groups who were buying it. As a result, *Izod Lacoste* lost its target audience, sales plummeted, and the upscale *position*, or void, was filled by *Ralph Lauren's Polo* brand.

Another example relates to an actual situation that occurred with a prospective client in the Spring of 1991. This prospect specialized in providing flavored and bottled teas made from all natural ingredients. Because of the nature of the *product* and the *price* they had to charge to manufacture it from top-quality, healthy and natural ingredients, the company *positioned* the product for upscale, health-oriented buyers. Initially, the company reached targeted buyers by smartly placing its products in exclusive food markets located in upper middle-class neighborhoods. In *building-block* terminology, its *distribution* strategy was in harmony with its *positioning*, *product*, and *pricing* strategies. One day, one of the owners of this company called me. In a very happy and excited tone of voice, she explained that she had an appointment with the buyer from the local *7-11* chain of convenience stores. I asked her why she thought a relationship with *7-11* would be good for her company. She replied by saying that *7-11* is a large chain which potentially represents a large volume of business. I told her that I thought that selling to *7-11* would hurt her product's *position* as an upscale beverage that would, in turn, tarnish her company's corporate image. If she secured *7-11* as a distributor, she would alienate her upscale customers — including her distributors.

She didn't really understand what I meant until the following week when she called me to tell me that I was right. She had met with the buyer of the *Mrs. Gooch's* chain of upscale, all-natural, health-oriented stores. This buyer asked her about the other stores with which she was doing business. To "impress" this buyer she mentioned her potential deal with *7-11*. After grimacing, the buyer told her that *Mrs. Gooch's* would never carry any products sold in a *7-11* store. This buyer knew that the image, or position, of *7-11* products, the corporate image of *7-11* stores, and the profile of its customers were incompatible with those of *Mrs. Gooch's*. Since *7-11* was a convenience store *distributor* that sold certain fast-food *products* (not associated with health) to younger, mostly male customers. *Placement*, or *distribution*, of this healthy line of bottled teas in such stores would tend to taint the *corporate image*, *positioning*, *product*, and *pricing* of both *Mrs. Gooch's* and my prospective client.

As an anecdote, this prospective client did not become a client. As with many small companies, even though they badly needed help with their marketing, the owners did not want to invest money in marketing advice. In an effort to help them anyway, I brought their situation to the attention of my *Advertising and Promotion Management* class at the University of Southern California. My students voted to help this company as part of a school project in exchange for some free bottles of herbal tea.

QUESTIONS TO KEEP IN MIND

When developing the Marketing Mix, it is important to keep the following questions in mind.

- *Who are the market targets (customers, prospects, and suspects)?*
- *What do they already have in their minds regarding your industry, company, competitors, and products?*

- *What do they think about your company and your products?*
- *Where are they located?*
- *What do they need and want?*
- *How much do they need and want?*
- *How are they doing the job now?*
- *What competitors are they considering?*
- *What do they like and dislike about competitive products?*
- *How much are they willing to pay?*
- *How do you reach them most efficiently and effectively?*
- *What are the costs?*
- *What is the expected ROI?*

The answers to these questions are obtained by using a *Marketing Information System* to collect the appropriate information from the marketplace. The data is collected and analyzed. Any gaps in knowledge are filled with additional *Market Research*. Both *primary market research* (such as conducting focus groups or surveys) and *secondary market research* (reviewing published studies) is utilized to bridge these knowledge gaps.

MODIFIED BY MARKETPLACE REALITIES

Upon collecting the necessary information, the mix might need to be modified by certain marketplace realities. These typically include *environmental factors*, such as competition and government regulations, and limited *company resources*. That is, because of competition and company resources, a company may choose to spend marketing dollars by offering the product at a lower *Price* rather then spending the same dollars on more advertising in a particular publication — a *Promotion* strategy. The point to remember here is that the variables in the marketing mix often compete for the same limited resources — financial and human.

STRATEGY FORMULATION

Once the necessary modifications are made to these answers, the *marketing variables*, or *building blocks*, become the *marketing strategies* of the company's *Marketing Plan*. That is, *positions* are chosen, *products* are defined, *prices* are set to certain values, *distribution channels* are selected, the *promotion* mix is determined, and *marketing information system* mechanisms are designed to collect information and measure strategy effectiveness. Even though these variables become defined over the planning horizon covered by your *Marketing Plan*, they should continue to be thought of as variables. The reason is that strategies should not be rigid and impossible to change. If your *marketing information system* tells you that they are not working as planned, they can, and should, be changed — assuming sufficient investigation and analysis is completed before making final decisions.

Because of the importance of these marketing strategies to an organization's marketing, each of them will be examined in detail in subsequent chapters.

TIPS and Exercises

1. Find articles and examples of the marketing mix of strategies used by successful companies.
2. After you understand why the mix worked for them, try to create the proper mix for your organization.

Chapter 4

DNA of Corporate Image

"Too many in science don't realize that Perception is Reality."

INTRODUCTION

The image of organizations and individuals is extremely important to their success as well as the success of the products with which they are associated. Because of its importance, this chapter focuses on *Corporate Image Marketing*.

Throughout recorded history, writers, philosophers and artists have understood the importance of image. Since it is very difficult and time consuming to understand the inherent nature of people, companies, and other *things*, we have to rely on our *impressions* for making decisions. *Arthur Andersen*, *MCI/Worldcom*, *Martha Stewart Living Omnimedia*, *Imclone*, *Enron*, and *ValueJet* are just a few examples of organizations that either went out of business or suffered tremendous losses because of their inability to properly repair a damaged corporate image.

In business, decisions are made very quickly. Because of this fact, first and subsequent impressions are very important. An old cliché warns — you never get a second chance to make a first impression. An astute marketing manager needs to recognize this and insure that every impression made by the company is as positive as possible. If it isn't, *life* will be made more difficult and expensive for everyone — especially those who have primary contact with the public such as the sales people, the customer service representatives, repair technicians, accounts receivable clerks, credit and collections staff, and public relations personnel. They will have to *dig themselves out of a hole* before making the initial sale, while appeasing irate customers, when repairing products, when they try to collect money due, and before generating repeat business. *American Airlines* recognizes the importance of first impressions to their image and business. They tell their newly hired flight attendants during a five-week training program, *"The first impression passengers get as they board a flight is going to set the entire tone of the flight."* In recent years, *American* has made a commitment to improving their level of service across the board from the point of making the initial reservation to the point of retrieving luggage. This strategy has paid off in increased customer and employee satisfaction. Not surprisingly, they continue to be one of America's most successful airlines and the market leader.

WHAT IS MEANT BY AN ORGANIZATION'S IMAGE?

Image refers to the impression that an organization makes in the minds of its publics. In other words, it is the first thought that *pops* into the minds of all those who do business with the company when they think about that company. Using a more formal definition, *corporate image* is *the collective impression made by an organization on its various publics*. These publics include market targets (comprised of customers, prospects, and suspects, or those who fit the profile of prospects but have had no contact with your organization) employees, past employees, job candidates, vendors, board members, media, governments, financing sources, the surrounding community, and competitors. While many companies are conscious of the image they portray to prospects and customers, a large number of them often forget their other important publics — employees (past, present, and future), media, suppliers, stockholders, board members, governments, regulatory agencies, universities, and surrounding communities. Companies should not forget these other groups for the simple reason that they all have the potential to become customers, employees, and important referral sources for new business.

Years to build and minutes to destroy

The important point to remember about *corporate image* is that it is *hard to build* and *easy to lose a good one* and *very difficult to rebuild a damaged one*. Unfortunately, in business, bad news travels fast. Robert L. Crandall, former president of *American Airlines*, has recognized, *"it takes years to build a reputation, and a few minutes to destroy it."*[1] Moreover, the factors that cause a negative image, if not corrected, can have a devastating impact on business. A survey conducted by *Opinion Research Corporation* of Princeton, New Jersey reported that 87% of those interviewed said that "when choosing between products of similar quality and price, they base buying decisions on the reputations of the companies in question." As reported in the *Wall Street Journal on Marketing*, only about 4% of dissatisfied customers complain to a company. The other 96% who don't bother to complain usually stop buying the product and also disparage it to 9 or 10 other people within a week. By passing the negative word to others, unappeased complainers form the top of a *negative word-of-mouth pyramid* publicizing negatives about your company and products to as many 250 people. In contrast, complaints that are resolved quickly usually lead to repeat purchases and stronger relationships. *General Electric* claims that its typical satisfied caller passes the word to five other people within 10 days.[2]

Broken bone analogy

This means that complaints that are resolved quickly and negative situations that are turned into positive ones result in a stronger and more positive relationship with the customer than would have occurred if the customer had no complaint in the first place.

Why does the repair of a broken relationship result in a closer bond with your publics? Similar to a broken bone that heals stronger over the break, the repair of a broken relationship means the relationship has been tested, and your company has passed the test. Buyers know that products can malfunction and companies can make mistakes. What they need and want are organizations and people who will help them through these difficult situations. Those who do will earn their loyalty and be rewarded by repeat business and referrals. Those who don't will lose their business and subsequent referrals.

This concept of *turning a negative into a positive*, therefore, should be a central tenet of every organization's marketing strategy.

WHAT AFFECTS A COMPANY'S IMAGE?

Virtually *everything a company and its representatives do affects its image*. Unfortunately, many technical product-focused companies either forget this or they don't understand it in the first place.

Image can be adversely affected by such transgressions as unreliable products, mistakes, association with controversial issues, socially unacceptable acts, layoffs, plant closings, bad publicity, disgruntled employees, unscrupulous competitors, bad service, long waits on the phone, *bad-taste* Web sites, signs and packaging, a poorly-chosen name, "cheap-looking" stationery, and impolite or uncooperative treatment of prospects and customers by company personnel.

Conversely, it can be helped by such positives as community assistance programs, public television and arts sponsorships, aid to universities and hospitals, donations to worthwhile causes, good treatment of various publics, a good name, good service, quality stationery, good-looking buildings and signage, plant tours, and congratulatory ads.

CREATING YOUR IMAGE

To create an image for your organization, you should start with a mission statement. The problem with most mission statements is that they are too general and do not give proper direction to all those who need to communicate your image — people in your various publics.

Mission Statement

Your mission statement should do the following three things:

1. Make it clear to the world what your company does, or why you exist.
2. Identify your target audience.
3. Define what makes your organization unique.

Corporate Identity Tools

Most companies have three tools they can use to create their corporate identity — name, logo, and corporate image slogan.

Name

Often, the *first point of contact* with an organization is its name. Therefore, the selection of a name is a very important decision. A good name tends to contribute to a positive image, be consistent with an organization's line of business, be easily remembered, and properly position the company relative to key competitors. A not-so-good name may hurt a company's image and/or confuse its various publics. And name confusion can be very detrimental since it may diminish the return on the company's investment in marketing. That is, the dollars spent may be benefiting the other company whose name is the subject of the confusion. The confusion over *Goodrich* and *Goodyear* is a good example. Even worse, the other name, or names, with which it is confused may have negatives associated with them.

Be cautious about using your name. Often the name of the founder or owner is used as part of the company name. While this can work, as in the case of *Dell Computer* or *Hewlett-Packard*, it can also have many disadvantages. Firstly, unless it is used in conjunction with other words that are descriptive of the business, it may be difficult for various publics to know what the firm does from its name. Secondly, using a personal name can cause needless customer fears. One of the many concerns customers have with companies who sell products that require after-sale service is the fear they'll go out of business and not be around to support and service their products. In today's marketplace, using a personal name for a new company often fuels such fears since a personal name normally implies the firm is a small *mom-and-pop* family business. Small implies less stable since many small companies find difficulty surviving against much larger competition. Thirdly, it's more difficult to establish useful graphic images and positions in the minds of prospects with personal names. Finally, if the person whose name is associated with the company receives bad publicity, as in the case of Martha Stewart, the effect on the company's sales and profits can be devastating.

New companies. For new companies, an effective name should create images of innovative, state-of-art, growing, in demand, etc. If possible, it should also give an indication of the type of business or industry the company is in, or it should be descriptive of the type of products and services the company sells.

Avoid names that limit your future. *Apple* is a computer company that built its early success in the education and computer-hobby market. In this market, its name served it very well. It has had considerably more difficulty, however, penetrating the *Fortune 1000* market. Many of the decision makers in these large companies have associated the name *Apple* with *fun*, *games*, and *education* and not with serious business computing. While *Apple's* loyal following and quality products have helped to overcome initial purchasing resistance in the business market, the company has lost a significant number of sales and share of the market to *IBM* PC compatibles, in no small part, because of the image created by its name. Recognizing this problem, the company has shifted emphasis from *Apple* to Macintosh. In fact, on many business-related products, the *Apple* logo has shrunk relative to the *Macintosh*, *PowerPC*, *iMac*, and *PowerBook* names.

Study the most successful companies. When selecting a name, it's useful to look at the names of successful companies in similar businesses for ideas. Understanding how their name has helped them to achieve success will help you to create a successful name. When trying to establish a new identity, a company should be careful about using initials because they may cause confusion when the organization is not well known. Once well-known and established, initials can work as in the case of *IBM*, *MS-NBC*, or *BMW*.

High-technology and bio-tech. There are *lots* of standard prefixes and suffixes used in high-tech names that can be combined to formulate new names. Some examples include the following: *Com*, *Comp*, *Digi*, *Data*, *Elec*, *Quan*, *Memory*, *Mem*, *Micro* for prefixes, and *mation*, *tron soft*, *ix*, *ics*, *ex*, *rex*, *rox*, *on*, *ec*, *ic*, *in*, *al*, *tel*, *el*, *com*, *storage* for suffixes. For DNA or life sciences companies, prefixes such as *bio*, *pharma*, or *gen* are rather common and *gen*, *ex*, *ec*, or *tech* are examples of common suffixes. It is not necessarily good to be common. It is better to communicate what you are or the benefit you provide.

Learning from the best consumer products companies. With regard to consumer-product companies, names vary widely. Some of the more descriptive names include: *Coca Cola*, *Home Depot*, *Thrifty Drug* stores, and *Burger King*. Professional firms still typically use the names of founding partners, but some are beginning to recognize the value of attaching a descriptive "handle" or slogan to let the market know what they do and what makes them unique.

Testing for objectivity. Once several potentially *good* names are selected, they should be tested (i.e. you should use your *Marketing Information System* to do some *Market Research*). There is no need to hire some expensive research firm to do this. You can ask friends, business associates, prospects, customers (if the company is a going concern that is changing its name) vendors, and even competitors. They're in a more objective position to evaluate the name than the founders who created it. What these objective sources have to say should be seriously considered against the more subjective instincts of the top executives of the organization. Even so, you should not ask friends or people in the target audience if they like a certain name. Many assume you created it, and may not give you an objective answer. What you should do is provide each person in the test group a list of names in different order, and ask them for their first word association with each name. The names that produce the desired association, or image, should be the ones you use to make your final name choice. If, for some reason, you are stuck with a name that is not the "perfect" choice, you have the logo and slogan to use as tools to help communicate the desired corporate image.

Avoiding marketplace confusion and legal conflicts. The final selection(s) should then be scrutinized against a search of other names in the same industry. The objective is to make sure that the name does not conflict with other trademarked names being used for similar products. This can be done by going to the library, by hiring a search firm, using an in-house attorney, or an outside legal counsel. The outside lawyer will probably be the most expensive and will most likely hire a *search firm* to do a computer search anyway. A patent attorney should be used if the firm intends to formally trademark the name that has been selected. In any event, the newly-selected name can be protected by having an article or a notice published establishing the date the name is first used. Also, use in *interstate* or *international commerce* can help to protect the name of products sold beyond state lines and national boundaries. Until such time as a trademark is registered, uses of the name selected should have a ™ as a superscript following the name. If and when the trademark is officially registered, the name will be followed by a superscripted ®. After getting a trademark registered, however, it can be lost if the name becomes too generic, the company does not challenge uses that fail to affix the registration notice, or the name is challenged in court. Examples of the former include trademarked names that have been used generically such as *Kleenex*, *Xerox*, and *Google*. It is ironic that companies desire to be thought of generically, but if that happens, they are legally in danger of losing their trademark.

Logos and Stationery

In conjunction with the name, it is important to think about a logo and stationery. They are often the first symbols of your company that your publics will see. Because of their importance to creating a first impression and lasting image, they represent two very important marketing decisions that affect corporate image. Unless a talented designer is on staff, the company should seek outside professional help. The best ways to find firms who specialize in logo and stationery design are to either (1) ask your ad agency or marketing consultant (if you have a good one), or (2) pick examples of good-looking and successful logos and stationery, and find out who created the designs. Once this list is compiled, the firms identified should be interviewed with regard to their fees and their understanding of your industry and products.

Before making a final selection, one should make sure that the designers offer several alternatives from which to choose. If possible, one should get the designer to quote a *fixed fee* for the project. If the budget for this is limited, one way to obtain near-professional designs at a very low cost is to sponsor a competition amongst students of a respected design school. Who knows? It's possible that the winner might be a candidate for employment some day. In any event, once the alternatives are designed, it is necessary to test their acceptance amongst the company's publics via your Marketing Information System. Again, objectivity is the key, and it is best to find a sample of critics that most closely approximates your prospects and customers.

Think of the logo as a stamp that will imprint an image of your company in the brains of your publics. Remember, it will appear on stationery, business cards, signs, brochures, packages, business forms, company checks, company trucks and products. Therefore, it is important. Along with the name, it will serve to create an image or position your company and products.

Slogans

The third tool in your corporate image tool kit is the slogan. If you are locked into a name and logo that are not ideal, you can often counterbalance these with a good positioning slogan. There are lots of slogans used by companies, but few good ones. For many years, *Coca Cola* used "It's the Real Thing" to distinguish the company from other cola companies, such as *Pepsi Cola*. It also used the benefit-focused slogan "The pause that refreshes." *Lexus* uses "The passionate pursuit of perfection."

Contact Handling

After the impressions made by your company name, logo, slogan, stationery, signage and other company communication tools, probably the next impressions that affect your company's image are the ways in which visitors or callers are treated. If a company wants to position itself as competent and service-oriented, it must act competently and offer good service at all levels of the organization. Any discrepancies between what the company says it is and what its various publics see and experience will tarnish its image and hurt sales. Such discrepancies could also be interpreted as *misrepresentations* and erode the trust between your company and publics. Without trust, the company will be unable to develop the relationships it requires to build a successful business.

If your company is market-driven, every employee will be trained to extend the utmost courtesy and helpfulness to all who call or visit. Every personal contact (whether a prospective customer, someone trying to sell something, or a prospective employee) should be regarded as a potential *unpaid sales person* for your organization. If *positively impressed*, they will become a member of your firm's "sales army" — recommending your company and products whenever they encounter potential buyers. If treated poorly, the company risks losing their assistance. Even worse, they could make unflattering and damaging comments about your company. Remember, bad news travels fast, and can be quite damaging. Don't forget the *positive* and *negative word-of-mouth pyramids*.

Unfortunately, many companies don't understand this. They look upon the receptionist position as a low-level, low-paid job. They don't understand that the receptionist is the first human voice that most people encounter when they call or visit your company. Consequently, the receptionist often plays a big part in the firm's image. Because of this, receptionists should be well-trained, like what they do, be personable, and be specifically instructed to take special care of customers and treat all others with respect, dignity, and personal attention. Additionally, a good receptionist can be trained to assist in sales, support, and service. They can be a big help with these functions. In addition to making the job more interesting and responsible, this broadening of duties enables your company to justify paying a higher salary and getting the caliber of person required to do a good job.

Taking Care of Your Other Publics

While some companies understand that it is important to treat their customers and prospects well, very few think about doing the same for other publics. Employees, job applicants, past employees, vendors, media representatives, and *walk-ins* should all be treated well. The reason is very simple. They may be customers or employees some day. Whatever their status, all contacts can become *unpaid ambassadors* and *sales people* for your company. If treated poorly, they are likely to become the opposite, looking for every opportunity to disparage your organization and hurt sales — resulting in up to 250 negative impressions.

Unfortunately, members of these other groups are too often neglected. Job applicants who walk in off the street without an appointment or send in a résumé are often the most neglected. They are made to feel as if they are an annoyance rather than a potential employee or ambassador for your company. How much time and effort does it take to treat them well? An offer of coffee, a courteous smile, or assistance are small gestures that can result in large returns. Just as with the receptionist position, many companies neglect the personnel function even though it is one of the most important functions in the company. Well-paid, personable, talented and creative people should be hired for the personnel department. Moreover, top executives and managers should test the performance of this function periodically. Assuming they won't be recognized, they should *walk through* the process to find out how prospective employees are being treated. If they will be recognized, they should send trained surrogates in their place. They should also try to *fit* the interviewing of walk-ins into their busy schedules whenever possible. If this is not possible, they (or their secretaries) should at least visit the lobby to greet walk-ins and set up appointments for a later time. If executives follow these suggestions, they can perhaps save the large sums they are currently spending on outside search firms each year — raising overhead and prices needlessly. The question is, how many potential *Einsteins* does a company lose by its personnel policies? Also, how much bad will is created by the ways people are treated by most personnel departments?

The best and most successful companies understand this. They understand that the personnel function is critical to their image and continued success, they treat every contact with courtesy, and they make sure that they return all calls and letters as quickly as possible. They do this because each employee is trained to do it. It is part of their fabric and culture and it memorialized in company policy and procedure manuals. It's no surprise that such companies consistently dominate their industries.

In addition to job applicants, past and current employees are often neglected. When this happens, a company's image can be greatly tarnished. It's well known that employees who are treated well perform better. Yet, many companies look upon their employees as *property* rather than contributors to the company's success. Even though they work for the company, it's important to make sure that they are consciously thought of as one of the company's important publics. From a marketing perspective, it is important that they receive, and are allowed to give input to, such important company activities as suggestions for product enhancements, new products, and any other activities that help to improve the company. And if an employee decides to leave the company, a conscious effort should be devoted to making his or her transition as easy as possible. Moreover, the company should do everything possible to insure that their last memories of the organization are as good as possible. The reason is that they'll take their memories with them wherever they go, and they'll talk about their experiences with previous companies. They should be looked upon as ambassadors rather than traitors even if they go to competitors. After all, they may someday become customers or return as wiser employees. And it is *never* a good idea to antagonize them.

What has been said for the above publics applies to all the others. It's important that companies consciously think of treating them well and turning them into *ambassadors of good will* and *unpaid sales people*. They include: vendors, past vendors (you may need them again), members of the board, solicitors, media, government organizations, stockholders, financial institutions, neighbors, and virtually any groups or individuals that come in contact or do business with your company.

Product Quality and Customer Service

After satisfying the prerequisites described above, one of the best ways to create a positive image is to offer excellent products and superior after sale service. This is especially critical in technology organizations since much of the focus is on the technology and on the service to keep the technology working. The important point to remember is that customers should not have the *"door slammed in their faces"* after the sale is made. If treated well, they will buy more and recommend the company to their friends. Each call for help and service should not be viewed as an annoyance. It should be viewed as an *opportunity to strengthen the relationship*, talk about new products, and increase sales. And even if more business is not forthcoming immediately, happy customers, more than any other group, will be effective unpaid sales people for your company and products. That's why customers should be treated exceptionally well. They can offer testimonials in sales presentations, provide memorable quotes that can be used to create effective advertising, be a source of positive word-of-mouth advertising, and help the company's image in many other ways.

PROTECTING YOUR IMAGE

After you create a good image, it is very important that you develop strategies to protect it. There are three classes of strategies that need to be implemented to protect your image from serious damage — (1) Rumors, (2) Facts, and (3) Day-to-day negative occurrences.

When the damage stems from a Rumor

Rumors relate to untruths that others spread about your organization. They can seriously damage your sales, profits, and reputation if you do not handle them properly.

Pepsi Cola suffered damage to their image and a decline in sales as a result of a rumor that used syringes were found in containers of their soft drinks. *McDonalds* was plagued by a rumor in the Mid-West that their burgers contained red worms. Someone began spreading rumors that *Procter & Gamble's* logo is a satanic symbol.

From a Corporate Image viewpoint, what is the most-effective way to handle such rumors? Spokespersons for the company should do, or not do, the following:

1. *Do not publicize the rumor*. Denying rumors through the media only serves to spread them to a broader audience. It also causes the skeptics in the marketplace to believe they are true.
2. *Provide proof that the opposite of the rumor is true (without acknowledging the rumor or giving it further attention).* If there are rumors that there are hypodermic needles in *Pepsi* containers, publicize facts showing that all bottles are washed, sterilized, turned over, and inspected in the manufacturing process to insure that the product is consistently pure and safe. For the red worms in hamburgers rumor, publicize the cleanliness of *McDonalds* restaurants and the fact that they all use only 100% USDA-inspected beef. For the rumor that *Procter & Gamble's* logo is a satanic symbol, publicize the history and meaning of the logo.
3. *Vigorously prosecute, without publicity (if possible), those who created and spread the rumor.* You need to set examples so others won't be encouraged to spread additional rumors.

When the damage results from a known Fact

Perhaps the best way to understand what marketers should do when the negative situation is a commonly-known fact is to look at actual examples of the proper and improper handling of these situations.

Proper Handling Examples

The proper handling of a negative situation based on fact is exemplified by the way the executives of *Johnson & Johnson* handled the *Tylenol* scare. Someone was contaminating Tylenol capsules with poison. As a result, several people died, and the sales of the product were suspended. Rather than *"sweep the problem under the rug"*, the company took immediate action to correct the situation. The Chief Executive of the corporation went on national television, showed concern for the victims and their families, suggested that viewers not buy Tylenol in capsule form, and outlined a *plan of action* to solve the problem and to insure that future products would be safely contained in tamper-proof packaging. As a result of this competent and quick action, sales of Tylenol not only returned to their previous levels, but also began to exceed them. The company succeeded in *turning a negative into a positive* — an essential Corporate Image Marketing strategy.

Lee Iacocca was able to do the same when the media reported that some *Chrysler* cars were being sold as new after they had been driven a few miles by *Chrysler* executives. Lee went on national television, admitted the problem, and proposed an immediate solution.

Improper Handling Examples

Examples of the improper handling of negative publicity resulting from actual occurrences that only served to cause further image damage are numerous. Some include: The denial of wrongdoing by *Sears* and *Winston Tire Centers* — both of which were found to be guilty of doing unnecessary repairs and overcharging customers by the State of California, *Intel's* problems with the *Pentium* chip, *Perrier's* handling of reports that their processing of water was contaminated by benzene — a known carcinogenic, *Dow Corning* problems with breast implants, *Toshiba's* problems with *illegally* selling U.S. technology, the Tobacco Industry's handling of the reported health risks from smoking and nicotine addiction, and the former Soviet Union's handling of the Chernobyl nuclear power accident. All of the above suffered considerable damage to their Corporate Image.

Procedure for controlling image damage from true facts

What is the proper procedure for minimizing the image damage from negative situations that are based on fact? The chief executive of the company, and not some public relations person, should do the following in an effort to turn the negative into a positive:

1. *Acknowledge or admit the problem.* Failure to admit the problem will only cause your publics to no longer trust you.
2. *Apologize to those who are affected.* Customers and other publics like it when companies take responsibility for their problems.
3. *Limit the Scope.* Explain that the problem has been investigated and is limited to certain individuals and locations (as is appropriate and true). Usually, problems are created by certain individuals, departments, or divisions who deviate from company policies.
4. *Outline a solution that will prevent this problem from reoccurring.* To re-establish trusting relationships with customers and other publics, they have to be assured that the company has taken measures to insure that the problem is not likely to reoccur.

Everyone should act like an owner

Whether or not you own stock in the company, you should look at your organization as your company. Assuming ownership is perhaps the best way to maintain a positive attitude and work ethic. Moreover, employees who treat the company as their own are more likely to be promoted into a key management positions by the people who do own the company. In fact, those who act as owners are likely to be owners some day via stock options, promotions, and other opportunities.

Understand that Perception is Reality

To maintain a positive corporate image, everyone in your organization should be trained to understand that, to your important publics, perception is reality. In technology and scientific companies, this notion is critically important because too many technical people tend to dismiss the importance of marketing's role in shaping the perceptions of people in the marketplace. Because this is such an important business and marketing concept, a more lengthy explanation is provided.

What you see is not always what you get

Since the beginning of time, when man looked at the horizon, he saw a straight horizontal line. The perception was that the Earth is flat. As scientific instruments and knowledge advanced, scientists were able to prove that the Earth is a spherical globe. A person viewing the horizon from the surface of that globe is really seeing a small segment of a very large circle that looks flat, but is, in fact, round.

Early scientists had a difficult time convincing their constituents that the Earth is indeed round. In fact, Galileo was imprisoned by *the Church* and lost his life for his discovery of this reality. Unfortunately, for him and other scientists, perception was the victor over the reality.

Once vehicles with cameras were sent into space, the photographs of the Earth's spherical shape was proven to be the reality.

Similar to physicists, the gulf between perception and reality presents problems for marketers. Sophisticated marketers know that, in most business situations, perception is reality. For example, when *Coca Cola* conducted blind taste tests for a new formula of its signature beverage, the new formula won the tests, but lost the buying public. *Coca Cola* was forced to bring back the old formula — the one that lost the taste tests. The perception did not represent the reality. *Coca Cola* learned that people "taste" with their eyes and minds as well as their tongues.

What is reality?

People are not equipped with the tools they need to distinguish perception and reality. They equate reality with what they can detect with their senses. This presents a problem since much of reality is not detectable by human senses. Some examples are provided in the following paragraphs.

The electromagnetic spectrum. People can only see what is in the visible part of the electromagnetic spectrum — from red at the lowest frequencies to violet at the highest. Most of the electromagnetic spectrum, however, is not visible to the human eye — from radio and microwaves at the low frequencies to ultraviolet and x-rays at the high-end. This means that humans cannot see most of what constitutes the reality of this spectrum. Moreover, within the visible part of the spectrum, there are an infinite number of different colors. Yet, most humans can detect only 267 different colors.

Audible frequencies. Just as human eyes can only see a small part of the electromagnetic spectrum, human ears can only hear a small fraction of frequencies. People who have pets know that these animals can often hear things that humans cannot. Subsonic and ultrasonic frequencies are used for medicinal purposes but are not detectable by human hearing. The reality is quite different from the perception.

Elements. The elements of the periodic table are certainly part of reality, but many of these elements are colorless and odorless gases such as oxygen, hydrogen, and nitrogen. They exist and are necessary for life but they cannot be seen, smelled, or tasted. To humans, the perception is that the element is not present, but the reality is that it is.

Motion. All matter is made from molecules, atoms, and subatomic particles that are constantly moving, but humans cannot detect the motion. Similarly while humans sitting in a chair someplace on earth don't sense any motion, they are rotating with the surface of the Earth at from 700 to 1,000 miles per hour. The Earth is simultaneously revolving around the Sun at thousands of miles per hour, and the Sun is moving about the center of the galaxy at millions of miles per hour.

Solid matter versus empty space. When a human looks at a living or inanimate object, he/she sees a form that looks solid, continuous, and at rest. That is only a perception, however. The reality is that the molecules and atoms that make up this form are largely derived from empty space and rapidly-moving atoms and subatomic particles.

The forces of nature. The forces of nature that govern the universe — known by scientists as the electromagnetic, gravitational, strong and weak forces — cannot be seen by people. Yet they affect the motions of the stars, planets, and all the matter that constitutes the universe.

How you look and sound to others? Perhaps the most obvious example of the confusion between perception and reality relates to the fact that we humans are not able to see ourselves exactly the way we look to others. We only get to see a mirror image of ourselves in a mirror, pond, or other reflective surface, or a snapshot of how we look in an often unrealistic posed instant of time. Also, the way we sound to ourselves is quite different from the way others hear us. Most people are quite amazed the first time they hear themselves on a tape recorder. What is the perception and what is the reality — the way we look and sound to others or the way we look and sound to ourselves?

The answer to the question "What is reality?" provides us with an opportunity to learn an interesting marketing lesson. If we take the market-driven view, we should listen to others because they are the only ones who know how we look and sound to the world outside of our own minds. To see and hear ourselves, in reality, we have to listen to others. Stated another way, from the marketing point of view, the customer's perception is the reality. This is perhaps the way marketers should answer this question.

The Marketing notion of perception and reality. Those who really understand marketing tend not to distinguish perception and reality. They understand that perception is reality, and vice versa. For example, they know that buyers want to believe that using a certain perfume or deodorant will make them more attractive or feel better about themselves. Because of the perception that the product will provide these benefits, it often does. The perception becomes reality. Those who use the perfume and deodorant feel better about themselves. When they feel better, they look better. Consequently, they act and become more attractive. It is not important whether the product instantaneously causes the desired effect or acts as a placebo, the important point is that the desired result is achieved.

Using the convergence of perception and reality. In light of the above discussion, marketers need to use perception and reality to their advantage when developing and executing corporate image and other marketing strategies.

ENHANCING IMAGE

In addition to creating and protecting your image, you also should do whatever you can to enhance your image in the minds of your publics. You do this by taking every positive about your company and products (awards, positive articles, and testimonials) and publicizing it to a wider audience.

IMPORTANT CORPORATE IMAGE ISSUES

To develop and implement successful corporate image strategies, you should group your strategies into three categories — *create*, *protect*, and *enhance* and think about the following points:

1. Virtually everything a company and its representatives do affect its image.
2. Everyone in your organization should be made aware of this point.
3. A company, through its marketing and the behavior of its representatives, must do whatever possible to consciously maintain a good image in the minds of all its publics.
4. Members of all publics should be looked upon and treated as if they were unpaid ambassadors and sales people of the company.
5. Every person in the company should be trained to be conscious of the factors that affect its image and to counteract any negatives that could serve to tarnish that image.
6. Trained marketing personnel should quickly and honestly deal with anything that endangers the image of your company.
7. A concerted effort should be made to turn negatives into positives, not with just words, but with useful actions.
8. A good Corporate Image will help to increase revenues and lower costs. A bad one will do the opposite.
9. You are more likely to positively influence your company's corporate image as well as your own if you (1) act as if you own the company and (2) view your company as a row boat whose oars everyone must row in synchronization in order for personal and company goals to be achieved in the most efficient and effective way.
10. It is important to understand that, in the context of developing a positive corporate image and successful marketing program, perception is reality.

[1]Robert Crandall, *Los Angeles Times*, September 4, 1988, pg. 1 of Bus. Section.

[2]John Goodman, *Wall Street Journal On Marketing*, pg. 146.

TIPS and Exercises

1. Create corporate image strategies for your company (mission statement, corporate identity tools, training, communications, and quality control).
2. Create "protect" strategies including those for rumors, facts, and day-to-day issues that occur.
3. Create "enhance" strategies to promote positives about your company to a wider audience.

Chapter 5

DNA of Positioning

"Make it clear to market targets why they should only buy your products."

Positioning is one of the most important yet most misunderstood and neglected concepts in marketing. You may be thinking — "If it is so important, why is it neglected and misunderstood?" Perhaps the reason is that most marketing textbooks that are used in universities only recognize the *4 Ps of Marketing — Product, Price, Place and Promotion.* As you can plainly see, *Positioning* is not one of them. And if you are surprised about this, don't be. These same marketing textbooks either don't mention or don't give proper weight to *Corporate Image* or the *Marketing Information System* either. This means that most people who have learned marketing in school have not learned close to half of the seven important building blocks of marketing!

No wonder (1) marketing is so misunderstood, (2) so many marketing mistakes are made by some of the highest paid executives in the largest organizations, and (3) so many people say that they don't teach you the most important "things" in school. With regard to the third point, it is no surprise that the book *What They Don't Teach You at the Harvard Business School* was a best seller.

Getting back to positioning, perhaps the best place to start your understanding of this important building block of the *DNA of Marketing* is with a discussion as to what positioning is.

WHAT IS POSITIONING?

Different marketing *gurus* attach different meanings to the term *Positioning?* In *Positioning: The Battle for Your Mind*, Al Ries and Jack Trout define Positioning as *"... what you do to the mind of the prospect."*[1] William L. Shanklin and John K. Ryans, in their book *Marketing High Technology* describe positioning as a process that "...allows the high-tech marketer to determine the various industries or buying groups that can use the products and array them in an ordered fashion."[2] While different, both serve to provide understanding of how the term is used in business. The various perspectives from which *positioning* can be viewed are provided below.

(1) **Empty spaces in the Marketplace.** *Finding and filling unsatisfied market needs, niches, or cachets.* This is a view of positioning in relation to the unfilled positions, open spaces, or unsatisfied needs in the marketplace.

(2) **Buyers with Similar Needs.** *Identifying and targeting specific market segments as groups who are most likely to buy your product.* From this perspective, positioning is viewed in terms of groups of buyers who have similar needs and wants.

(3) **Image of the Product.** *Creating an Image for the product in the minds of prospective buyers.* From this angle, positioning is expressed from a company and/or product perspective. The marketers create an image for each product that fills a need in the marketplace.

(4) **Uniqueness or Defensibility.** *Creating a unique position that can be defended against competitors.* As in the military sense, the best positions need to be defensible. Once you establish this position, it should be very difficult or impossible for competitors to take this position away from you. The advantage of a defensible position is that prospective buyers have very clear reasons why they should buy *only* from you. These clear reasons tend to lower your promotion costs and boost your sales. If you can say something positive about your products that your competitors cannot say about theirs, you can create a defensible position. *Figure 5-1* graphically illustrates the concept of looking for unique niches, or empty spaces, in the marketplace.

(5) **Competition or Market Share.** *Pursuing an Image of the product in relation to, or separate and apart from, the competition.* This expresses positioning in terms of competitive positions. Examples include: "We are the market leader;" or "At Avis we're number two, but we try harder." Unfortunately, too many marketers use competitive positioning in a negative way by disparaging competitors. Such disparaging is considered unprofessional and bad form. Moreover, it tends to reflect negatively on the disparager. The reasons include: (1) some market targets know and like your competitors, and by "knocking" competitors, you will also alienate them; (2) others think that those who try to benefit by knocking others have nothing positive to sell; and (3) still others who don't consciously know why it's wrong for you to "bad-mouth" competitors, know it unconsciously — causing the same negative result. *Figure 5-2*, a typical pie chart, graphically illustrates the concept of positioning from a market share or competitive point of view.

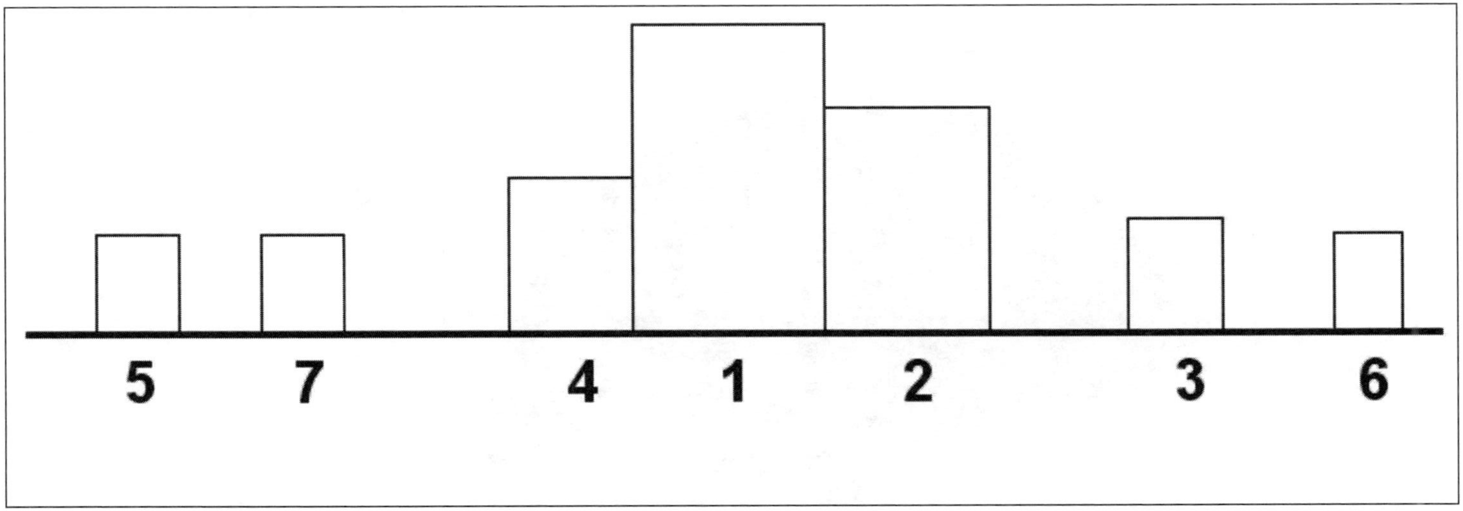

Figure 5-1. Positioning based on available niches and/or uniqueness. 1. Crest is the market leader of the general "fluoride" toothpaste market. 2. Colgate is also big but is usually second after Crest. 3. Arm&Hammer has come on strong with a baking soda position. 4. Aquafresh is also in the general market with a "fresh breath" position. 5. Topol has a unique small niche with the "smoker's tooth polish" position. 6. Mentadent has created the "peroxide for whiter teeth" position. 7. Tom's of Maine has the "health/all natural" position. 8. Many other, not shown, are "also rans". 9. The market leaders try to cover all positions by offering different variations. For example, Crest offers baking soda, peroxide, and other versions.

Note: the sizes of the blocks representing the position are not drawn to scale and the numbers are used for reference only and do not represent market positions.

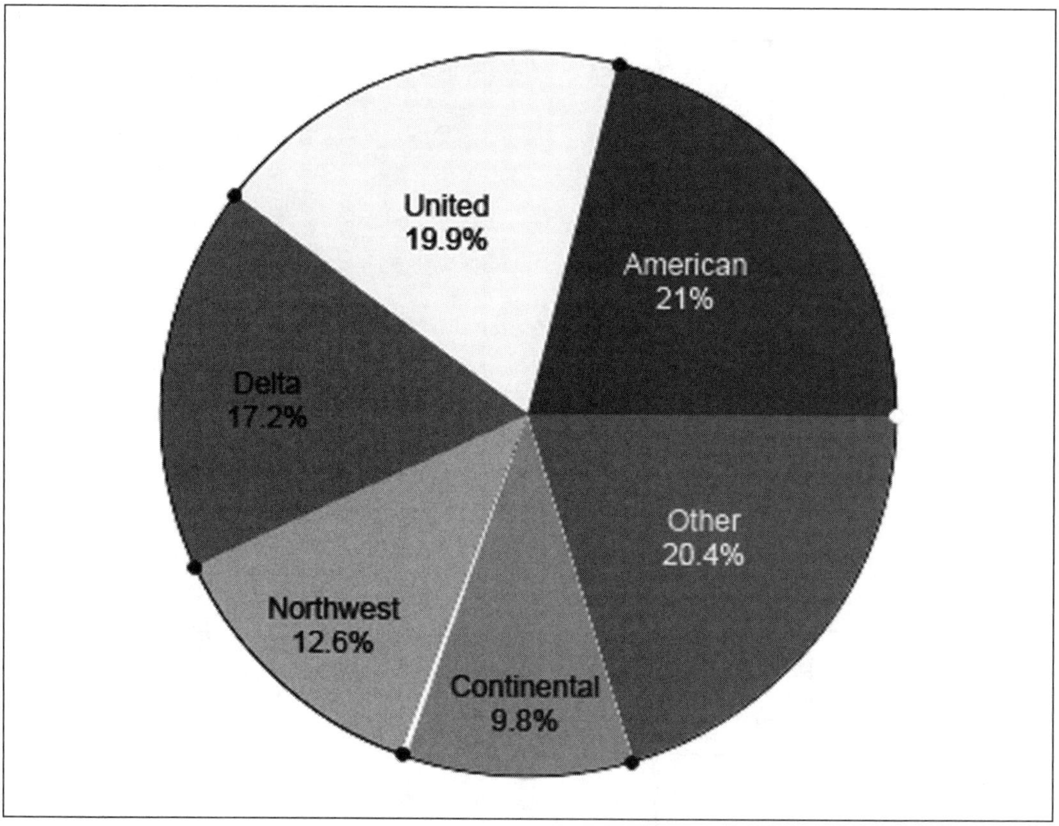
United
19.9%
American
21%
Delta
17.2%
Other
20.4%
Northwest
12.6%
Continental
9.8%

Figure 5-2

(6) **Other Products in Your Product Line.** *Creating an image in terms of, or separate and apart from, other products in the product line.* This views positioning in terms of your other products. For example, in many product lines there is a low-priced, medium-priced, and high-priced model; or the introductory model, intermediate model, and deluxe model. The important point here is to position products in the product line so that there is *little or no* overlap in their markets. The amount of overlap is commonly called *cannibalization*. Just as cannibals eat other people, if positioning is not done properly, one product can eat, or take business away, from others in the line. By insuring that the images of the various products in your line do not overlap, you help to avoid confusing buyers and competing with yourself.

COMPREHENSIVE DEFINITION OF POSITIONING

Since it incorporates all of the others, perhaps the most appropriate definition of *Positioning is the systematic process of finding a window, or niche, in the prospect's mind and filling that window with a memorable benefit that is difficult or impossible to copy.* Since that is quite long and perhaps too difficult to remember it is best to think about *positioning* as made up of two components. A good metaphor for these components is a *lock* and *key*. The *lock* is the *target market segment with an unfilled need*. The *key* is creating an image of the product that fits that *lock*, or *unfilled need*, better than anyone else. That is, if you can create a *"do not duplicate" key*, you will unlock enough of the potential from that market segment to achieve the goals of your plan.

WHY SHOULD POSITIONING STRATEGIES BE DEVELOPED FIRST?

Once you set up a *marketing information system* and create the *corporate image* you want, you are ready to work on your "5 P's" strategies. Of all the P's, it is very important that high-tech marketers develop *positioning strategies first*. The reasons include the following:

1. In the *market-driven* approach, it is important that the *position* of the product fill the identified need or niche in the marketplace.

2. It is much easier to fit the product to the image, or *position*, than fit the image to the product. The position is the *image blueprint* the product needs to follow.

3. Once *positioning* is created all the other strategies tend to fall into place. That is, the product can be designed and priced properly, distributors can be chosen, and promotional strategies can be developed to communicate the mix of strategies in order to get people in the target audience to buy the product.

For example, Reuben Mattus decided to develop *Hagen-Daz* ice cream when he noticed that, *"The quality of ice cream had deteriorated to the point that it was just sweet and cold. Ice cream had become cheaper and cheaper, so I just went the opposite way."*[3] Upon establishing the high-end position, he knew he had to create a quality *product*, charge a top *price*, *place* the product in the marketplace via quality retail *distribution*, and use high-end *promotional* vehicles to communicate the benefits of the product.

MINDS ARE "BOGGLED" BY TOO MUCH INFORMATION

To properly understand *Positioning*, it is important to realize that prospects are overexposed to information in the marketplace. Think of all the advertising generated by the multitude of Web sites, e-mail, newspapers, magazines, TV and radio stations, billboards, busses, bus benches and shelters, taxicabs, newsletters, direct mail advertising (too often known as "junk" mail), cable TV, yellow pages, association directories, fax machines, etc. Studies show that this information amounts to an average weekly exposure of 20,000 ad messages per person at the rate of nearly 3,000 per day! Obviously, this is too much for any human brain to process. And, it's getting worse all the time. According to Peter Large, in *The Micro Revolution Revisited, "More new information has been produced in the last thirty years than in the previous 5,000."* He goes on to present an even more interesting statistic — *"The total of all printed knowledge doubles every eight years."*[4] This information is not provided to alarm you, but to convince you that everyone is inundated with too much information. Understanding this is *step one* to understanding *Positioning*.

Many companies either don't understand or refuse to recognize this fact when marketing their products. They think that their products and technologies are superior; and because of this view, they believe that prospective buyers will magically discover, and line up to buy, them. While this scenario is a possibility with some products and technologies, it is certainly *not* a probability. Moreover, once serious competitors enter the marketplace, this *inbred* thinking becomes a blueprint for disaster. If company marketers don't consciously recognize that their prospects are being constantly bombarded with too much information when they create their marketing programs, they are likely to design messages that are too easily *lost in the information jungle*. Again, understanding and remembering that there is too much information in the marketplace for anyone to absorb is an important first step.

LOOK FOR THE OPEN SPACES AND BE FIRST TO GET THERE

One way to help cut through the information maze, is to *step around* it, or to focus on specific niches or market needs that aren't being satisfied. Going for open positions in the marketplace help to avoid clashing with entrenched competitors. It also gives companies a window in time to develop products and establish themselves in one of the strongest positions — being first in the minds of prospective buyers. For example, most people remember the first American in space — Allan Shepard, or the first to orbit the Earth — John Glenn, or the first to walk on the moon — Neil Armstrong. They have more difficulty remembering those who were second, third, etc. The same is true with the first President of the United States, or the first baseball player to hit 60 home runs in a season, or the first British Rock 'n Roll band to *invade* the United States and the world.

Companies that invent new products and technologies have the inside track on the *first position*. Some are able to take the advantage of being first and to maintain a *leadership position* while others lose them to more savvy marketers. An example of the former is *Xerox*, which owns the *copier position*. When prospects think of copiers, most think about *Xerox*. They often refer to the act of copying as *Xeroxing*. While not the first copier company, *Xerox* was the first company to come out with the superior technology of xerography that produces plain paper copies. An example of the latter (savvy marketers who take the first position away from weaker marketers) is *IBM*. While certainly not the first computer company, *IBM* owns the computer position because it was *first to get its message into the minds* of most prospects. *Univac* was first to the marketplace, but didn't succeed in getting its message across to the majority of the market. The lack of marketing-oriented thinking is the primary reason. *Univac* concentrated on the technology. *IBM* concentrated on the people using the technology. Since people buy computers, it's important to be first in their minds. Once *IBM* turned on their marketing machine and entered the mainframe computer market, the computer business became known as *IBM and the seven dwarfs*. Univac is not only one of the dwarfs, it later merged with *Sperry-Rand* and the resultant company has since changed its name to *Unisys*. Unfortunately, many believe it is still one of the dwarfs.

WHAT MAKES YOU UNIQUE? WHAT ARE YOUR STRENGTHS?

To help identify openings, available positions, or market niches, it is important to start by identifying what makes your company and your products unique. List everything you can think of that qualifies as a *unique characteristic* or feature on a piece of paper or computer screen. If nothing else, this list might help you to devise promotional strategies for your company and products. To the right of each unique feature, list the unique benefits each provides to your key target markets. Even better, ask your customers to tell you what they like about your products and how they benefit them.

The next thing you should do is list the *strengths and weaknesses* of your company and products. Do the same for all of your major competitors. Compare your company's list with that of your competitors. In addition to helping identify unique benefits, this exercise will help you to be able to position the key *benefits* of your company and products relative to those of your competitors. It may also serve to identify some promotional strategies that can be used at a later time.

FOCUS ON SPECIFIC TARGET MARKET SEGMENTS

Whether or not your company's products are first, you can position yourself as first and foremost in the minds of certain segments of the market, if you focus or specialize in serving those segments. Even after hundreds of computer stores had been established in Southern California, *The Writer's Computer Store* became a success by positioning itself as the place for writers to go for their computers. *Sony* was able to achieve success in the digital camera marketplace by positioning its *Mavica* camera as an easier to use digital camera. With this positioning strategy, they were able to serve the biggest segment, or lock, in the market (those who put ease of use above all other benefits) and quickly achieve a 40% market share. While a late entry in the PC business, *Dell* was the first computer company to sell PCs through direct marketing channels. *Topol* targets smokers with its tooth polish — smartly avoiding much larger industry leaders such as *Crest* and *Colgate*. *Secret* was positioned as a deodorant for women.

No company or product can be *"all things to all people."* Many smaller companies, fall into the trap of trying to cover everything with their limited marketing budget. As a result, they try to appeal to every possible segment of the market at once, but end up not appealing to anyone. While their intention is to save money by covering a wider market with the same message, their message becomes too diluted to be effective. Instead of saving money, they wind up losing their identity, and many end up losing their entire investment.

To get into the minds of market targets, marketers have to get their attention. They have to let targeted segments know that the company is focusing directly on them, understands their business, and specializes in filling their needs. If the message is too general, it doesn't get the attention of these targets, and they don't feel that the company is qualified to take care of their specialized needs and interests.

TARGET BASED ON PRODUCT LIFE-CYCLE STAGE

In addition to targeting specific market segments, it is also important for the high-tech marketer to understand that each target market is made up of *sub-segments* that respond differently to the introduction of new and innovative products. In particular, each of these sub-targets will adopt new and innovative products at distinctly different times in a product's life cycle. Behavioral scientists and market researches have identified five distinct sub-segments of a typical target market — (1) *Innovators* (aka the *Avant-Garde* segment), (2) *Early Adopters*, (3) *Early Majority*, (4) *Late Majority*, and (5) *Laggards*.

The *innovators* are the *avant-garde* group that is the first to adopt new products and services. They have a tendency to be young (in mind if not in body), well-educated, successful, from higher social and economic groups, and willing to take risks. They rely primarily on impersonal and scientific information sources and have a tendency to socialize and communicate with other innovators. In technology markets, innovators like to be the "first on their block" to acquire new versions or models of hardware and software. They are not afraid of the inevitable "bugs" that are inherent in new models and upgrades. Some even like to be the first to find bugs and report them to manufacturers. On the other hand, many can be quite cynical and vocal about bugs or design flaws in new models and versions.

The *early adopters* are similar to the innovators, but they are more cautious. As a result of this attribute, they are typically the trusted *opinion leaders* and trend-setters of most groups — i.e. the ones to which the majority looks for guidance, and therefore, a good index of the ultimate success of a new product. They read and travel more than members of subsequent groups and are likely to be influenced by scholarly sources of information such as technical journals, special interest magazines, university professors and the *avant-garde* group. They can be positively influenced by company marketing and sales personnel if they are approached in an intelligent and professional way.

The *early majority* is typically above-average in education and social position. They rely primarily on word-of-mouth advice from early adopters and can be positively influenced by your marketing in making decisions to buy new products. As their name implies, they are part of the largest segment of buyers — usually comprising one-third of the market. Therefore, their acceptance of a product can often "make or break" the success of that product.

The *late majority* are average or below average in social status, income, and most other leadership categories. They often require more coaxing, or peer pressure, before they will try a new product or life style. More often than not, they reject change until its benefits are proven by either the *early majority* or their peers. They are important because they also typically comprise one-third of most markets.

The *laggards* are typically at the lower end of the economic and social spectrums. They are bound by tradition and accept innovations only after they have become so widely accepted that they are considered traditional. By the time they accept a new product or innovation, it is usually in the maturity or decline stage of its life cycle and is being replaced by newer products. This group can be particularly important for targeting when the company needs to clear its inventories of older products to make room for new models.

Figure 5-3 graphically relates the adoption of new and innovative products by these subgroups to the Product Life Cycle.

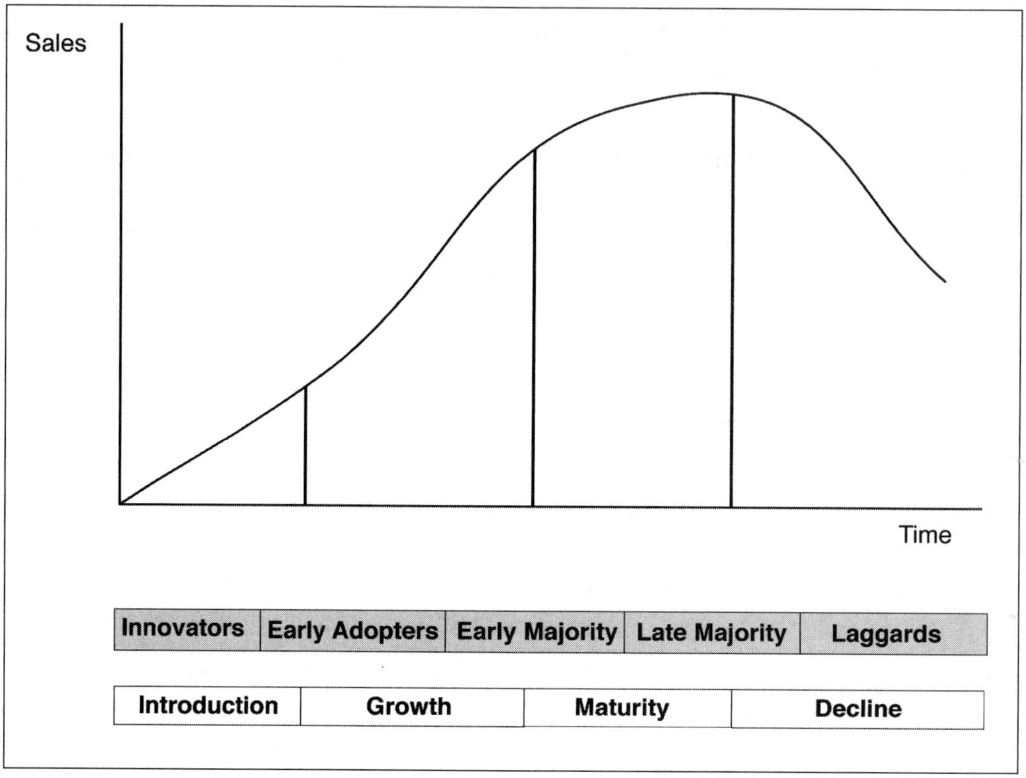
Sales
Time
Innovators
Early Adopters
Early Majority
Late Majority
Laggards
Introduction
Growth
Maturity
Decline

Figure 5-3

It should be noted that the descriptions of the above sub-segments may not apply universally to all groups. For example, in some consumer-goods markets, such as clothing and music, product-trends may actually be started by those who are at lower socioeconomic levels. Astute marketers should have good *Marketing Information Systems* that enable them to more specifically segment and profile their prospects and customers.

In any case, by understanding the existence and characteristics of the different sub-segments enumerated above, marketers can more precisely position and target products at the various stages of their life cycles.

CUTTING THROUGH THE INFORMATION JUNGLE

In addition to targeting specific market segments, the marketing strategists have to understand how to cut, or blast, through the wall of information clutter in the marketplace (which you may recall averages 20,000 messages per week) and get their messages into the minds of their market targets. Many accomplish this by employing the *KISS principle*, which is an old acronym for *Keep It Simple Stupid*. That is, they keep the message simple, concise, easy to understand, easy to read, focused on the needs of the target audience, unique, and non-confusing. The message has to be unique and benefit-focused to get through the information clutter and into the minds of prospects. It has to cut through the layers of noise and the defenses prospective buyers have built to filter this clutter. Because these layers can be very thick, it has to be sustained and repeated in order to get through and be remembered.

Since technology companies are dealing with complex or sophisticated products, they often think that the only way to communicate is through complex messages. The opposite is true. The more complex the product or service, the simpler the message should be. Even if the audience is technical and can understand complex concepts, many are too lazy or preoccupied to think in sufficient depth to absorb your message. Also many of the executives who write the checks are not as technical. Even if they are, they are likely to be too busy to take the time required to understand complex messages. On the other hand, simple messages can reach everyone in the target audience. They do not discriminate.

RECOGNIZE THE MARKET'S PERCEPTION OF YOUR POSITION

Too many unsophisticated companies *brag* in their marketing literature that they are number one, the leader, and the best. They use superlatives, but they don't recognize that superlatives have to be proven. The reason is that most prospects have been barraged by so many similar claims, most of which have proven to be false, that they are naturally skeptical about them. Either prospects already know your products are number one and wonder why you are bragging, or they don't know and *wonder why they haven't heard*. To avoid placing these doubts in the minds of prospects, it is best not to use superlatives in the company's marketing unless, of course, proof is provided. Moreover, this proof should not be company claims, but should be the result of customer testimonials or recognized and respected independent surveys, studies, and awards that can be easily verified.

If your company is not number one, it should recognize its position and develop its marketing strategies accordingly. One of the most famous and effective positioning strategies was the *"We're number 2, but we try harder"* campaign of *Avis* years ago. If the company tried to position itself as the number one company in the rental car industry, it would be lying and would lose customers since most people who travel know *Hertz* has been number one for many years. Instead, *Avis* developed a stronger and more effective position by recognizing it was number 2 behind *Hertz* and by using this fact to lay claim to the "better service" position represented by the slogan "We try harder".

The mistake a lot of companies make, especially smaller companies, is that they refuse to accept their position. In some cases, they operate from an inbred, egocentric view that they are number one. Perhaps this is a carry over from high-school football rallies. Whatever the source, it is important to recognize and understand that *it is not what people in your company think, but what people in the marketplace think of your company and products*. Once your company recognizes its position in the industry, it can develop powerful and effective *Positioning strategies* to market its products. Remember, all big companies were once small companies. Small companies get bigger by satisfying customers and not just themselves. As always, both sides must win.

NON-LEADER POSITIONING STRATEGIES

What are some effective positioning strategies if your company is not first or the leader in its industry?

Lower Price

The most obvious is price. The industry leader usually offers higher-priced products. This leaves the l*ower-price position* available. One key problem with a lower-price position, however, is that it leaves the company open to a cycle of *"cutthroat"* competition. That is, it is very easy for a competitor to join in and offer a lower price since lowering one's price does not take much skill or unique talent. To stay competitive, the company usually has to match or beat the competitor's price. The competitor responds, and the cycle escalates into a *price war* in which everyone's profit margin approaches, or even passes, zero. In such situations all competitors lose. While the customers may win in the short run by paying lower prices, they often lose in the longer run since they don't receive the service and support they need (many of the quality, service-oriented companies are forced out of business by the *cutthroat* competition, and the one's that remain can't afford to offer service at the lower prices). This is the problem with the *lowest price position*. There is always someone who offers a lower price — escalating the situation into a *price war* in which *all sides lose*. Since a business is successful only if both sides win, the *lowest-price strategy* is often a very weak positioning strategy — especially if the lower price is the only advantage. It should be noted that it can work, but it's a risky position. It is very difficult to defend — especially in a very competitive market. When it does work, other marketing strategies are typically used simultaneously. That is, *positioning* and *product* strategies related to better service or better product, *place* strategies providing more convenient ways to find, buy and use the product, or *promotion* strategies that communicate an incentive to buy quicker give the customer reasons, *in addition to price*, for buying.

This latter point underscores another common problem with the lower-price position. Unless the other building blocks are at work to establish the credibility of the product, a lower price position usually translates to the perception that the product is inferior or the company is desperate to sell its products. For example, if a product with a well-established position from a reputable company is sold by a trustworthy distribution outlet, market targets will run to buy it when the price is reduced or put on sale. On the other hand, if an unknown product from a not-well-known company is sold by a store or person with questionable credentials, a lower price merely confirms the buyer's suspicions of inferiority.

Quality & Service

A strong non-leader position is the quality position. A non-leader, especially if it's a smaller company, can typically offer more personalized service and support, or it can offer more quality or features for the same price. This position can allow a company to build up a loyal following and to expand its business irrespective of price competition. The reason is that most people go back to a company with which they are comfortable and that provides them with quality products and service. That is, as long as the company continues to do a good job, customers will remain loyal. Moreover, they will spread the "positive word" about the company and products to their friends and associates. Most people return to the same hair stylist, doctor, dentist, cleaner, restaurant, computer company, phone company, and pharmacy where they get good service. Size or price is often not as important to them as service because they know that good products and good service effectively lower their costs. The quality gives them greater use and enjoyment out of the product — effectively saving them time, money, and aggravation. If the service begins to falter, however, they are prompted to look elsewhere for competitive products.

Specialist

As mentioned above, companies that are not the leaders can also establish a strong position as a specialist. That is, they can focus on specific target market segments. If they are effective marketing themselves to these segments, they will get their specialist message into the minds of key targets that have specific needs. The danger of the specialist position is that it can backfire if the targeted market segments have economic difficulties resulting from recessions, strikes, high interest rates, droughts, and other unforeseen difficulties. Economic downturns have particularly hurt companies whose business is dependent on such industries as real estate, entertainment, oil and gas, and farm products in drought-stricken or natural disaster areas. To protect against this problem, companies should diversify and establish the specialist position in other markets once they've succeeded in one target market. This is particularly important in industries where business is seasonal or cyclical. The company should seek to select targets whose needs follow different seasonal or cyclical patterns — for example, targets who prosper in times of high-interest rates should be balanced with those who flourish in periods of low interest rates; segments whose seasonal demands peak during the Fall should be complemented with buyers whose needs reach their zenith in the Spring.

Innovator

Companies that are not industry leaders can be industry innovators. They can target those customers who want to buy the "latest" products, be at the forefront of technology, or be the "first on their block" to own new and innovative products. These market targets typically prefer products and companies that are *innovative* over those that are industry leaders or have the lowest prices. Many high-tech companies fit comfortably in this niche.

To be successful with this position, however, innovative companies need to understand that they have to properly market their products. Innovation alone is not sufficient for success. The high-technology graveyard is filled with the remains of innovative companies that were unable to compete with such less-innovative marketing powerhouses as *Microsoft*, *IBM*, and *Intel*.

The important point to remember is that whatever position you choose, your company and products have to be properly positioned in order to be successful. As with the company, the position of the product should start with its name.

THE IMPORTANCE OF THE PRODUCT NAME

Just as with the company name, the product name is critical to the successful positioning and marketing of the company's products and services. In fact, according to Al Ries and Jack Trout in their book on Positioning, *"The single most important marketing decision you can make is what to name the product."* While many would dispute this claim, there is no doubt that the name given to a product or service is a far more important decision than most company decision makers realize. The name of the product is typically the first point of contact between the customer and the product. As such, it's the first message that gets into the prospect's mind about the product, and its importance, therefore, cannot be diminished.

To be most effective, a name for a product should have one or more of the characteristics listed below.

Be Descriptive

Many technology companies fall into the trap of giving products technical sounding names typically comprised of a series of letters and numbers such as *Nissan 300ZX*, *Mazda RX70*, *Panasonic KX-F250*, and *Ford F-150*. With sufficient advertising and publicity, these names can get into the minds of prospects and stay there. However, they are less likely to penetrate the information clutter and remain in the prospect's mind as more meaningful names such as *Nutrasweet*® (instead of the generic Aspartame) for an artificial sweetener, *Diminicol*® for a cholesterol-lowering food ingredient, or *Microsoft* microcomputer software. These names are descriptive of the products that they represent. It doesn't take much guesswork to understand them. And it takes less money invested in promotion to get them to *stick* in peoples' minds.

Knowing the importance of getting and keeping the public interested in the space program, *NASA* hasn't given space vehicles technical names. Instead, they have chosen names such as Friendship, Freedom, Voyager, and Challenger — names that have meaning and can be remembered by the public.

The same is true of the computer software industry. Names of popular programs include: *Word*, *Windows*, *Photoshop*, *Freehand*, and *Illustrator*. In many cases, the names of popular programs are descriptive of the software's function.

Be Concise

As with all marketing, a name should be as short and as concise as possible. Again, it has to cut through the overgrown information jungle. As exemplified above, most of the successful names are *four syllables or less*. Remember the KISS principle.

Avoid Confusion

Most families don't give their children the same, or similar, names. If they did, life at home would get quite confusing. More importantly, the identity of those children would be affected for their entire lives.

Many companies are so *hung up* on their company name that they insist it appears in all product names. Just as in families, this often causes confusion among different products. For example, *Alka Seltzer* (for relief of upset stomachs) and *Alka Seltzer Plus* (for relief of cold symptoms), *Macintosh II*, *Macintosh IIx*, *Macintosh IIcx*, *Macintosh IIvx*, *Macintosh IIci*, and *Macintosh IIfx* are names of products that have caused confusion. Once again, it's often hard for many prospects (those who don't buy and some who do) to distinguish between different products when the only distinction in the name is the model or product number.

In addition to causing confusion, the failure of one model can *drag down* the image of the company and negatively affect the sales of all other products that contain the same name, or *handle*, on every model.

Avoid Pluses since they can often become big Minuses

The naming of *Alka Seltzer Plus* caused a big dispute between the manufacturer and its ad agency at the time. In fact, the ad agency resigned because of it. The ad agency, *Doyle, Dane and Bernbach*, tried to convince the VP of Marketing of *Miles Laboratories* that it wasn't a good name choice. Problem number one was who would ever want to buy regular *Alka Seltzer* with *Alka Seltzer Plus* on the market? The agency felt that prospects would begin to look at regular *Alka Seltzer* as *Alka Seltzer* "Minus". Problem number two was *Alka Seltzer* is for stomach upsets and *Alka Seltzer Plus* is for colds. Well, the ad agency was right. Instead of cutting into the markets of cold medicine competitors such as *Contac*, *Sudafed*, and *Dristan*, *Alka Seltzer Plus* achieved its sales by seriously *cannibalizing*[5] the regular *Alka Seltzer* market. While the marketers of the company thought they would take advantage of the millions of dollars a year they were spending on the *Alka Seltzer* name, they didn't foresee the more-costly damage that would be done to *Alka Seltzer's* market share.

IBM's introduction of the *PCjr.* was another attempt at *trading off* a successful name. The product didn't have a clear and separate identity even though prospects knew, from the "*jr.*" suffix, that the product was something less than the PC. The product was not successful, not only because of the name, but also as a result of inferior product features and quality. It was less than the PC — much less than one would expect from a *junior* version. The egocentric thinking behind the idea that *"all you have to do is put the IBM name on it, and it will sell"* was proven wrong. The PCjr. is an example of flawed marketing from *IBM*. More significant than the losses that resulted, it proved that there were *"holes"* in *IBM's* armor. That is, it showed competitors that *IBM* is not the invincible giant that everyone thought it was. This opened the door for other manufacturers to make *PC clones* that ultimately took considerable *market share* away from *IBM* in the personal computer market.

Relate the New to the Old

When introducing new products based on unknown technologies and concepts, it is often effective to select a name that relates the new and unknown to the old and familiar. In this way, it is easier for prospects to understand and accept the new product. For example, one of the first word processing programs to appear on personal computers was called the *Electric Pencil*. The first automobile was called the *horseless carriage*. The first telegraphs and telephones were referred to as the *wireless*. These names were easily accepted and understood because people were already familiar with the names and concepts of the older products that were replaced by the new.

Of course, this positioning concept can also be used for non-technical products. Seven-up was successfully positioned as the *uncola*. Numerous other products are described by what they do not include — *sugarless* gum, *tubeless* tires, *no-fat* salad dressing, and *decaf*-coffee.

SOME LEADER POSITIONING STRATEGIES

If a company's products are *number one*, the *number one* or *leader position* is a very strong *positioning strategy*. In many industries, leaders secure twice the market share of the number two company and twice again as much as the number three brand. Moreover, as with political candidates, these relationships are not easily changed, unless the company (or the candidate) *makes serious mistakes* that cause customers (and constituents) to switch to competitors. To maintain a leadership position, therefore, a leader has to avoid making big mistakes while simultaneously avoiding complacency and conservatism — admittedly *a tough job*, but somebody has got to lead, and it might as well be you.

Leaders Should Act Like Leaders

Leaders should set the standards by which others in the industry are measured. As is true of all companies, they should avoid *"putting down"* or dismissing the competition. They should *never* adopt the egocentric position that there is no competition. Smart leaders know that there are always at least two competitors — (1) Substitute products that perform similar functions and (2) the buyer can choose to buy nothing. As with all companies, leaders should avoid even referring to competition in their marketing. A leader doesn't need to mention competitors. If asked about competition, they should be as quiet, confident, and *matter of fact* as possible by taking a position such as, "They are good, but we are better, and here are the reasons why..." The reasons should be proven by data from independent, credible, third party sources.

Leaders should *position* themselves as spokespeople for their industries just as political leaders are spokespeople for their constituencies. They should demonstrate leadership by educating prospects about their products, technology, and industry rather than by telling prospects that they are the best.

Without saying they are the best, leaders have subtle and innovative ways of communicating their leadership position. *Harvard* refers to themselves as *The Business School*. *MIT* is *Tech*, or *The Engineering School*. *Coke* is *The real thing*. *Xerox* is *The Copier Company*. The *PC* refers to *IBM*. Real leaders never have to tell people that they are number one. They are above that, and customers usually know who the industry leader is. If there ever is a need to show that you are "number one" or "the best," you should use verifiable data from credible, independent, third-party sources.

Leaders Can't Do Everything

While often more savvy than their competitors, leaders sometimes succumb to ego weaknesses. That is, after building successes in one industry, they often think, with all their muscle and power, they can easily duplicate their success in another industry. This thinking often leads to big mistakes. With all its resources, leaders at *IBM* thought they could unseat *Xerox* in the copier market, but they failed. *Xerox* thought they could be successful in the computer business, but they weren't. *AT&T* thought the same but they haven't been successful in their efforts with computers. *IBM* thought it could *make a big splash* in the phone business, but it hasn't. Leaders have to recognize that it is not so easy to unseat well-entrenched leaders in other industries. While it does happen, it doesn't happen very often. The reason is that they become so closely identified with one product line that buyers have difficulty believing that they can also be proficient with other unrelated products. Furthermore, the unsuccessful efforts to try to make it happen can be very costly — running into the multiple millions, or even billions, of dollars. In most cases, it is better for the leader to invest this money in those areas in which it has considerable strengths (remember the SWOT model).

Must Respond to Innovations

Leaders have to respond to innovations — especially those that can threaten or change their business. A notorious example of a leader who failed to respond, is *Penn Central Railroad*. It failed to recognize the importance of air travel. With 20/20 hindsight, most marketing experts realize that the company positioned itself too narrowly — as a railroad company, rather than as a transportation company. The company failed to recognize the competitive threat posed by other innovative forms of transportation. It also failed to recognize the opportunities that they represented. As air travel, a superior technology for medium and long distances, and the personal automobile, a more convenient alternative for short distances, became more and more accepted and affordable, the need or demand for railroads to carry traveling passengers has grown ever smaller. At one point, the railroad companies had the capital to open airline divisions. Now most rail travel in the United States is subsidized by the Government.

On the other hand, an example of a leader that continues to respond to innovation is *IBM*. After *IBM* got into the computer business, it became *The Computer Company* for large mainframe computers. In 1956, when upstart *Digital Equipment Corporation* began developing smaller computers powered by the new transistor technology, *IBM* didn't only look at *Digital* as competition, it looked at the company's technology as an opportunity. After insuring that the smaller minicomputers were not some new fad, *IBM* quickly followed suit with its own line of minis. Then, in the early 80's soon after *COMPAL*, *Apple*, *Radio Shack*, and others became successful manufacturing and marketing even smaller computers, known as personal computers, *IBM* entered the market with its own *IBM PC*. It didn't take long for *IBM* to become *"The PC"* with its *"own"* (although developed by *Microsoft*) operating system called *PCDOS* (which stands for Personal Computer Disk Operating System). The reason is that the company usually acts like a leader that responds in a positive way to innovation. *IBM* is committed to owning *"The Computer Position"*. It's no wonder *IBM* grew from sales of $500,000 in to a volume over $70 Billion within 25 years, whereas *Penn Central* is a mere shell of its former self. Yes, *IBM* has had some difficult years and made some serious marketing mistakes due to its corporate ego. However, in the early 1990's, it began to recognize its errant ways and take corrective action. Unlike *Penn Central*, it began to act like a leader again. *IBM* recently decided to get out of the PC business and concentrate on computer services. They are acting as a leader again and getting out of this low-margin business.

Must Walk a Tightrope

While some companies can be criticized for being too narrowly defined and not responding to innovation, others can be criticized for *jumping* into too many businesses with conflicting positions that they don't understand. The real answer is that companies have to *"walk a tightrope"* investigating and responding to new ideas and innovations while not jumping at every opportunity that comes along. There have to be good reasons to get into new businesses, and the company has to be prepared to do so. It has to pursue those opportunities that match its inherent strengths, and avoid those which correspond to its weaknesses or pose threats from well-entrenched competitive positions (the *SWOT* model applies again). Good companies go from one successful venture to another — using the capital generated from each success to build another successful operation. They don't continually jump from sinking ships to lifeboats, or turn those lifeboats into luxury liners.

MAKE SURE POSITIONING IS IN HARMONY WITH OTHER STRATEGIES

Positioning your company's products as being of the highest quality but offering them at discount prices will confuse prospects and hurt sales. Similarly, offering top-quality products through discount distribution outlets or advertising them in throw away newspapers will cause the same kind of confusion. For example, *Gucci* products are typically found in swank shops on *5th Avenue* or *Rodeo Drive*, not at *K-Mart* or *99¢ Stores*. The reverse is also true. Discount products are not found in the most prestigious shops. Why? The *image*, or *Position*, of the *products* would be in conflict with the products themselves. Product image, or *Position*, has to fit with the *Corporate Image*, *Product*, *Price*, *Promotion*, and *Distribution* strategies. If it doesn't, the resultant confusion will hurt sales because *confused prospects don't buy*.

SUMMARY

Many of us have the benefit of 20/20 hindsight to look at the positioning mistakes made by some very large and respectable companies. The important point to realize is that they were mistakes that could have been avoided and turned into successes if the companies followed the rules. What are the rules? Some of the more important ones are summarized below:

1. Understand that there is too much information and confusion in the marketplace.
2. Think of *Positioning* as a systematic process for finding a window, or unique and defensible place in the minds of your publics (the lock), and filling that window with a memorable benefit that is difficult or impossible to copy (the key). Also think of *Positioning* as (1) the Image of the Product, (2) the Product's Position Relative to the Competition, (3) Targeting specific Market Segments with common needs, and (4) the Product's Relationship to other product's in your product line (avoid cannibalization).
3. Find a unique market niche or opening, and be the first to fill it.
4. Turn the *"first-mover"* advantage into a long-term leadership position.
5. Recognize and understand the company's *position* in the marketplace from the point of view of your target audience.
6. If not first, focus on specific market segments, or create specific niches such as products with more features and benefits, better quality, better service, etc.
7. Design all messages to *cut through* rather than add to the information jungle.
8. Make product names, logos, slogans and other image-building elements as descriptive and unique if at all possible.
9. Make sure that *Positioning Strategies* work with all other marketing strategies.

Best of luck.

[1]Al Ries and Jack Trout, *Positioning: The Battle for Your Mind*, pg. 201.

[2]William Shanklin and John Ryans, Jr., *Marketing High Technology*, pg. 53.

[3]Los Angeles Times Staff and Wire Reports "Reuben Mattus; Ice Cream Maker Behind Haagen-Dazs, *Los Angeles Times*, January 30, 1994, pg. A26.

[4]Peter Large, *The Micro Revolution Revisited.*

[5]*Cannibalization is a marketing term that refers to the process by which one product takes sales away from another that is produced or marketed by the same company.*

TIPS and Exercises

1. Draw a horizontal line and put boxes for each of your competitors on the line similar to *Figure 5-1*. Try to draw box sizes that fit the relative sizes of your competitors. Try to identify the positions that each of these products occupy in the minds of people in your target market segments. If you don't know what they are, ask people in those segments.
2. Identify the segments in your target audience that have unfilled needs and document what those unfilled needs are.
3. Ask those segments what their unfilled needs are (what they are not getting from the products they currently buy that they would like to get).
4. Create images of your products (goods and services) to fill those needs better than those of competitors (focusing on the unique aspects of your products that fill those unfilled needs or do things competitive products do not do).
5. Try to create names, logos, and slogans for products that communicate those images.

Chapter 6

DNA of Product

"It's the Star of the High-Tech Show... The center of attention."

WHAT ARE PRODUCTS?

P*roducts are the goods and services developed to satisfy the needs of your target market and to achieve the goals of your Marketing Plan.* In *market-driven* companies, target market needs are discovered using the company's *marketing information* system. They are developed into new products with the help of the organization's *new product development system* discussed in *Chapter 2*.

Product-driven bias

Too often, products are not developed in this way. They are the "brainchild" of an inventor who assumes everyone in the market will want the product. In reality, market targets will only accept a product if it provides them with clear benefits or solutions to their problems that are not provided by other options. To be successful, marketers need to focus their companies on developing products that customers want — not products that inventors think they want.

The most obvious strategy in the Marketing Mix that needs help from the others

Because the *Product* is the most visible and tangible of your marketing strategies, it is often given the most attention. Unlike the others, it's the only component of the *marketing mix* that market targets can really see, hear, touch and smell. As a result of this attention, the other variables in the mix are often neglected to the detriment of the successful marketing of the product. Moreover, as is often the case with the star of any show, it is perhaps the most misunderstood component in the *marketing mix*.

It is a Marketing Variable

The fact that *Product* is a variable may come as a surprise to some, but it's true. *Product* begins its life as a variable — not a well-defined object or service. During the *new product development* stage it remains a variable until it is introduced to the marketplace. At this time, it becomes a well-defined strategy that, in the case of a tangible good, has a particular shape, size, and color, along with other physical characteristics. In the case of a service, the product is also a well-defined strategy in terms *what the service is, who is to provide it, when, where, and how it is to be delivered*, and so forth. However, even after the product is defined, marketers should understand that it can be changed. That is, if your *marketing information system* tells you that market targets prefer a different size, shape, color, price, image, or package, the product can (and, in most cases, should) be changed to accommodate them.

The Device, "P of Marketing," and Complete Product

Another factor that causes marketers to misunderstand the *product* variable is their confusion between the *device*, the *product as a P of Marketing* and the notion of a *complete product*. What most technology marketers refer to as the *product* is really only the *physical portion* of the product. As William Davidow says in his article, *The Ascendancy of High-tech Marketing, "Customers buy products, not devices... Marketing turns devices into products."*[1] What he is saying is that most people confuse the "physical" component of the product — the device — with the *complete product* because it is the most visible and tangible part of a complete product. Marketing often adds packaging, product literature, operator instructions, after-sale support and customer service to convert the *device* into the *P of marketing* known as *Product*. Even after these components are added, the *Product* is not complete. To transform it into the *core component* of a complete product, marketing must do the following: (1) Give it an identity, or *Position* that is often represented by the product name, logo, and positioning slogan, (2) Provide it with a *Price* so buyers know what they have to pay to acquire the product; (3) *Place* it in marketplace through distribution channels that make it convenient for market targets to find, buy and use the product; (4) Associate it with the company's reputation, or *Corporate Image* (or separate it from the company's reputation if the association is likely to be risky or confusing); (5) Imbed a *Marketing Information System* mechanism in the product so that its performance in the marketplace can be measured and any problems can be quickly traced to their source and corrected (examples include a lot number that traces a product defect to a faulty ingredient or an employee number that traces poor service to a weak employee); and (6) Communicate the benefits of these attributes to the marketplace via personal selling, advertising, and other forms of *Promotion*.

In a nutshell, the *complete product* is the *product variable*, or *P of Marketing*, plus all the other building blocks of marketing loaded into it (*corporate image*, *marketing information system*, *position*, *price*, *place*, and *promotion*). In turn, the product, or P of marketing, is the *device* plus such other product components as packaging, warranties, product literature, customer support, and service. *Figure 6-1* graphically illustrates the differences between the *device*, the *product as in the P of marketing*, and the *complete product*.

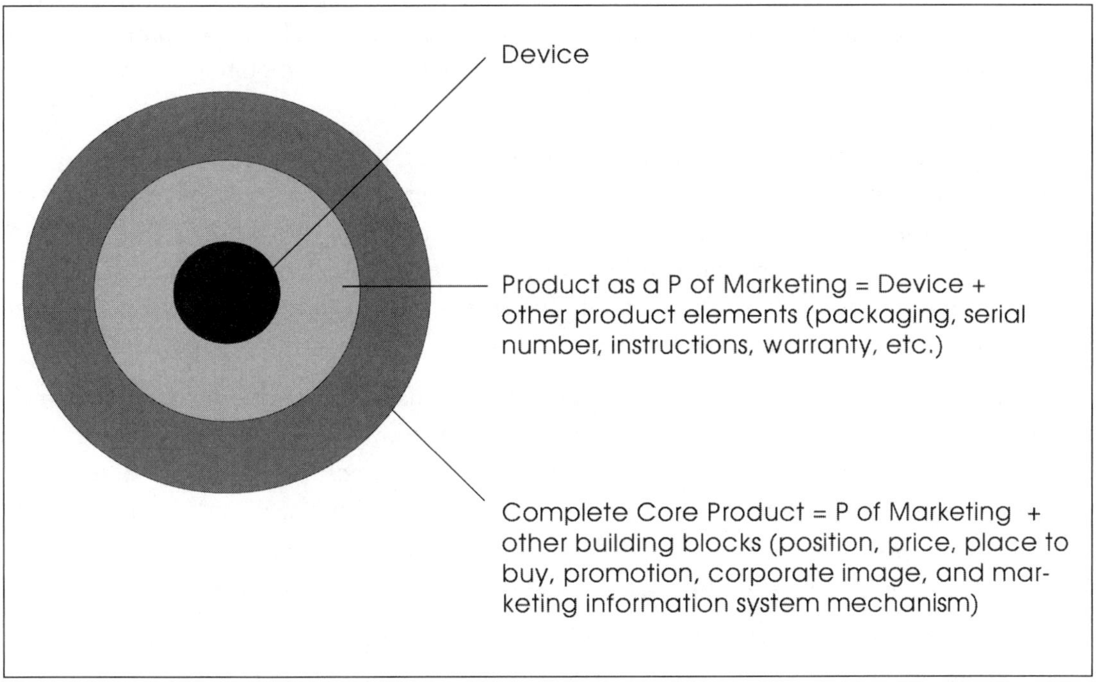
Device
Product as a P of Marketing = Device + other product elements (packaging, serial number, instructions, warranty, etc.)
Complete Core Product = P of Marketing + other building blocks (position, price, place to buy, promotion, corporate image, and marketing information system mechanism)

Figure 6-1

Once you understand the difference between the *device*, *product as a P of marketing*, and the *complete product*, there is another product concept that is important to understand — the notion of the *core* and *peripheral* components of product.

Core and Peripheral Components

The successful marketer should look at every *product* as having two main components — a *core* product component and a *peripheral* product component. The *core* component is the same as the *complete product* discussed above. The *peripheral* component is *customer service*.

If the product is tangible, such as a personal computer, the *core* component is the physical computer and related software. The *peripheral* component relates to how buyers are serviced by the company during the process of *finding*, *buying* and *using* the product. The reason that more than one company may be involved in this process is that the customer may buy the product from one company, such as a retail dealer, but may need to contact the manufacturer directly to complain, buy accessories or replacement parts, or get the product serviced.

If the product is a service, the *core* component is the main service provided by the company whereas the *peripheral* component relates to how the customer is treated when finding, buying and using the service. Taking the example of the Internet, the *core service* is providing reliable access to the Internet. The *peripheral service* is related to how well customers are treated when they call up to compare prices with other service providers, sign up for the service, install the service for the first time, use the service, call with billing questions, or complain.

Whether the core component of the product is a tangible good or a service, more and more products are perceived as commodities primarily because the companies that create them are finding it increasingly difficult to *position* their products as unique from their competitors. In many of these cases, the *peripheral service* component can be used to distinguish company products from those of competitors.

In any case, marketers should realize that good *service*, or taking good care of customers, is essential to the successful marketing of any product. Because the subject of customer service is so important, it will be discussed in greater detail in *Chapter 12* of this book.

Table 6-1 below graphically illustrates the concept of core and peripheral components for products that are goods and services.

Table 6-1

Core and Peripheral Product Components for Goods and Services

Core Product Component	Peripheral Product Component
When the product is a Tangible Good. Example: DNA test kit.	*Service component:* How well the buyer is treated while searching for, buying and using the DNA test kit.
When the product is a Service. Example: Consulting Service.	*Service component:* How well the customer is treated when comparing consultants, asking for a proposal, during the consulting process, upon receiving the deliverables and the invoice.

Upon understanding this core and peripheral component concept, it is important for technology marketers to have an idea as to what makes a product *high-tech.*

WHAT MAKES A PRODUCT HIGH-TECH?

There is little agreement as to what qualifies a product to be classified as *high-tech.* The *U.S. Bureau of Labor Statistics* classifies an industry as high-tech if it has twice the number technical personnel and spends twice the money on research & development (R&D) as the national averages for U.S. manufacturers. Many believe this classification to be inadequate because it fails to account for the following:

1. *Indirect R&D inputs* from products and devices, such as computers, which are used in the manufacture of the end products.
2. *Foreign averages or inputs,* which are becoming more and more important as most manufacturers move toward a global economy.
3. *Many high-tech companies who don't do their own R&D* but who buy, sell and service products resulting from the R&D of others.
4. *High-tech service businesses* such as Internet Service Providers, Bio-tech consultants, Computer Chip designers, and other high-tech service businesses.

If we look at the way the term "*high-tech*" is used in everyday language, we find that it has evolved into a much broader meaning. It is used in reference to styles of art and design, lettering, furniture, music, clothing, hair, athletic shoes, and virtually anything that looks or sounds new, modern, metallic, computer-like, machinelike, or contemporary.

Because there seems to be no definitive specification for *high-technology*, we have latitude in developing our definition. Let's say that a high-tech product is any product that requires educating the prospect as to what the product is, or what it does, before they feel comfortable buying it. Using this expansive definition, a large number of goods and services could be classified as high-tech.

Why is this definition useful? It is useful because it works. If we educate prospects as to what our goods and services can do for them, we will be more successful marketing them. The more technical the product, the more education is required in its marketing.

Now we can move on to exploring the different models that can be used to develop products.

PRODUCT DESIGN ALTERNATIVES

As with all marketing decisions and strategies, products should be designed to meet the needs of the target audience. Depending on those needs and the nature of the product, product designs typically fall into one of three basic models — the *Standard product model*, the *Diversification product model*, and the *Hybrid model*. These models are explained in the following sections.

Standard Product Model

The *standard product model* is based on the idea that, while buyers have different needs, there is a core set of basic product capabilities that all of them require. In such cases, it makes sense to design the product so that every customer buys at least the same *standard product* as a starting platform. Instructions on how to put together, use, and care for the product are provided in the form of an *instruction sheet*, *booklet* or *manual*. For those who need additional capabilities, *options* are designed so they can be easily added to the standard base, or core, product. Add-on items that add minor functionality, are offered as *accessories*. Consumable items that are essential to the use of the product are provided in the form of *supplies*.

Modular structure

The standard product model is modular in structure. That is, every configuration shares the same basic unit. Those who need more can add the options and accessories they need. Products that are designed using the standard product model typically receive their identity from the name of the company. This means that the *corporate image* variable is the main differentiator or source of *positioning* for the product. Another way to state this is that the image of the company, or *corporate image*, is inseparable from the image, or *position*, of the product. The original *IBM* PC is an example of this product design and positioning philosophy. Options and accessories could be added, many of which were made by others, to give greater functionality to the *IBM* PC platform, and the identity of the product was almost totally dependent on the *corporate image* of *IBM*. Later *IBM* PC clones were substituted for the original, but the *IBM* design standard was followed.

Services

While there are some differences, products that are services follow the same pattern. Everyone is offered the same basic service for a given price. Those who have additional needs can pay for the *options* and *extras* as they need them. For example, an Internet service may offer the same core product component to all customers for a basic monthly price. The product might include unlimited access to the Internet, an e-mail account, Internet access software, nominal Web space, and technical support to get started. Some customers may want additional space for their Web page or more technical support. Others might desire virtual domain hosting so they can use their own personal domain names. Still others might require higher-speed DSL or Cable access. These extras can be offered as options that the customer may or may not select.

In the course of their evolution, ice cream, cameras, personal computers, and stereo systems have followed this model. For example, with cameras, most people started with a basic unit. Those who needed a special lens or flash attachment could add it. Those who wanted a special case to carry the camera could purchase one. Of course, consumable supplies such as film could be purchased, consumed, thrown away, and repurchased as needed.

Standard Product Model Advantages

The examples above point to certain advantages of this *standard product model* design. They include the following:

1. Customers buy just what they need and want.
2. The product design usually does not force them to buy, and pay for, more than they want.
3. As their needs grow, the product can grow with them.
4. Since they have only one standard model to stock, manufacturers and distributors do not need to guess which basic items customers will buy — allowing them to hold down their inventory costs and pass the savings on to their consumers.

5. Because standard products don't have unique options built-in, they often cost less and have a base price advantage over other designs. Therefore, companies can promote this advantage in their advertising.

Standard Product Model Disadvantages

Of course, for some market segments, this design also presents certain disadvantages. They include:

1. Some customers prefer to have the unique features they need built-in to one compact unit.
2. Some customers do not really know all the capabilities they need and want until they begin using the product. Many discover that built-in features that they never thought they would use (those that would be options on standard product models) are "indispensable" to their use of the product.
3. Because they typically contain fewer unique features, *standard product* designs tend to be more difficult to position, or distinguish from competitive offerings.
4. In some cases, not including certain "important" functions in the *standard model* can anger customers and cause them to feel that the company's products are inferior to those of competitors. For example, when customers want to buy a product, they may become annoyed when they are repeatedly told, "That feature is extra," or "that is optional."
5. When customers add options and accessories to add the functionality they want, the business can go to competitors.

To avoid these disadvantages, many marketers turn to the *diversified product model* when designing their product strategies.

Diversified Product Model

Using the *diversified product model*, each product in the product line is designed to be unique and separate from other models. The uniqueness is designed into the product. You cannot take one of these products and add options to turn it into another diversified product. Moreover, products that follow this design model typically have identities, or positions, that are separate and apart from the identities of the company's who make them.

Procter & Gamble has used this model in the design of their products. *Tide*, *Bold*, and *Cheer* are all detergent products made by the company. Each has its own position, or image, that is not directly linked to the identity of the company. Moreover, you cannot add options to one to turn it into another. *General Motors* and many other automobile companies have also used this model in the design of their products. In particular, *General Motors* designed different models to appeal to the different segments of the buying public. Since the middle class is the largest segment in America, *General Motors* created three separate product lines

— *Buick*, *Oldsmobile*, and *Pontiac* to satisfy the demand for cars from this group. For the smaller upper and lower-class segments, *GM* developed one product line each — *Cadillac* for the upper segment, and *Chevrolet* for the lower. Ford did the same with *Lincoln*, *Mercury*, and *Ford* for the upper, middle, and lower-class segments respectively.

Of course, when one observes actual consumer behavior, one might find some in lower socioeconomic groups buying *Cadillac's* and upper-class buyers buying *Chevrolets*. This can easily be explained by understanding that some customers will buy products that were originally designed for other segments, for reasons of status, anonymity, utility, conservatism, frugality, and a variety of other tangible and psychological reasons. For example, members of lower-class segments may wear designer clothing or buy luxury cars because they want to impress others or psychologically escape from their reality; whereas members of upper-class segments may wear blue jeans and drive utilitarian cars either because they don't want to draw attention to their wealth or they don't need to prove their status to others. This does not negate the validity of creating products with unique identities. It gives buyers good reasons for selecting one product over another, and allows them to select the segment with which they want to identify (whether or not they are members of that segment).

The advantages and disadvantages of the *diversified product model* are virtually the opposite of those of the standard product model discussed above. As the world has become more and more competitive, more and more companies have gravitated to the diversification product model out of necessity — to establish unique identities for their products that are separate and apart from those of the competition and take up more shelf space in distribution channels. Success with this model, as with all marketing, requires a good understanding of *positioning* since products have to be properly positioned if they are to be sold successfully in competitive environments.

Even though the diversification product model has grown with the competition, many who use this model have also found the need to add options and accessories to each of their products in the line. Therefore, the diversification product model has evolved into a *hybrid* of both models discussed so far.

Hybrid Model

The *hybrid model* for designing products uses elements of both the *diversified* and *standard* product models. That is, each product has unique functions designed into it, but it also has options and accessories that provide additional functionality to each product model to satisfy the differing needs of buyers. Using the automobile market as an example, you can buy a model of *Chevrolet* and add options such as a CD player, aluminum alloy wheels, more expensive metallic paint, a sunroof, and a variety of other options to add functionality to the already diversified product. It is still diversified because you cannot add options to turn a

Chevrolet into a *Buick* or *Cadillac*, but you can add what you want to customize the car to your specific needs. Because of its versatility, this model has become popular for many products such as cars, cameras, computers, bicycles, and modular furniture.

PRODUCT FAMILY

Irregardless of the product design model which your company chooses to best meet the needs of customers, an entire line of products is likely to be developed to satisfy the different needs, or available positions, in the marketplace. These lines are often built from a group of related products that can be thought of as *product families*. These product families, in turn, are constructed from a variety of product family members. Some of the most common of these products members are discussed below.

MEMBERS OF A TYPICAL PRODUCT FAMILY

By knowing the various products that comprise a typical product family, the marketer has the ability to create additional products for sale that satisfy the unfilled needs of buyers and bring in additional revenues and profits for the company — another "win-win" situation.

Core Product

At the center of a typical product family is a basic, *core product component* that *commonly meets the needs of most prospects in a particular target market segment*. This core product can be based on either the standard, diversified, or hybrid product models. The product line could be an *Apple Macintosh* with a core product in that line being a specific *Powerbook* model. It could also be a *Buick* product line with a *Buick Skylark* as the core product. The core product could also be a cellular service, or an already-diversified flavor of ice cream.

Options

Since the *core product* usually does not fulfill the needs of all prospects in the target market, *options* are provided to give features and capabilities to only those who want (or want to pay for) them. The seller of the *Apple Macintosh* computer might offer an optional DVD drive. The buyer of a *Buick* may be able to select an optional sunroof or a CD-player. The customer of the cell-phone service could sign up for greater monthly usage at a lower per-minute rate or add Internet access. The buyer of a cup of chocolate marshmallow ice cream (an already-diversified product) could elect to add chocolate sauce or nuts.

Accessories

While often confused with options, accessories are really different. They are designed to help a person use the product, but they typically don't fit into or become a part of the product.

They are extra or outside the concept of the basic product and its options. Examples of accessories for personal computers might include dust covers, carrying cases, and mouse pads. For automobiles, accessories are likely to include floor mats, car covers, inexpensive security devices, such as *The Club*, and steering wheel covers. Cell-phone service providers might offer phone covers.

Supplies

Supplies are *consumable items that are necessary for the proper functioning of the basic product and its options*. A starter amount of these may or may not be included with the standard product. Examples of supplies for computer printers include ink cartridges, laser toner cartridges, and special paper for the printer. For cars, supplies often include gasoline, motor oil, transmission fluid, car cleaning solutions, spark plugs, and brake pads. Cell-phone services might offer phone batteries.

Shipping, Delivery, and Installation

Because of their size, weight, complexity, or nature, many products require shipping or delivery and installation. While these are sometimes separate services performed by different people (and separate companies), delivery and installation often occur together. Delivery includes making sure all the product components ordered by the customer are taken to the customer's site in good working order and condition. Installation refers to the process of putting the delivered product family components together to form a working unit or service. Many services, such as window washing and plumbing services, have delivery and installation built into them. They cannot be performed without the inclusion of delivery and installation at the customer's site. Marketers should understand that many technology sales have been reversed because of problems caused by delivery and installation personnel. Therefore, it is important to the success of your company to make sure that they are properly trained to be courteous and helpful to customers in addition to being competent. This is an area where many companies try to save money by hiring less-skilled people. They forget that these positions are often the first point of contact after the sale is made. Moreover, delivery and installation often represent the first services that a customer receives. Consequently, a good first impression is critical to the success of the sale and to the continued good relationship with the customer.

There are several ways of helping to insure successful shipping, delivery and installation. If these methods are not already employed, it is the marketer's job to put them in place. They include the following:

1. Have the sales person send or e-mail a standard *installation letter* to the customer in advance of the delivery or installation. This letter should clearly delineate what the installers will and *will not* do and how payment will be handled. It is important to avoid

the situation where the customer is surprised or expects more than the delivery or installation person can deliver.

2. Before the product leaves the company's premises, the person responsible should complete a *Shipping* or *Delivery/Installation Checklist* so that each item ordered is *checked out* to insure it is in good working order and is *checked off* as it is loaded into the shipping or delivery vehicle. The time to find out it doesn't work is in your shop. Not at the customer's premises.

   In those cases where the product is a service, the service provider should make sure he/she has all the materials and tools required to properly perform the service. A checklist for this purpose is also recommended.

3. Upon delivering and installing the product, the installers should demonstrate that the product works, and have the customer *sign a copy* of the *Delivery/Installation Checklist.* This will be an important piece of the customer's file that proves that the system was delivered and installed properly.

   For service providers, a *Service Provider Checklist* should be signed by the customer to verify that the service has been performed to the customer's satisfaction.

4. Have at least one item on the checklist be a question such as, "Were the installers (or service providers) courteous, and did they complete the installation or service to your satisfaction?" In this way, the company can obtain feedback on their service as well as remind the installers of their responsibilities. It can also serve as a good way to measure installer performance and to communicate to the customer that good service is the intent of the company. Another purpose for this question is to protect the company from any frivolous complaints from unscrupulous customers at a later time.

5. If, for some reason, the delivery and installation does not go well, you should not despair. This situation should be viewed as an *opportunity to turn a negative into a positive.* Apologies, flowers, a give-away item, and other forms of saying you're sorry can become a great advantage. Most people understand that mistakes are unavoidable. When they occur, studies show that the company's positive handling of them can serve to forge an even better relationship with the customer. Conversely, if handled improperly, they can start a terrible chain of events that endanger the successful completion of the sale and the ongoing relationship with the customer. Even worse, the improper handling of mistakes can cause negative *word-of-mouth* advertising that will cost the company a lot more than the loss of that one sale. In some cases, it may even lead to costly litigation.

Training

Many high-tech goods and services, musical instruments, art materials, and education services, require training of customers after the sale. The sophisticated nature of most high-tech products and musical instruments dictates the need to train users on their proper operation and care. In the case of personal computers, training is normally required on both the hardware and the software. It is critical to the successful use of the product. For educational services, training is an inherent part of the core product. For DNA-testing products, training of laboratory workers is often mandatory.

Support

Most products that require training also require after-sale support. *Support* refers to the *assistance given to customers after the product is purchased or the training class is completed.* This service can be delivered over the phone, online, at the customer's site, or at the company offering the service. What many marketing and sales personnel sometimes forget is that the sale is not final until the customer is trained, supported and satisfied. Even if companies have policies of no returns after installation, those that understand marketing will accept the product back within a reasonable time after shipping if the customer is not satisfied.

Service

Many use the word *service* as a general term for all services performed before, during and after the sale. In the context of the *product family*, service refers to the *repair and maintenance* of the product. *Repair* is a service performed in response to a product breakdown, whereas *maintenance* is a service routinely performed to prevent a breakdown. In many companies, the *intangible* service is turned into a *tangible* product by means of a *service contract* that delineates the services that will and will not be performed according to the contract. The *will not* usually includes clauses to protect the company from misuse or abuse of the product.

Product Information

While often not considered part of the product family, various types of product information are an essential part of most products. They include the following:

Brochure: The introduction of the prospect or customer to the high-technology product family is often achieved via the brochure or catalogue. The brochure should contain a picture, or graphic representation, of the product (in the case of a service, this could be a picture of company personnel providing the service), a description of features and benefits, a listing of product specifications (or capabilities in the case of a service), and a brief history of the company (or its founders if it is a new company). It should represent a compilation of marketing variables and strategies working together to help sell the product. Because the brochure can be expensive and product prices often change rapidly, pricing is one variable that should not be specified in most brochures. Price is usually alluded to in brochures with such words as *low-cost*, *economical*, *good value*, or *cost-effective*. Although it is part of any product family, the brochure is really a promotional tool. Therefore, it will be discussed in greater detail in *Chapter 9* on *Promotion*.

Warranty: An important component of many products is the warranty. The *warranty gives the customer protection against any defects in materials and workmanship for a period of time* usually ranging from 90 days up to one year. In the case of a service, it usually assures the customer of service to their satisfaction. It should be noted that some warranties are as short as 30 days and as long as 5 years, or in rare cases an entire lifetime. The warranty embodies both the *Product* and *Pricing* variables, and can be used to help *Position* and *Promote* the product. While assuring product protection, it also acts to change the effective price of the product. In other words, if products from two different companies are basically similar and have the same list price, the one with the longer warranty will have a lower effective price since the customer will *not* have to pay for a service contract over the additional period.

Manuals and Instructions: Many high-tech products require written instructions to guide the user in their proper operation and maintenance. These written instructions are often provided in the form of *owner's* or *user's* manuals. Too many companies fail to give these manuals the importance they deserve. This is shortsighted because incomplete or unreadable manuals can cause the user a great deal of grief and ill will toward a company. Moreover, confusing instructions only cause customers to call the company more frequently. These additional calls, in turn, serve to tie up company resources requiring more customer support people, more phone lines, and more office space to house these additional resources. Manuals that accompany many high-tech products are notoriously bad. In many instances, they are written by technical people who write them in a hurry or don't know how to communicate or write in ways that users understand. Marketers should understand that a well-written manual can often have an important affect on the perception of the product in the marketplace. In addition to generating positive word-of-mouth advertising, it influences the *ease-of-use* rating users give to products in published surveys, studies, and magazine articles. Positive mention in these sources can go a long way toward making more sales for your company. Furthermore, they can be quoted and used to advantage in promotional media. Conversely, a company that markets its products as being *easy-to-use* when product manuals are, if fact, *difficult* to read runs the risk of being labeled as dishonest. Such a label, of course, causes serious corporate image damage and serves to negatively impact sales.

Upgrades

Upgrades are improvements in core products that enhance their performance. Some upgrades fix problems, or *bugs* as they are sometimes called. Others add necessary or requested features. Some are offered to customers at no additional charge. Others, usually the ones that include new features, have an additional charge associated with them. Still others are included under the provisions of service contracts. No matter how they are offered, they are looked upon as an essential part of some product families. Marketers should recognize this and make sure that upgrade policies and strategies are part of the their *product strategies*. Marketing and sales personnel should also insure that they communicate the upgradeability of the product, along with the upgrade history of the company's products, to prospects and customers.

Microsoft introduced one of their upgrades, *Windows '95*, as a new product. The marketing of this upgrade was so successful that customers were lined up outside stores at midnight to be amongst the first to purchase the product. It is no wonder that *Microsoft* has maintained a leadership position in the microcomputer software marketplace for so many years.

Up until now, the above discussions have concentrated on the products or product components that fit into a *product family*. Larger companies, or companies that have a variety of different products, cluster these *product families* into another level of product hierarchy called *product lines*.

PRODUCT LINE

The *product line* is comprised of a number of products or product families — each of which appeals to one or more specific target market segments. The purpose of having a whole line of products in the *product mix* is to cover more of the needs of different target market segments, strengthen positions, counter (or *get ahead of*) competition, and increase market share. Companies that have the resources, offer multiple product lines to either broaden existing positions, or to go after completely different target market segments. The interrelationships between products, product families, and product lines depend on market needs as well as the company's size, resources, opportunities and positions. Using American automobile companies as an example, *General Motors* offers a variety of product lines that appeal to different market segments. As discussed previously, Cadillac was intended for the high-end market. Buick, Oldsmobile, and Pontiac for the middle segments, and Chevrolet is positioned for the low end of the market. Each of these product lines offers different *automobile models* that can be viewed as the core products of their respective product families. For example, the Buick Skylark has its own family of products and product elements including options, accessories, supplies, product literature, manuals and other product components.

The consumer giant, *Procter & Gamble* (known for its *brand marketing*) considers each of its products as a different *product line* with its own unique position. What is interesting about this approach is that the positions of these product lines are so strong that most consumers don't even associate them with *Procter & Gamble*. For example the top-selling laundry detergents *Tide*, *Cheer*, and *Bold* are all *Procter & Gamble* products — each with their own market niches and identities. *Tide* is an *"old friend"* that is a reliable detergent with a long history. It is often positioned to get clothes *white*. *Cheer* has had different positions — most recently making colors look brighter or getting clothes clean in warm and cold water (*all temperature Cheer*). *Bold*, as its name implies, removes those *tough stains*.

The product line should cover the needs of the identified target markets. And the products within these lines should complement each other as much as possible. It is important that products are not in conflict — causing one product to hurt another. It is particularly critical that marketing strategies be devised so that one product does not seriously *cannibalize*, or eat up, the market share of another. As mentioned in *Chapter 5* on *Positioning*, the choice of the name *Alka Seltzer Plus* served to cannibalize the standard Alka Seltzer market rather than take away market share from competitors. It is difficult to completely avoid a small amount of cannibalization resulting from one product in the line taking some business away from the other. However, good marketing strategies will minimize this from happening and will help to insure that the contribution from each product will be additive to the overall sales of the company.

Figure 6-2 graphically represents the relationships between the product line, product family, and the various notions of product discussed above.

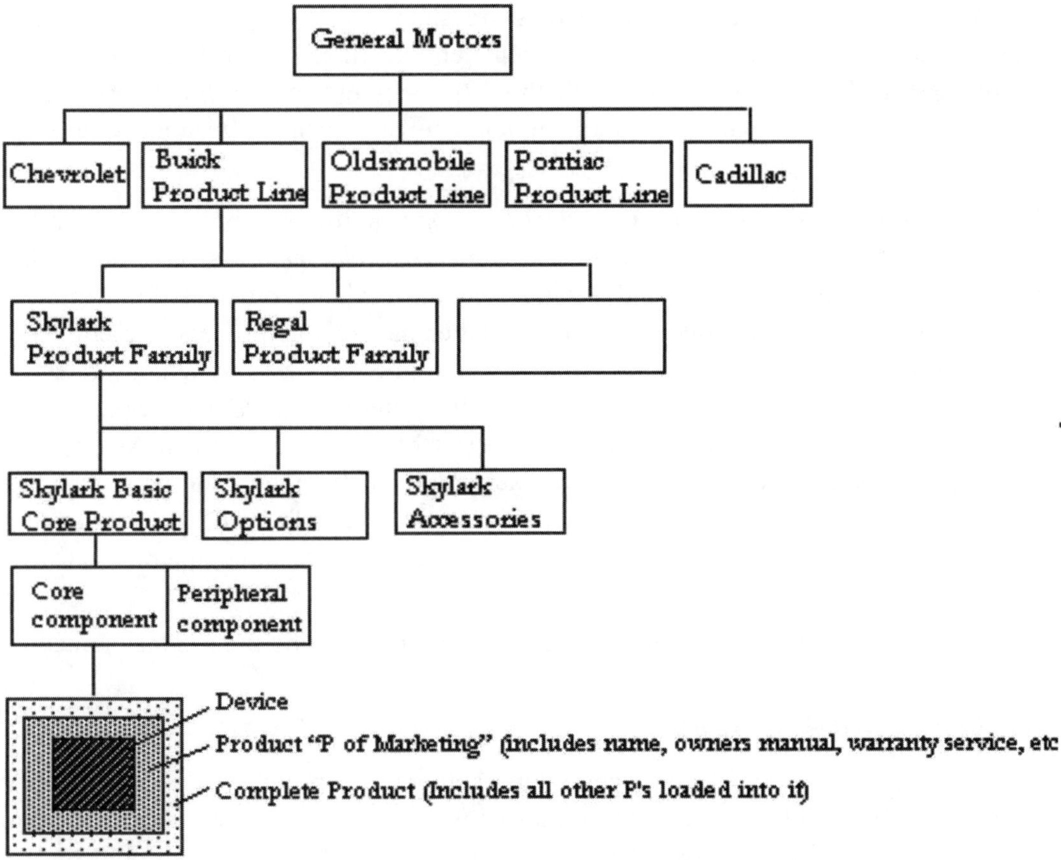
General Motors
Chevrolet
Buick Product Line
Oldsmobile Product Line
Pontiac Product Line
Cadillac
Skylark Product Family
Regal Product Family
Skylark Basic Core Product
Skylark Options
Skylark Accessories
Core component
Peripheral component
Device
Product "P of Marketing" (includes name, owners manual, warranty service, etc
Complete Product (Includes all other P's loaded into it)

Figure 6-2

With these relationships between the *product*, *product family* and *product line*, it is useful to look more closely at the *product strategies* that help to successfully sell the product in the marketplace.

PRODUCT STRATEGIES

The product strategies of most companies are shaped by many factors including the company philosophy, research and development, engineering, the professional talents of company personnel, and other internal factors. To help insure success, they should be primarily shaped by external sources in the marketplace such as customers, prospects, competitors, and suppliers.

As discussed in the section on *New Product Development*, the new product ideas from the above sources are put into the company's *New Product Development System* at one end, and after several levels of screening and testing, the most viable products for commercial development come out of the other. During the latter part of this process, the company is simultaneously conducting *Market Research* to determine the best marketing strategies to insure the success of the viable products. For each product, a *position* is selected to take advantage of openings in the marketplace that aren't being properly filled. As part of the positioning strategy, a name and message are selected to penetrate the information jungle and get the product into the minds of target prospects. At this point, the collected information is put back into the system to help finalize the design of the product for commercial release.

The following are the factors that should be considered in finalizing the Product strategy.

Has the Best Name Been Chosen?

Because of its importance to the successful marketing of the product, the name selection is reviewed again. If feasible, it is tested again to see what the marketplace thinks of the name. Does it properly position the product in the mind of the marketplace? Is it confused with names of competitors? Does it describe the product or service or the benefit it provides?

Physical Characteristics

To the extent that the physical characteristics of the product are not dictated by the technology, they should be designed to accommodate customer preferences — particularly in regard to such aesthetic and user considerations as shape, color, texture, and location of user controls. The physical characteristics of most services are dictated by the overall design of the service — including the design of the office, uniforms, company vehicles, and the capabilities and training of the people providing the service.

Aesthetics

As insignificant as color may be to a project engineer or researcher, it can be very important to the person who makes the buying decision, and it often adds functionality to the product. The marketer should do some *market research* to determine where the product is likely to be used. If it is used in an office, its shape and color should be compatible with the objects in the office. While *IBM* is sometimes referred to as *Big Blue*, a reference to the color of most its original mainframe computers years ago, most of its products that are used today are designed to fit the decor of the environments in which they will be used.

The color of the product's skin is not the only color consideration. The color of other components, such as displays, buttons, and wires, may also be significant. Two major factors should be considered when making color decisions for a product — function and aesthetics. In describing the reason for the multicolored display on its color correction system, the CEO of one company told the author of this book, "*There is really no functional need for the color display in the system, but our clients like it. It's good show business.*"

Color, of course is not the only aesthetic decision to be made. There are many others. Shape, texture, and feel are some of the more obvious ones. In addition to their contribution to aesthetics, some characteristics perform other functions. For example, some find amber computer monitors to be easier on the eyes. With the proper software, color monitors aid operator efficiency by helping users to distinguish between different selections. Considering the fact that there is limited desk space and elbow-room in most offices, manufacturers are designing their products to have smaller and smaller *footprints* and profiles (the space taken by the product on the desk). Why? That's what customers want. They want smaller, quieter, lighter, easier, more powerful, more portable, and less power-consuming. They want everything, and whether you offer it to them or not, some competitor will.

Services also must consider aesthetics in their product designs. In addition, to making their offices, service delivery vehicles, and other service elements as attractive as possible, most professional service organizations require their professionals to follow commonly accepted dress, grooming and behavior codes. Many organizations, such as medical equipment, computer repair, and copy machine service firms require their personnel to wear special uniforms. These uniforms (1) enable employees to do their job more effectively, (2) help to position and promote the company more efficiently, (3) make it easier for customers to identify company representatives, and (4) make service personnel more attractive or official-looking.

Cultural Differences

If the product is to be sold internationally, color and other aesthetic elements become even more significant. Some foreign cultures attach special meaning to colors, symbols, and other visual elements. Philip R. Cateora and John M. Hess report the following in their book *International Marketing*:

> *"A prominent international manufacturer of water-recreation products learned an expensive lesson in Malaysia. Its home office received heated requests from its Malaysian distributors to stop shipments on all products colored green. The distributors reported that numerous customers associated the firm's colors of green with the jungle and illness... The whole idea of color to an Asian is coupled with beliefs... To the Chinese, red is very lucky, but a Thai prefers yellow as a lucky color."*[2]

American automobile makers continue to complain about unfair competition from Japan. Although they have been trying to exert pressure through political channels to get the Japanese to buy more American cars, most have refused to put the steering wheel on the right side of cars for export to Japan (to accommodate the fact that the Japanese drive on the left side of the road). While they may believe that such an accommodation wouldn't be cost effective, the Japanese have no problem moving the steering wheel for the American market. The refusal of *Detroit* to recognize and respond to a really important customer need, as well as the attitude that it represents, is one of the reasons that many Japanese refuse to buy American automobiles. If American auto makers spent as much time and effort responding to customer needs as they do to lobbying politicians and paying lawyers, perhaps they could improve their performance and contribute more to the American economy.

Market Segmentation Considerations

In most markets, there are target market segments that have different requirements. Some of these requirements can be accommodated by the options offered on the *standard product* within the same product family. Others require a completely separate product line often for reasons of positioning. That is, some people want a *top-of-the-line* product regardless of cost whereas others are more cost-conscious wanting a product that *gets the job done* for less money. How does a company best accommodate these different requirements of different target market strata? Offer totally separate product lines with their own identities. The *big 3* Japanese automakers recognized the varying needs of different market segments when they decided to introduce separate luxury automobile product lines. After surveying the market, they knew that the upscale segment of the car market would not buy luxury models that were part of the *Toyota*, *Honda* and *Nissan* product lines. These lines created images of reliability, good value, and economy, but they did not communicate an image of luxury. Therefore, they introduced separate lines with separate positions, or identities. Hence *Lexus*, *Acura* and *Infiniti* were born.

Human Factors

The term *Human Factors* refers to the considerations involved in making products easier and more efficient to use. The size, shape, and location of operator controls; the color and viewing angle of displays and lights; the angle of keyboards, steering wheels, and pedals; the weight of pens, doors, and packages; the shape of electronic mice, furniture, and vacuum cleaners; and the position and location of On/Off, Reset, and channel-changing switches and buttons are all examples of human factors considerations that go into the design of products.

With products that are services, human factors typically relate to how the service is communicated. Is the menu written and formatted in a way that the customer understands the options available and how to best communicate those options? Too many mistakes are made in restaurants because of human factors considerations. If you are in a service business, you can think of what you can do to help insure that mistakes are avoided in the rendering of your particular service.

While many companies stress human factors in their marketing literature, human factors are too often neglected in the development of products. An example of this is the original *IBM* PC keyboard. It's hard to believe that the same company that designed the elegant *Selectric* typewriter keyboard is also responsible for the original *IBM* PC keyboard. The location of "*Shift*" and function keys, and the size, shape, and location of "*Return*" and "*Backspace*" keys are some of the human factors *offenses* embodied in the original PC keyboard. Some believe that *IBM* purposefully put this inferior keyboard on the PC so as to avoid cannibalizing the market for its much more expensive and profitable high-end systems. Whatever the reason, the design of this keyboard was responsible, in no small part, for customers giving their keyboard business to alternate suppliers.

It should be noted that, no matter how well a product is doing in the marketplace, the marketers and product designers should not do anything that is going to point customers toward competitors because some customers will not return. Poor human factors give competitors an open space, or position, through which they can *put their foot*. Once they have their foot in the door, it's difficult to get them out.

Product Performance

Product performance typically refers to the speed and precision at which a product does the tasks it is designed to accomplish. In addition to giving customers what they want, the performance designed into a product, is affected by cost, competition, and a variety of other factors. Marketing input is critical to determining the performance that will be designed in the product. *Positioning* affects the determination because a *high-end* product will have to exhibit superlative performance. *Price* is also an important factor since it will dictate the cost that can be designed into the product. If price is no object (and it usually is), quality and performance can reach the highest possible levels. The performance designed into the product is usually the result of a price-performance trade-off as determined by the desires of the market targets. For example, many travelers would like to take advantage of the timesaving benefits resulting from the supersonic speed capabilities of the *Concorde* aircraft. However, American travelers and their neighbors on the ground have decided that they would rather pay less to travel on the much slower subsonic models and avoid the "sonic booms" associated with supersonic aircraft.

Quality/Durability

As with performance, the quality and durability built into the product has to fit with the product's position and the desires of the marketplace. It confuses people to pay low prices for the highest-quality products, and vice versa. In the first case, they are mistrustful. They ask themselves what's wrong with the product? In the case of high-prices for lower-quality products, they feel cheated and become very angry.

Quality/Price Trade-off

There is also a trade-off between quality and price. That is, while everyone wants the highest quality for the lowest price (within the constraints of proper positioning) most people will only pay for what they feel they can afford. Using the air travel analogy, manufacturers could build aircraft that are even safer and more comfortable. However, most travelers either can't afford, or are not willing to pay for, these extras. They believe the margin of safety and the spacing between seats of today's aircraft that allows for an affordable ticket from Los Angeles to San Francisco is preferable to a greater margin of safety and more comfortable seats at 10 times the price per ticket for the same trip. An example of this preference is the fact that, over the years, the first-class sections of most aircraft have gotten smaller and smaller to accommodate larger and larger tourist class sections. On the other hand, some people are willing to pay a lot more for better food, more leg room, and other benefits of flying first and business class — even though they are going to the same destination at the same time.

Total Quality Management

Due to the ever-increasing demands of customers and competition, companies are increasingly incorporating *Total Quality Management* (TQM) and *continual improvement* concepts in their product strategies. These concepts were developed by the late W. Edwards

Demming. While originally neglected by most U.S. companies, Demming's TQM concepts were readily learned and adopted by Japanese companies. The result has been that, in a very short period of time, the label *Made in Japan* has been repositioned from its meaning of inferior quality to becoming synonymous with the very best quality in the world.

The key elements in a TQM philosophy include the following:

- **Concentration on customer satisfaction.** Satisfying customers becomes the main focus.
- **Setting High Standards.** Using what *Xerox* calls *competitive benchmarking*, companies compare themselves with the best companies in the world and try to match or beat the standards set by them.
- **Continuous Improvement.** Employing what the Japanese call *kaisen*, everyone in the company is mobilized to do whatever they can to continually improve the product.

Many are good at designing products that work according to specifications, but few give sufficient consideration to the servicing or repairing of the product after the sale. Visions of technicians spending hours working on early generation copiers, minicomputers, and phone equipment with their tools spread all over the floor are vivid in the minds of many in every marketplace. Even more vivid is the *down time* and disruption this situation causes.

Some products break down more frequently than others, but almost nothing makes a customer angrier than the disruptions caused by difficult-to-service products. This anger can quickly turn into negative word-of-mouth advertising, damage to the images of the product and company, and lost sales. Probably the best way to avoid this situation is to have the marketing department educate and sell the product designers on the importance of making *ease-of-servicing* a critical parameter in the product design. Otherwise, marketing will have to waste more time in *image damage control* when the complaints start rolling in.

The laser printer and copier technology designed by *Cannon* is a good example of the incorporation of serviceability into the design of the product. The *Cannon engine*, as it is called, is at the heart of many of today's laser printers and copiers. The engine is designed so that 80% of its moving parts (the components that are most likely to fail) are incorporated in the disposable toner cartridge of the printer or copier. When the cartridge is depleted of toner, signaled by a warning code when the toner reaches a low level, it is merely replaced by another cartridge containing new moving parts. This design gives sales people a distinct advantage not only at the time of the initial sale but also at the time when good references need to be called for testimonials on the product. In addition to answering one of the market's primary objections about printers and copiers — frequent breakdowns — it also takes the *mess* out of toner replacement. From the point of view of sales people, in addition to limiting angry customer reactions and breakdowns, the serviceable design gives them another profitable replacement part to sell — toner cartridges.

Delivery and Installation

Marketing input and consideration should be given to the delivery and installation of the high-tech product. The following are some important questions that should be considered into the design of the product:

1. How many are required to deliver and install the product?
2. Will it fit within standard shipping containers and vehicles?
3. Will it withstand the shock from mechanical handling devices used by *UPS* and other common carriers?
4. Can it fit within standard freight elevators and office or shop doorways?
5. Are there any special power requirements or distance limitations?
6. Does the product require any special environment or site preparation?
7. Can the customer hook up and install the product without installer assistance?

Packaging

The packaging of the product is also an important marketing decision. Packaging of products usually serves several purposes including: *protection* of the contents, *aesthetics*, *identification* and *location* of the company, and *information about what is inside*, and *directions how to properly use or handle it*. With many products, protection is an important issue — especially if the product is to be shipped and handled by persons outside the company. Products damaged on arrival don't create happy customers, and they can run up company repair, replacement and redelivery costs needlessly. Aesthetics of packaging for all products are important — especially if they are distributed through retail channels. Since customers of many products are urged to keep the packaging for future movement or shipment of the product, there will be ample opportunity for the packaging to work for, rather than against, the company's marketing programs. Good-looking packaging makes good impressions and attracts attention when the product sits on shelves. Company logos, slogans, and identifiers are important for the same reasons. Information about the origination point should appear on the packaging in the event the paperwork gets lost and/or the product has to be returned because the customer was not available to accept it at the time of delivery. In addition, warnings about the proper handling of the product such as *This Side Up* can avoid a lot of needless headaches resulting from the inadvertent mishandling of the product.

If the product is for export, special packaging may be required. It is best for you to know this in advance so you can plan for it in the product development stage. Unfortunately, many companies don't start thinking about special export packaging until a foreign order is received.

Legal Issues

Before the product is even developed, a thorough search of conflicting patents and trademarks should be made by qualified sources. In addition to patent law firms, there are companies that specialize in such searches — sometimes for nominal fixed fees. When the legal budget it limited, you can save a lot of money by contracting with a search firm directly rather than having your patent attorney do this kind of work. Patent attorneys will typically mark up all outside service fees by their standard overhead rates. They will also add in billings for their time to correspond with the search firms. You can have someone in your company do this work for much less, but they should keep the patent attorneys apprised of what they're doing so there is no wasteful overlap. Internet searches can greatly facilitate this process.

As soon as you begin using the product name, you should put a ™ as a superscript after the first occurrence of the name on every document in which it is used. Each of the documents on which it is used should include dates on them so that the *date of first use* of the name can be easily established. This includes all marketing literature, correspondence, logos, memos, and advertisements. This will protect your company from others using your name for a similar purpose. Generic names cannot be trademarked unless they refer to a product whose definition is far removed from the meaning attached to the generic name. *Chair* cannot be trademarked in reference to an object on which people sit, but could be trademarked if it refers an unrelated product, such as a line of clothing.

Once a trademark is registered, all of the places where ™ appeared must be changed to an *R in a circle*, or ®. This symbol "tells the world" that the name is a registered trademark.

In addition to trade-marking names and patenting inventions, it's a good idea to protect all software, manuals, important product literature, and technical documents by copyrighting them. This can be done by filing a copyright application and prominently displaying the word *Copyright* followed by the date and the name of the company (or individual) who owns the copyright on all title pages and labels of the copyrighted material. Once notification is received that the copyright is registered, a *C in a circle*, or ©, can replace the word Copyright on all materials.

To protect the company against abuses of sales, support, or service contracts, they should be drafted by a capable business attorney who specializes in such contracts. To save legal fees in the future, you can store these original drafts on a word processor so that when changes are made, you can easily make them without paying your attorney to do so. The marketing department should make sure that all terms and conditions on contracts can be easily read and understood by customers and vendors — two of the company's important publics. Many company personnel avoid the issue of explaining contracts at the time of sale because they feel such legal matters scare prospects away. This should not be a concern if the contracts are well-written and the sales people are properly trained as to how to explain them. It's much easier to discuss these issues before, rather than after, the sale when there is a misunderstanding. An easy way to do this is to give prospects a copy of all contracts and suggest that they read them over and call if they have any questions. As with all company documents, the aesthetics and readability of contracts should be taken into account.

As a final general comment about legal issues, it is best to take care of them as far in advance as possible since the costs of doing so will be minuscule compared to lawsuits from patent, trademark, or copyright infringement or from customer charges of misrepresentation and contract infringement.

Government Regulations and Approvals

Often government regulations and laboratory testing play a big part in defining the product. There is *U/L approval* for electrical equipment, *FDA approval* for bio-tech and pharmaceutical products, *FAA approval* for objects that fly in the air, *FCC approval* for communications devices, *Export licensing* requirements (many restrictions apply to certain types of high-tech equipment), *product liability* laws, etc. For a product to be successful and to avoid costly litigation, it should adhere to all government regulations — Federal, State, County and City.

Taxes, Duties and Tariffs

Taxes, duties and tariffs need to be considered at the time of product development since they will add cost to the product — particularly if the product is exported to a foreign country. These will play a part in the quality-price, performance-price trade-offs already discussed.

Power and Television Requirements

While it may seem like an insignificant detail, many firms designed products without considering the possible need to have them work with both *60* and *50-cycle* power. The time to think about this is at the beginning and not after the product design is completed. Markets are becoming more and more international. Although the United States, Canada, and Japan use *60-cycle* power, Europe, Australia and many other parts of the world base their power on *50 cycles*.

In addition to the numerous difficulties associated with different power standards, there are other differences that cause problems. For example, television sets in the United States,

Canada and Japan are based on a *525-line broadcast standard*; whereas Europe, Australia and other places have a *625-line standard*. With High-Definition Television, or HDTV, there are many more standards. This means that most TV monitors purchased in one country cannot be used in any other that follows a different standard.

Costs

As with all business decisions, costs are a very big concern in developing and defining the high-technology product. In addition to concern about the *target price* of the finished product, the cost implications of every decision have to be estimated at virtually every step along the way. At each juncture, the developers have to decide whether it will be more cost-effective to make the component or buy it from an external source.

It is important to note that this *make or buy* decision has marketing implications beyond the affect of cost on the final price of the product. It can also affect product confidentiality and the customer's attitude toward the product. For example, if a customer discovers that a significant portion of the product is made by another company, this customer may try to go directly to the supplier. Also, the position the product occupies in the mind of the customer could dramatically change, causing the customer to buy elsewhere. This has occurred in certain cases where customers learn that a product they thought was made in their home country turns out to have significant portions manufactured in other places.

Competition

The competition often plays a big part in helping to define what goes into high-tech products. Most companies want to *keep up* with or *beat out* their competitors. Therefore, they may need to make changes to their products to give themselves competitive advantages. While it is good for companies to stay ahead of their competitors, they should not forget that their primary mission is to satisfy customers, not to beat the competition. After all, the best way to maintain an advantage over competitors is to keep customers happy and not give them any reasons to look elsewhere.

FAB TABLES

For every product in your product line, you should create an FAB Table. FAB is an acronym for *Features*, *Advantages*, and *Benefits*. As shown in *Figure 6-3*, a FAB Table should have four columns in the following order — (1) *Features* (inherent characteristics of the product, such as size, color, weight, speed, etc.), (2) *Benefits* (what those features do for the target audience… small enough to fit anywhere in your office or home, fast enough to run today's most advanced programs, etc.), (3) *Advantages* (unique features and benefits that your competitors' products do not have), and (4) *Return on Investment, or tangible time and money savings*, (derived from taking the features, benefits, and advantages in the previous three columns and using credible data to translate them into time and money savings). For example, *Datapro Word Processing Reports* did a study that showed that a secretary using a word processor could do three times the work she could do on an electric typewriter in the same amount of time. This data was used in the fourth column of a FAB table to illustrate the time and money savings of a word processor over electric typewriters (which were competitive products at one time). This FAB table can greatly facilitate the success of your marketing. The two most important uses are (1) It can help those who will create and execute your marketing communications (ads, brochures, Web sites, etc.) and (2) It should be given to your sales personnel for placement in their Sales Notebooks so they can intelligently show customers how your products will benefit them — including make them more money than those of competitors. All good marketers know that features do not sell as well as benefits. Your product FAB tables can save a lot of time and money for those, in and outside your company, who create your marketing communications and sell your products.

FAB TABLE

Product	Features	Benefits	Advantages	Tangible Benefits Over status quo and direct competition

Figure 6-3

SUMMARY

It is virtually impossible for one chapter of a book to cover all the issues that you should consider in developing your company's product strategies. Nonetheless, those that are presented in this chapter should give you a solid foundation upon which you can develop a comprehensive product strategy for your company.

The important point to remember is that the Product is a variable as are the other ingredients in the Marketing Mix. The needs of the marketplace and the resources of your company help to give it definition in the form of a Product strategy. This strategy, however, is subject to change as the needs and conditions of the marketplace change. There are many examples of this. Railroads were largely supplanted by air travel and automobiles, impact printers have lost significant market share to laser printers, and typewriters gave way to word processors. To quote an old cliché, "the only thing that is constant is change." It is important not to forget this nature of products and the world. The successful marketer always looks into the marketplace, anticipates, and prepares for change.

[1]William Davidow, "*The Ascendancy of High-Tech Marketing*", *Electronic Business*, May 15, 1988.

TIPS and Exercises

1. Outline your product line.
2. Outline new core products, services, options, accessories, and supplies you could add with little difficulty to help fill the unfilled needs identified in the previous chapter to round out your product line.
3. Evaluate the "peripheral" customer-service component of your products, and make suggestions for improving your customer service. If you need help, ask you customers how you could serve them better.
4. Think of things you are throwing away now that you could turn into products.
5. Create FAB Tables for each of your products. Give copies to those who create your marketing communications and those who sell your products for you.

Chapter 7

DNA of Price

"It's never low enough... It's never high enough..."

WHAT IS PRICE?

Simply stated, *Price is the amount of money the buyer is willing to pay and for which the seller is willing to sell the product.* We should add to this definition our standard ending "*...in order to achieve the goals of the marketing plan.*" When we add this phrase, we are building the *both sides win* philosophy into our definitions.

It's a measure of value

It should be noted that Price can refer to an exchange of something other than money for a product. For example, in the case of bartering, a price is paid in the form of other goods and services. In *start-up* companies, many founding employees, work for reduced wages and stock options — trading current labor for future benefits that may or may not be realized.

It's the "best" and "worst" understood of the marketing building blocks

In some ways, it is the best-understood marketing variable since most people have a lot of experience comparing and paying prices whenever they go shopping for food, pharmaceuticals, clothes, household items, and industrial products. In other ways, as with the product variable, it is only superficially known. At times, it can be the most mysterious, frustrating, and difficult to understand of all the variables. The reason is that, unless you have a good *marketing information system*, price often behaves, and effects, other variables differently that you expect it will. Moreover, even after you have done all you can, it sometimes works differently than you predict it will.

Needs to be coordinated with other variables in the mix

In particular, Price must be very tightly coordinated with your other marketing strategies — particularly *Positioning*, *Product*, *Distribution*, and *Promotion* strategies. For example, you wouldn't expect to see a high-priced, quality product sold for an unbelievably low price in a discount store or advertised in a "*throw away*" paper. High-priced, quality products are sold through exclusive distribution channels and are advertised in the highest-quality media. If not, the various messages conflict with each other. This conflict only serves to confuse your customer, reduce sales, and potentially ruin the product's position your company's image in the minds of your publics. This happened to *Izod Lacoste* when they flooded the market with their "alligator" shirts. Rather than continuing to sell them through exclusive retail outlets, the company (then owned by *General Mills*) made them available to any reseller who wanted to buy them — including discount stores. The intensified competition, and the availability through discounters lowered the "street price" of the product. This, in turn, lowered the product's image in the minds of buyers causing the company to lose its upscale position. The void, of course, was quickly filled by *Ralph Lauren's* "Polo" line.

Because *Ralph Lauren* has not made the same mistake to date, *Izod La Coste* has had considerable difficulty trying to regain its market share.

Examples of the connection to other building blocks

There are many other examples of the interdependence of Price and other building blocks. *Porsche* automobiles have a much higher price tag than *Volkswagens*, and you'll never see them sold next to each other even though they are made by the same company. The same is true for *Cadillac* and *Chevrolet*, *Lexus* and *Toyota*, *Lincoln* and *Ford*, *Infiniti* and *Nissan*, and *Acura* and *Honda*. Upon introducing its line of PC's, *IBM* was very selective in picking dealers to sell its products. Additionally, those dealers that were selected had to agree to some very strict rules and conditions including: they were not allowed to reship or sell the systems to any other unauthorized resellers; they had to service any PC brought in for repair even if the PC was purchased elsewhere; and they had to have at least one full-time service and support technician at each location authorized to sell the product.

Price boundaries

At the high end, price is determined by *what the market will bear*, or the maximum price that market targets will pay for the product. At the low end, it is usually bound by how much is required to *cover the costs* of making the product. Actually, there are cases where products are sold below cost. These will be discussed later in this Chapter. For many new products, the price is set somewhere between *what the market will bear* and a minimum acceptable return on investment. The reason is that a maximum price will usually limit sales to only the high-end segment whereas a price set at cost provides little or no incentive to introduce the product. For new products, a *what the market will bear* price is common for a few important reasons — (1) the product is usually not available from other sources — allowing the company to have a monopoly position for a period of time, (2) research and development costs need to be amortized over initial production runs causing the prices of these first-generation products to be higher, (3) economies of scale have not been realized, and (4) members of the innovator segment of most markets want to be "the first" to buy the product no matter what the price.

Graphic representation

A graphic representation of Price is shown in *Figure 7-1*. As shown in this figure, Price is usually comprised of several different components including *cost of goods*, *amortization* (or allocation to each unit of product) *of research and development* and other costs, and *gross profit*. Depending how the company's accounting system has been designed, there may be other cost or expense components included in the Price of the company's products. There are rules and laws which govern what can be included in the actual inventoried *cost of goods*, which are capitalized on the *Balance Sheet*, and what has to included in the company's *general and administrative expenses*, which are expensed on the *Profit and Loss*, or *Income*, *Statement*. Since the rules and laws are always changing, it wouldn't be useful to discuss them in this text. A course on *Cost Accounting* is recommended for those who are interested.

Price Graphic
PRICE
Gross Profit Margin
Amortized Costs
Cost of Goods Sold
Zero Point

Figure 7-1

WHAT FACTORS AFFECT THE PRICE OF A PRODUCT?

Too many marketers put far too little thought into setting the price of their products. Many simply copy those of competitors. Others just add what they think is an adequate profit margin on top of their costs. Still others guess what the price should be. Too many price their products too low. The definition of price given at the beginning of this Chapter can serve as a good starting point for establishing the price of a product.

Understanding the definition of Price

The first part of the *price definition* incorporates the concept of *what the buyers are willing to pay*. Having a good *marketing information system* or doing some competent *market research* is critical to making this determination. Focus groups, well-designed surveys, and objective price tests are techniques that can be used to find out what price market targets are willing to pay.

Reflecting, the *both sides must win* philosophy of business, the second part of the definition reflects the *amount of money for which the company is willing to sell* the product. This is also important — especially in the case of a new product for which the market has no clear perception of its value. Since this concept of *value* is also often misunderstood, it perhaps deserves further explanation.

Value

Value incorporates the *Price*, *Product*, and *Positioning* marketing variables, and can be affected by all the others. The expression "*One person's junk is another's antique*" helps to communicate the concept of value. For one person, the product has little or no value. It is considered, or positioned in that person's mind, as junk that occupies valuable space. Either that person is not in the target market for that product or does not understand its value to others. The other person, on the other hand, is in the market for the product or does understand its value to others. Old baseball cards, furniture, cars, paintings, sewing machines, musical instruments, athletic shoes, computers, and radios are just some of the products that have been discarded by some for little or no money only to be resurrected by others who have made small fortunes collecting, selling, and trading them. In marketing terminology, the *product* is *positioned* as *worthless* or *valueless* by one and *valuable* or *priceless* by another. The first sets the *price* at or near *zero*. The second buys the product from the first and resells it for a "*what the market will bear*" price.

Value can also be affected by the other building blocks of marketing — *distribution*, *promotion*, *corporate image*, and the *marketing information system*. That is products are perceived to have a higher value if they are sold by reputable distribution outlets, promoted in prestigious publications, made by well-known and respected companies, and if the maker and seller of the products collects feedback (using a *marketing information system*) to determine if buyers are satisfied with the product.

In general, buyers will consider products to be too expensive unless their value is clearly established. Value simply reflects how much a product is worth in the mind of the buyer. When the buyer has little or no idea of the value of a product, it is up to the marketplace or the seller to establish the price and educate the buyer on its value.

Price establishes the value of new or unknown products. Many marketers clearly do not understand this concept of value. For example, when they introduce a new product to compete with one that is already established as the market leader, they typically offer it at a lower price. This simply positions the product as inferior — especially since the marketplace has no way, other than price, to value a newly-introduced product. What they should do is offer it at the same or a higher price and communicate its additional value. If they want to give buyers an incentive to try it, they can offer a special introductory discount — using the *sales promotion*, rather than the *price*, variable alone.

Once you understand the concept of value and its effects on price, it is useful to examine the other factors that should be considered in establishing the price of your product.

Quality/price trade-off

There is always a trade-off between price and the quality or durability built into the product. That is, in order for some products to fit within the window of affordability for *targeted market segments*, the quality has to be brought to a level that is somewhere below the maximum possible. In other words, if the company makes the product with "*too much*" quality, a majority in the target audience will not be able to afford it. Contrary to popular belief, it is usually the customers who determine where the price/quality trade off is. While all of us would like computers that never fail or cars that can withstand a 60-mile per hour crash without harm to its passengers, most of us would not be able to afford them. Therefore, we've decided to "take our chances" with lower quality so that we can afford having our own computer and our own car.

There are cases, usually in non-marketing oriented companies, where the quality-price trade-off is out of balance. The first case is that of a company offering an inferior product that does not meet customers' minimum standards of acceptance for a *not-so-inferior* price. Colloquially, this might be referred to as a "*rip off*". This is an unstable situation that cannot last. Either the company will fix this problem, or customers will stop buying and spread the negative word about it. If the latter happens, the company will be put out of business. The other case is that of a company that offers a superior product for a very low price, which you should know by now is not good *Positioning*. This case might occur when the company does not know what the product really costs. That is, it hasn't identified all the costs that go into making and selling the product. This is also an unstable situation. Even if sales are brisk, the company is likely to lose money on each sale. Eventually, it will have to realize and correct its mistakes or go out of business. Another problem often arises out of this second scenario — prospects don't believe the quality is superior because the price is too low. They are skeptical of bargains — especially if the product brand is not well known. Consequently, they don't buy.

R&D and Start-up Costs

Unless the company has a good reason for pursuing a loss strategy, the price should, at a minimum, cover all direct and identifiable costs. With pharmaceutical, high-tech, other R&D-intensive products as well as products from start-up companies, there are usually high *Research & Development* and *start-up* costs. The price of such products should be set to help recoup these high costs after a reasonable number of units have been sold. Therefore, in determining the price, the company should calculate how many units it expects to sell over a reasonable period. It should then spread, or amortize, such costs over all units so that each product sold *carries* or *helps to make back* its fair share of start-up and R&D costs. While most companies are fairly good at knowing the direct costs to make each unit, too many are not as good at incorporating these other less-obvious costs.

G&A Expenses

In addition to start-up and R&D costs, there are also other costs that are lumped into one *bucket* called *General and Administrative Expenses (G&A)* or affectionately called *overhead*. While they are not typically included into the *cost of goods sold* — a key determinant of price, it is important to consider these costs when figuring *break-evens* and setting prices.

Profit

The word profit has been given a bad name by those in favor of other economic systems and many others who are ignorant of what the word really means. Profit is not synonymous with *rip off* or *gouging* as many would like you to believe. Profit is the "food" of an organization — essential for its health and growth. Without it, the company would die. And when the company dies, so do all the jobs and paychecks. The following also disappear when a company dies: the taxes that the company pays to help fund local, state and federal governments who, in turn, help to educate potential employees; the money that the company would pay to its vendors for goods and services; the contributions to State Disability Insurance, FICA, etc.; and all the opportunities for providing goods and services that help people. Profit can also be looked upon as a *reward* that goes to the company for its good performance.

It is true that some companies cheat, steal, don't treat their people well, pollute, and don't pay their fair share of taxes. This should not surprise you. Companies are like people. There are so many in the world that there are likely to be bad ones as well as good ones. The important point is that *profits have little or nothing to do with the reasons why the bad ones are bad*. If you understand this, you are on the right track to a successful marketing or business career. The reason is related to the fact that, by definition, bad companies are not marketing oriented. A company cannot sustain profits very long if it commits bad acts, such as overcharging customers, to achieve its profitability. Eventually, all of the company's publics will abandon it. The good employees will leave, the customers will stop buying products and engage in *negative word-of-mouth* advertising, suppliers will stop supplying products, and the government authorities will prosecute violations. Marketing-oriented companies don't alienate their publics — not just because they're "*nice guys*," but also because it wouldn't be good business.

Marketing-oriented companies make good profits. They use them to make the company grow — they add new facilities and refurbish old ones; they hire new employees; they reward and promote employees who contribute to the company's growth; and they pay dividends to stockholders that furthers interest in the company's stock, and makes it easier to raise additional capital for continued growth.

From the above discussion, you can see that building a "*reasonable profit*" into the pricing strategy is essential for the continued growth and prosperity of the company.

Competition

Many look at competition as a necessary evil. Marketing-oriented companies should perhaps view quality competition in a more positive light — as a challenge that makes the game of marketing and business more fun. Just as with any game, it would be boring if there wasn't a competing team on the other side that was also trying to win the same game. More importantly, good competitors push the company to make better products. Just as world-class athletes are driven to be their best by competing with other world-class athletes, world-class companies are pushed to produce their best products to beat those created by their most formidable competitors. A popular term for this process is *competitive benchmarking*.

With regard to *Price*, competition forces the company to be *price-competitive* and therefore more efficient in doing better marketing, controlling costs and allocating its resources. This, in turn, usually means a lower price to the customer and greater sales. Without competition, a company might be inclined to charge the maximum price, or what the market will bare. This might limit sales to only the higher end of the market. It also makes the company less competitive in world markets.

In addition to affecting price directly, competition also has an indirect affect on price. The reason for this is that the competition, through their marketing efforts, help to educate the marketplace on new products and technologies. They also help the company to "*legitimize*" the product — an important function when introducing a new technology. As a result, the education and market awareness costs are shared rather than shouldered by one company. This cost sharing, in turn, helps to hold down the price since no one company has to pass it on through the price of its products.

Of course, it should be noted that competition could tend to increase marketing costs — especially in markets where the product tends toward becoming a *commodity* item. In such markets, companies have to spend extra marketing money to differentiate their products from those of the competition. If marketing is done cleverly, the company can actually realize bigger returns on their marketing dollars by figuring out ways of using the marketing outlays of competitors to their own advantage. For example, they can design a comparative campaign along the theme, "*This is theirs. Now look at ours. You be the judge.*" *Avis* did this with *Hertz*, with their "*we try harder*" campaign. Virtually everyone in the computer industry does this with whoever is the market leader. They get the attention of prospects by comparing themselves with the market leader. Without this comparison, their company name or product might continue to go unnoticed. Of course, when comparing you to competitors, it is not a good idea to mention competitors directly by name. This only gives them *free advertising*.

Irresponsible competitors can negatively affect pricing for everybody. They are the ones who enter the market with a *get rich quick scheme* that usually never works and *ends up* hurting everyone — customers, responsible competitors, and themselves. They typically jump into the competition late with a *cutthroat* pricing strategy that quickly generates sales, but little profits. Responsible competitors lose significant business. This forces them to cut services or use inferior components to compete. Customers don't get the products or add-on services they need to make them work. The resultant *negative word-of-mouth* advertising from the lack of service combined with the *skinny* profits eventually cause the irresponsible parties to go out of business, but only after they have caused serious damage to the industry. Some industries take many years to recover — if they ever recover at all.

Government Regulations

There are government regulations that affect pricing decisions. They delineate what you can and can't do. Marketers should review current regulations because they change periodically. Relevant price regulations should be communicated to all marketing and sales personnel since they have to be formally instructed to follow the rules when quoting prices to prospects and customers.

There are two regulations that are worth noting in this text. The first is the *Robinson-Patman Act (1936)*. Simply stated, this Act "outlaws discriminatory pricing practices that substantially lessen competition, tend to create a monopoly, or injure, destroy or prevent competition." It should be emphasized, however, that this Act does not prevent a seller from passing on different cost savings to different customers in the form of different prices. That is, customer A might be offered a better price than customer B because customer A agrees to buy a larger volume at one time, thereby improving selling and order processing efficiencies which, in turn, lowers costs. Similarly, if customer A decides to buy now rather than wait, he/she may be offered a discount to reflect the lowered sales costs in making the sale.

The second regulation worth noting relates to the repeal of the *fair-trade* laws. The fair-trade laws enabled suppliers of brand-name products to impose a fixed resale price on their customers — distributors and dealers. Effectively, this meant that any company or individual who sold a brand-name product had to sell it for the price, which the supplier established as the list price. These fair-trade laws have been repealed. Now it is illegal for a manufacturer or a reseller to set a fixed list price. This is why many products, or advertisements of products, use the words *suggested list price*, *manufacturer's suggested retail price*, or *MSRP*. Companies can set prices for the products that they sell to their customers. They can also *suggest* an end-buyer, or retail, price. They cannot, however, fix a price that their resellers must charge their customers.

Following all governmental regulations is the most prudent course of action. While you might find this an obvious statement, many companies have opted for another course — pleading ignorance or thinking they could "*get away with it*." The resulting fines, legal fees, and damage to image have proven that negligence or deliberate avoidance is a very bad business strategy. Without mentioning specific names, scandals have done irreparable damage, in the form of tarnished images, lost sales, and lost sales opportunities to the organizations involved.

What's included in the price?

An important consideration in formulating the pricing strategy is determining what will be included in the base price of a product. Since what's included is also an important part of the product strategy, both strategies have to be closely coordinated. On the one hand, you want to fortify the product with features and extras to beat those offered by the competition. On the other, you want to hold prices down to a range which is within the window of perceived affordability of your target market segments and is not too far from those of competitors.

As a *general rule*, the *more the product is like a commodity*, with standard features that can be purchased from many sources, *the more important the price becomes*. Conversely, *the more unique the product is*, *the less important the price*.

Using the personal computer example, you have to decide whether or not a warranty, starter supplies, training, support, delivery and installation, will be included in the base price. If you don't include enough of these, you risk angering buyers who discover that many items required to make the product truly functional are *optional* charges. If you include too many, you have to charge a higher price to cover costs and meet profit requirements, and you risk losing buyers because they perceive your price to be high relative to your competitors. Since the personal computer has become more of a commodity item, price has become very important. Therefore, the trend has been to *unbundle* options from the standard product so that the base price of the standard product is as low as possible. This lower price is then used in advertisements and quoted over the phone to meet or beat that offered by competitors. In order to successfully compete on price, however, the product features have to be similar to those of your competitors.

The trend with high-technology products has been to offer more power for a lower price, commonly referred to as "more bang for the buck." The situation you want to avoid is the one in which you are losing business because your price is higher than your competitors and your prospects and customers don't *perceive* the extra value for the higher price. Similarly, you want to avoid losing business because you've unbundled so much that your basic product's lack of functionality angers prospects and customers. Your marketing information system should give you the information you need to make the right decision — if you have a good one that requires your attention.

Elasticity

The elasticity of price, or demand, is an economist's phrase that refers to the change in quantities purchased prompted by changes in price. A *high degree of elasticity* means a small decrease in price will trigger a large increase in the quantity of product that will be purchased. Conversely, a *low degree of elasticity* describes a situation where, no matter what the change in price, the quantity purchased will be nearly the same. During the *energy crisis* of the early 1970s, many believed gasoline to have a very low degree of elasticity. In many cities, it seemed that consumers would line up around the block, sometimes for hours, just to purchase gasoline to run their automobiles irrespective of the price. *Figure 7-2* shows a graphic example of high elasticity (large quantity change in response to small price change); whereas *Figure 7-3* shows an example of low elasticity (small quantity change in response to even a large change in price).

Relating the concept of elasticity to technology products, the products with a *higher degree of real uniqueness* tend to be *less elastic* whereas the *commodity* products tend to be *more elastic*. Patented biotech products that create a *barrier to entry* to competitors command higher prices because they are unique and not available elsewhere. Marketers should know the relative elasticity of products in their product lines. This knowledge comes from experience, observation of the marketplace, and various market information system techniques. The easiest and most straightforward technique is to simply ask your target audience — particularly your prospects and customers.

Psychological

Since they are critically important, psychological factors should be given proper consideration in developing pricing strategies. The product's *position*, or image in the marketplace, will play a critical role in giving the marketer pricing flexibility. If prospects perceive the product as unique or of the highest quality, the price should be relatively higher than those of less-unique or lower-quality products, and vice versa. Unless the product is a well-known brand, low pricing for a high-quality product will hurt the product's position and adversely affect sales. Even if the product is a known brand, some prospects will be skeptical about buying. They'll wonder what is wrong with it. They'll think it might be an imitation or an off-brand disguised to look like the *original*.

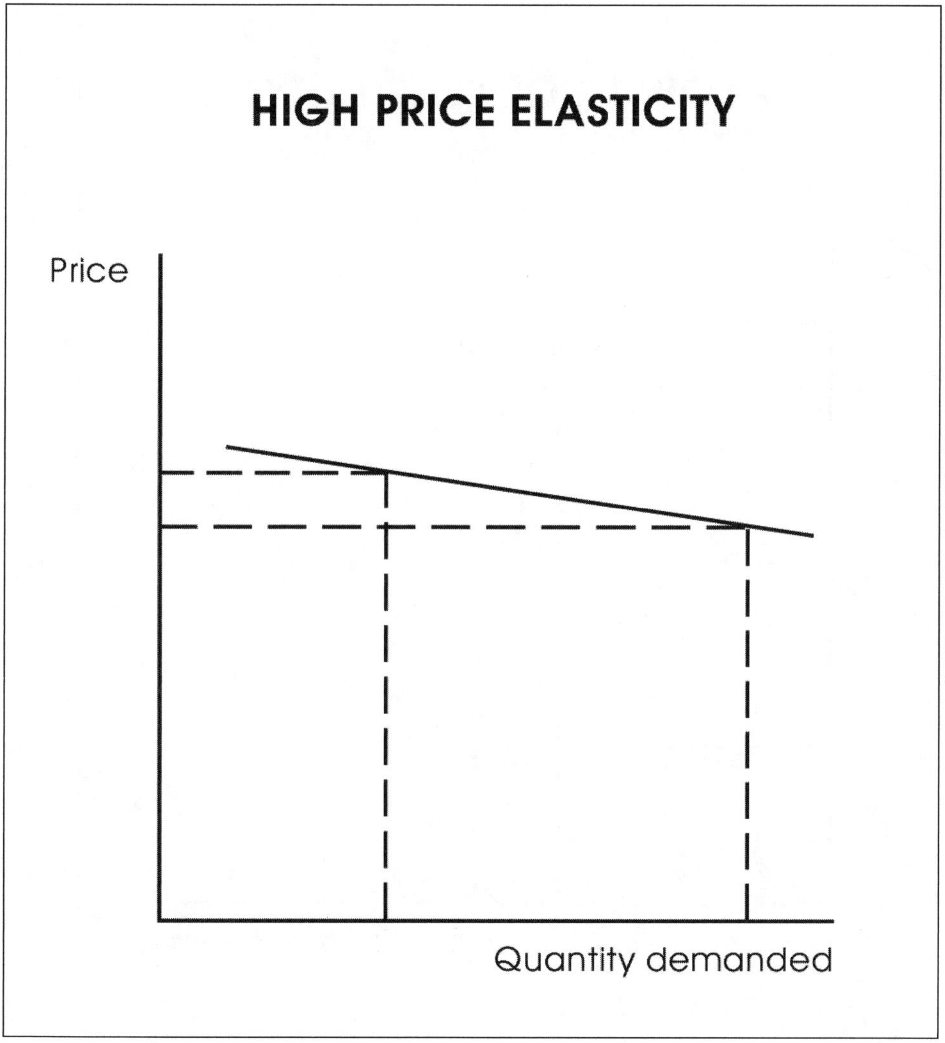

Figure 7-2

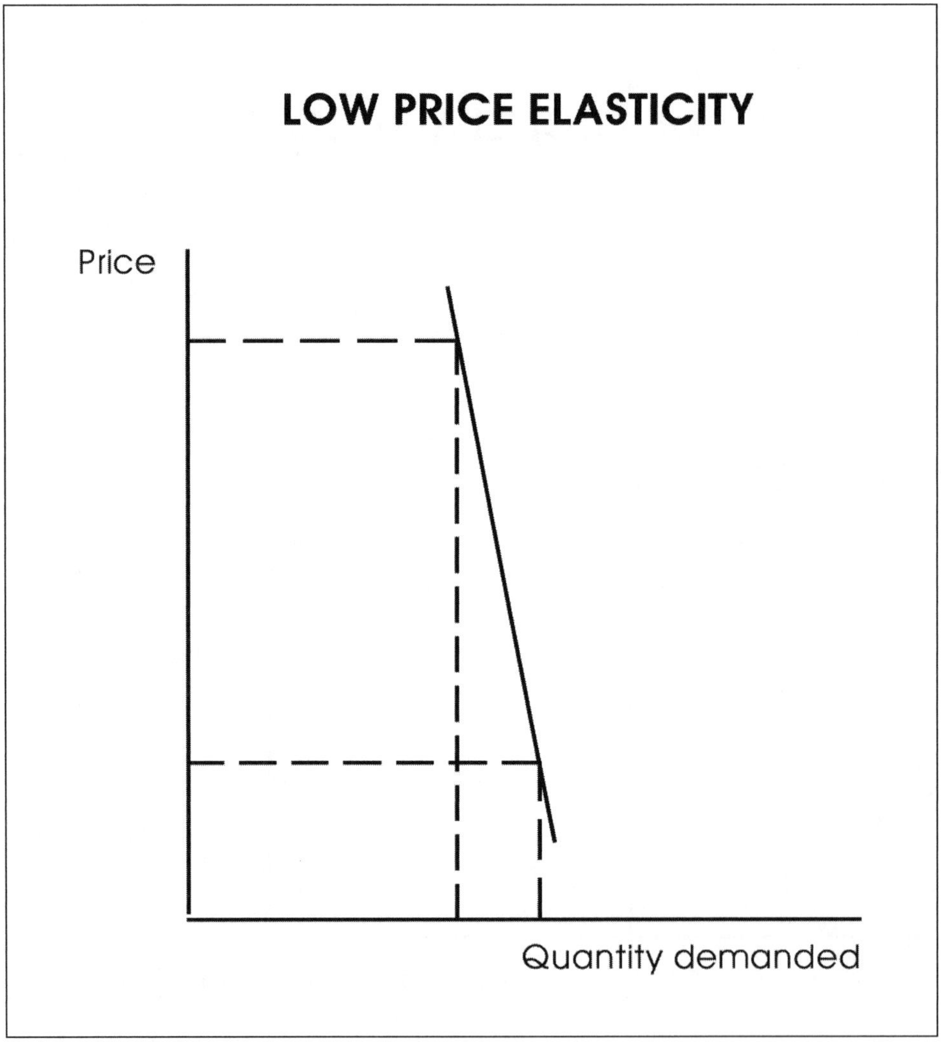

Figure 7-3

In general, the more the product is perceived as unique, the more flexibility the marketer has in pricing the product. Conversely, the more the product is perceived as a commodity, the less the flexibility in pricing. This is one of the reasons why it is critical for marketers to take extra care in positioning products. Without good positioning, the company feels more pressure to compete via lower prices. Lower prices usually mean lower profits and greater vulnerability to even lower-priced competitors. Because it is so easy to change prices, relative to making changes to other marketing strategies, a *lower-price* strategy is often the easiest marketing strategy to beat.

Most-Significant-Digit Pricing

An additional psychological factor that marketers should understand is *most-significant-digit pricing*. This factor relates to the notion that buyers focus on the most significant digit of a price, and often ignore the other digits. This means that a price of $99.95 appears to be much lower than $100 even though it is only 5¢ lower. When selling a tangible product, therefore, sophisticated marketers will price the item using the *most-significant-digit pricing* method — especially if the product is being sold directly to consumers.

Supply and Demand

Similar to the concept of elasticity, supply and demand considerations can greatly affect the price of a product. If demand exceeds supply, there is a shortage of the product. Shortages tend to increase the prices of products since suppliers know they can sell out even at higher prices. Demand and price is less elastic. If supply exceeds demand, there is a surplus. Surpluses tend to lower prices since suppliers have to offer buyers an incentive to buy the excess products. Some companies create an artificial shortage so that they can raise their prices without losing sales or eliciting complaints from customers. Many believe the *energy crisis* in the early 1970's was the result of an artificial shortage created by the oil companies to soften customer resistance to the desire of these companies to increase gasoline prices above the *psychological barrier* of one dollar per gallon. A similar situation occurred in 2004 with the two-dollar per gallon barrier. Others feel the same about restaurants that make patrons wait for a table when there are many empty tables in plain view. Some technology companies have been accused of using the same tactics to create more interest in their products and maintain relatively high prices for them. Whatever the source, marketers should understand that *uniqueness, shortages* and *waiting in line* for products tend to cause prices to rise. Many economists define the economic price as the point where supply and demand curves intersect (see *Figure 7-4*). Any price below the economic price will cause a shortage, and any price above the economic price will cause a surplus. Therefore, according to the theory, if there is a shortage, the company should raise the price to lower demand to the point where supply and demand curves will intersect. The problem with the theory is that, in practice, it is very difficult to collect the information to accurately draw the curves. Therefore, most companies estimate the economic price through trial and error, observation, market research, and the application of statistical techniques.

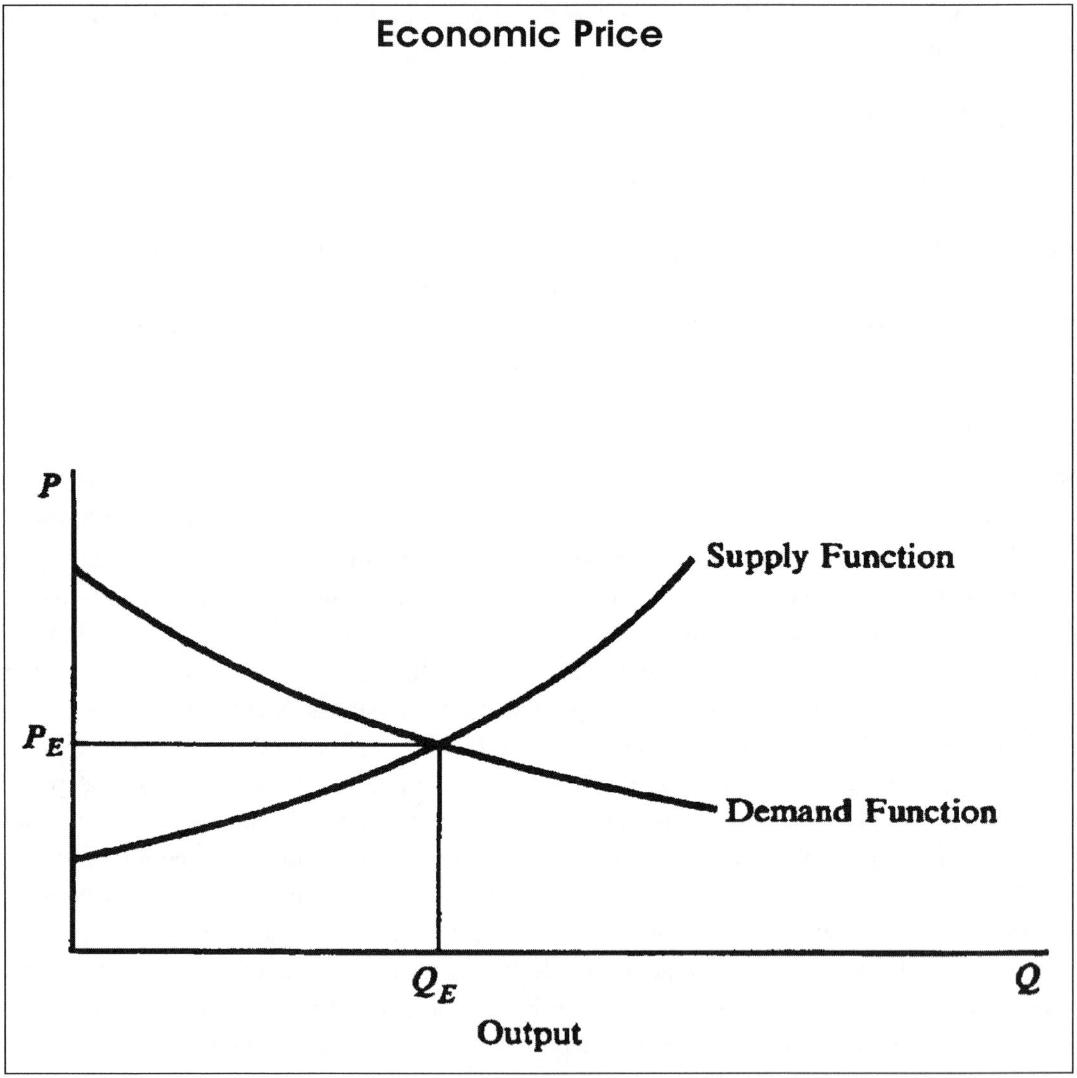

Figure 7-4

Product Life Cycle

The stage of a product's *life cycle* can affect the pricing strategy. For example, most new technology products are priced higher for a variety of reasons including patent protection; demand exceeds supply; there is typically little or no direct competition; the company needs to recoup heavy R&D, marketing and other start-up costs; the company has not yet achieved economies of scale that often come in later stages of production; and the marketplace has come to expect that prices of most technology products will go down over time. On the other hand, in those cases where there is *not* significant pent-up demand or the company has a strategy of building market share as rapidly as possible, companies may offer special *lower* introductory pricing. The idea is to get people to try the product or build up such a large market share that competitors will not be encouraged to enter the marketplace. If they do, they will have a difficult time achieving a significant market share.

Products in the *growth* and *maturity* phases of their life cycles are typically affected by the other factors already discussed above. Products that are in the late maturity or decline phases of their life cycles are typically priced lower to sell them quickly and clear the way for newer products.

Avoid Inconsistencies

Pricing inconsistencies should be avoided when developing your company's pricing strategies. While this advice seems to be rooted in simple common sense, you'd be surprised at how many firms have been guilty of serious pricing inconsistencies.

Bundles

Often, several products in a product family are bundled together and sold as a package. Using the personal computer example, a package might consist of the standard configuration computer, printer, warranty, delivery, installation, starter supplies, training and support for up to 90 days. This package should be priced so that *the price of the bundle is less* than the sum total of the individual prices of items in the package. The reason is that the cost of selling these items as a *package is lower* than selling them individually. The package price also gives buyers an *incentive* to buy everything together *now* from the company rather than purchase the pieces over time, possibly from competitors. Surprisingly, you can find products whose package prices are greater than, or equal to, the individual prices of each of the items in the package. This causes confusion, resentment, and gives the buyer reason to doubt the capability and sophistication of the seller.

Volume Pricing

Again, because the costs of selling multiple units of the same product at one time are less, companies typically offer *volume pricing* schedules whereby purchasers of progressively larger quantities are rewarded with increasingly lower prices.

Service Problems. While common in most industries, volume pricing can cause many problems. In too many cases, the higher volume customers are discounters who sell large quantities, but who can't afford to give the service and support necessary to maintain satisfied customers (because of thin margins created by their discount pricing). Those customers who become dissatisfied blame everyone in the distribution chain — especially the manufacturer whose name is on the product. This ill will hurts the corporate image of those involved, starts a chain of negative word-of-mouth advertising, and requires the companies in the distribution chain to divert resources from productive activities to *damage control* efforts, such as fielding and answering complaints. The end result is that the intended benefits from volume pricing are often outweighed by the high costs of dealing with the negative fallout that it produces.

Gray-market problems. Another problem caused by volume pricing in various markets is that buyers who seek to maintain their lower prices order much more than they can sell. This surplus is typically *dumped* into what's called "*gray market*" activities in violation of contractual agreements and contrary to the intent of the original volume pricing strategy. This *dumping* or *transshipping*, as it is sometimes called, puts product into the hands of unauthorized resellers who are outside the control of manufacturers and who often don't play by the rules. Their activities cause market instabilities that end-up hurting everyone in the distribution chain.

Bill-back problems. An additional problem caused by volume pricing is that it puts everyone in a difficult and uncomfortable situation when resellers don't achieve their contractual volume commitments. Manufacturers typically *bill back* resellers who don't achieve their volume commitments. This bill-back is based on the difference between the higher price corresponding to the actual quantity purchased and the lower price corresponding to the quantity that the reseller is contracted to purchase. The problem with this situation is that it causes a strain between the two parties, and bill-backs are often difficult to collect.

Value of service-oriented resellers. Since many high-tech and biotech products require after sale support and service, pricing schemes should be modified to recognize that many low-volume resellers are doing a better job than high-volume resellers. That is, they are providing the support and service necessary to maintain satisfied customers for everyone in the distribution chain. While their volumes don't warrant economic consideration in the form of price breaks, their support and personalized service activities actually provide greater economic benefits. Price breaks, therefore, should be given to resellers for services provided that take the burden of providing them "*off the back*" of the manufacturer.

Solution to bill-back problem. High-volume resellers should be given discounts retroactively as they *earn* quantity price breaks rather than on the first units that they buy. This avoids the embarrassing and difficult task of "*billing back*" and collecting from customers for quantities not achieved. It also helps to alleviate the pressure on resellers to *transship* surplus products to unauthorized resellers.

Summary of benefits of volume pricing. With these potential problems, why is volume pricing so pervasive in many industries? There are several answers including the following:

1. Volume pricing gives resellers an incentive to commit to buying larger quantities now.
2. It *locks* resellers into buying your product now rather than competitive products later.
3. Most sales incentives are based on meeting volume milestones.
4. Many products are still looked upon as devices or objects rather than complete products.
5. Volume pricing does reflect certain economies of scale in the sense that selling and manufacturing costs go down as volumes go up.
6. Reputable resellers should be given price breaks as rewards for selling larger volumes.
7. Volume pricing goes far back into history and culture as a pricing scheme for selling items in quantity.

Because of these historical and economic foundations for volume pricing, it should not be abandoned. However, it needs to be reevaluated in the context of the *end-result* objectives that many companies want to achieve. There are many qualitative criteria, such as support and service provided by resellers that should also be considered in designing pricing strategies. Volume pricing, without consideration of these qualitative aspects, will *backfire* in marketing many products that require after-sale service.

Remember, good marketing seeks to maintain the *best possible relationship* with customers. Price inconsistencies do nothing but strain this relationship.

Avoid competing with customers

One of the quickest ways to anger customers is to compete with them on price in their own markets. Unfortunately, too many companies do just that. How does this happen? Resellers in the distribution chain work hard to sell a manufacturer's products to customers. They spend time educating customers on the benefits and advantages of a manufacturers' products. Customers buy small quantities from the resellers. If customers need many additional units, they contact the manufacturers directly to obtain better prices. Manufacturers can offer much lower prices because they don't have to give any margin discounts to resellers (i.e. no middlemen are involved). They also don't have the expenses associated with educating and training the customers (the resellers have already done this for them). The manufacturers make the deals with the end-user customers directly, cutting out the resellers. Resellers get angry and complain to manufacturers and eventually take their business elsewhere (if they have a choice). Manufacturers, while getting the short-term volume business from the end-users, lose the longer-term, larger-volume business from the resellers.

Additional Considerations

Before embarking on a pricing strategy, it is very important to *think through* all the ramifications of your strategy — including the likely reactions of your competitors.

Also, while it sounds obvious, you should make sure to notify all your sales personnel of any price changes. You'd be surprised at how many price changes are known to the marketplace before sales people who work for the company are told about them. This causes embarrassment, leaves your sales people unprepared, makes them look bad, and reflects negatively on your company. All personnel who are in a position to quote prices to buyers should be informed of price changes, should be explained the reasons for the changes, and should be told how to position these changes before the new prices are communicated to the marketplace.

In most cases, *Price* is a very powerful variable that when set to the proper level can trigger buying actions quickly. In order to be effective over the long run, however, it must be coordinated with all the other variables and strategies. To further your understanding of price, it is useful to look at some pricing strategies that you might apply in the marketing of your products.

PRICING STRATEGIES

As with the other marketing strategies, pricing strategies should aim to achieve the goals of the Market Plan. The key targets embodied in your Plan should be *measurable* — relating to either profit requirements or market share.

Profits and Market Share

Market share refers to a company's penetration of, or percentage of total sales in, a particular market — either expressed as a percentage of actual sales or market potential. The larger its market share, the smaller the share of its competitors. As discussed previously, even if a company has little or no competition in a new market, it typically does not own a 100%

share of that market because of such factors as limited resources to cover the market, alternative products, and the lack of awareness of the product on the part of certain market segments because they may be difficult to reach or they may not come in contact with the company's marketing. Since the pricing strategy for maximizing profit in the *short-run* can conflict with that of achieving market share, it is important to understand the difference.

As mentioned previously, a company needs to earn profits for its continued health and well-being. Therefore, when does building market share become a more important goal than achieving short-term profit? The answer is simple — when it is necessary to achieve long-term profits. Studies show that companies that achieve a significant market share in a crowded field of competitors are almost always profitable whereas companies with a very small share of the market often lose money.

The actual percentages that represent significant shares vary by *industry* and by *size of market*. Percentages required for dominance in domestic, or localized, markets are typically twice those of worldwide markets. Averaged over many industries in domestic markets, a 20% share is considered dominant. In the worldwide automobile market, *Toyota's* 10% share of the world market is considered significant. In the domestic beer market, *Anheuser Bush's* 48% share is so dominant it is more than twice the share of its nearest competitor — *Miller*.

As market share or volume rises, the cost of doing business decreases due to the economies of scale in production, marketing, and finance. The decreases in cost can be quite dramatic — reaching levels as high as 20 to 30 percent every time volume doubles. These lower costs translate directly into higher *bottom-line* profits.

Another important benefit of building market share, of course, is that it is often done at the expense of competitors. Every percentage point captured is a percentage point taken away from an existing or future competitor. The more points, the greater the opportunity for sales, growth, lowered costs, profit and control.

What the Market Will Bear

In markets where there is little or no competition, a pricing strategy that maximizes profits on each product sold is often used. This strategy sets the price at the highest possible level. It is employed when the company knows it has a "*window in time*" before competitors are able to enter the market. The company tries to realize the highest profits possible in the shortest amount of time to recoup high start-up R&D, production, and marketing costs before margins are threatened by price competition.

This pricing strategy is best utilized when the company and/or product...

1. Is extremely well-positioned.

2. Has a monopoly.
3. Uses a new and patented technology that is not easy to emulate without violating the patent.
4. Occupies the high-end or exclusive position.

Notice how each of the above conditions is closely linked to creating a *defendable positioning strategy* that makes it clear to buyers why they should only buy your product from you.

It should be mentioned that even if these conditions are present, there are situations where you may not want maximize short-term profits. Such situations are often related to the fact that high profits will attract serious competitors. You don't want them to enter the market at a time when you need to build market share and establish a leadership position.

Therefore, when you employ a *what the market will bear strategy*, you should employ *supporting* strategies that protect your market share from such competitive threats as lower prices, more features, or performance advantages. These backup strategies will tend to incorporate various combinations of the appropriate building blocks of marketing as exemplified below.

1. *Corporate image:* Stress your market leadership.
2. *Positioning:* Emphasize the unique and important benefits and advantages of your product.
3. *Product:* Boost customer service, incorporate better quality, or include more for the same price — thereby lowering the effective price. Also, protect your product legally with patents and trademarks if you can.
4. *Pricing:* Lower effective prices below maximum levels (perhaps by #3 above).
5. *Place:* Fill up shelf space or distribution channels to lock out competitors.
6. *Promotion:* Increase market awareness of your benefits and advantages, and develop personal relationships with market targets.
7. *Marketing information system:* Collect data base information to build customer relationships and follow-up on customer satisfaction.

Profit Target

Rather than entice competitors to enter the market with the promise of large profits resulting from a *what the market will bear strategy*, many companies employ a pricing strategy that satisfies the *profit targets* established in their Business Plans. In such cases, they simply add the established *profit target* percentage to the cost of each product to determine the desired price.

Leader

While the leader has the luxury of having greater flexibility than followers in setting pricing strategies, the leader has to be careful to insure that the marketplace understands and perceives the value associated with higher prices for products that are perceived to be similar. Buyers will typically pay more for products from leaders since they believe that leaders offer such benefits as:

1. *Quality* (buyers presume that leaders have achieved their leadership position by providing higher-quality products and customer service).
2. *Longevity* (they believe leaders will be around to take care of them).
3. *Comfort* (they reason that all those buyers can't be wrong).

The *Strategic Planning Institute* surveyed the performance of 2,600 companies over 15 years through its *PIMS* (Profit Impact of Market Strategy) Program. It found that companies that are leaders in customer service charge an average of 9 percent more for their products and grow twice as fast as companies whose customer service was not rated as highly.[1]

However, if the leader gives the market any reason to doubt its leadership position — usually through image erosion, its inability to keep up with important product innovations from serious competitors, supply problems, or pricing that is out of line with quality competitive offerings — buyers will be prompted to try alternatives. The success of newer online computer services and Internet service providers, *VHS* (rather than *Sony Betamax*) format VCRs, and *IBM PC Clones* provide examples of competitive products that capitalized on mistakes made by market leaders.

Lower Price

If a company does not hold a leadership position in a competitive market, it is usually at a serious disadvantage. To compete, marketers of non-leaders often employ a strategy based upon offering lower-priced products. They believe that if they don't beat the price of the leader, they will lose business. While this belief is logical, offering lower prices rarely solves their competitive problems. Why? The paragraphs below will explain.

Indefensible Position

From the point of view of positioning, the *lower price strategy* is not a defensible position. That is, any competitor without much thought, effort, or resources can easily lower their prices and take this position away. A more successful strategy is to formulate a unique position that competitors are unable to easily take. *Topol* did this with smokers tooth polish. *Arm & Hammer* did it with baking soda toothpaste. *Tom's of Maine* did it with an all-natural toothpaste. These companies knew that they could not compete with the market leader, *Crest*, which is made by *Procter & Gamble (P&G)*. Rather than compete head-on with giants *P&G* and *Colgate* for the general-purpose fluoride position, they created other unique positions and supported them with similar or higher, rather than lower, prices.

Inferior value

The lower-price position presents another problem for products. It typically communicates to the marketplace that the lower-priced products are of a lower value. That is, since most buyers usually know the market leader, they already have a reduced perception in their minds of non-leader products. By pricing non-leader products lower, the company is reinforcing the notion that it has an inferior value. On the other hand, if it were to offer products priced higher than those of the leader, buyers are more likely to think or believe that these products are superior to those offered by the leader. For example, a non-leader salad dressing may have healthy, all natural ingredients that taste better and therefore cost more. The non-leader clothing may be handmade with better quality materials. The non-leader consulting firm may use experienced professionals rather than recent college graduates to work on the client's project. The non-leader computer company may charge more for customized software or personalized service.

Weakest and Most Difficult to Defend

As discussed above, the *lowest price* is a very common pricing strategy when the product has become a *commodity* — available from many competitors and not perceived to be unique. When used alone, without the support of other marketing strategies such as positioning and product quality, *lowest price* is the weakest strategy because virtually any competitor can easily offer a similar product at an even lower price. Conversely, the same competitors would have considerably more difficulty changing their positions, products, distribution channels, and promotional strategies in a very short period of time.

Superior and Higher-price

A superior or higher-price strategy should support the upscale or superior-quality position. This strategy is good for both *high-end* market leaders and smaller boutique companies. By pricing their products higher than those of well-entrenched market leaders and by supporting these prices with upscale positions and higher-quality products, small boutique companies have the opportunity to carve out a successful niche in the marketplace. When they were first introduced to the marketplace, both *Hagen-Daz* and *Ben and Jerry's* ice cream were from very small companies that had little chance in making significant dents in the market shares of much larger market leaders. By offering their products at higher prices and by supporting them with upscale positions and good product quality, both companies became very successful. If they had introduced these products at lower-than-market-leader prices when they were unknown, the marketplace would have a difficult time of placing a value on their products. Moreover, they would have likely gone the way of hundreds of other unknown companies who made the mistake of pricing their products lower, which only served to confirm their "inferior" status in the minds of buyers.

Follow the Leader

In some markets where products, such as airline travel or personal computers, are perceived as commodities, non-leaders have to follow the pricing of leaders in the short run. That is, if *American Airlines*, the domestic market leader, lowers its prices, non-leaders typically have to follow if they don't want to lose business. The reason is that the market leader is perceived to be better or amongst the best in the minds of buyers. If they lower prices below non-leaders, most will select the leader because they believe they are getting a better value for less money. The Corporate Image of the leader serves to legitimize the quality of the product. In the long run, for the reasons given above, non-leaders should work on other more defendable marketing strategies. For example, *Alaska Airlines* has competed successfully by offering better customer service and *Southwest Airlines* has competed more successfully by offering low-cost and efficient air service to cities and airports that many of the other airlines do not regularly travel. In the short-run, because they may not be perceived to be as good as the leader, non-leaders may have no choice other than to follow the leader.

It should be mentioned that a *follow the leader* strategy does not always relate to the lowering of prices. It also applies to the leader raising prices. For example, in late 1993 when *Hertz Corporation*, the market leader in rental cars, announced that it was raising its prices by 12% in major cities across America, the rest of the rental-car industry followed suit. The *Wall Street Journal* reported that "Slim profits in the car-rental industry will force even small players to increase their prices in line with Hertz..."[2] Prior to the price increase, the non-leaders knew that if they raised prices above the leader, without giving buyers other good reasons to select their product, they would lose substantial business to the leader.

Match Competition

A match the competition pricing strategy is almost identical to the *follow-the-leader* strategy discussed above. The major difference is that a competitor, other than the leader, is the one who makes the first pricing move. Using the airline example, if *Continental Airlines* or *Northwest* lowered prices, other airlines may or may not match them. Whereas the others would have to follow *American's* lead in the short run, they may not feel the need to match *Northwest's* or *Continental's* lower prices. The primary reason why others may not follow them is they are non-leaders who have had serious financial difficulties in the past. Both of these factors tend to diminish their corporate image. As a result, competitors would probably watch for any decrease in their own business before they feel the need to employ a *match the competition* pricing strategy in the short run.

Loss Leader

A *loss-leader* pricing strategy involves the pricing of certain products at, or below, cost in order to attract buyers who will, at the same time, buy more-profitable products. While losing money on the *loss leader*, the company hopes to more than compensate for the item loss with their profit on the entire order. This strategy is often employed by retail establishments, Internet, and mail-order companies that want to *pull* customers in the stores, to their Web sites, or encourage them to order several items at one time from a catalogue. The *loss leader* item is usually a desirable, yet relatively inexpensive item that is often purchased with a higher-priced, more-profitable product. The result is that the buyer pays less for the loss-leader product, and the seller meets overall profit requirements by making money on the aggregate order, or entire *shopping cart*.

Predatory

In many cases, *predatory* pricing also involves selling products at a loss. The idea is for the company that employs the predatory pricing strategy to quickly build up market share and drive competitors out of business. Japanese manufacturers of integrated circuits, or *chips*, were accused of practicing predatory pricing. American manufacturers complained that their Japanese competitors *dumped* chips on the world market at prices below cost just to drive American manufacturers out of business. As a significant share of the world's manufacturing and service origination has shifted to China and India, Chinese and Indian companies are regularly accused of doing the same. The fear is that once market share is achieved and those responsible for the predatory pricing practices gain control of the market, they will raise prices to abnormally high levels to pay back their losses and achieve much higher longer-term profits. That's why predatory pricing has been ruled illegal in the United States. However, because it is very difficult to prove and because other countries may not recognize American laws, it is still used as a pricing strategy throughout the world.

It should be noted that many American manufacturers have also been accused of this type of pricing strategy. *IBM*, *Microsoft*, *American Airlines* and a variety of other companies, large, small, known and unknown, have been accused at one time or another of predatory pricing practices to drive competitors out of business so they could later raise prices and make greater-than-ever profits.

Maximize Revenue Contribution

In cases where it is possible to estimate the *demand curve* for a product, a *maximize revenue contribution* pricing strategy is a good choice. It sets the price at the point where the *% of the market that will buy* multiplied by the *gross profit (P-C)* of the product will yield the greatest amount of revenue contribution to the company. An example of this strategy is illustrated in the following *Table 7-1*.

Price = P	Demand =D (%who will buy)	Revenue Contribution=RC and Cost=C. RC=(P-C) x D (Note: Assume C=$10)
$10	90	0
$20	80	800
$30	75	1,500
$40	70	2,100
$50	65	2,600
$60	60	3,000
$70	40	2,400
$80	20	1,400
$90	10	800
$100	5	450

Table 7-1.

As shown in *Table 7-1* above, the $60 price is shown to produce the greatest revenue contribution, and would be therefore chosen under the *maximize revenue contribution* pricing strategy.

Specials and Discounts

Companies that produce commodity products try to build market share by differentiating their products. While this is typically accomplished via positioning and promotional strategies, it can also be done by using a short-term discount or a "special pricing" strategy. Advertisements that communicate a one-time-only discount, holiday-season special, special introductory offer, and rebates are commonplace in various print and broadcast media. These are all short-term *sales* promotions. That is, they are offered to prospects in order to prompt a *quicker buying action*. While they are considered *promotion* strategies, they are mentioned here because they involve, and must be closely coordinated with, pricing strategies. The important points to remember about these discounts and specials include the following: (1) The reasons for the special prices should be logical and clearly communicated to buyers; (2) Specials should be offered for only a *limited time* period (i.e. they should *really be special*);

and (3) Buyers should not be made to expect them frequently; otherwise, the special prices will become the new *de-facto prices* of the products. When this happens, buyers will either wait for the next special price before buying, or they will demand discounts every time they order.

SUMMARY

To avoid being surprised about the effect of your pricing strategies, you should do your *homework*. This means doing market research and developing a good *marketing information system* to continuously collect, analyze, report and take action on pricing and other data. Your system should continuously monitor the prices of competitive and alternative products, survey the opinions of targeted customers and prospects before introducing new pricing, and take the appropriate action upon collecting and properly analyzing the data.

You want to make sure that the resultant total derived from the multiplication of your price by the quantities you expect to sell covers your costs and generates the profit, market share and other goals you have targeted in your Marketing Plan.

[1]Rolph Anderson, *Essentials of Personal Selling*, Prentice Hall, 1995, pg. 346.

[2]Douglas Lavin and Robert Johnson, *Prices for Rental Cars Are Set to Climb Sharply,*≈ Wall Street Journal, September 29, 1993, page B5.

TIPS and Exercises

1. Survey the pricing strategies of your competitors.
2. Identify the cost of sales percentage and gross profit percentage for your products, and compare these with your competitors.
3. Find out what your customers think of your pricing strategies.
4. Look for ways to round up prices (that is from say $44 to $49.95) without causing a negative reaction from your customers.
5. Look at your best sellers and determine if they have unique positions.
6. Identify your products that are considered commodities and try to give them unique positions and raise their prices accordingly.

Chapter 8

DNA of Distribution

Placing your products in the marketplace

"Making it convenient for customers to find, buy and use your product."

WHAT IS DISTRIBUTION?

D*istribution*, or *Place* — to carry on the alliteration of the P's — refers to the *methods and processes of making it convenient for customers to find, buy, and use your products*. Just as the heart pumps blood through arteries to all parts of the body to sustain life, the company *pumps* product through *distribution channels* in the *market territory* to create sales and sustain the health and growth of the business. In the above definition, the words *convenient*, *find*, *buy*, and *use* are all very important to the distribution of high-technology products.

Convenient to Find

People are more likely to buy products that are convenient to find. In some cases, products are convenient to find because they are sold through many different distribution outlets located near your prospect's home, work, travel route, or vacation spot. In other cases, products are convenient to find because a communication of some kind has told prospects where they could find and buy them.

Convenient to Buy

In addition to being available in a nearby store, office, or direct channel, products are made convenient to buy because the distribution outlets that carry them have ample convenient parking, are well-lighted and secure, have products conveniently displayed, accept many forms of payment including most major credit cards, and do not require customers to wait in long lines to purchase them. In the case of *direct marketing*, products are made convenient to buy because prospects have received an e-mail, catalogue or direct mail piece that has a convenient link, toll-free number, or a postage-paid response card the prospect can use to directly order the product. Other direct marketing channels that make it convenient for prospects to order the product include Web sites, direct response ads, and shopping networks — all having multiple response channels, such as toll-free phone and fax numbers, postage-paid response cards, e-mail addresses, Web URLs, or on-screen menus, from which prospects can select the avenues through which they find it most convenient to respond.

Convenient to Use

The buyers of high-tech products often need the advice of a knowledgeable sales or customer-service person to help them with their selection. Computer stores, medical equipment outlets, cellular phone centers, and sophisticated electronic appliance stores are just some examples of distribution outlets that *add value* by helping prospects select the products that best meet their needs. After purchase, some products, such as DNA test kits, computers, and software, may require a service person to train customers on the use of the product as well as answer their follow-up questions. Some products, which are either large or complex, may require delivery or installation. Once delivered and installed, convenient warranty, maintenance, or repair services may be required for the continued successful use of these products. When the computer or test equipment doesn't work, a customer needs to be able to quickly and easily get it fixed — preferably from a helpful and friendly service person from the place where they bought it or the manufacturer. Because these *convenient-to-use* services are essential for the successful use of many products, manufacturers need to make their availability an important criterion in selecting distributors and channels.

DISTRIBUTION GOAL

As explained above, the goal of distribution is to make it as easy as possible for your market targets to find, buy and use the product. The limitation on achieving *perfect* distribution is the company's distribution budget. That is, no company has the resources to put all of the company's products within easy reach of *all* market targets. People in small towns who are not close to transportation centers or major distribution points cannot be easily reached by most companies. Even the largest banks can't afford to put a branch on every corner, and the largest computer and telephone equipment companies cannot justify putting sales offices in every city around the world. However, with the help of advanced technology, the Internet, and good systems, a company can establish direct marketing channels to cover many areas that were formerly difficult or impossible to reach. In the 3rd Quarter of 1997, *Cisco Systems* and *Dell computer* respectively sold $9 million and $3 million worth of product each day via the Internet.

As with all marketing strategies, the company has to do an ROI (Return on Investment) Analysis to determine the most cost-effective and efficient distribution methods to cover the marketplace. Even if this analysis is not comprehensive or precise, making the effort to measure the costs and returns related to your distribution alternatives, can provide significant payoffs. For example, after doing a "quick and dirty" ROI analysis, the author of this book made one adjustment to a client's distribution. This resulted in a 35% increase in sales and profits within 90 days!

THE POWER OF DISTRIBUTION

Companies that have control over distribution in various industries have a considerable amount of power that can be translated into greater sales. At a time when breweries were largely local because it is not economical to ship a product that is largely water over long distances, *Anheuser-Busch* went into debt to build large new breweries in major metropolitan areas to economically reach 80% of the US population. Based on this change in distribution, the Company quickly grew their market share from single digits to 41% of the domestic beer market. By 2004, *Anheuser-Busch* commanded a dominant 48% of this market.

Another example of the importance of distribution is *Time-Warner*. *Time-Warner* has control over its own large distribution network for records, films, videos, and publications. This network gives *Time-Warner* an advantage over other entertainment companies in getting product to consumers. In fact, because of the company's importance and size, many competing companies have agreements with *Time-Warner* to distribute their products. In other words, *Time-Warner* has control of an important distribution pipeline.

Due to its development and control over one of the two on-line reservation systems used by travel agents, *American Airlines* controls the pipeline for flight and reservation information. This control has played no small part in *American's* rise to the number one domestic airline in the United States.

ADDING VALUE

Each level of a distribution system has a definite reason for existing, or as the French would say, *a raison d'être*. In general, the key reason for existing in a distribution system is to *add value*.

Manufacturers

The manufacturer's reason for existing is obvious — to make the product. That is, the manufacturer buys raw materials, subassemblies, and labor and *adds value* by combining these resources to create a new product. If manufacturers can economically cover the marketplace by selling and shipping product directly to end buyers, they will. To perform the manufacturing function profitably, manufacturers typically need to earn a 50% gross profit margin as a rule of thumb. This translates to a 100% markup of their costs to make the product. If they can't economically cover a particular market, they require the assistance of *middle people*. The most common middle people are distributors and dealers.

Distributors, or Wholesalers

Classically, *distributors* — also called *wholesalers* — add value by performing a *warehousing* function. Since many manufacturers cannot efficiently sell products in small quantities, and many *dealers* cannot afford to buy in large quantities, the distributors bridge the gap. They buy products from manufacturers in the quantities manufacturers need to make money. They warehouse them, and sell them to dealers in the quantities that they can afford to buy. For performing this function, they typically make a 10 to 15% gross profit margin. To realize a 15% gross profit margin, the distributors need to mark up the cost of the product from the manufacturer by 18%.

Dealers, or Retailers

The *dealers*, also known as *retailers*, add value by performing a convenience function for the end buyer. That is, they stock the products that the end buyer wants to purchase, they help the end buyer select the products that best fit their needs, and they provide convenient locations with access to safe transportation and parking. They also accept returned merchandise and perform other essential functions required by end buyers. Depending on the complexities involved in servicing the needs of customers, dealers typically need a 30 to 50% gross profit margin to make money. To achieve a 33.3% gross profit margin, the dealers have to mark up their costs (the price they pay to distributors or manufacturers) by 50%.

Other Middle People

There are other specialized types of middle people who may be involved in distributing a company's products. They include manufacturers' representatives, jobbers, and franchisees. Whatever they are called, they add value by representing the manufacturer or by performing the function of one of the middle people discussed above. Their functions will be discussed in more detail in the next section.

Adding Value Summary

There are two key points about adding value and middle people that are very important for marketers to remember.

1. *All middle people exist to add value.* That is, they add something that the distribution level above does not provide, but which the level below needs.
2. *You can eliminate the middle people from a distribution system, but you cannot eliminate their function.* For example, many end buyers may try to save money by buying products *wholesale*, or skipping the retailer. To do this, however, they often have to sacrifice convenience, flexible payment terms, saving time, and other "*value adds*" that the retailer provides. Similarly, if manufacturers cut out distributors from their distribution systems, they will have to invest in warehouse space and more sales people to service the larger volume of smaller orders received directly from dealers and end buyers.

DISTRIBUTION CHANNEL STRATEGIES

There are many different ways of distributing products throughout the marketplace. Depending on the products, the industry, and a variety of other factors, the *depth* and *breadth* of the *distribution system* will vary. The breadth of the system refers to the number of different distribution channels involved in distributing the company's products. The *depth of the chain* is the *number of layers of sellers between the manufacturer and end buyer* in each channel. *Figure 8-1* represents a multiple-tiered distribution system with depth and breadth. Some products are sold direct to end-users by the company's sales people or direct marketing systems that involve no *face-to-face* selling. Others are sold first to distributors who, in turn, warehouse them and re-market them to dealers or *OEMs*. These resellers *add value* by adding something to them, repackaging them, or simply making them conveniently available to end buyers. To give you a better understanding of distribution, it is useful to explore some of the most common channels and methods.

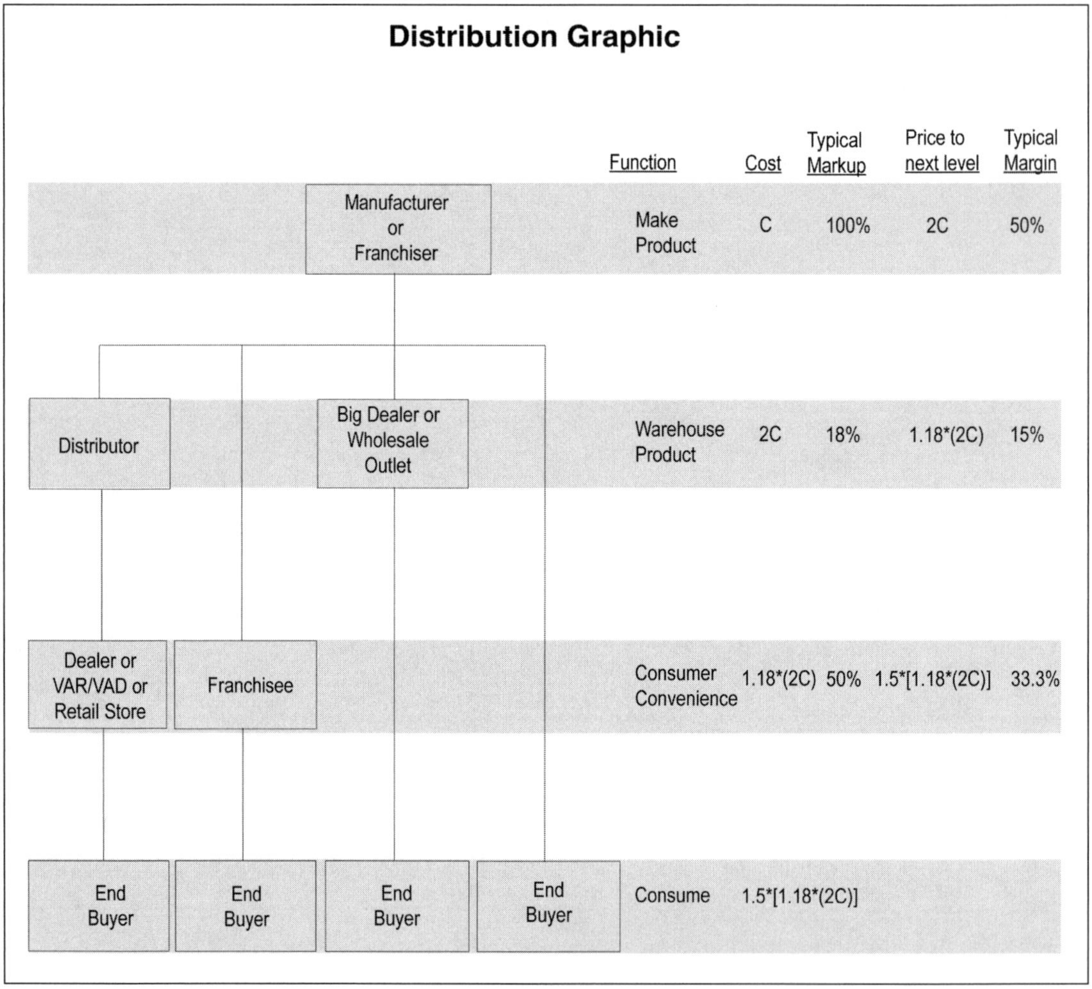
Distribution Graphic
Function
Cost
Typical Markup
Price to next level
Typical Margin
Manufacturer or Franchiser
Make Product
C
100%
2C
50%
Distributor
Big Dealer or Wholesale Outlet
Warehouse Product
2C
18%
1.18*(2C)
15%
Dealer or VAR/VAD or Retail Store
Franchisee
Consumer Convenience
1.18*(2C)
50%
1.5*[1.18*(2C)]
33.3%
End Buyer
End Buyer
End Buyer
End Buyer
Consume
1.5*[1.18*(2C)]

Figure 8-1

Direct to end buyers

If your company has the resources and systems to cover the market economically, the best method of distribution is to sell direct to the ultimate users of the product. The reasons for this include the following:

1. The company *does not have to share the proceeds of the sale* with another company.
2. It *does not have to relinquish any of its control* over the product to others.
3. It *does not have to reveal trade secrets* about proprietary products.
4. It *does not have to deal with problems introduced by middle people* in the distribution chain, such as misrepresentation of the product.
5. It *can communicate directly with the marketplace* to efficiently determine what customers want via an effective marketing information system.

Having the resources to cover the market is not always a function of the size and strength of the company. Small companies can usually do a good job of covering the market under the following conditions:

1. The market targets are easy to identify and reach.
2. The product is unique, and prospective buyers can easily learn about it through articles in publications that they regularly read.
3. The product is proprietary, and distribution through resellers would jeopardize company secrets (and therefore *end up* costing more).
4. The company builds custom products for a small number of customers or clients making it difficult to distribute them any other way.
5. The company develops and installs an efficient direct marketing system.

Manufacturers' Representatives

Many smaller companies don't have easy-to-reach or well-defined markets. They also don't have the resources to hire, train, motivate and keep a sales force on staff to cover the all their key markets. To reach markets beyond their grasp, these companies contract with manufacturers' representatives. Manufacturers' Representatives are *agents*, who unlike resellers, never buy, *or take title to or ownership of*, the products. They are *sales people for hire* who work for their own companies, who in turn, represent the products of many different manufacturers. They *operate on an extended contractual basis* to negotiate sales between buyers and sellers. For their efforts, they receive a commission, or percentage of each sale. Their contract usually gives them an exclusive territory in which to sell. It also allows them to represent non-competing but similar lines of products from other manufacturers. Since they are not directly employed by the manufacturer, these reps usually do not have the authority to change prices or terms of a sale. As a result, they typically work closely with *inside marketing or sales* personnel who work directly for the manufacturer. Once reps sell products, the manufacturer ships them directly to the buyer. Manufacturers' reps never buy products and resell them, as do distributors and dealers.

Since manufacturers' representatives are *not* employed by your company and are shared by many different manufacturers, the common problems with them include the following:

1. Motivating them to spend sufficient time selling your company's products.
2. Getting them educated on the features and benefits of your products.
3. Insuring that they accurately represent your company and products to buyers.
4. Controlling their actions to the benefit of your company.

As with any sales people, proper *incentives* in the form of proper commissions must be provided to encourage these reps to spend time *pushing* your products. If your incentives are inadequate, they will most likely spend most of their time selling products from those client companies that offer them bigger commissions.

It should be mentioned that smaller companies are not the only ones who use the services of manufacturers reps. Large companies use them to cover territories that are outside of their economical reach — particularly in remote areas and foreign countries where local languages and customs dictate the need for local firms. It should also be explained that, even though they are called *manufacturers reps* and typically represent *manufacturers*, some have been known to represent others in the channels such as distributors and dealers.

Distributors

As discussed in the section on Adding Value above, *distributors* are *resellers who typically purchase larger quantities of product from the manufacturer and sell them in smaller quantities to dealers and other smaller resellers in the distribution chain*. Their main function is to warehouse the product — that is, keep *enough stock on hand* to supply their dealers' needs on short notice. Distributors have large warehouses stocked with lots of inventory from a variety of different manufacturers. The dealers buy from them because they don't have the resources or space to purchase large enough quantities directly from the manufacturers.

Dealers

Dealers add-value by performing a convenience function. They exist to provide convenience services to end users, such as delivery, installation, training, support and customer service. Dealers also have locations with parking that are more convenient to end buyers.

Value-added Dealers

Value added dealers (VADs), value added remarketers (VARs) and original equipment manufacturers (OEMs) are similar to normal dealers in that they buy product from manufacturers or distributors and sell them to end users. They *differ*, however, in *the amount of value that they add to the product*. In addition to the traditional services provided by dealers, they also add proprietary products, such as their own manufactured software and hardware, to the manufacturer's original product. In some cases, they even re-configure and repackage the product with their own shell and logo so that it does not even look like the original product to which the value was added. *IBM* did this with a printer manufactured by *Epson*, a popular Japanese manufacturer. By simply adding a grounding connector and an *IBM* logo to the *Epson* printer, the company transformed the product into an *IBM* printer. Many VADs, VARs, and OEMs also typically sell their products to very *specific and specialized market targets* such as doctors, lawyers, the military, architects, and retailers.

Franchising

Franchising refers to the *transference*, or *licensing*, *of product rights from the franchiser* (usually a manufacturer or distributor) *to the franchisee* (usually a dealer). Typically, the franchisee has to pay a rather high initial franchise fee to the franchiser for rights to sell the franchiser's branded products using the franchiser's logo, uniforms, layouts, and goodwill. The franchise contract usually requires the franchisee to conform to a pre-designed store or office layout, dress code, product line, and set of procedures and policies. In addition to the initial fee, the franchisee often has to pay royalties on earnings to the franchiser as well as buy materials and products from the franchiser.

Formerly the domain of fast food companies, franchising has found its way into the distribution of many different products.

Because technical products tend to be much more complex than fast foods, franchising has not proven to be a favored method of high-tech distribution. It is much easier to standardize and control the quality of a hamburger that is consumed on the spot than it is to regulate the quality of a high-tech product that requires training, ongoing support and service.

Retail Store

The skyrocketing costs of labor combined with the rapidly declining costs of technology have prompted companies to look for lower-cost ways of distributing their products. Several have chosen the concept of retail stores. Computer stores, phone stores, and Internet service locations are examples of high-tech retail distribution that have sprung up all over the world. In the 1960's, nobody would have dreamed of walking into a retail store to purchase a computer. Today it is commonplace. Due to declining prices and rising labor costs, it is more cost-effective to service customers from retail stores than to send sales and service people into the field to cover the market. Travel time, response time, and auto expenses can all be saved. One sales person can invest the time saved to service more customers via the phone, e-mail, and in-store customer visits. For many customers, the convenience and the money they hope to save is worth the effort of visiting the store.

The retail store also gives a prospect who may be *nervous* about buying certain products a comfortable and non-threatening way to view and compare them. It is much less intimidating to walk into a store than to make a special appointment with a professional in an *ivory-tower* office building. Furthermore, it is more feasible for a company to demonstrate its wide variety of products to prospects in a retail store environment than to bring them to prospects' offices or homes.

Although retail store space is more expensive than other commercial space, the street-access and marketing visibility of the retail store often more than pays for the difference in cost. Having the company's sign prominently displayed in key retail locations can serve as a very inexpensive advertisement of the company name, logo, and products. Even if they don't bother to drop in, prospects who drive or walk by the store location will at least become familiar with the name and logo so that when they see them in an ad, a letter, or mailed brochure, they will be more likely to feel comfortable with the company and products. In a sense, the signage and other visual look of the retail store serves as an *advertising exposure* that makes an all-important marketing impression on all passersby.

While some companies have been successful selling high-tech products via stores, many have not. *IBM*, *Gateway*, *Xerox*, *Businessland*, *AT&T*, *COMPAL*, *GTE* and many others too numerous to mention have all opened and closed stores. The reason? Economics — the same reason used to justify retail selling in the first place. These companies discovered that you need *difficult-to-find* qualified sales and support people with an even higher level of knowledge and sophistication than you do operating out of an office. The reason for this is that you can't pool them the way you can in a large office. Each store has to have its own set of *superstars*. Moreover, they found that it was impossible to generate enough business to justify their high labor and operating costs. Also, once the superstars educate prospects on the virtues of the product, these prospects comparison shop and purchase products from lower-cost discounters and mail order houses that don't have these professionals on staff.

Retail stores have been proven to be a good method of distributing high-tech products if these products don't require significant before-sale and after-sale services. The lower the price and the closer the product is to a *McDonald's* hamburger, the more the retail store is an effective distribution channel for high-technology products. As computers and cellular phones grow more sophisticated, reliable and easier to use, the viability of retail stores as a successful method for distributing them will rise accordingly.

Virtual Store

Large Internet portals, such as *eBay* and *Yahoo* have launched virtual stores. This can be a very inexpensive way to reach a large audience. Using a model similar to the one used by shopping malls, the portal companies rent virtual store space to their tenants. The tenants pay a monthly rental fee, plus a percentage of their gross sales and other nominal charges to reach the large numbers of visitors to these portals. Even big corporations, such as *IBM*, rent virtual stores to benefit from the large traffic generated by these portals.

Other types of Distribution

There are many other variations on the basic forms of distribution discussed above. A few of them are presented below to make you aware that they exist and to allow you to decide if they are appropriate for your particular products and style of business.

Jobbers

Jobbers are distributors who are also known as service wholesalers. Jobbers are resellers who buy product from the manufacturer and resell it to the dealer, performing such marketing functions in the process as branding, financing producers, and extending credit to dealers. Jobbers were popular in the days when manufacturers and dealers were much less sophisticated.

Consignment

Consignment is a form of distribution in which a manufacturer or wholesaler gives the dealer product with the hope that buyers will purchase it once they see it displayed or demonstrated. In this case, the dealer does not take title or pay for the product until it is sold. This method of distribution shifts most of the costs of handling and inventorying product from the dealer (*the consignee*) to the manufacturer or wholesaler (*the consignor*). It can be a necessary distribution strategy for any product or company that is not known to the marketplace. It is a *try it, you'll like it* form of distribution. Phonograph records and books, particularly those of lesser-known artists and authors, are often distributed by this method. Clothing, foods, and many other products have also been distributed by this method, particularly when they are new to the marketplace.

Service/Delivery Personnel

Some companies have achieved great success by giving incentives, in the form of commissions, to delivery and service personnel who are already calling on customers. While they typically do not have the product knowledge or education to sell many kinds of products (if they did they'd be on the sales staff), they are very effective at selling supplies and add-ons. Since they are already calling on customers anyway, giving them product to distribute is an added plus. One problem with this form of distribution is control over inventory. It is critical that tight controls be kept on all such products available for sale by this method of distribution. Without controls, some delivery and service technicians might be motivated to realize the entire revenues from sales of untracked inventory rather than just the commissions. Another potential problem is getting service personnel to concentrate on servicing customers. If they are getting commissions on selling supplies and add-ons, there is a danger that they'll *push* these products at the expense of fulfilling their main duties of servicing customers. If the company does service at a highly-technical level, using service personnel for distribution should be carefully evaluated before, and closely watched after, deciding on employing this distribution strategy. On the other hand, if service personnel are largely performing routine delivery, service, and maintenance functions, using them for distribution of products on commission is less likely to interfere with their main duties. If it does, you can always decide to take action accordingly. You might even find that you would be better off switching the most successful ones to sales anyway.

Vending Machines

Vending machines can be a very useful form of distributing products. Most people are familiar with using vending machines for drinks, snacks, games, rides, phone calls (pay phones), and music ("juke" boxes). Other uses of such machines have included dispensing rental car keys and contracts, postage stamps, pictures, money (ATMs), and change. In most cases, the customer puts money or a credit card into a machine, selects a product, and the machine dispenses the product with change, if appropriate. The advantage of these machines is that they replace the need for a human being to sell and dispense the product and they can be placed in locations that are convenient to the target audience. They also serve as their own special form of advertising the product — constantly reminding those who pass by of the product inside. The main disadvantages of vending machines are that they sometimes malfunction or run out of product. When this happens, unless there is a human supervisor nearby who can rectify the problem, the customer is likely to become very frustrated. Some frustrated customers have been known to vandalize these machines — especially when their money is inadvertently "eaten" or improper change is returned. Technical products are not typically distributed using vending machines, but marketers should never rule out this option — especially for supplies that may be needed at odd hours when people are not available to dispense them. *Quiagen* uses this a *quasi vending maching* by distributing via a *Qia-Cabinet* located in customer laboratories.

Mail Order and other Direct Methods

Many products have been sold via the mail. Products that require installation, delivery, training, and support are probably not best distributed by this method, but many commodity products can be effectively distributed via mail order. On the other hand, *Dell*, *Cisco*, and *Intel* have been very successful selling their technical products via direct channels. In order for a company to have a successful direct channel, its marketing department should produce an attractive, clear, concise and accurate Web page, catalogue, brochure, direct response ad, or mailer that makes it easy for prospects to directly order products. The more response channels listed in the communication, the higher the sales. That is, the most effective direct mail operations list toll-free phone and fax numbers, e-mail addresses, and Web page URLs as well as provide postage-paid response cards that encourage prospects to select the response channel they prefer.

Internet

As the use of the "information superhighway" continues to grow and customers become increasingly (1) comfortable with ordering products over the Internet and (2) frustrated with traffic, parking, and safety related to shopping through traditional distribution channels, the distribution of product via the Internet is expected to accelerate. The Internet is perhaps the most convenient distribution channel ever invented — especially for products such as software, books, music, photographs, manuals, and articles that can be easily represented and downloaded in digital form.

FACTORS AFFECTING THE SELECTION OF DISTRIBUTION CHANNELS

To better understand how to devise the most appropriate distribution strategies for your products, it is helpful to look at the important factors that are likely to impact the distribution channels you select.

Control desired over product

The more control that you need over your product, the less you should choose distribution alternatives that involve outside companies. If your product is *proprietary or top secret* and you need to restrict information to as few people as possible, you probably don't want to use outside agents or dealers. Even though you can bind them contractually to maintain your trade secrets, it is very hard to control information once it leaves the confines of your company. Additionally, when people outside your company are distributing your product, it is difficult to control their actions. Even if the product is not proprietary, you want *outsiders* to represent your product accurately and honestly. While you can tell them to do so, you have little control over them if they don't. Your only remedy is to switch reps, distributors, or dealers.

Resources available

If companies have the resources to hire, train, motivate, and compensate good sales people, they develop their own sales force to maintain control and confidentiality over their products. If they don't have the resources and if control is not a big issue, they will typically seek outside distribution through distributors, dealers, manufacturers reps, and others. Even if they do use these outside sources, they will need *inside sales people* on staff to work with them.

Geography

Many companies distribute their products locally through their own sales people, but through outside distribution sources in other areas. The reason is that supporting a sales staff in remote areas can be much more expensive. That is, either you have to maintain remote sales offices staffed by some of your strongest people (the farther away the office, the stronger the personnel required), or you have to pay rather large travel and lodging expenses to send sales people into these areas.

Local Knowledge and Culture

In market areas where target market segments practice different cultures or speak different languages, outside distribution sources that are known in these areas become more important. It is difficult enough to communicate with prospects and customers when cultures and languages are the same. When they are different, communication becomes *exponentially* more difficult. Even the largest companies use local distribution sources in foreign areas, or they hire foreign nationals educated in their home country to run their foreign offices.

Desired Speed of Market Penetration

Due to the ever-changing and highly-competitive nature of most products, it is often important to get them into distribution channels as rapidly as possible. In most cases, penetration can be achieved more quickly if well-established *outside* sales companies are employed to distribute them. These companies are already in the marketplace calling on your market targets with experienced sales people. By distributing your products through them, you avoid the long lead times typically associated with finding, hiring, training and motivating your own sales force. Once your company and products become established in this market, you can shift to other more direct distribution methods. Of course, companies that have a well-established and trained sales force in a market territory can penetrate that territory more quickly using their own sales force.

Competition

You may select a particular distribution strategy to distinguish your company and products from the competition or to avoid *bumping* heads with your main competitors. In other words, if a distributor is known, to be pushing a competitor's products, you might find another distributor who is willing to concentrate on yours. Of course, you can also displace your competition, but this is often harder to do — especially if the competition is firmly entrenched in the marketplace.

Return on Investment

As with all marketing and business decisions, companies should select distribution strategies that will yield the highest *return on investment.* Sometimes companies forget that they need to make the investment before they realize the return. The old cliché, "*you have to spend money to make money*" is what you should remember here. Sometimes a larger investment will yield a much larger return. Therefore the expected return (or numerator of the ratio) has to be carefully considered as well as the investment (or denominator of the ratio). While it is impossible to forecast the expected return with complete accuracy, it is possible to *pencil out* different scenarios to determine the ones that appear to be most promising. Also, once a good *marketing information system* is put in place (which will be discussed in a later chapter), the effect of various distribution strategies can be measured so that new plans of action can be taken to improve the company's distribution.

DISTRIBUTION IN PRACTICE

No matter what the size of the company, the overall distribution strategy is typically a *mixture* of different approaches that work in different markets. For example, you might decide that the most cost-effective distribution strategy is to *sell direct locally*, and *sell through foreign distributors abroad*. The strategies selected seek to optimize the return on investment at the time they are selected. Because situations change so rapidly in today's marketplace, however, these situations have to be reviewed continually with the help of a well-designed *marketing information system*. All companies make mistakes. The good ones have good systems for detecting mistakes and quickly correcting them. Distribution is one strategy area that has to be constantly monitored to insure that the market is being properly covered in the most efficient and effective ways possible. Inefficiencies in this area can cost the company a tremendous amount of money — money it can't afford to throw away.

Even the largest companies have problems with their distribution strategies. Distribution problems often stem from one of the following:

1. A poor understanding of the fundamental concepts of distribution.
2. The lack of trust between the different entities of the distribution network — i.e. between manufacturers, distributors, dealers, and manufacturers reps.
3. The failure of the organizations in each channel to understand their role in the distribution system.
4. Poor supporting systems for the distribution function, such as inadequate computer, shipping, paperwork and filing systems.
5. A lack of timely communication between the organizations in each channel.
6. The failure to provide for backup should primary systems breakdown.
7. Improper information flow between the various levels in each channel — manufacturers, distributors, dealers, and end buyers.

Companies that solve their distribution problems are better able to control their destiny in the marketplace.

DISTRIBUTION AS A COMPETITIVE WEAPON

Companies that dominate their industries with large market shares can use distribution as a competitive weapon. They are able to gain control over distribution channels and effectively *lock out* competition from certain markets. Many companies do this by dominating the *prime shelf space* in stores and on the Internet. Big airlines do this by buying up all the available gates at major airports and by dominating computer screens of on-line reservation systems. Large high-tech companies, such as *Microsoft*, *Intel*, *Hewlett-Packard*, and *IBM*, do this by establishing their products as the *industry standard* to which product developers and competitors must conform just to compete successfully.

NON-LEADER DISTRIBUTION STRATEGIES

If your company is *not* an industry leader or a dominant company, you have to formulate other distribution strategies to compete effectively. Often times, your only alternative is to join forces with the *big distributors* in your market and pay them to distribute your products. This is common in the entertainment industry where the giant firms, such as *Universal* and *Time-Warner*, will distribute records, films, and other software for smaller companies. As an alternative strategy, you can sometimes make alliances with small distributors who are in competition with these *big distributors* and who have a vested interest in *pushing* your products to compete with them. You can also try to distribute your products on your own by using the methods already discussed.

SUPPLY-PUSH AND DEMAND-PULL STRATEGIES

Whether or not you are a dominant company or an industry leader, your distribution strategies have to be coordinated with your other marketing efforts. As such, you have to decide whether your strategies will concentrate on *pushing product through* your distribution channels or *pulling customers* through the turnstiles of your distributors.

Supply-Push

Using a *supply-push* strategy, manufacturers utilize their sales force and other promotional strategies to encourage distributors to take quantities of their products. Using their own promotional strategies, the distributors, in turn, *push* these products to their customers, the dealers. These dealers then utilize their marketing resources to aggressively market them to their customers — the end buyers. In this way, product is, in effect, *pushed* through the distribution channels with each distribution layer encouraging the one below to buy larger *supplies* of product.

Demand-Pull

Using a *demand-pull* strategy, manufacturers utilize promotional strategies, such as advertising and publicity, to create a strong demand for their products — pulling customers into stores, offices, and Web sites. Encouraged by advertising and other promotions, customers flock to retail outlets to buy the promoted products. To satisfy the increase in demand, dealers order more from their suppliers, the distributors. Distributors, in turn, order more from manufacturers.

Combination

Of course, it should be noted that many companies employ both *supply-push* and *demand-pull* methods. They *push* their distributors to take more products via personal selling efforts, price incentives, promotions, and contractual commitments. They also *pull* end buyers through their distribution channels via attractive product offerings, clever positioning, aggressive pricing, and competent promotion strategies, such as media and cooperative advertising.

In order for any of the above channel and distribution strategies to work efficiently in ever-increasing competitive environments, high-tech marketers need to have the supporting systems to insure timely deliveries of supplies coming in and products going out. The following section describes some of the more important supporting systems.

DISTRIBUTION SUPPORTING SYSTEMS

Once customers order products, they want them "yesterday." In some cases, they will settle for today or tomorrow, but rarely will they tolerate next week or next month. This means that marketers need to insure that they have the proper systems in place in order to meet the ever-increasing demands of their customers. If they don't, they know that some competitor will.

System Components

At the heart of most distribution supporting systems is a computer with powerful software that enables the company to integrate its purchasing, inventory, manufacturing, order processing, customer service, and delivery systems. Tied in with the computer system is a telephone/fax and e-mail system that enables the company to receive orders and feedback from customers as well as place orders and expedite delivery from suppliers. The reference to manufacturing and inventory systems may appear, at first glance, to be irrelevant to service companies. In fact, companies whose products are services need similar systems. For service companies, the "manufacturing systems" are replaced by systems for developing and providing the service. The "inventory systems" are supplanted by systems for insuring the availability and scheduling of trained personnel to perform the service. That is, instead of having product sitting on a shelf, a consulting or law firm will have consultants or lawyers available to perform the service.

Just-in-Time Delivery

Just-in-time delivery means that a company at any level in the distribution chain can order parts, subassemblies, or complete products on short notice and have them delivered very quickly. For example, *Mazda's* plant in Hiroshima, Japan has 120 parts suppliers located nearby. As a result, *Mazda* can have 80% of its components delivered within 30 minutes of the time they are needed on the assembly line. This means that *Mazda* can avoid the costs of carrying expensive inventory in costly storage facilities. *Mazda's* storage facilities are those of its nearby suppliers who can deliver quickly. In fact, in most Japanese factories, suppliers drive their trucks into the assembly plant and drop off the parts and subassemblies next to the assembly line where and when they are needed. From this example, you can see that a system model for just-in-time delivery requires the following ingredients:

- Close relationship with suppliers.
- Plant location near key suppliers.
- Facility design that allows for quick and efficient delivery.

- Good communications links with suppliers via phone and Internet.
- Good purchasing and receiving systems.

The inventory carrying, storage, obsolescence, breakage, and other costs saved by just-in-time delivery can be invested in other areas of the company or passed on to customers in the form of higher quality and lower, more competitive prices. Combined with other Total Quality Management (TQM) techniques, such as continual improvement, *Just-in-time delivery* methods can result in even better customer service and lower costs of doing business.

Examples

Many companies have grown more successful because they implemented good systems to support their distribution efforts. To punctuate the points above, two examples will be offered below — *Dell Computer* and *General Electric.*

Dell Computer

Michael Dell was a student at the *University of Texas* when he started *Dell Computer.* He started by buying surplus computers and components and reselling them from his dorm room. When he began to realize revenues approaching $250,000 per month, he decided to leave school and devote full-time to running his company. His company grew quickly to Fortune 1000 status and reached $1.7 billion in less than 10 years. He did this by building good direct marketing support systems that enabled his company to distribute products directly to end buyers without going through more conventional distribution and dealer channels. His direct link with customers enabled him to collect accurate marketplace information, quickly fill customer orders, and better service customer needs. As mentioned previously, *Dell* was selling one, two, and three million dollars worth of product each day from its Web site alone in each of their first three Quarters of 1997.

General Electric

To compete in the cutthroat electric appliance market, *General Electric* developed a *Direct Connect Program* in the late 1980's. This program required the redesign of its information and management systems. Instead of requiring dealers to buy and inventory full truckloads of appliances to get the best pricing, *GE's Direct Connect* system gives dealers instantaneous access to their on-line order processing system round-the-clock. Rather than stock appliances they can't afford to carry, dealers can now check availability and order directly from *GE's* on-line inventory. With this system, *GE* can deliver appliances to 90% of the country within 24 hours. Dealers who are part of the program get the best prices, faster delivery, lowered inventory and handling costs. For its part, *GE* has lower paperwork, inventory, and marketing costs. Its marketing and distribution costs alone have been lowered by 12%. Moreover, by having direct links to dealers, *GE* is able to capture accurate sales and marketplace information on-line.

By investing in good distribution supporting systems, both *Dell* and *GE* have been able to better service their customers, obtain accurate and timely marketplace information, increase sales, lower costs and increase resultant profits.

SUMMARY

Distribution is an important but often neglected and misunderstood function of marketing. Companies who understand distribution and formulate competent strategies, can gain critical advantages over their competitors.

Distribution should cover the marketplace in the most efficient and cost effective ways possible. This is usually achieved through a combination of direct sales, direct marketing, and multi-tiered distribution in remote, foreign, and difficult-to-reach markets. Companies who dominate distribution channels can have control over their markets, use it as a competitive weapon, and make money from competitors who need to use their distribution resources.

The questions to think about when formulating distribution strategies include:

- Where are the market targets located?
- How do you efficiently and effectively get your products to them?
- What's the most *convenient way for them* to buy your products?
- Who are the competitors, and what distribution strategies do they employ?
- Can a good distribution strategy be employed to effectively *lock competitors* out of key markets?

One final point to remember about distribution is — if your competitors are controlling certain channels of distribution, you might want to look for other channels rather than compete directly with them. *Southwest Airlines* did this by initially flying to cities and airports that were not adequately covered by industry leaders, such as *American*, *Delta*, and *United*. Because *Southwest* has been so effective, other airlines are developing strategies to compete with them in these markets.

TIPS and Exercises

1. Identify the distribution channels you currently use.
2. Compare these to the distribution channels used by your competitors.
3. Determine if the resellers in your reseller channels have sufficient incentives (discounts off list) to want to push your products.
4. Try to develop distribution strategies to lock in your customers and lock out your competitors. Off-line, try to get exclusives on distributor shelves, and online try to select a good domain name and employ effective natural and paid search strategies.
5. Determine if there is any competition between your channels, and if there is, try to create strategies to avoid channel contention.
6. Ask your resellers what you could do to help them sell more.
7. Try to identify additional channels you could use without much additional investment.

Chapter 9

DNA of Promotion

"When it doubt, tell the truth..."

Mark Twain

WHAT IS PROMOTION?

Probably the most interesting, creative, and *difficult to do well* of all the fundamental building blocks of marketing, *Promotion* is *the process of communicating the benefits of complete products to market targets so they will be prompted to take a buying action.* To understand this definition, marketers can benefit from a clarification of the terms *complete product, benefits, and buying action.*

Complete Product

As discussed in *Chapter 6* on the *Produc*t variable, a complete product is much more than a device or service that is developed by engineers or others. Based on information collected from the marketplace, the *device* or *service* is augmented by other elements to create the *Product building block.* To make it complete, a *Corporate Image*, *Position*, *Price*, *Place* where prospects can find it, *Promotional strategy* informing prospects about it, and *Marketing Information System* mechanism are added to form a complete core component (see *Figure 6-1*). To transform this *complete core component* into a truly *complete* product, the *peripheral component* of customer service is added (see *Figure 6-2*). Therefore, what gets promoted is a *complete product.* That is, when a product is advertised, or promoted in some other way, customers usually need to know a lot more about it than what the *Product building block* tells them. They often also want to know about the following:

1. *Corporate Image.* What about the product's parents? Does it come from a good family? Buyers often want to know about the manufacturer and reseller.
2. *Positioning.* Is the product right for them? Is it made to satisfy their needs? Does it have something unique that other competitive products don't have? Does the product have a positive history and track record?
3. *Pricing.* Can they afford it? Is it priced to support the level of quality and status they may be seeking?
4. *Place.* Once prospective buyers are comfortable with the product, its parents, image, and price, they often need to know where they can buy it.
5. *Promotion.* Since the promotion vehicle reflects on the image of the product and its parents, buyers are often influenced by the image of the medium used to inform them about the product. They don't expect a quality product to be advertised in a low-quality, "throw-away" newspaper.
6. *Marketing Information System mechanism.* Studies show that buyers prefer products from companies that attempt to measure their satisfaction or give them the opportunity to voice their opinions about the product and company.

7. *Customer service.* Buyers are often concerned about how well the company will take care of them after they buy the product (this of course has been defined as the peripheral component of the product).

For these reasons, promotion has to be concerned with communicating the benefits of the *company*, *product*, *position*, *price*, *place*, and *marketing information system*.

Once marketers are comfortable with this concept of the *complete product*, they are ready to conquer the other elements of the *promotion definition* that may need further explanation — *benefits* and *buying actions*.

Benefits and Features

While “benefits” is a term that most think they understand, inexperienced marketers often confuse “benefits” with “features.” Quite simply *features* are inherent, or built-in, characteristics of a product. No matter what language people speak or what they want the product to do for them, everyone can agree on a product’s features. A product has a certain size, weight, shape, color, performance characteristics, and specifications. These are its features. On the other hand, *benefits* tie the product's features to the specific needs of the target audience. They explain the product’s features in terms of how they will benefit the customer. Each buyer might be seeking a different key benefit from the same product. Furthermore, it is also possible that the same feature might benefit different prospects in different ways. A few examples are provided to help you to better understand features and benefits.

Car Example

When expressing the room available in the back seat of a car, an ad or a sales person could communicate this as a *feature* — in terms of cubic feet or meters. Unfortunately, most car buyers cannot visualize how this feature will satisfy their needs for back-seat space. If the space were communicated in terms of benefits to a particular buyer, say a family of four with some tall members, it could be expressed as “enough room for a 6-foot 4-inch person to fit comfortably in the back seat.”

Mattress Example

The creative director of an ad agency that represents a large, well-known mattress manufacturer conducted market research to develop a strategy to sell his client’s products. Upon interviewing prospective buyers, he discovered that mattress buyers identify with one of two key groups — those who buy a mattress for *comfort and luxury* and those who buy the same product for *health reasons*, such as to provide back-support. This means a mattress could be positioned and sold to one audience by communicating the comfort and luxury benefits, and to the other by communicating the health benefits. If marketers examine the market for mattresses in the United States, they will find that the *comfort and luxury position* is owned by *Simmons* with their *Beautyrest* product line, while the health position is owned by *Sealy* with their *Posturepedic* line.

Computer Example

High-tech companies, such as those who sell computers, have a tendency to communicate the technical features without explaining the benefits to the buyer. Technical jargon may work when communicating to a technical audience. What many high-tech marketers fail to realize, however, is that they could sell a lot more product if they also took the time and trouble to explain technical features in terms of the benefits to the less technical buyer. Even though technical people may play a part in a purchase decision, more often than not, a non-technical person makes the final decision or writes the check. Communicating in terms of features, a computer sales person may explain "this desktop computer has 1 gigabyte of RAM memory, a *Pentium* processor running at a clock rate of 2 GHz, and 100 gigabytes of hard-disk storage." After highlighting each feature, the same sales person could just as easily explain, "to do your accounting and word processing, this system has enough RAM memory to run all of today's popular programs, it has enough disk storage to hold your programs and data for several years, and it runs at a fast-enough speed so that you will rarely have to wait for the computer." As described in this example, the most successful promotions provide both features and benefits so as to communicate with those who need to know one, the other, or both.

Buying Action

A *buying action* is *any action that leads the prospect closer to buying the product.* While most recognize the purchase of a product as a buying action, many fail to understand that *buying actions* often involve smaller steps such as calling a toll-free number, visiting a Web site, or filling out and returning a postage-paid reply card for more information; calling the company for an appointment to see the product; visiting a retail outlet to view or try out the product; or making a mental note to see a product some time in the future. Sophisticated marketers recognize that the buyers of many high-technology products cannot and will not buy upon first contact. This is analogous to asking someone to marry you upon your first meeting. Buyers will buy once they are comfortable that the product satisfies their needs better than other alternatives. Since technical products tend to be more complex, prospects may need to take a series of smaller buying actions that acquaint them with the product and the company before they are truly comfortable taking the ultimate action of buying the product.

Once you truly understand the definition of the *Promotion* building block, you are ready to move on to exploring some of the most-common types of promotion.

TYPES OF PROMOTION

Marketing novices equate promotion with *advertising* or *sales*. Marketing professionals know that advertising is only one component of the *promotion mix*. In addition to Advertising, promotion covers many other activities including the following:

- Personal Selling
- Sales Promotions
- Direct Marketing
- Publicity
- Trade Shows
- Seminars
- Specialty Advertising
- Newsletters
- Customer Referrals (also known as Word-of-Mouth Advertising)
- Networking
- Collateral materials, such as brochures and price lists
- Stationery/Business Card Design
- Product Slogans and Logos
- Personal Gifts
- Packaging Design
- Books, Manuals, and Operating Instructions
- Phone Handling (including voice and fax)
- Web Page Design and online advertising
- E-mail, Search Engines, and Weblogs
- Office Design
- Product or Point of Purchase Displays
- Business Forms Design
- Reception and Treatment of Visitors

Basically, promotion involves virtually *any form of communication that impacts the sale of the product or image of the company.*

It is presented as the *last* "P" in the marketing mix because it should be *developed last* after the other strategies have been formulated. The reason for this is that promotion is the company's vehicle for communicating its other marketing strategies to the marketplace. That is, once a *position* is chosen, the *product* is ready for introduction, the *pricing strategy* has been devised, and *distribution* channels have been established, *promotion* is used to effectively and efficiently communicate these strategies to the company's various publics. It is utilized to explain what the product is, how it uniquely satisfies their needs, how much it costs, where they can buy it, and how well the company will take care of them.

MAIN OBJECTIVES OF PROMOTION

To clarify the above characterizations, some of the objectives of Promotion are listed below.

1. *Provide information* to the market about your company and products.
2. *Pre-sell the product.*
3. *Hook* or prompt prospects to take a buying action.
4. *Pull prospects through the turnstiles.*
5. *Give* prospects an *incentive to buy now.*
6. *Educate* the company's various publics on its products.
7. *Create interest.*
8. *Get* the *prospect's attention.*
9. *Project a favorable image*, personality, culture of the company.
10. *Get publics to remember* the company and its products and services.
11. *Develop* a *positive relationship* with publics.
12. *Position* the company and its products apart from other choices.
13. *Plant seeds* that will grow into sales.
14. *Communicate* with company publics.
15. *Tell* prospects *where* and *how* they can *buy* the product.
16. *Get prospects to make a small commitment* leading to the larger commitment of buying.
17. *Drive benefits* of company products *into the minds* of publics.
18. *Drive* company and product *names into the minds* of publics.
19. *Develop loyalty with all target market segments.*
20. *Collect valuable information about the company's customer base and the marketplace.*

AIDA MODEL

Another way to think of the objectives of promotion is to relate them to an *AIDA Model*. This model organizes the objectives of promotion into the following four sequential steps:

1. *Attention*. The first step to get the attention of market targets.
2. *Interest*. The next step is to develop their interest in your products and company.
3. *Decision*. After generating interest, you want them to decide to buy your product.
4. *Action*. Finally you want them to take a buying action leading to purchase.

This model can help marketers to focus on the sequential steps in the promotion process and to think about where their market targets are in this process. That is, in cases where the market is well aware of, and interested in, the product, marketers can focus on getting market targets to make a decision and take action. On the other hand, in those situations where the product is not well-known, marketers may have to educate their audience to get their attention and develop their interest before they are ready to take the subsequent buying actions.

Once marketers are able to assess the communication needs in each of their market segments, they can select the promotional tools and develop the promotion strategies that will best satisfy their objectives — achieving the goals of the Marketing Plan. One of the more popular tools in the promotion tool kit is advertising.

ADVERTISING

The subject of advertising all alone can fill many books. This text aims to give you a good enough understanding of advertising that you will be able to apply advertising methods with success to the marketing of your products. A good place to start is a definition of Advertising. Advertising is *communicating the benefits of the product and company, usually via paid outside media, in order to prompt a buying action*. In light of this definition, it is useful to examine the types of advertising that professionals typically employ.

Types of Advertising

There are many ways of advertising your company and products. As new communications technologies and ideas are developed, new forms of advertising are being created all the time. Some of the more popular ones are presented below.

Print Media • Magazines

Magazines and trade publications are a popular form of advertisement. A company's products can be presented attractively in color or in black and white, and the message presented has *shelf life* that goes beyond the frequency of publication. That is, whether published weekly, monthly or quarterly, magazines are often saved long after they are issued. After reading them, many pass them to their friends and associates. Offices keep them for quite a while in lobby areas, and long after most people throw them away, libraries keep them on file for historical record. This long life of magazines and trade publications makes them an attractive means of spreading your message to various publics.

For many products, focused trade magazines are a particularly effective source of advertisement. The main reasons are (1) they cost less than general readership magazines and (2) they are aimed at specific target market segments. Examples of focused trade magazines are *Science*, *Marketing Computers*, *Film* and *Video Magazine*, and *Macworld*.

Airline magazines are particularly effective for travel and office products such as personal computers, copiers, cellular phones, and fax machines since many business people in the target market often read these magazines to pass the time of their plane flights. If your products are marketed nationally or internationally, you can select an airline magazine that covers this market. If your products are sold within a smaller geographical area, you can find local commuter airline magazines that allow you to focus rather efficiently on specific geographical areas.

Print Media • Newspapers

Newspapers can be very effective for promoting products that appeal to a wide audience, but unless they focus on specific niches, that are typically not as effective for promoting specialized or complex products. With rare exceptions, they have a general readership, and are not very well focused on specific target markets. Most of them have a very local reach. In major cities, in particular, ads in newspapers are very costly — with full-page ads costing many thousands of dollars. Also, because of their frequency of issue (usually daily), ads in newspapers tend to have a very short shelf life.

Industry newspapers and journals that focus on specific target markets can be very effective. However, you should find out which of these your market targets read most often. Examples of industry newspapers are *The Daily Journal* (Los Angeles lawyers), *Daily Variety* (Entertainment industry), and *Data Training* (Corporate training industry).

It should be mentioned that local newspapers, while not always the best venue for advertising technical or specialty products, are an excellent source of market information. They often contain special articles on specific industries and businesses. Additionally, they give marketers a better understanding of the local factors that influence prospective buyers in a particular geographic area.

Broadcast Media

Products that are widely-used by large numbers of people are the best candidates for advertising in *Broadcast Media*, such as *television* (TV) and *radio*. The reason for this is that broadcast media reach a very general audience. Therefore, they are good for advertising such products as soap, toothpaste, cars, cereals, and other products that most people buy and use. In fact, as its name implies, the *Soap Opera* is a type of television program that was originally created to advertise soap and other consumer products to the large numbers of housewives who were home taking care of children in the 1950's and 1960's.

Because of the high costs and unfocused reach of most *broadcast media*, they tend to work better for general-purpose consumer products that have a large target audience. Conversely, broadcast media are usually not good vehicles for advertising niche products that appeal to technical, eclectic, sophisticated and smaller audiences.

Even so, high-tech companies, such as *Boeing* and *IBM*, routinely do corporate image advertising on television. Since most people know that advertising in broadcast media is expensive, television and, to a lesser extent, radio give instant credibility to products that are advertised on their "airwaves." Therefore, television can be effective in boosting the corporate image of technical and smaller companies.

Cable TV

With all of the cable TV channels and the ability to focus on specific groups of prospects, cable TV holds promise as an effective source of advertising products that appeal to technical and special-niche audiences. Many large companies even have their own networks. Marketers should research the extent to which their prospects view cable TV and evaluate this potential source accordingly. Of course, another question to consider is whether or not the cable stations your prospects watch offer advertising. Many do not.

Infomercials

A special type of broadcast advertising is the *infomercial*. The *infomercial* is a very long commercial — often up to 30 minutes — that seeks to provide in-depth information about the product. It often uses a celebrity to endorse the product or explain its benefits. The problem with *infomercials* is that they suffer from a bad *corporate image*, or reputation. That is, many of the products advertised in this way have fallen short of expectations. In fact, some of the creators of these products have been indicted for fraud and other abuses of law. As a result, many consumers have developed a tendency to question the credibility of products that are advertised via infomercials. Marketers need to weigh the positives and negatives of *infomercials* when they evaluate this form of advertising.

Video, CD-Rom, and DVD

Taking advantage of the proliferation of VCR, CD and DVD players in homes and businesses, many companies have produced video commercials that advertise the benefits of their products and services. This advertising method can be particularly effective promoting more complex and technical products since they can be shown in action as the video explains their benefits and advantages over other alternatives. Videos are particularly effective when used in conjunction with follow-up sales calls. The videos can explain the basic benefits of, and interest the prospect in, the product — thereby saving valuable sales person time. The sales person can then follow up on the prospect's interest to close the sale.

Advergames and Product Placement

As people are overloaded with more and more ad messages every day, many are skipping ads and commercials. To counteract this problem, marketers are increasingly turning to relatively new promotional methods that have been proven to be very effective in promoting products and companies — *Advergaming and Product Placement.*

Product placement refers to putting an advertiser's product in a movie, TV show, game, or other content. As people pay attention to the content, they cannot help but see the advertiser's products that are placed in the show or movie. For example, if the actor is drinking a soda, it might as well be the Advertiser's brand. This becomes a win-win situation for all involved. Advertisers get their brands in the mind of their target audiences in a more subtle, believable, and natural way. The originator of the content creates a believable and realistic experience for customers, and the consumer gets a richer more believable experience.

Advergaming is riding the growing popularity of games. In some cases, advertisers products are placed in the content of the game. In others, games are created specifically to teach players about the benefits of the advertised products. Unlike ads and commercials where advertisers compete for the attention of an increasingly disinterested and skeptical target audience, players seek out advergames because they are fun to play and they may win prizes.

Internet

Even though it is in its infancy, the Internet continues to prove that it has the potential to become the greatest promotional channel ever invented. It has virtually unlimited potential constrained only by the current state of technology, access, and the learning curve required to become proficient. As technological advances diminish these limitations, marketers need to continually reevaluate the "highest and best" uses of the Internet for their promotional purposes. Currently, the highest and best uses of the Internet for promotion fall into the following categories: e-mail, search, Web sites, Weblogs (blogs), and advertising links.

E-mail. E-mail has become a very effective way to communicate with market targets. Unlike other forms of communication, e-mail can provide a rich communication (especially if attachments, links, or html-enriched graphics are included) that a recipient can view at will when it convenient. The negative side of e-mail is *Spam — commonly defined as unwanted and unsolicited e-mail.* By 2004, the average user of e-mail estimated that 75% of received e-mails were unsolicited and unwanted. While solutions continue to be developed to solve the spam problem, none has proven to be completely effective.

Search. By 2004, search had grown in importance as both a promotional and research, or marketing information system, tool. By simply typing a search word or string of search words, a prospect can find answers and company advertisers willing and able to provide them.

Web sites. By creating a Web site, marketers have the ability to economically reach far beyond the local geographies that limited businesses since the beginning of time. The power and potential of Web sites is enhanced by the ability of people finding your site via search and e-mail. Any e-mail or search results can have a link that will transport a prospect to your Web site. Of course creating the content of the site is critically important and requires disciplined use of the 7 Building Blocks of Marketing, the Universal Marketing Structure™ and Universal Web Structure.™ These latter two structures will be presented in more detail later in this chapter.

Weblogs or Blogs. Blogs are running dialogues in "diary-like" form that make it possible to have a continuous feedback loop between market targets and advertisers. They provide an alternative way to spread information and commentary outside of mainstream media. Because they are informal, direct, and candid, they tend to have greater credibility than other forms of promotion. Blogging has driven the adoption of yet another technology, called Real Simple Syndication (RSS), which allows blog readers to track freshly posted information without having to browse through a long list of home pages.

Outdoor Advertising

Billboards, bus shelters, benches, and sides, and taxicabs can be an effective method of advertising. Because this type of advertising reaches a very general audience, it is best-suited for products that appeal to a broad audience and/or a specific geography.

Yellow Pages

While the *Yellow Pages* also address a rather general audience, this form of advertising has proven to be very effective for technical, industrial, and consumer products. The reasons for this include the following: a Yellow Pages listing has a shelf life of at least one year; prospects who look in the Yellow Pages are usually *ready to buy* the product; and small companies can appear as large as big companies through their trademark ads in the Yellow Pages.

In recent years, the Yellow Pages have become more sophisticated in the options that are offered. A listing can be in special consumer, business, or neighborhood directories. There are regular listings, boldface listings, listings in red, trademark listings, or display ads. Although many directory sales people claim a display ad is the most effective, more than a few marketing experts believe that a *trademark listing* can be as effective, and in some cases more effective, for a lot less money. The trademark listing stands out because it puts your logo, address, phone number and/or slogan in place of the regular listing. Because it appears alphabetically in the column where your regular listing would be, it can be more easily found than a display ad, which is sometimes out of sequence on a different page. Since all trademark ads are the same size, a smaller company can appear as large as the largest company. Also, the trademark listing allows a company to establish a more professional image by avoiding association with the local pizza places, fast food restaurants and plumbers that often dominate display listings in the Yellow Pages.

There are now many different Yellow Pages directories from different companies. All of them tell you that *theirs is the best*. You should go with the one that gives you the best coverage. While it would be inappropriate to endorse one over another, studies show that the one that is distributed by your main phone company is the one that is most widely used. Depending on the degree of coverage overlap, you might consider advertising in more than one directory. You never know which one a “hot” prospect might look in first. Of course, if you put in place a good marketing information system, you will be able to measure which directories pull in customers and which do not — allowing you to make adjustments in subsequent years.

Industry Directories

Industry-specific directories are very good sources for advertising products to highly-targeted audiences. The reasons include the following: they are typically inexpensive, they cover specific market niches, and they usually have a life of at least one year. They are most useful in those industries in which they are used frequently. For example, *The Parker Directory* is used daily by people in the California legal community because it lists all the names, addresses and phone numbers of courts, practicing judges and lawyers throughout the state. The *Writers Guild Directory* is a frequently-used directory in the entertainment industry. If your target audience uses such a directory frequently, you should seriously consider advertising in that directory. At the very least, you should familiarize yourself with the various industry directories your target audience uses regularly. You should keep these on file in the company's marketing library for future consideration.

FAX Machines

With the rapid spread of FAX capabilities in the office and the home, a new type of advertising is being employed. An advertiser's FAX system can be programmed to dial up and transmit complete ads to the FAX machines of selected market targets. While this can be effective, it can anger prospects if it is not used discreetly and with their prior permission. As with electronic mail, many prospects don't want their systems tied up with advertisements — particularly if they are using them to complete their own work under deadline pressures. Before using this promotional method, it is recommended that prospects be contacted to obtain their permission before sending them promotional material.

A more effective use of FAX technology is the *Faxback* service. Using Faxback, a prospect can fax a request to your firm, and your company's FAX machine can automatically fax a brochure or some other promotional piece back to the requestor. This is more effective for the simple reason that the prospect is making the request, similar to *opting in* for receiving e-mails and e-Newsletters.

Electronic Shopping

As mentioned previously, electronic shopping networks have become a popular way of advertising and distributing certain consumer products. They have considerable potential since the buyer can view the product as well as receive a detailed description. However, more expensive and complex products are not likely to be effectively promoted by this method. The price and the complexity of such products usually dictate the need for a face-to-face demonstration followed by questions and answers to and from a knowledgeable sales person or an interactive Web/e-mail exchange. Furthermore, the work schedules of those interested in complex products are typically incompatible with the time slots of electronic shopping programs. In the future, with the advent of interactive television in the office as well as the home, electronic shopping might prove to be a more effective high-tech advertising vehicle.

Other Advertising Methods

There are many other advertising methods that can be employed to promote a company's products. The more important of these, such as *Direct Mail*, will be discussed later in this Chapter. A few others are mentioned here to give you an idea of the alternative methods that you might find appropriate to your business. They include such methods as skywriting, distribution of leaflets, door-to-door solicitation (*Avon* and *Fuller Brush*), and physical bulletin boards.

Selecting Advertising Media

Which of the above advertising types should you select to advertise your products? Once you select the types, which specific media should you choose — that is, what print, broadcast, online, outdoor, direct, or other media would be most appropriate for your business? Unfortunately, too many marketers don't know the answers to these questions because they don't understand the underlying concepts that drive media selection.

Step One — Identify your market targets. The key to selecting the appropriate types of advertising and media is to first define the target audience. As discussed in the sections on *positioning* and the *marketing cycle*, you should have a good definition of your target markets. If you don't, you can conduct some market research. If you have an established company, you can profile your existing customer base. Then you can look for prospects that match this profile.

Step Two — Match market targets to media candidates. Once you know the target audience, you can use your marketing information system (do some market research) to determine where you can best *reach* them. Publications, such as *Standard Rate and Data Service*, or *SRDS*, have this information for most print, broadcast, and direct media.

Step Three — Collect specific cost and market research data on specific candidates. You can contact the publications and other media sources directly and ask them to send you a *media kit*, which usually contains an advertising *rate card* and extensive market research data on the audience that they reach.

Step Four — Compare costs. Advertising costs are typically compared by looking at the *CPM* for each media source. *CPM* stands for the *cost for reaching one-thousand prospects*. For example, if the target market for a particular product is small and well-defined, the CPM for sending a direct letter to each prospect is probably far less than the CPM for advertising in a magazine or on a TV program. For the marginal cost of the mailer and a postage stamp, each prospect can be efficiently reached by a direct mail campaign. On the other hand, if the product is a consumer product, such as soap or toothpaste, which most people in a market territory might buy, the CPM for TV advertising is likely to be less than that of direct mail. That's why many consumer products companies advertise their products on top-rated prime time TV shows even though commercial time might cost them upwards of $450,000 for one 15 to 30-second spot. While TV commercials are very expensive, they may prove to be the most efficient and least costly way to reach each prospect in a very large audience. The CPM numbers for various media can be determined by (1) contacting each media source and requesting their media kit or (2) looking up the data in *Standard Rate and Data Service*, also known as *SRDS* (available in print and online). Once these figures are obtained, they may need to be modified to reflect the fact that the market segments reached by these media do not exactly coincide with your target audiences. For example, a publication may reach an audience that includes all PC users, but your product may only work with *Pentium*-based PCs. Therefore, to more accurately compute a CPM figure for that publication, you need to estimate the percentage of PC users that have *Pentium*-based PCs and apply this factor to the published figures.

Step Five — Select the media. After comparing the CPM's and the other advantages and disadvantages of the various media alternatives, the media is selected that is likely to most efficiently cover the market while meeting other important advertising objectives. What are other objectives? For example, since certain broadcast media often bring some extra credibility to the advertiser, a marketer may decide to select a TV ad rather than another media type that has a lower CPM simply because increasing the company's credibility may be an important objective that is not factored into the CPM comparison. The goals of the Marketing Plan should guide your decisions.

Step Six — Determining Frequency. Once the previous steps identify the media to best *reach* your target audience, you need to determine the optimal frequency. Frequency is necessary for a number of reasons. When the ad runs, people in the target audience may (1) not be available, (2) speak a different language (likely to also affect content decisions), (3) be too distracted or disinterested, (4) need repetition to sufficiently understand and remember the ad's message, (5) not be ready to buy (their *buying window*™ is not active). Once you know the frequency, you have the last major piece of the puzzle to develop your ad budget.

By better identifying your target audience and keeping the proper reach and frequency in mind, you are likely to do a much better job of selecting the right media vehicle for your ad messages.

Reasons for Advertising

Too many “self-appointed” marketers think that all you have to do is “build a better mousetrap” and buyers will “beat a path to your door”. Anyone who truly understands marketing knows that this kind of thinking is wrong. While most of the people who work for a company have a wealth of knowledge about its products, it is naive to assume that everyone else does. Therefore one of the reasons for advertising is to *provide information* about your company and products to the marketplace. Some additional reasons include the following:

Image, Good Will, and Buyer Comfort. Providing information is not always enough, buyers want to feel comfortable that they are buying the right products from the right company. Advertising, if properly executed, can help to build a positive image of your company and products as well as to develop a lasting relationship with your various publics. Because of this need to feel comfortable, buyers will often bypass generic products to buy advertised brands.

Communicate Benefits. In a competitive environment, after providing product information and developing good will, advertising needs to communicate the benefits of the product. Buyers are far more interested in knowing what your company and products will do for them than how great you think your products are.

Position, or Differentiate, from Competition. Because your competitors may also talk about benefits, you need to position your products to clearly differentiate them from competitors. If you give your target audience easy-to-understand reasons for buying your product from you, more often than not, they will.

Drive Lasting Perceptions into the Buyer's Mind. To sustain your positioning and success, your advertising has to create strong and positive perceptions about your products in the minds of your target audience. If the product is something *intangible*, such as a service, it should seek to create the *aura of tangibility* so that buyers will better remember it. Conversely, if the product is *tangible*, it should seek to create intangible advantages that can be remembered. Alvin Toffler recognizes this in his book, *Future Shock*, when he says,

> *"...goods are increasingly designed to yield psychological 'extras' for the customers. The manufacturer adds a 'psychic load' to his basic product, and the customer gladly pays for this intangible benefit."*

For example, *Tide's grease-releasing formula gets clothes* "white." *Cheer gets them* "*whiter than white at all temperatures.*" *Bold gets those tough stains out and makes clothes* "*bright.*" Zenith "*puts the quality in before the name goes on.*" These images are important intangible thoughts that help buyers distinguish otherwise similar tangible products. A computer is a device that only becomes a useful product when such less tangible ingredients as software, training, support, operator manuals, and service are included. *Compal*, an early pioneer in the microcomputer industry, made these intangibles tangible by having them printed on a laminated silver-card, called "*The Compal Difference*" (see *Figure 9-1*). This card also recorded the customer's serial number, the name of their support person, and the phone number to call for assistance.

THE COMPAL DIFFERENCE

Congratulations on purchasing a system from COMPAL®

You have joined a rapidly growing group of business professionals who recognize the importance of the service COMPAL provides.

Anybody can sell you a computer or word processor. Some provide on-site repair service. Still fewer give you adequate training and support. Only COMPAL provides you with the assurance that, with one single phone call, you will get all the help you need.

That's because COMPAL recognizes there is a big difference between selling systems and making them work for you in your business.

With each system and software package you purchase, COMPAL provides:

- **TRAINING**—Training specialists will teach you at your own speed until you learn.
- **SUPPORT**—Customer support representatives will answer all your system and software questions over the phone.

As part of the On-site Service Contract, COMPAL will provide:

- **REPAIR SERVICE**—Technical Specialists will repair malfunctioning hardware at your office.
- **LOANER COMPONENTS**—If hardware problems cannot be solved on the spot, COMPAL will provide loaner components until the malfunctioning part can be fixed.
- **SOFTWARE UPGRADES**—As an extra bonus, COMPAL will give you upgrades to COMPAL software packages at no additional charge (there is only a small handling charge to cover mailing costs). Since most of the system capability is in the software, your system is virtually never obsolete.

COMPAL®

Figure 9-1

Prompt a Buying Action. The ultimate reason for advertising is to prompt prospects to take a buying action or be predisposed to buying when a sales person calls on them.

Important Considerations

When creating advertising or promotional pieces, the following considerations are very important to keep in mind:

Be Conscious of Corporate and Product images. The advertisement should be in line with the company's image and the product's positioning strategy.

Strive for Quality over Quantity. Because of image, smaller or less frequent ads of high-quality are usually preferable to larger more frequent ads of low-quality. The quality of the ad reflects on the quality of the company and products.

Focus on Targets. Ads that focus on *specific target markets* are typically more successful than ads that try to be "all things to all people". Clear positioning, once again, is a very important consideration.

Appeal to the Audience. Understanding the characteristics and needs of the target audience will help to get the advertising message in the minds of these targets. For example, accountants are typically interested in saving money while real estate developers are interested in making more money by closing more deals.

Keep the Message Simple (KISS Principle). In addition to targeting specific audiences, your ads should focus on one idea at a time. Ads should also be as straightforward and simple as possible.

Tell the Truth. Just as some people lie, some companies do too. Irrespective of issues of morality and integrity, lying is bad marketing and bad business. While some buyers fall for lies, many others will not. Moreover, when discovered, lies destroy the trust between the company and publics resulting in lost sales and tarnished images. Lying, even if not deliberate, is a big strategic mistake.

Tell the Believable Truth. Telling the truth is often not enough. You have to tell the *believable* truth. That is, if you make *hard-to-believe* claims in your marketing pieces, you should back them up with independent, credible proof.

Reach the Audience. As discussed earlier, you can best reach an audience by identifying your targets, finding what media they consume, comparing the CPM and qualitative factors for each of the media candidates, selecting the media, and running your advertisement. Of course after you run your piece, you need to use your *marketing information system* to measure and analyze its effectiveness so that you can repeat successes and avoid duplicating mistakes. As a reminder, to match the profiles of your market targets with those of the media, you can look up information on media audiences in SRDS or you ask each media candidate to send you their audience profiles in media kits. These are often available online. You should also ask your customers and prospects to identify their favorite media.

Get their Attention. Once you determine the proper media, you have to grab your prospect's attention. You do this with catchy, clever, creative and *simple* messages. Nobody likes to read, watch or listen to anything that is boring or unnecessarily long.

Get into their minds to generate Interest, Decision, and Action. Recalling the *AIDA model*, once you get their attention, your message should *get through* to them and encourage them to buy. The message should answer an objection, solve a problem, or *push* one or more of their "*hot buttons*." An example of a "*hot button*" is service response time. Someone who has just waited two days to get his or her copy machine serviced is *ready and waiting* for anyone who can improve response time. Response time, therefore, becomes a *hot button*.

Stay in their minds. Getting into their minds once or twice is not enough. In fact, it can sometimes be worse than not advertising at all. Many buyers will think something happened to the company. To be effective, *advertising has to be repetitive and cumulative*. Ads in media that work should be repeated as frequently as possible. Repetitive good ads build awareness, relationships with targets, brand recognition, loyalty, and lead to buying behavior.

Avoid Anything Offensive. It's *common sense* to avoid offending groups of people in ads. Yet many ads are offensive. They poke fun at people's race, religion, gender, and political affiliations. Such offensive references should be eliminated, not only because they are improper, but also because they can *needlessly hurt sales* and the *image of the company*. This has nothing to do with *political correctness*. It has everything to do with common business sense.

Avoid Negative Concepts. Negatives in ads often backfire in many different ways. Sometimes, they insult many in the target audience. Other times, people associate the negatives with the product and company being advertised. Two examples of negative headlines from actual ads are: "At your age, you should be making more money." and "The *Lap Top for people with brains enough to know the difference*." The first is from a bank ad that was pushing a higher CD rate for people 55 and over. The second is from a manufacturer of lap-top portable computers priced at $1,000 less than popular competitors. Both ad headlines are very *negative* and *insulting*. Some people will respond because useful information is provided in the ad, and they won't find these headlines offensive. Many others will not respond because of the negatives.

Don't disparage or mention the competition. Ever since the FTC ruled in 1979 that ads that disparage competitors' products aren't necessarily illegal, many advertisers have chosen to "*knock*" their competition in ads. Although it may be legal, it's *not* very smart marketing. Disparaging the competition, per se, causes many buyers to question the motives and integrity of the company doing the "bad-mouthing". It puts little suspicions and doubts in the heads of buyers that, in turn, cause them to hesitate buying. It also prompts the competitors being disparaged to escalate their own comparative advertising efforts to the possible detriment of your company. Most importantly, just mentioning a competitor by name is a mistake. Why? Mentioning their name gives them free advertising. You've probably heard the phrase, "Bad publicity is better than no publicity at all." This is often true, and since you are doing the disparaging, the audience doesn't believe you anyway. Hence, you are doing your competitor a big favor.

It is acceptable and even advisable to do comparisons that say something to the effect, "Ours is better and here are the reasons why..." Factual comparisons can be very effective, but these should be done in a positive rather than a negative way, and they require proof to be credible.

It should be noted that most advertisers don't intend to blatantly disparage or lie. More often, they exaggerate or say something in a way that is hard to believe. To the intelligent, somewhat cynical, already skeptical, and overburdened buyer of products, exaggeration is no different from lying. In any case, it often produces the same results — lost sales and negative *word-of-mouth* advertising.

Avoid using superlatives such as "We're the best," or "We're number one." Buyers have heard the message "*we're the best*" or "*our product is the best*" so many times that they turn their minds off when they hear it again. Certain words such as "*best*" should be avoided at all costs in advertisements unless, of course, the word is quoted from an authoritative, independent, and respected third-party source such as an industry expert, an acknowledged survey, or definitive study. If it is used in an ad, it should be *proven* in the ad or it should be easily verifiable by the reader. That is, the authoritative source that uses the superlative should be referenced in the ad so that the reader can verify its authenticity. The only case where verification might be omitted in an ad is if the superlative is a well-known and easily proven fact such as "*Winner of the Academy Award for Best Picture...*". If the superlative refers to a feature, such as speed ("it's the fastest") the speed should be listed in the ad with a verifiable source. This proof is essential for avoiding skepticism and hesitation on the part of prospective buyers.

There is another danger of using unproven superlatives in marketing. Since many products change rapidly, competitors may make their products better or faster during the time it takes your company to conceive, produce, and distribute the ad (which often takes months — an eternity in high-tech industries). Moreover, most publications have a *shelf-life* of at least a month. As a result, it could be several months after the superlative was first used that a prospect will get to *consume* your message. By that time, the superlative *best*, *fastest*, or *biggest* may no longer be true. While your company never intended to lie, the end result is the same as if you did.

Another reason for avoiding superlatives is *psychological*. If buyers know you are the best, they'll question why you're having to restate it in your ad. They will tend to think you are insecure, and this is not good for your image. If they don't know, they'll wonder why they haven't heard it before. This kind of wondering causes hesitation in buying.

Summary of Advertising Do's and Don'ts.

When creating advertising, marketers should follow the guidelines set forth below.

Advertising Do's.

1. *Know your product and your business.* If you don't know it, it will be hard to communicate it to an ad agency or to your target market segments.
2. *Do some market research to determine how best to reach your market targets.* This does not have to be sophisticated or expensive research. You can simply investigate the kinds of media your key prospects consume, their likes and dislikes, and their "hot buttons". You can find this information simply by asking or surveying them, looking in SRDS (Standard Rate and Data Service), or asking media sources for audience profiles.
3. *Tell the truth.* Lying or exaggerating will only get you and your company into trouble in the long run, if it doesn't in the short run.
4. *Focus on specific targets.* The message should be directed to a specific audience. It should not try to be *all things to all people*.
5. *Keep the message simple (KISS principle).* The simpler the better. Complex messages don't get into the prospect's mind. Prospects "*shut off*" either because they don't understand the message or they're more attracted to other simpler messages.
6. *Say one thing at a time.* In addition to keeping the message simple, communicate one idea at a time. More often than not, communicating more than one at a time will weaken the chances of each one getting into the minds of prospects.
7. *Your message should appeal to market targets.* Many companies select messages that they like, but ignore the likes and dislikes of target audiences. Since the market targets are the buyers and company personnel are already *sold*, the messages should appeal to the market targets. Messages that communicate benefits — i.e. what your product will do for them — are the most effective.
8. *Always be positive.* Positive messages put buyers in a positive, buying frame of mind.

9. *Grab their attention.* Create a message that is clever, attractive, creative, and simple enough to grab their attention.

10. *Get into their minds to create interest, a decision, and action.* After you catch their attention, you get into their minds by answering an objection, solving a problem, or pushing a "hot button" to get them interested enough to decide to buy your product.

11. *Stay in their minds.* Advertising works by repetition. It has a cumulative effect.

12. *Make sure all ads have a look of quality.* Quality ads reflect well on your company and products. Fewer and smaller high-quality ads are usually better than larger, more frequent low-quality ads.

Advertising Don'ts

1. *Don't use negatives.* Negatives cause buyers to question and hesitate. This does not mean you can't use the word "no", but it does mean that you shouldn't use it in a negative context.

2. *Don't be offensive to any group*. Be sensitive, and avoid offending anyone, particularly on issues of race, religion, gender, sexual orientation, national origin, body size and shape, intelligence, politics and other sensitive topics.

3. *Don't "bad-mouth" competition.* You can use comparisons as long as you provide proof, but don't disparage of competitors.

4. *Don't use unproven superlatives such as "best."* You can use other words that give the same impression, but avoid superlatives. However, you can and should use them if you provide verifiable proof from objective sources.

Keeping these *"Do's and Don'ts"* in mind is very important for developing successful advertising. However, to create an effective ad, another piece of advertising knowledge is required — the *structure of a good ad.*

Structure of a Good Advertisement

Good ads sell your company and products. To consistently create good ads, it is helpful to follow a definite structure. Because this structure universally applies to all marketing, it has been named the *Universal Marketing Structure*™, or the *UMS*™, by the author of this book, who recognized the pattern and created the structure. The UMS has the following sections — each with its own function and purpose.

Headline. The headline should contain the main benefits of the communication. If it does not, it should at least entice the reader, viewer, or listener to receive the main benefits in another part of the communication. It should have a "*hook*" that "*catches and pulls*" market targets into the communication. It should be truthful and concise, position the product, and identify the target audience. The reason it's a good idea to put the main message of the communication in the headline is that studies show that *five times* as many people read the headline as read, or pay attention to, the other parts. For the same reason, it's often a good idea to put the name of the product and the company in the headline — especially for products and companies that are *not* well-known.

Photo or Graphic. As expressed in the cliché, *a picture is worth a thousand words.* Therefore, if a picture or graphic is used in a communication, you should make sure that the message conveyed reinforces rather than detracts from the main message of the piece. A good use of a photo or graphic is one in which the main message is made more tangible, or understandable. The photo or graphic should make the product look as good as possible. It should reinforce the chosen *Position* of the product and the *Corporate Image* of the company. A photo or graphic can also help to reference the size of the product, or function as a graphical element that breaks the text up into "bite-sized pieces" so that the reader won't "choke" while trying to absorb all the information. A bad use of a photo or graphic is one that conflicts with the main message of the piece, confuses the reader, or adversely affects the product's or the company's image.

The Body. The body of the communication should support the headline and offer clearly-stated *benefits* of the product that summarize, explain, and clarify any listed features. It should focus on the main message presented in the headline and not introduce awkwardly distracting or unrelated messages. It should be concise, read and flow like a story.

Close. The Close has four important functions to perform as described below.

1. *Reinforce the headline.* Since the headline typically contains the most important message of the piece, the close should reinforce this message because it is the last thought left with the reader.

2. *Solicit a buying action.* All communications should ask readers, listeners, or viewers to take an action that will lead them to an eventual purchase. For example, it might ask the reader to call a toll-free number for more information, stop in to see the product at a local dealer, send in a coupon, visit a Web site, buy before the end of the month, or take some other buying action.

3. *End the piece.* People feel uncomfortable when a communication ends abruptly without a proper conclusion. Some people even get mad when a favorite song or program is interrupted with a commercial, news flash, or some other unexpected interruption. The same is true of ads or marketing pieces. To avoid making prospects feel uncomfortable, confused, or angry, the close should end the piece — unless of course, a "cliffhanger" ending is deliberately intended to build interest in the next edition of a series.

4. *Marketing Information System mechanism.* All marketing communications should prompt the prospect to respond in some positive way. When the prospect does respond, the company needs to identify the source of the response so it knows which messages are working and which are not. Therefore, all ads or marketing pieces need to have a mechanism built-in to facilitate this measurement. Examples of a marketing information system (MIS) mechanism include a code on a business reply card, a specific extension attached to a toll-free phone number, or an operator asking a caller "Where did you here about us?" In each case, the ideal is to identify the exact medium that prompted the response. For a publication, the code should tell the company the publication name, page, issue date, and other relevant information. Of course, the problem with relying on the phone answerer to ask the caller "Where did you hear about us?" is that either the phone answerer might forget to ask the question or the prospect might forget where he or she heard. The solution is proper training or using a more automatic mechanism in the piece.

Layout or Format. The layout of the piece should be designed to facilitate communication of its main message and recognize that all prospects are either busy or lazy. It should help to make the piece attractive and alluring, be clean and uncluttered, and have highlighted (boldfaced, bulleted, or italicized) sub-headlines so the reader has the option of focusing on certain points or reading the entire piece. It should have the look of quality. Cheap-looking ads cause readers to question the quality of products and the sophistication of the company. In English-speaking cultures, it should read left to right and top to bottom, and it should be easy to follow. Every consumer of the piece should be fed the information in the sequence and with the emphasis that was intended by the advertiser.

Signature. The signature of the piece is usually represented by the company's (or product's) name, logo and slogan. Similar to a signature on a letter, the signature of the communication proudly takes responsibility for it by signing the company's (or product's) name. It also helps to graphically frame the ad, and to formally tell the reader that he/she has reached the end. In addition to the company name and logo, the signature may also include a slogan that consistently positions the product or company in the minds of buyers.

Intangibles. There are many other elements that can facilitate the communication. Colors, types fonts, shapes, creativity, uniqueness are just some of them. These elements make the communication something extraordinary. They make it more attractive, entertaining, and enjoyable. They are called intangibles here because many of them are difficult to isolate, measure, and repeat with certainty. This is why creative professionals are hired to create ads. Some have a knack for creating marketing communications that attract customers and increase sales.

The best ones, however, use some system such as the UMS™. David Ogilvy, the legendary head of the *Ogilvy Mather* ad agency whom *Time Magazine* called "the most sought-after wizard in the advertising business," says in his book *Ogilvy on Advertising*, "The silly thing is that there are just about infallible formulae for constructing advertisements..."[1]

In-House Advertising vs. Using an Ad Agency

Marketers often have to decide between doing their own in-house advertising and using an outside ad agency or marketing firm.

The factors that point to doing advertising yourself include those listed below.

Good in-house talent. If you are fortunate enough to have talented marketers, copywriters and graphic artists along with the proper equipment, you have the capability to do much of your own advertising.

High volume. Having high volumes of advertising helps to justify hiring the proper talent and acquiring the necessary equipment to do in-house advertising.

Important to retain control. In-house advertising is often the only choice if a product is classified, proprietary or if there is some other reason why it is important to retain close control over inside knowledge about the product.

Difficult to find an Ad Agency to understand the product. With high-tech products, in particular, it is often difficult to find a marketing firm or agency that understands the product well enough to properly advertise it. The disappointing performance of most high-tech advertising is too often the result of this dilemma. The ads are typically written by either (1) technical people who understand the product but don't communicate well or (2) creative people who communicate well but aren't technical enough to understand the product. If an agency that has the capabilities to understand high-tech products cannot be found, it is sometimes preferable to develop communications in *house* or look for specialized consultants to bridge the gap.

Maintain better cost controls. Doing advertising in-house usually enables you to maintain better control over costs. Although many ad agencies will give fixed price estimates, very few of the good ones will commit to them. If you are able to obtain a fixed fee commitment from an agency, make *extra* sure that the fixed fees cover *all advertising costs* for the project including materials, printing, folding, delivery, etc.

The circumstances under which use of an Advertising Agency is preferable include the following:

You don't have advertising talent. If you don't have professional advertising talent on staff and you don't have the resources to hire such talent, you have to go outside for your advertising.

You need and want objectivity. Outside advertising talent gives you objectivity that is difficult to achieve with in-house sources. Staff talent is often constrained by internally popular ideas and management pressures that hinder objectivity.

Influx of new, creative ideas. Ad agencies often bring with them an influx of new and creative ideas that come from their full-time exposure to others in the advertising business.

Shift responsibility for mistakes. In political environments, it is often useful to blame an outside agency for ad campaigns that don't work. It is also sometimes politically and psychologically easier to switch ad agencies than it is to fire your own people when a campaign does not achieve the desired results.

It's Best to Share Advertising Responsibility

Advertising works best when your company shares advertising duties with an outside agency. Since agencies are expensive, they should be given tasks that they do best while your company does the rest. For example, if your company has a good ad copywriter who understands the product better than the agency, it will be best served by having him or her write the copy (subject to review by the agency) and having the agency execute the graphics, ad production and placement in selected media. They've got the equipment, the access, the experience, and the time to do the professional art and graphics required for formal brochures and media ads. They may not, however, have sufficient technical understanding to write ad copy without significant input and a large time investment from your company.

A close working relationship between your company's marketing personnel and the ad agency will produce the best results. It is important for the *senior marketing people* in your company to *have final say* over the work done by the ad agency. The ad agency should *not* be given "free reign" to do whatever it wants. Firstly, "*free reign*" is never free. Secondly, in the absence of constraints, many ad agencies let creativity overshadow the company's main marketing objectives and exceed budgets. The output of the agency must be "*in-synch*" with the marketing goals of the company as expressed in the marketing plan.

Guidelines for Selecting an Advertising Agency or Outside Marketing Firm

Even before your company has the resources or desire to hire an ad agency, it should begin the process of looking for one. The reasons for this are (1) it takes time to find the right one, and (2) your company should be ready to move forward in a hurry once the assistance of an ad agency is needed.

The following should be considered in selecting an ad agency:

Track record. Does the agency have a successful track record? You should obtain and call references. If it doesn't, you might want to give them a chance, but you should get something in return such as lower fees, more personal attention, or some other benefit for taking the risk.

High-tech experience. If you have a high-tech product, you should determine if the agency has any high-tech experience. In particular, you want to know if the copywriters on staff have sufficient technical backgrounds to comprehend the technical complexities of your company's products. If they don't, you might end up with advertising that is good at selling soap, but flops with high-technology goods and services.

Industry experience. Does the agency have a track record in your industry? If not, are they willing to learn about your industry without charging you for their education? In the absence of a track record that makes you comfortable, the agency should be willing to invest in learning your industry without squandering your resources.

Understand your business. During your interviews, has the agency demonstrated an understanding of your business and uniqueness? They should. If they don't, you might give them another chance, but you probably want to look further.

Comfort. How comfortable are you with the people with whom you will be working? If you are not comfortable at the outset, it won't get any better later on. To have a good working relationship, you should be comfortable with the agency people with whom you will working very closely.

Ability to Control. Will you be able to control the actions of the ad agency, or do they demand complete control? You have to retain control even if you trust the agency implicitly. After all, it's your company, your products, your reputation, and your money. On the other hand, if you don't really understand marketing very well, you might want to defer *some* creative control to the agency. Better yet do some reading. You might want to read a book I wrote entitled *Creating Your Own Marketing Makes Good $ and Sense*. Another good one is David Ogilvy's book *Ogilvy on Advertising* referred to earlier in this chapter. Also, you might want to take a course on marketing or advertising from a local college, university, or professional trade organization.

Trial Relationship. Whichever agency you choose, you should let the relationship develop slowly. Suggest a trial period during which you start your relationship with one or two small projects. Based on the success or failure of these projects, you can decide what additional relationship, if any, you wish to develop.

How much advertising should you do?

No matter how much advertising you do, *you can never do enough*. In light of the fact that all companies have limited resources, you should start out with a budget that provides at least the minimal coverage you need to achieve the goals of your marketing plan.

CPM

As discussed in *Step 4* of a previous section of this chapter on "Selecting Advertising Media," one logical way to compare and budget for advertising placement costs is by comparing the *CPM's* of your various advertising alternatives. This concept can be extended to include all marketing costs — development as well as placement — for each insertion of an ad. Furthermore, the CPM, or cost per reaching 1,000 of your targeted prospects, can be used to compare all promotional costs. The only caution here is that some promotional costs may yield qualitative as well as quantitative benefits. An example of a qualitative benefit might be the boost in *Corporate Image*, or prestige, derived from advertising in a top-quality publication or on a popular TV program. These qualitative benefits should be considered when evaluating your advertising mix.

MIS

From the start, you should have a *marketing information system* in place to measure the effectiveness of your advertising so that you can repeat and expand those strategies that prove to be effective and curtail or revise those that don't.

Advertising Budget

Many companies base their advertising budget on a percentage of projected sales. Depending on the industry, the competition, and a variety of other factors, a budget between 5 and 10 percent of projected sales is a useful place to start. Others set aside a higher percentage of projected sales — especially during the start-up phases of new companies and the introduction of new products. Leading consumer marketing companies have very large advertising budgets. For example, in 1996, *Procter & Gamble* spent nearly $2.8 billion on domestic advertising, which represented roughly 16.3% of domestic sales, nearly 8% of worldwide sales, and almost 92% of worldwide earnings. Typically, the Company spends roughly 10% of projected sales on advertising. This number was approximately $3.4 billion by year 2000.

Initial outlays for advertising should be based on the amount required to sufficiently cover the marketplace to meet marketing plan goals. After the initial outlay, the effectiveness of the various advertising strategies should be measured using your Marketing Information System. Based on these measurements, strategies should be revised in an effort to improve advertising performance on the *next iteration*. That is, those strategies that have produced results (leads, sales, and profits) should be fortified while those that have not should be modified or eliminated after you have analyzed why they didn't work.

In summary, to help determine the right mix and amount of advertising, an interactive process should be followed which involves the following steps:

1. Creating messages and selecting media to properly cover the marketplace.
2. Monitoring and measuring results.
3. Analyzing results to determine the reasons for successes and failures.
4. Revising strategies and budgets to create more successes and avoid failures over the next marketing cycle.

Step 1 above has been covered in these sections on advertising. *Steps 2* through *4* will be given more attention in a subsequent chapter on the *Marketing Information System*. The important point to remember is that with each implementation of advertising strategy, mechanisms have to be put in place to monitor results and prompt corrective action. With this in mind, it is useful to move on to discussions of the other promotional strategies.

SEMINARS

Seminars are a very effective way to promote your products — especially if they are high-tech. They provide an excellent forum for:

- Educating prospects on the features and benefits of products.
- Tailoring a program to address the specific needs of a particular target market segment.
- Providing an opportunity for one skilled presenter to "sell to" many prospects at one time.
- Giving the presenter sufficient time to explain the key benefits and differentiators.
- Soliciting testimonial references from happy customers or clients.
- Attracting qualified prospects — if they take time from their busy schedule to attend the seminar, they are most likely very interested.

Preparation

To help insure the success of the seminar, careful planning and preparation should be employed. The following steps provide useful time sequence to follow:

Select the Seminar Topic

The topic should be selected and *positioned* so as to generate sufficient interest and attendance. It should be aimed at your target audience. For example, a seminar for Internet service providers, laboratory scientists who specialize in DNA testing, surgeons whose areas of expertise is cosmetic laser surgery, or video editors who do special effects for television commercials.

Select a Date and Time

Date: The seminar should be scheduled at a date and time that is convenient for target prospects. Care should be given to select a date that does not conflict with holidays, trade shows, fiscal year end closings, or normal "days off" for target prospects. For example, Wednesdays are bad for many doctors because many traditionally take that day off.

Duration: Shorter duration seminars are often more effective than all-day seminars. Firstly, it's difficult for most prospects to commit time to sitting in a seminar all day. Secondly, most people get restless after an hour or two (most movies are cut to between 90 and 120 minutes for that reason). Thirdly, prospects prefer a focused and concise presentation to one that takes all day (but which could have been done within two hours).

Day of Week: Usually, seminars should avoid Mondays and Fridays. Mondays are important "getting started" or "recovering from weekend" days. Moreover, many people tend to be in bad moods on Monday. Friday is the beginning of the weekend so many people have their minds on weekend plans and would have a difficult time concentrating on seminar presentations. That leaves days in the middle of the week — Tuesday, Wednesday and Thursday. Assuming it doesn't conflict with special industry meetings, Tuesday is probably best because prospects are less likely to schedule social plans on Tuesday than later in the week. Also, it gives three more days during the week for sales personnel to follow up on the interests generated in the seminar and to keep them "*hot*." This is essential because weekends have a tendency to "*cool off*" prospects and wipe their memories clean from the previous week. If possible, duplicate seminars might be scheduled for another "middle day" of the week in the event that serious prospects have other commitments on Tuesdays.

Time: The best times for short duration seminars are very early in the morning, late afternoon, or early evening before dinner. During these time periods, the prospect misses the least amount of productive work time, and does not have to miss dinner. Of course, this may not be a good time for some businesses. The key is to find out what is the best time for your target audience.

Select a Location

If company offices are attractive and convenient, they are one of the best locations — particularly if you are selling products that are not easy to transport. In your offices, you are in your own territory. You know where everything is located; you know how to "*work around*" problems that arise; and you have support people readily available if any equipment should malfunction during the seminar.

If offices are not attractive and convenient, you might want to consider renting a banquet room at a hotel that satisfies the above criteria. Depending on the geographical spread of prospects' offices, good locations are usually near airports, freeway intersections, and any other known and easily accessible landmarks. Late afternoon traffic patterns should also be considered when making the selection and setting the times.

Often a good location strategy is to hold the seminar at the "*nicely appointed*" offices of a happy customer or client. The customer can serve as a testimonial for your product and can show the seminar attendees how he/she is actually using the product. However, you should be sensitive to any competitive problems that this might create between different prospects. In some cases, the hosting customer may not want competitors wandering around his/her facility. In others, some competitors may feel uncomfortable visiting other competitors.

Invitations

Once all the details of subject, time and location are determined, you should have invitations printed. Engraved or printed invitations on quality "invitation-style" panel cards are most effective. Some companies are finding even greater success with a "new" technique — that of printing invitations on postcards that have an attractive picture on the other side. They claim that, with an attractive post card, prospects are more likely to attend and less likely to throw away the card — even after the event has been held.

Invitations should contain the pertinent information: Subject, date, time, location, whether or not food and drinks will be served, and instructions to R.S.V.P. to a specific person and phone number by a specific date. Any parking, elevator, or other special instructions should be enclosed with (but probably not included on) the invitation.

Food and Drinks

Arrangements should be made in accordance with caterer lead times for food and drinks. Lavish, expensive food is not required for a successful seminar. Of course, the food and drinks selected are likely to have an impact on your corporate image.

Mailing

Invitations should be mailed so that they arrive on the desk of the prospects no later than *two weeks* before the date of the seminar, with *three weeks being preferable* in some cases. This means that they should be mailed no later than three weeks before the date of the seminar. Less than two weeks notice creates calendar conflicts, more than three weeks increases the likelihood that prospects will forget about the seminar or its importance.

Whenever possible, stamps should be affixed to the envelopes. Secretaries are more likely to forward stamped envelopes than those that have the "*mass-produced*" look of bulk mail, although a stamp machine is an acceptable alternative in most cases.

R.S.V.P.

Instructions to RSVP are important. If food is being served, the instruction should ask for an RSVP no later than a week in advance of the seminar. It is best to have prospects RSVP to a specific person and phone number. In addition to making the process more personal, that person can better maintain an accurate list of those who have responded. The respondent's name, company name, and phone number should be recorded on the list. This is important for reconfirmation of attendance at the seminar, future follow-up, notification of changes or cancellations, and *sign-in* on the date of the seminar.

Follow up

Follow up is essential to successful attendance at the seminar. You will find that respondents who've RSVP'd that they will attend often need reminding or coaxing. Sales people should follow up at least once — one or two days before the seminar to reconfirm attendance. During the follow-up process, sales people can also "*flush out*" competitors posing as legitimate prospects. Every effort should be made to politely weed out competitors before the seminar because they can and will try to steal your prospects or disrupt your seminar if you let them.

The sales people should also use the follow-up opportunity to build *relationships* with prospects and to find out what they want from the seminar.

Rehearsal

The roles of each of the people involved in the seminar should be clearly delineated. If possible, a "walk through" rehearsal should be conducted to insure that everything is coordinated properly and that the props and equipment are in good working order. You'd be amazed at how many problems and mistakes are avoided by this walk through. Remember the more you prepare and plan, the more the prospects will be impressed with you and your company.

Seminar Presentation

After proper planning and preparation, the following steps should be followed to conduct a successful seminar.

Greeting and Screening

On the day of the seminar, properly-trained reception personnel should be assigned to welcome attendees and make sure that they either sign a guest book with their name and other key contact information or provide a business card with this information on it. Greeters should have welcoming and friendly personalities, but they should not be afraid to enforce procedures that turn away competitors and others who should not be at the seminar — politely explaining the reasons. After the seminar, your sales staff will use the information collected for follow up, and your marketing department will use it to measure the success of the seminar. If the information is incomplete or improperly collected, it will waste valuable time and cause your marketing and sales personnel to not trust such information in the future.

Presentation Folders

Your marketing department should prepare an information package that contains information about the company, products, publicity and awards, and a seminar agenda or outline. This should be given to attendees as they sign in.

Presentation

The presenter, or presenters, should be knowledgeable, confident, and skillful at speaking, but *not* be too polished. Speakers that are too polished give a plastic, unreal, and "*canned*" appearance that raises questions about their sincerity. Presenters should command the interest and attention of the audience by being sharp, concise and clear in their presentation. They should be responsive to questions from the audience, but shouldn't allow any attendees to dominate the floor. Speakers must retain control at all times. Giving competent presentations are aided by guidelines known as the *8 Be's of Successful Presentations*. These guidelines are summarized below and can be more easily remembered by the acronym PRESENTS.

1. **Be Prepared.** Knowledge and preparation form the basic foundation for a successful presentation. It is best to prepare the questions you are going to ask in advance and make sure everything you use to demonstrate the product, or give the presentation, works. Also be prepared for failure. Have a backup strategy if something does not work, and know exactly what you are going to say. The speaker should use the situation to his or her advantage

rather than become flustered. Attendees tend to think that the way you handle a difficult and unpleasant situation is similar to the way you will react to their problems during your business relationship.

2. **Be Results-focused.** Prospects are interested in the *benefits* your product will provide them. Of course, it is best to always translate benefits into time and money if at all possible. Time and money are the most tangible benefits that prospects can most easily understand and believe.

3. **Be Exciting.** Think of how you can add something to your presentation to make it exciting. The first sentence out of your mouth should really grab the prospect's attention and get them interested.

4. **Be Succinct.** Prospects are either busy or lazy. Consequently, they don't want you to waste their time. While you need to cover important product benefits that satisfy their needs, you want to stress the "hot-button" bullet points and forget the boring details — unless, of course, the audience specifically requests them. A good guiding principle is "*when it doubt, cut it out*." Also, it is a rule that the higher the position of prospects in their organizations, the less detail they want in a presentation or demonstration.

5. **Be Educational.** Prospects take their time to listen to your presentation because they want to learn something. It is therefore up to you to teach them what they believe is important. Without having any specific intelligence on the attendees, you can assume that they are all interested in issues that improve their performance, make their lives easier and more enjoyable, save them time, and make them money.

6. **Be Newsworthy.** Most people like new things. Therefore, to grab and maintain their attention, your presentation should be newsworthy. If there is nothing really new about your product, you can (1) introduce them to a new use of your product, or (2) relate your product to a newsworthy item that is of interest to them.

7. **Be To the point.** Since you can be succinct in your presentation but wander from the main topic, it is important to stick to the main points in your presentation — those points that the prospects feels are important. Focus will keep their attention. Wandering will lose them.

8. **Be Seated.** This is just another reminder to keep your presentation as brief as possible. Just as football teams practice two-minute drills, you should have 2, 5, 10, and 15-minute versions of your presentation. Moreover, you should practice delivering your presentation with a stop watch to insure that you stay within these time frames. In some cases, you may need to deliver longer presentations, but you should let the prospect initiate them.

Sales Assistance

Before, during and after the seminar, sales personnel should be stationed at convenient places in the room to answer any questions that arise or to help the presenter with any props used in the presentation.

At the end of the presentation, the presenter should introduce the sales people and encourage prospects to ask them specific questions as well as enjoy the food and drinks.

Clean Up

If the seminar is presented in the company's offices, arrangements should be made for clean up so that the facility is in presentable condition for the next day's work. Marketing *good impressions* don't end with the seminar. Bad impressions can do a lot of unwanted and unintended damage.

Follow-Up

After the seminar, follow up is critical. In fact, it is best for sales people to schedule the next step (which may be a phone call or face-to-face demonstration) with prospects before they leave. To this end, sales people should have their appointment books and *lead cards* (see *Figure 9-2* for a sample lead card) handy so they can record the next step to be taken. It's best to "*strike while the iron is hot*." Prospects cool off after they leave a seminar or demonstration and get colder as more time passes. Therefore, even if it is not possible to schedule the *next step* on the day of the seminar, sales people should call the next day to find out prospect reactions, answer any questions, and schedule that next step.

Lead Card

ENCORE VIDEO INDUSTRIES

Name: ____________________ ***Date:*** ________

Position: ____________________

Firm: ____________________

Address: ____________________

____________________ ***Zip:*** ________

Business phone ________ ***Other phone*** ________

Comments: Degree of Interest: Hot___ Warm___ Cool___

Where did you hear about us?

☐ newsletter ________
☐ show ________
☐ sales call ________
☐ magazine ________
☐ word of mouth ________
☐ seminar/speech ________
☐ mailing ________
☐ other ________

System Type

☐ EPR
☐ PRISM
☐ FVS 100
☐ other ________

Front

Follow-Up History

Date of Contact | Action Taken | Objections/Interests/Next Step

Back

Figure 9-2

Some companies do a good job of conducting seminars. Fewer do a good job of follow-up. Without follow-up, the efforts invested in the seminar will largely by wasted.

Seminar Summary

Seminars are one of the most effective ways of promoting products that require some education of the prospect before a sale is likely to be made. More than media advertising, they enable companies to focus on specific market targets, and they provide a good forum for educating and selling many prospects with a single coordinated presentation by the company's most effective presenters.

TRADE SHOWS

Trade shows can be a very effective source of new business. They use the marketing principle of *cumulative attraction* to draw large numbers of prospects. Cumulative attraction is the principle by which *many companies located close together will draw larger audiences than the same companies separated by some distance*. Prospects are attracted by the opportunity to find out about the products of many different companies without spending the time and effort to travel between their offices. Moreover, prospects can conveniently comparison shop and make quicker buying decisions. Many auto retailers understand this principle. That's why they often locate their showrooms in close proximity to each other.

Shows that target specific niches are particularly effective for technical companies whose products have been developed for these niches.

Objectives

There are many good reasons for a company to participate in a trade show. Some of the more important ones are provided below.

Sales

The ultimate objective of any trade show is to generate sales. While some trade shows allow customers to actually buy products at the show, many ones do not. Whether or not the trade show permits customers to walk away with the actual goods displayed, sales are often *closed* at trade shows.

Leads

In the absence of making sales at the show, the next best objective is to obtain *leads* that will hopefully turn into sales. Sales people working the show should have a sufficient number of blank l*ead cards* (see *Figure 9-2*) on which they can staple prospects' business cards. If the prospect does not furnish a business card, the sales person should make sure that they fill in the necessary information on the lead card, making sure to note the *next step* on the back.

If the show is very busy with heavy traffic, the sales person should have clever ways to avoid spending too much time with any one prospect. If the sales person senses that the prospect is very "*hot*" and insists on spending time asking questions, the sales person should spend the time. As the saying goes, "*a bird in the hand is worth two in the bush*." Also, you don't want to lose prospects that visit competitors after leaving your booth.

However, if you spend too much time with one prospect, you may lose many others who also may be "hot." Therefore, the preferred strategy is for the sales person to use the show to obtain leads, and to schedule appointments with those "*hot*" prospects at a more convenient time away from the hectic and distracting environment of the show.

Image

In addition to making sales and generating leads, an important objective of participation in a trade show is to spread the company name and enhance its image. Companies who don't attend important trade shows miss opportunities to drive their *name* and *position* in the minds of attendees. If they are known, they are conspicuous by their absence. If they are not, they are less likely to become known.

Find Employees

Shows attract many of a company's publics in addition to prospects and customers. It is sometimes a good source of generating media attention, finding employees, vendors, and other groups of people who can help your company. Therefore, the sales people and others who have booth duty should be trained as to how to properly handle *non-prospect* inquiries. The most impressive and successful companies always give the impression they are always prepared.

Trade Show Do's

There are proper and inappropriate ways of participating in trade shows. Some of the more important "Trade Show Do's" are presented in the following paragraphs.

Select a Great Location

The marketer who is responsible for making trade show arrangements should select the *best location* possible. This involves having a location strategy, and reserving the selected location as early as possible. Depending on the company's strategy, the "*best*" location will vary. For example, a company with superior, well-positioned products may want to locate next to its largest competitors. A company may want to locate next to the industry leader to get the "*spillover*" or walk-by traffic that the leader generates. On the other hand, a smaller company may want to avoid being next to an industry leader for fear of being overshadowed and overlooked. A company whose products work with those of another company may want to be next to that company. A company that cannot afford to have a large "*island-style*" booth, may want good visibility at the intersection of two isles. Because there are so many factors and considerations, it may take some experimentation to discover the "*best location strategy*" for your company. Thinking about it, considering all the factors, and applying some logic will usually put you ahead of your competitors.

Train and Rehearse

As with seminars, it is important to properly prepare people who are going to participate in the show. Yet, few companies do this properly. It is important that the objectives of the show and the procedures to achieve those objectives are discussed and rehearsed. It is an important detail that should be part of the company's show marketing strategy.

Assign and schedule trade show duties

Everyone assigned to participate in the show should be provided with a *booth-duty* schedule that coordinates booth duty, breaks, and visits to competitor booths. Prior to the show, the show manager should obtain a copy of the show directory, highlight key competitors and vendors, and assign each participant to visit a fair number of them when they are not working in the booth. When visiting competitors, they should be instructed to pick up competitive literature and to find out as much as they can about competitive products. As part of the *Marketing Information System*, each participant and attendee should turn in a report that summarizes the strengths, weaknesses, new product offerings, and other important information for each of their assigned competitors. This will help them learn more about competitive products as well as collect valuable information for your company.

Create a Booth to Enhance Your Corporate Image

The first "thing" prospects and other publics will notice about the company at a trade show is your booth. Therefore, careful attention should be given to the design of your booth. It should be both attractive and make people feel comfortable. If the company has a limited budget, a smaller high-quality booth is preferable to a big one that makes the wrong impression. A classy, good-looking booth can be made from low-cost, lightweight panels combined with decorative items such as live plants and furniture.

As with all marketing instruments, the booth should be positioned to create the correct image of the company and to get the company's message into the minds of its key publics.

Therefore, well-positioned, benefit-focused headlines that include your product and company names should be prominently displayed on the most visible parts of your booth. If you walk any trade show, you will be amazed at how *poorly* most booths communicate. There is a simply test to determine if your booth is working for you. If people who walk by know what your company and products do for them (without asking you), your booth is working. If not, your personnel will have to waste their valuable time explaining this over and over again, and you will lose this benefit of communicating these important points to all those who walk by and are unable to talk with your booth staff.

Get Business Cards

It is important to obtain business cards from booth visitors and affix them to company lead cards. It's especially critical to obtain correct names, phone numbers, fax numbers, company names, and addresses. Nothing is more frustrating than having a “hot” lead with no way to follow up. Business cards also serve to uncover competitors posing as prospects.

Fill out lead cards

In those cases where booth visitors claim to have run out business cards, you can have them provide their information on lead cards. Even if prospects produce their business cards, they should be affixed to *lead cards* so you can capture other important information such as notes on the products in which they are interested, their degree of interest, appointment date and time, the next step, objections, competition information, new product suggestions, and other pertinent data.

Dress for Success

While your booth should make a good first impression, the impressions made by personnel in your booth are even more important. Men and women should both wear professionally-tailored suits. For men, white or blue solid-color shirts are preferable. It is important to remember that everything and everybody representing the company affects the company's image. Professional duty at a trade show, or in the office, is not the appropriate time to make personal fashion statements or exercise personal freedoms. It is a time to impress people, and to make the job of selling and earning sales commissions as easy as possible. The old cliché *you never get a second chance to make a first impression* is good to remember.

Follow up

It is important for senior marketing professionals to make sure that the sales people properly follow up on leads generated by trade shows. This usually involves meeting with the

Sales Manager and determining a follow-up strategy. It also requires that a manager follows up on the *follow-up* to insure that it is being done properly.

Measuring Results

As with all marketing strategies, the success of each trade show should be measured so that you can decide whether or not to participate in the same show again. Leads, presentations, and sales resulting from show contacts should be measured and reported by the sales staff to a senior marketing (or trade show) manager. The specific mechanisms for doing this will be covered in *Chapter 11* on the *Marketing Information System*.

Trade Show Don'ts

There are many "things" you should not do at trade shows. Some of the more important ones are summarized below.

Don't Waste Precious Time

Too many show visitors who are not serious buyers will waste your time. They include competitors, vendors who are interested in selling something to your company, and "looky loos," who visit lots of trade shows but rarely buy anything. They can and will take valuable time away from qualified prospects. Always be polite, but find a nice way to explain that you cannot spend too much time with them at the show. Weed them out, or test their interest, by offering to set up a meeting with them after the show. You can explain that there are too many distractions at the show to devote the attention they deserve. It is best to set up an appointment next week when the show is over so that you can efficiently concentrate on properly satisfying their needs. Also, ask for their business cards. If they don't have them, ask them to fill out lead cards. This usually *flushes out* the competitors and *looky loos* because they either don't want you to know who they are, or they don't want to spend their time filling out a card because they are not serious buyers. It's ironic, they have no problem wasting your time, but they refuse to extend you the courtesy of providing the information you need.

Don't Disparage the Competition

While you should never make negative remarks about your competitors, a trade show provides a very compelling opportunity to do so. Avoid this opportunity. Feel free to compare your company's products to the competition, but do so in a factual and professional manner. Take the approach that their products are good but yours are better.

Don't Give Away Your Best "Stuff" At the Show

Save your best product literature and your best closing pitch for a more opportune time — unless of course you have a legitimate "hot" prospect. The best sales people get prospects interested at the show with less expensive introductory literature and information. They send additional more expensive collateral materials with a cover letter as a follow-up after the show, or they hand out this material during a subsequent appointment. They save the best literature for closing opportunities. There are several good and important reasons for following this strategy. They include the following:

1. Visitors to trade shows typically pick up plastic bags that are offered as promotional items by various vendors. They stuff your expensive literature in these bags along with free promotional gifts. When they return to their office or home, most keep the free gifts and throw out your expensive literature without ever reading it. Since your most expensive literature can cost several dollars a piece to produce and print, their actions are equivalent to throwing significant amounts of money in a waste basket. However, the biggest waste is not the lost money. It is the lost opportunity to introduce your products to them.

2. If legitimate prospects think that you have provided them with your best material, you may never have the opportunity to develop a relationship with them. They will simply visit your competitors trying to find products that outperform yours as described in your literature — without giving you the opportunity to explain why yours might be better.

3. Since show visitors are bombarded with so many different companies and products at a trade show, they are likely to forget who you are. This is analogous to being introduced to many new people at one time during a party. Most people rarely remember the names of the people at the party. After the party, memories fade more. The best way to get someone to remember you, your products, and your company is to (1) impress upon them the key benefits of your product that will satisfy their needs and (2) set up an appointment to meet with them after the show is over.

4. The trade show is analogous to a "one-night stand." That is, it is difficult to build serious business relationships with prospects after only a single, often hurried meeting. You have to provide them with the appropriate introduction, get them interested, and set up other meetings away from the distractions of the show to build the rapport needed for a serious business relationship. Sales, or relationships, that begin too quickly often end just as quickly.

WALK-INS

Many companies have a significant number of people from their various publics walk into company offices without an appointment. Rather than view these walk-ins as ambassadors who can help to spread the positive word about their company and products, most companies treat them as an unwanted interruption. It is true that they can be annoying — especially when they come in during a busy period — but they should be treated as potential buyers or ambassadors of good will. After all, companies spend a lot of money on advertising just to reach these important publics. When someone walks in to your office, it doesn't cost you anything to reach them. In fact, it costs very little — maybe a smile, a little politeness, and a cup of coffee — to make a good impression on them that, in turn, can generate positive word-of-mouth advertising.

The promotional strategies of the company, therefore, should have specific procedures for handling walk-ins. These procedures should include the following:

1. Greet them with courtesy, and determine what they want.
2. Find the most appropriate person(s) to speak with them.
3. If that person is busy, have his/her secretary or associate set up an appointment to meet at a later time.
4. Offer them coffee or other complimentary refreshments while they are waiting to speak with someone.
5. Don't make them wait for very long. The days of making people wait to indicate rank and importance are over (if they should have ever existed at all).
6. Make sure that they are treated as well as possible.
7. View them as an opportunity to win them over as a friend of the company and a source of free, positive word-of-mouth advertising.

Because of the way most companies treat walk-ins, the company who follows the above steps will positively distinguish or position itself as a *special* and *unique* company in the minds of walk-ins and other publics. As you will learn, the "word will get around" that your company is special — the one to buy from, work for, sell to, loan money to at favorable rates, buy stock in, and, in general, do business with.

WORD-OF-MOUTH ADVERTISING

Most companies are too passive with regard to generating referrals. Of course, they love to have them, but they do not do enough to get them. The following steps should be considered to encourage referrals.

Good Products and Service

The first steps in generating referrals are to (1) provide *good products* and (2) make sure that your products are provided with good customer service. You provide such good service to customers that they will tell their associates and friends without solicitation. Studies show that it is five times more expensive to find new customers as it is to sell to existing ones. In fact, every experienced marketer and sales person knows that "*Prospects = Costs whereas Customers = Profits*." This means that a marketer's efforts to convert prospects into customers can be quite costly whereas selling existing customers should be as simple as taking orders.

Rewards

The next step is to reward customers for referrals that turn into hot prospects or sales. It does not have to be monetary reward, such as a *finder's fee* or commission. The reward can be in the form of a *thank you* over the phone or e-mail, a thank-you note, flowers, a promotional gift, lunch, or dinner.

Incentives

An incentive is a bonus that is publicized to all customers and earned. That is, it is similar to "*frequent flyer*" incentives offered by the airlines or to a free wash for every 10 paid car washes. To make sure that customers don't misinterpret such incentives, the marketing department should be very careful in wording and publicizing them. For example, acceptable wording might be as follows: "As a special Holiday thank you, we are offering a gift certificate worth $50 to customers for each referral who buys our model 8200 laser printer in the month of December." Notice, this incentive is offered to all customers, and it is not excessive. Large incentives may backfire since some prospects might think your products are being recommended only because of the incentive offered.

Testimonials

Whenever customers say *nice things* about your company or products, you should ask them if they wouldn't mind putting their words in writing and sending them to you in a letter. For each testimonial, you should have them sign a *legal release* that allows your company to quote them in your marketing materials without charge to your company. Above all, make sure you thank them verbally and in writing and that you provide any other allowable promotional rewards, such as t-shirts and coffee mugs, that also serve to advertise your company and products. Some organizations don't allow their personnel to accept these.

In summary, referrals are a highly-effective way to market most products — especially in high-technology and industrial markets. Prospects are more likely to trust friends and associates than sales and marketing people who benefit from selling them products. Additionally, referrals can have a pyramid effect whereby each satisfied customer spreads the word to others who, in turn, do the same. Companies should actively participate in the referral process by taking extra good care of customers and by rewarding them in non-offensive ways for spreading the word to their friends and associates.

PUBLICITY

Good publicity is even more effective than good advertising. It has the air of objectivity. It is usually more believable. It is often better remembered, and it tends to prompt quicker buying actions.

Whenever possible, it should be quoted in company advertising. This will multiply the positive effect of the publicity and create even greater buyer awareness.

As with word-of-mouth referrals, publicity should be pursued actively. What steps should the marketing department take to foster positive publicity? The following list includes some of the most important ones.

Identify Media

The primary media that influence market targets should be identified and entered into a mailing list or data base. The essential information in this data base should include the following: The editor's name, technical editor's name, name of the media, mailing address, fax and phone number, e-mail address, Web address, circulation figures, and target audiences reached. Additional useful information might include the editor's birthday and any special comments about the media.

Establish Media Contacts

The marketing department should make an effort to meet with and get to know the editor, technical editor, and other key personnel who work for each of the media identified above. These media people should be invited to company functions receive company newsletters and general-purpose mailings.

Obtain Press Kits and Editorial Calendars

Most media offer press kits that include editorial calendars free of charge. These provide information on submission of materials (ads and articles) for publication. The editorial calendar will list the upcoming issues that will focus on special topics. Those issues with topics that correspond to your product areas are the ones you should target for your ads, press releases, and articles.

Send Press Releases at Regular Intervals

Press releases related to your products and achievements should be sent to the media list on a regular basis. If available and applicable, an 8 x 10 *glossy* photo of the product, key executives, your facilities, or special events should accompany each press release. If an article is written, the photo will serve to make the product more tangible as well as make the publicity more visible and effective.

Submit articles on your company and products

Good writers in the company should be identified and encouraged to write articles about your company and products. The marketing department should get these articles placed in the magazines on the media list — especially in those issues that focus on your areas of expertise. If your company does not have personnel to write articles, you can outsource this function. You should have a list of proven writers ready, inside and outside your company. You usually want to aim for an issue that is two or three months into the future since it will take that long to write and submit the article in time for publication deadlines.

Contact Broadcast Media

Worthy news items should be released to broadcast and online media. Products that are new, unusual, or revolutionary are good candidates for attracting interest from these media. If your company or products are featured in a Webcast, radio or TV broadcast, the program should be taped, duplicated, and distributed to sales and marketing people so they can use the publicity to interest new prospects and close sales.

Consider Hiring a Public Relations Firm

Consideration should be given to hiring a *public relations* firm for publicizing your company and products. A good PR firm can do wonders for a company who has newsworthy products if they have established contacts with the key media that your market targets frequent. The same criteria used for choosing an ad agency should be applied to the selection of a public relations firm.

Public Display

All positive publicity should be publicly displayed in the lobby and in the halls of company offices. The best articles should be permanently framed and displayed in areas that are frequently visited by your market targets.

Publicity should also be displayed in attractive *Portfolios* located in the lobby and other public gathering places. While prospects are waiting in the lobby to speak with someone from your company, they can browse through your publicity. The positive publicity that they see helps to sell them on your company and products. Reprints of particularly favorable articles should be made for dissemination to your publics.

These portfolios, or notebooks, should also be made available to sales personnel for use in their sales and closing presentations.

SALES PROMOTIONS

Sales promotions are *special offers* aimed at getting the prospects to buy and the resellers to sell your products quicker. They often involve a discount, rebate, bonus, coupon, or some "*giveaway*" for acting before a deadline or expiration date. They can be very effective at prompting buyers to purchase products sooner than they ordinarily would.

Types of Sales Promotions

There are many different kinds of Sales Promotions. The following is a representative list.

1. *Discounts.* A reduction in price is offered if the prospect orders within a certain period.
2. *Bonuses.* Bonuses in the form of options, accessories, upgrades, or supplies are included at no additional charge if the prospect purchases by a certain date.
3. *Giveaways.* An item such as a coffee mug, pen and pencil set, flashlight, or some other item is offered if a purchase is made within a definite time period. These *Specialty Advertising* items, as they are called, typically have the name, address and phone number of your company on them.
4. *Coupon Response.* A discount, free booklet, manual, training course, or some other product-related item is offered if a prospect sends in a coupon from an advertisement. Coupons are a good way of measuring the effectiveness of an ad, generating leads, and collecting other valuable information for your *Marketing Information System*.
5. *Rebates.* A portion of the purchase price is returned to the buyer if the product is purchased by a certain deadline.

Sales Promotion Do's

When running sales promotions, there are certain things that good marketers should do. Some of the more important are provided below.

Care and Taste

When selling high-tech or industrial products, sales promotions should be conducted with great care and taste. You should avoid any sales promotions that might appear to be "cheap," low-class, or in bad taste. Sales promotions should be in harmony with your *corporate image* and *positioning* strategies.

Communicate a Good Reason For Doing

There should be a good reason for doing a sales promotion, and this reason should be communicated clearly to your target audience. Good reasons include: inventory or seasonal clearance, holiday special, seminar special, show special, new product introduction, old model clearance, end-of-year clearance (to meet sales quotas or lower inventory taxes).

Assign a Time Limit

Most sales promotions should have a definite time limit associated with them. If not, the discounted price will become the new *de facto price*, and the company will never be able to go back to the suggested list price. If sales promotions prove to be very successful, they can always be extended. The reason for the extension should be clearly communicated to prospects and customers. For example, such reasons as "Due to the heavy demand...", "Because many customers didn't receive notice of the discount...", and "Since we still have a couple of older models remaining..." are logical reasons for extending promotion deadlines.

Sales Promotion Don'ts

When conducting sales promotions, there are many approaches that marketers should avoid. Some of the more important ones are provided below.

Don't do anything to cheapen the image of your product or company

A misguided sales promotion can hurt the image of your products and company. You should think through the ramifications and sample the opinions of trusted members of your target audience before implementing sales promotions.

Don't insult the intelligence of your publics

Many promotions are really insulting. They treat intelligent adults as if they were *mindless morons*. This won't work with professional, high-tech or industrial products. Sales promotions should not make you look foolish by alienating members of your target audience.

Don't make it open-ended

All sales promotions should have a time limit clearly stated in the media in which they are placed. This point also has a legal foundation. You don't want a customer calling up a year after the promotion ended and demanding the advertised discount because there was no time limit listed. Time limits avoid these potential legal problems.

Don't use bad taste

As with all marketing, good taste should be used in all sales promotions. If coffee mugs, pens, or calendars are given as "*free items*" they should be attractive and exude good taste. The ads that provide information about them should similarly be done tastefully.

NEWSLETTERS

Newsletters, in physical or electronic form, are a very effective and inexpensive way for a company to communicate with its various publics. They are particularly good for letting customers know about new products, specials, and company achievements as well as reminding them about current products.

Maintain Good Relations with Company Publics

Because it can be routinely sent to each and every customer and company stakeholder, the newsletter is perhaps your best vehicle for staying "*in touch*" with customers and other publics. It is well-suited for telling customers about new products, upgrades, add-ons, specials, operating tips, company achievements, customer successes, and any other company or product news.

More than any other promotional method, newsletters provide an avenue for your company to maintain an ongoing relationship with your publics. By providing them with "family" news, they make members of these publics feel as if they are part of your company's family. In this way, newsletters help to create unpaid company ambassadors and sales people for your organization.

Take Newsletters Seriously

Because of their importance to maintaining good relations, your company should take them seriously and make every effort to do a good job producing them. This means that they should be published at *regular intervals* (quarterly is a good frequency), and an editor, a staff of writers, and perhaps a photographer should be chosen from the company's pool of talent or outside sources.

Small Budget

It should be mentioned that the newsletter is one promotional piece that does not require outside professional execution. It contains news, and people are familiar with receiving news in black and white on newsprint. Furthermore, with the rapid changes characteristic of many products, most people prefer timely and accurate news to *old information* that is beautifully presented. In fact, some of the most coveted newsletters are inexpensively-reproduced copies of hand-typed sheets. Publishing them electronically can save you paper, printing mailing, and associated friction costs.

Make them Inexpensive not Cheap

Inexpensive is a good marketing word. *Cheap* is not. Rather than appear *cheap* and risk damaging your company's image, you can produce newsletters of near-professional quality with a relatively inexpensive personal computer-based desktop publishing system. In fact, newsletters produced in this way can be made to look even better than some that are produced professionally. Electronic versions can be made to look good with very little investment — especially if the creator of the newsletter understands some basic electronic publishing software.

Newsletters Summary

In summary, newsletters are an effective and inexpensive means for a company to "*stay in touch*" with its various publics — especially market targets. They should be published regularly, with quarterly being a good frequency. They can be *inexpensive*, but should not look "*cheap*."

NETWORKING

Analogous to word-of-mouth advertising, networking refers to activities designed for people to meet, form business relationships and refer business to each other.

The concept of networking is not new. It is an old form of promotion embodied in the many clubs and associations that have formed over many years. The idea is that it is preferable to do business with people you know and trust than those you don't know.

Joining clubs and groups can be a very effective way of helping to market your company and products. In addition to the contacts made in these organizations, members have opportunities to speak to their local chapters as well as to regional and national chapters. Whenever speakers are introduced, their company affiliations are usually mentioned. This is an effective means of spreading information about your company and products to a large number of people. High-level leads and ideas are often generated during these networking activities. That's why it is usually a good idea for marketing and sales personnel to participate — especially in those organizations that have a significant number of people from your company's target audience.

COLLATERAL

Marketing literature, also known as collateral, is an essential part of every company's marketing program. Whether big or small, young or old, companies need literature that provides information about them and their products. In the context of the organization, literature typically refers to brochures, annual reports, product description sheets, product specification sheets, price lists, formal proposal booklets, and virtually any literature that is typically offered to your target audience. The same principles discussed in the section on *Advertising* apply to collateral.

Brochure

The term brochure, as described here, refers to the most important piece of literature used to describe your company and products. As distinguished from a description or specification sheet, the brochure is usually longer than one page (four to six pages being most common) and is professionally-produced on a higher-quality stock.

What should be included

- *Headline:* As with any ad, the brochure should have a compelling headline that expresses the main message and "hooks" the reader into reading the further.
- *Cover:* In addition to the headline, the cover should have an attractive photograph, graphic, painting or design that helps to communicate the benefits provided by your company and products. If it is a product brochure, it should have the name of the product prominently displayed with the company name or logo on the bottom of the page. Too many companies make their logos *too big* in media advertising and brochures. This communicates insecurity. If anything, the logo should be a little understated. If you look at brochures for *IBM* or *Xerox* products, the logos and company names are discretely sized.
- *Body:* In the body of the brochure, cleverly-worded sub-headlines should communicate the main messages (usually the benefits or advantages of the product) with support and detail for these being provided in the text following each sub-head. Readers, who don't have the time or the patience to read the entire brochure, should be able to pick out the main thoughts by reading the sub-headlines. Pictures of the product should reinforce the messages of the headline, sub-headlines, and text, and vice versa. If the product is attractive, pictures should be prominently displayed (preferably with professional models playing the part of people using the product). If the product and people using the product are not attractive, you can artistically enhance their photographs by using special lenses, interesting angles, filters, and screens. Sometimes illustrations or drawings can serve this purpose even better.

- *Close:* The close of the brochure should follow the same principles as an ad with reinforcement of the messages of the headline and supporting text and a strong solicitation for the reader to take some action — call, write, visit your Web page, e-mail, send in a business reply card, or visit.
- *Specifications:* On the last page after the close, product specifications should be provided so that technical evaluators of the product will have some of the information they need to give their input to the buying decision. If the product is a service, specifications are typically replaced with the credentials of the professionals who will be doing the work.
- *Logo:* Even if included in other parts of the brochure, the very last item on the last page should be the company name and logo followed by the company address, phone, fax, e-mail, Web site, telex or any other reference that might be useful.
- *Slogan:* If the company has a good slogan, this can appear with the logo or as the very last item on the last page. An example of a good slogan is that of *Zenith*, "*The quality goes in, before the name goes on*." A bad slogan would be, "*We're Number One*." Why is it bad? It is boastful, not credible, amateurish, and often inaccurate.

What should not be included

- *Price:* Brochures are very expensive, and prices change too often. Furthermore, it is not considered good form to put prices in main product brochures. As you will learn a little later, prices are best placed on *Price Lists* or on the less expensive *Product Description Sheets*.
- *Too Many Different Type Fonts:* Amateurish brochures and ads have lots of different type fonts and sizes mixed on the same page. This is enough to give the reader a headache. One or two type fonts should be employed, with possible italic or boldface variations for subheads. Three to five type sizes should be sufficient as delineated below:

    1. The biggest is the headline, with point sizes ranging from 36 to 72 points (note there are 72 points to the inch).
    2. Next are the subheads (or possibly quotes blown up in the middle of text for emphasis). These are often 12 to 14 points.
    3. Then the normal body text (typically 10 to 12 points).
    4. Followed by captions for pictures and graphics (often 9 to 10 points).
    5. The smallest of all, also known as *the fine print* (6 to 10 points), contains legal language that notifies the reader of trademarked names, disclaimers, and other required legal text that would detract from the piece if it were bigger.

- *Too Many Wild Colors:* A brochure should represent the image and position of your products and company. In professional and high-tech companies, the colors should be professional and understated — not wild, crazy, or trendy (unless, of course, that is your position). Remember the brochure is for the target audience, and not for people in your company.
- *Negatives:* As with all marketing, there should be no negatives about your company, products, or competitors.

PRODUCT DESCRIPTION/SPECIFICATION SHEETS

As contrasted with brochures, product description sheets contain single-page descriptions of products. They follow the same basic principles of ads and brochures. They are simply less expensive and abridged versions of brochures. They are used in cases where the higher-quality brochures would be awkward or too expensive to use, such as enclosed with folded letters or bound in proposals. These are often enclosed in the pockets of folder-style brochures.

A typical structure of a *Product Description Sheet* is as follows:

Side One: The cover, or front, side of the sheet should have a headline or name of the product. If appropriate, a picture or illustration of the product, should follow the headline, or name. The main text of the brochure should follow or surround the picture or illustration. For emphasis, sub-headlines (or main benefits) should be highlighted with boldfaced or italic print. The company logo should appear at the bottom of the page either centered or in the lower right corner.

Side Two: Side two should contain any model configurations and prices (prices can be optionally put on separate *Price Lists* depending on marketing strategies and policies), followed by specifications (these can also be put on a separate *Product Specifications Sheet*). Many product descriptions don't require using the second side. This is fine, as long as the text and pictorial information is properly spaced and not crowded. See *Figure 9-3* for an example of a *Product Description Sheet.*

Product Description Sheet

ENCORE VIDEO INDUSTRIES

EVI/5210
PMT Power Supply Boards
For the Rank Cintel Mark III

Make a Good Thing Even Better

The Rank Cintel Mark III has become the world standard for post production telecine systems on the market today. Encore Video Industries has introduced its EVI/5210[SM] set of PEC power supply boards to make it even better.

Now available for the Rank are precision PEC power supply substitutes which provide the highest levels of photomultiplier precision, stability and regulation.

Precision Power

Each of Rank's Red, Green and Blue PEC boards are directly replaced by our easy-to-plug-in precision PMT power supply modules. These high-performance linear power modules provide a precision source of high voltage according to the following specifications:

Regulation: 0.001% for ±1% variation in source voltage.

Stability: 0.0005%/hour; 0.02%/8 hours.

Temp Coeff.: 100 ppm/°C from 0 to 50° C.

Protection: Short circuit and arc protected. Self restoring.

Design: Designed to be used without external controls.

They also assist you in maintaining short and long-term precision color balance to a very high degree of accuracy.

Precision Adjustments

In addition to the three RGB PMT modules, we provide an EVI/5210 PMT Control Board to directly replace the Rank PEC Control Board. Employing a 20-turn potentiometer, this control board allows you to set precise PMT voltage levels for 35 or 16mm positive or negative film. However, it is not intended for use with external controls.

Easy to Calibrate

Since the calibration pots are conviently located on the front of the Control Board, you can easily change the board voltages without having to remove the board from the telecine.

An IP toggle switch is also provided so you can easily switch to the proper PEC levels established for Interpositive film.

To Order or For More Information

If you wish to benefit from the improved stability and greater precision offered by Encore's EVI/520 set of PMT boards, call Encore Video Industries at 213-466-7663. Or write EVI at 6344 Fountain Avenue, Hollywood, CA 90028.

Figure 9-3

PRICE LISTS

The content and look of price lists involve both *pricing* and *promotional* strategies. Price lists should be clear, concise, cleanly laid out and self-explanatory. Remember, under current laws, manufacturers and wholesalers cannot fix retail prices. The words "*Suggested List Price*" should therefore be used if a manufacturer or wholesaler is printing the price list for the retailer. The price list should also contain any required disclaimers. These disclaimers will vary depending on company and industry policies. The one disclaimer that should be at the end of all price lists is the following, "*These prices are subject to change at any time without notice.*" This protects the company from any litigious people who are in the habit of filing lawsuits to force the company to honor outdated prices.

To keep new prices separate from old ones, new price lists should also have a revision date in very small letters at the bottom of the list. In fact, it's a good idea to put a revision date on all marketing literature so company personnel can distinguish between the latest and outdated versions.

While you do not have to invest a great deal of expense in producing price lists, you should make every effort to make price lists as attractive and as professionally-designed as possible. Care should be given to coordinate the paper stock and color of them with those of other *Product Description* and *Specification Sheets*. The reason is that you may want to enclose such lists with these sheets and a personal letter or bind them together in a formal proposal. Coordination, not only looks better; it communicates coordination and professionalism to your prospects.

PROPOSALS

An important promotional tool for many companies — especially those doing business in high-tech, service industries, and the public sector — is the proposal. The proposal is prepared to describe how your company and products will meet the specific needs of a prospect. These needs are often specified in an *RFP*, or *Request for Proposal*, initial meeting, *SBIR* (*Small Business Innovative Research*) *Program Solicitation Manual*, and/or various other public and private sector publications.

Although the proposal is a unique promotional tool, it employs basically the same marketing strategies, principles and techniques as other forms of promotion. The proposal should…

Be Responsive to Needs

As with any form of promotion, the proposal must be responsive to the needs of the prospect. These needs are usually very clearly delineated in face-to-face meetings, the RFP, or the solicitation manual. Therefore, to insure success, the proposal should respond to every detail in the solicitation request. If, for some reason, you company cannot fulfill a particular detail of the specification, the proposal should positively explain how it would satisfy the need in perhaps a different way rather than ignore, or avoid, the point. Avoiding points is likely to cause the issuer of the request to become angry or no longer trust your company.

Employ Universal Marketing System™ Guidelines

The guidelines presented in the section on advertising should apply to proposals as well. A proposal should be attractive and make it easy for the reader to pick out the important points without forcing them to re-read the entire document. It should clearly position your company and products to differentiate them from competitors. It should be concise, clear, and to the point. Since the reader is going to have to read many proposals, the proposal should be designed to make the reading task as easy as possible — employing, lots of space, an easy-to-read type font, and pictures and graphs, where appropriate.

Stress True Cost over Price

Both private and public sector organizations often use the *RFP* as a means to get the bid price of the product(s) being solicited as low as possible. As a result, price is usually a very important part of a proposal's marketing strategy. In anticipation that other bids may be lower, your company should communicate that your proposed solution will cost less even if your price is higher than other alternatives. How can your cost be lower when your price is higher? Easy. Quite often, solutions that are priced higher (1) cost less to operate and fix than other alternatives, (2) include support and service — effectively lowing the cost of the product, (3) warranty the product over a longer period — lowering maintenance and service costs, and (4) most important of all, most quality products cost a little more initially but save so much more over the customer's use of the product — effectively lowering the cost to operate and use and maximizing the customer's return on investment.

Consider Greater Marketing Objectives

You should look upon the proposal as a promotional tool whose objectives go beyond that of winning just one project award. Even if your company is not selected, your proposal can make a good impression that enhances your chances of being selected for the next project. Furthermore, a well-done proposal will be better remembered, will most likely be kept on file for a longer time, and will help to develop a better relationship with the soliciting organization. If nothing else, it will contribute to a positive image of your company.

LOGOS, SLOGANS AND STATIONERY

Since the details of logos, slogans and stationery have already been discussed in *Chapter 4*, repetition of the detail will be avoided here. The important point to remember is that they greatly help to promote your company and products. Logos and slogans act as *stamps* that stamp images into the minds of your various publics. Stationery and business cards usually accompany the first forms of personal communication from representatives of your company. As a result, a great deal of care should be exercised when developing these elements of the promotional mix. Professional assistance should be sought — particularly in the final design and execution of these.

PACKAGING

In addition to its main function of protecting your *product*, packaging should be an important part of your company's promotional strategy. In most cases, it is the first part of the product that buyers see. Also, packaging can have a long shelf life. That is, it is likely to sit on the shelves of distributors and dealers before the product is sold; it will pass through normal shipping channels and make impressions on everyone involved along the way; it may be kept by customers in the event that the product has to be shipped to another location or back to the manufacturer; and some will even use it to carry belongings when moving. As a result, packaging should be as attractive as possible, carry the company's main message or slogan, have the company and product logos prominently displayed, and promote any awards won by the product.

With certain low-cost products, your company may pay more for packaging than for producing the core product. Even in the more typical case where the package consists of a cardboard box, the company should consider the box as a vehicle for "free" advertising. It affords the company another opportunity to convince the customer that he/she has made the right decision.

INTERNET AND WEB PAGES

No examination of promotion would be complete without a discussion of the *Internet* and the *World Wide Web* (*www*). From its modest beginnings as an informal network that connected *university*, *research laboratory*, and *Department of Defense* computers, the *Internet* has evolved into a worldwide marketing vehicle that is continually growing in importance as more people are connected.

Unique Characteristics

Unlike other promotional vehicles, nobody owns the Internet. It is a network of computers around the world with each Web URL having the opportunity to carry the perception of equal importance with all others. This means that very small businesses can seem just as big as the biggest multinational corporations.

Access to a large global audience

By creating a Web site, your business can list itself with a variety of *search engines* enabling prospective buyers from around the world who have access to the Internet to find you when they search for the kind of goods and services you sell. Because of its rapid growth, estimates as to how many people and companies are connected to the Internet are changing every day. Updated figures can be obtained at any time via the *Stats Toolbox* on the ClickZ Web site (http://www.clickz.com/stats/). Whatever the current number, you can be sure that it is a very large potential worldwide audience.

They can find out more about you

Prospective buyers who know something about your company can deliberately look for you on the Internet. If your *domain name* coincides with your company name, browsers can often find you without using a search engine. That is if your name is *IBM*, they might try http://www.ibm.com. If they guess correctly, they will go directly to your *home page*. They can also find you by doing an organic search via *Google* (*http://www.google.com*) or other popular search engines.

Depending on how you design your Web site, they can view your company history, obtain product information, read customer testimonials, download product brochures and newsletters, view video clips or animations of your product in action, complete surveys, put themselves on your mailing list, request that more information to be sent to them, order products, and in some cases download products that can be stored in a digital format such as software, magazines, newspapers, books, and music.

If your company is unknown to them, they can find you

Even if they never heard about your company or products, prospective buyers can stumble upon your Web site by searching for companies in your industry or the types of products you sell. If you use *paid search* — getting listed on popular search engines and paying search engine companies every time a searcher clicks on your link, they can link to your Web site when they are looking for a particular type of product. In this way, you can attract prospective buyers from around the world who might otherwise never know you exist.

Promotional Uses

In the context of promotion, you can promote your company and products in a variety of ways. Some of the more popular are listed below.

1. *Create your own Web site.* Your Web site can be an online brochure, a virtual store or office, or much more.

2. *List your site in the various search engines.* Prospects can find out more about your company if your company is known to them or they stumble upon your site even if they never heard about you before.

3. *Get owners of other Web sites to link to your site.* They might do this because you link to theirs or pay them for all referrals or sales made to referrals.

4. *Advertise on other Web sites.* You can advertise on other Web sites that you believe will attract your target markets by paying the owners of such sites a fee.

5. *E-mail outbound and inbound.* As with traditional direct mail, you can promote your products by sending e-mails, with or without attached product sheets and newsletters, to your target audience. You can also put your e-mail address on business cards, promotional materials and your Web site so people can e-mail you with questions and product inquiries.

6. *Create Weblogs.* Weblogs are being increasingly used as non-threatening ways to promote companies and products. Market targets that have access to your Weblogs can participate in multi-person exchanges about products, customer needs, and many other subjects related to your company and products. People in your target audience like the informal nature of Weblogs and can see what others are saying about your products, which often serve as credible testimonials.

7. *Develop personal relationships.* Web sites can enable your company to develop a personal, one-on-one relationship with your market targets. That is, unlike most other media, you can communicate directly with them, find out what they want, and respond directly and more quickly to their inquiries.

8. *Sell products directly.* Many Web sites are set up to sell products directly to buyers. Sites that incorporate good online systems design, allow customers to fill in their orders right on their own computer screens thereby saving company labor costs associated with order entry functions. Many high-tech products including personal computers are sold in this way. The success of *Intel*, *Cisco Systems* and *Dell Computer* selling products from their Web sites has been discussed previously.

9. *Distribute information and product.* Web sites enable companies to efficiently announce product upgrades, enhancements, recalls, and new releases. In the case of software, customers can download upgrades directly to their computers saving the company significant costs in labor, diskette and CD-ROM media, upgrade paperwork, manuals, and shipping.

Market Information and Research

In addition to being an effective source for promotion and distribution, the Internet is an excellent tool for collecting information about the marketplace and doing Market Research. Since this aspect of the Internet is more appropriately discussed in *Chapter 12* on the *Marketing Information System*, it will not be covered further here.

BOOKS, MANUALS, AND PRODUCT INSTRUCTIONS

While more typically identified as part of the product, books, manuals, and product instructions are also important promotional vehicles. Before purchasing certain technical products, some prospective buyers will ask to see associated books, manuals, and product instructions. The impression made by these can either help or hinder the sale. Of course, you want it to help the sale so you have to employ good marketing techniques for these too.

Some companies believe in providing books or booklets as part of their marketing strategy. These books usually offer product details about entire product lines or focus on products for specific target industries.

Similar principles that apply to your company's marketing literature should apply to product literature. In some technical markets, product literature is often a main vehicle for promoting products.

OTHER PROMOTIONAL STRATEGIES

Since virtually all forms of communication with your company's publics should come under the banner of marketing, there are many other promotional considerations that have not been discussed in detail. It would be impossible for any book to cover all of them — especially since more and more are being invented all the time. In an effort to achieve more complete coverage of this subject, a few of these are listed below:

CDs and DVDs

Brochures, catalogs, videos, and other information on companies and products can be provided on CDs, DVDs, and other new media. These are often used in conjunction with a direct mail (including e-mail) campaign or personal selling activities.

Phone Messages

To entertain callers while they wait to speak with an employee who is not immediately available, many companies have gone to a system that plays music while callers are on hold. While some don't believe this to be an important marketing decision, it is a marketing decision that affects the company's image nonetheless. In fact, studies have shown that some callers really get annoyed if they don't like the music being played.

Some companies have even chosen to play commercials while callers are on hold. This can work well or be a disaster, depending on how it is executed. You should understand that some people will be inclined to resent *sales pitches* while they are waiting on the phone. On the other hand, if cleverly and carefully done, this technique can work very well if the caller is provided with important benefits of interest or an incentive, such as a discount on the product being advertised.

Many companies have installed a "*voice mail*" system whereby callers are greeted with personal phone messages if the party being called is not available. After hearing the outgoing message, the caller can then leave a personal message much the same as on a personal answer machine. The tendency to use this type of system actually helps smaller companies who use answer machines instead of receptionists. That is, they can appear as big as the larger companies who use voice mail.

As to which method is preferred, it depends on too many variables to give a patterned answer. The phone mail system seems to be the least offensive, but marketing personnel will have to sample the opinions of callers via the company's *marketing information system* to find out which works best for them.

Office Design and Layout

While too many companies seem unconcerned with the look of their offices, it does make an impression — often a big one — on the company's various publics. Even though significant numbers of people don't possess "good taste," most can recognize aesthetically pleasing surroundings when they see them. Buyers like to visit nice places, and employees seem to like to work longer in surroundings that are pleasant. Because if its importance to a company's image and work efficiency, consideration should be given to the look of the office as part of the firm's promotional strategies. The most important consideration is that the look of your offices should fit your position. You don't have to have expensively-appointed offices if you are positioning yourself as a discounter or low-price leader. On the other hand, if your image is one of a quality-focused, exclusive operation, your office design and layout should reflect this position.

Signage

Signs are an important identifier of a company's location, physical and virtual. Those that are aesthetically pleasing contribute to your company's image, while those that are not cause some to question other aspects of your company. In addition to being attractive, signs should be visible and make an impact. Even those prospects that walk, drive, or Web-surf by are affected by signs and symbols that they see. Every time they see the sign, the company's name, logo, and slogan is recorded in their minds. Whenever they see an ad, receive a mailing, or are called upon by a sales person, they will be more receptive and comfortable because the name and images on the sign will already be recorded in their mind.

PERSONAL SELLING AND DIRECT MAIL

In-depth discussions of Personal Selling and Direct Mail, which has evolved into the much larger subject of Direct Marketing, are noticeably absent from this section on Promotion. While they are both important promotional strategies, they have grown into major topics that straddle distribution as well as promotion. Therefore, they require separate chapters, and they are covered in the next two chapters of this book.

[1]David Ogilvy, *Ogilvy on Advertising*, Vintage Books, New York, 1985, pg. 70.

TIPS and Exercises

1. Put your existing promotional strategies into categories such as Print (magazines, newspapers, etc.), Broadcast (Radio and TV), Outdoor (Billboard, bus benches, taxicabs, etc.), Face-to-face (selling, trade shows, seminars, speeches, etc.), and Online (Web sites, e-mail, search, Weblogs, etc.).
2. Create a table listing all your promotional media by category and identifying the CPM (cost of reaching 1,000 of your prospects through each of these media).
3. Given the above information, identify the most effective ways to reach each segment of your target audience.
4. Develop strategies that integrate your off-line promotions with your online to create a synergy between them.
5. Identify the promotional strategies of your key competitors and compare them with yours.
6. Evaluate if you should add those they are using that you are not.
7. Ask you customers and prospects what media they read, watch, listen to, and visit on the Internet.
8. Of the ones you do not currently use, investigate whether or not adding them might improve your CPM and audience reach.
9. From the above, create a marketing/promotional budget.

Chapter 10

DNA of Direct Marketing

"The most convenient way to reach those who are busy, lazy, or inundated with too much information."

WHAT IS DIRECT MARKETING?

The *Direct Marketing Association* defines Direct Marketing as *"An interactive system of marketing that uses one or more advertising media to effect a measurable response and/or transaction at any location, with this activity stored on a database."* If you can follow or remember that definition, you deserve a medal. Perhaps a more useful definition of Direct Marketing is *"The process of marketing products directly to end buyers without face-to-face interaction with sales people."*

BRIEF HISTORY

Direct Marketing owes its modern beginnings to *Direct Mail* whose creation is credited to Aaron Montgomery Ward who, in turn, began the *Montgomery Ward* catalog in 1872 as a way of selling his products by mail. As Direct Mail became more sophisticated, it incorporated other media and techniques, such as telemarketing, the Internet, Faxback services, and direct response ads, to boost sales response. In recognition of this diversification, the *Direct Mail Marketing Association* changed its name to the *Direct Marketing Association* in 1984.

DISTINGUISHING CHARACTERISTICS

Experts in the field claim that the *Direct Marketing* discipline involves three distinguishing characteristics.

(1) *No face to face selling.* The product is ordered and sent directly to the buyer without any face-to-face contact with a sales person or company representative.

(2) *Results, or responses, are measurable.* The effectiveness of any direct marketing strategy can be easily measured by simply counting the responses.

(3) *Use of a database.* The list to which mailings and e-mails are sent and from which phone calls and faxes are initiated is derived from a database that is compiled in-house or purchased or leased from a mail list vendor. This data base is updated with purchase-history data and other pertinent information as it is collected.

Since all good marketers should strive for the characteristics described in (2) and (3) above, the author of this book believes the first characteristic is the only one that truly distinguishes *Direct Marketing* from other types of marketing.

MAJOR DIRECT MARKETING MEDIA CHANNELS

As described above, *Direct Marketing* grew out of *Direct Mail*. Currently it employs a variety of media channels to market products directly to consumers. Some of the most popular are listed below.

- *Direct Mail.* A mailing is sent to a targeted audience selected from a database.
- *Inbound Telemarketing.* A toll-free number is displayed in ads, mailers, catalogs, and product packages to encourage the consumer to call up and order product.
- *Outbound Telemarketing.* A telemarketer calls a targeted list derived from a database to encourage prospects to order product or to follow-up on a prior interest.
- *Inbound Internet contact.* A prospect visits a Web site or sends an e-mail to ask for more information, order the product, provide information, register a complaint or compliment, or search for information.
- *Outbound Internet response.* A company representative responds to a Web or other inquiry by *e-mail, Weblog,* or some other electronic method.
- *Direct Response Ads.* An ad solicits an order directly.
- *Fulfillment.* Your company sends literature or ships product in response to inbound orders from the above sources.

INTEGRATING DIRECT MEDIA CHANNELS

To achieve their objectives, direct marketers often use an integrated combination of these channels. In fact, they follow a simple rule — the more response channels you provide, the greater the response. That is, some prospects prefer to call a toll-free number. Others prefer to visit a Web site, e-mail, or complete and mail back a postage-paid *business reply card.* Still others prefer to fax their response. Some prefer to write a letter or visit in-person. Many who are connected to the Internet like to order directly from a Web site by entering their own orders via an on-screen order form. The key point to remember is that the more avenues you provide, and the easier you make it for prospects to respond, the more they will respond.

Since each of these media elements requires a bit more explanation, they will be covered in the following sections.

DIRECT MAIL

The precursor to Direct Marketing, *direct mail* is an excellent vehicle for promoting a variety of products.

Advantages of Direct Mail

Direct mail affords many advantages. It enables marketers to do the following:

Focus on Specific Targets

Marketing literature can be sent directly to target audiences. Unlike media advertising, which is a *broad-brush* method that is difficult to focus on specific prospects, direct mail is a *"rifle-shot"* approach that enables you to focus on certain names and addresses that you have identified as belonging to your target market.

You can compile or purchase mailing lists from a variety of sources that enable you to target a specific industry, Standard Industry Classification Code (SIC Code), Zip Code, or market segments with other similar characteristics. You can even rent a phone directory by street address from the local phone company so that you can target specific businesses located nearby.

Enclose Product Literature

Unlike media advertising, where a new version has to be developed for each magazine's format, direct mail enables you to send the same product brochures and technical literature to prospective buyers with a carefully focused cover letter.

Begin a Relationship

Sending letters to targets is an excellent way to begin a marketing or business relationship. Unlike the interruptive nature of *"cold calling"* on the telephone, letters enable you to introduce yourself, your products and company, in a non-interruptive way. That is, a letter can be opened and read by the prospect when and if he/she chooses. Therefore, the prospect retains control — an important psychological advantage for many buyers. A letter can be reread for better understanding and saved for future reference. The product literature that accompanies the cover letter can have pictures of the product that, if properly composed, *"are worth a thousand words"* of print or dialogue.

Inexpensive Incremental Coverage

Unlike ads and many other promotional strategies that require substantial investments to increase coverage, direct mail enables marketers to inexpensively reach additional prospects. That is, for the price of a mailing piece and postage, one more prospect can be reached. If the company's sales force needs a discrete number of additional leads, it can invest a specific and often modest amount of money to reach them.

Prerequisites for Achieving Direct Mail Success

Even before a mailing is distributed in the marketplace, there are two key prerequisites for success — the Mailing Piece and the Mailing List.

The Mailing Piece

As with all advertising, the message should be carefully chosen and professionally presented. It should be simple, powerful, and memorable. Moreover, it should look important. A mailing piece that has the look of *junk mail* will be regarded as such and thrown away.

Types of Mailing Pieces

There are three recognized categories of mailing pieces — (1) *Solo* mailings, (2) *Self-mailers*, and (3) *Catalogs*.

Solo Mailer. This is simply a mailing that comes in an envelope. To be most effective, solo mailings should be personally addressed (no mailing labels) and contain a cover letter. Solo mailings also often include product brochures, special offer sheets, and response cards. They are designed for audiences that have the time and interest to read more information about the product or the offer. An important objective is to design a solo mailing so that the recipient will open the envelope. This should be done *without employing common tricks* such as (1) putting a mailing piece that looks like a check or money order inside a window envelope or (2) making a promise on the envelope that is "too good to be true" only to have the prospect be disappointed when they open the envelope. These tricks often backfire. They get recipients to open the envelopes, but disappoint them once they do. This only causes resentment and a lack of trust — not a good way to begin a business relationship.

Self-mailer. As the name implies, a self-mailer is usually a single mailing piece that is self-contained and does not come in an envelope. It is best used for "stand-up" audiences — those who typically receive the mail while standing up or working away from a desk. Also self-mailers are good for getting key headlines and messages directly into the minds of recipients who might throw away solo mailers before opening them. They tend to promote pass-along readership, and are therefore good for promoting meetings, seminars, and upcoming events that may interest several people in the same office. Common types of self-mailers typically include post cards, folded 6-panel brochures, and newsletters.

Catalogs. Catalogs are booklets that are used for promoting large numbers of products at one time. They have a long self-life since people often keep them for from several weeks to a year. Catalogs are usually more memorable, and they rely heavily on graphics with meaningful captions to do the selling. For maximum effectiveness, catalogues should have *toll-free numbers on each page*, along with other channels for readers to respond including e-mail, Web, and mailing addresses; fax numbers; and self-addressed, postage paid business reply cards. As with all marketing, the more channels readers have to respond, the greater the response will be.

In addition to the common booklet-style catalogs, there are three other common types of catalog mailers listed below.

(1) *Mini catalogs.* These are catalogs that are smaller in size and have fewer pages than standard catalogues. They are not intended for saving. Most people keep them no longer than a week. Drug stores, office supply stores, super markets, and electronics resellers typically distribute new ones every week or month.

(2) *Packets.* Packets are groups of individual small brochure-like pieces that often come together in an envelope or are bundled with utility and credit card bills. They are designed to prompt impulse purchases. Studies show that most people sort them into two piles — *keeper* and *throwaway*.

(3) *Card Decks.* Card Decks are bundles of individual post cards that are typically packaged in cellophane wrappers. They are designed to prompt impulse purchases, and are sent to everyone on a mailing list — which is usually purchased or rented from a magazine, newspaper, or mail list broker. One side of the card describes the product and makes an offer to encourage the recipient to purchase the product, and the other side contains the name and return address of the company along with prepaid postage — usually by permit.

Common Mailer Elements

To be most effective, all of the *Solo*, *Self*, and *Catalog* mailers described above should employ the following common elements.

(1) *Universal Marketing Structure*™ — outlined in the previous chapter.

(2) *Multiple Channels for recipients to respond* — including toll-free numbers, e-mail or Web site addresses, and postage-paid business reply cards.

(3) *Marketing Information System coding* — to measure the effectiveness, or response, of the mailing.

(4) *Solicit a direct buying action* — asking prospects to take a buying action and giving them everything they need to order directly.

Other Important Mailer Decisions

Before distributing a mailing piece, a number of other important decisions need to be made. The most common are described below.

- *Numbers.* How many are to be sent? This will depend on the numbers in your target audience, the size of your mailing lists, the number of times it will be sent, the number of leads required, and the quantity discount "breaks" your printer will charge to produce the mailing piece.

- *Business Reply Card (BRC).* Will a BRC or coupon be enclosed? There should always be some sort of response mechanism. As already discussed, the best results are achieved if multiple response channels are provided. Also postage-paid BRCs will be returned in greater number than those that require the prospect to affix postage.
- *Size.* Will it be a standard business envelope, post card, invitation, brochure, or some other size? The answer depends on the information to be included, the product being advertised, the costs of the various alternatives, and your positioning strategy.
- *Envelope.* Will it be placed in an envelope (solo) or an address label be affixed or laser printed onto the mailer (self mailers and catalogs)? This depends on so many different factors. Using an envelope avoids the problem where the mailing label covers some of the information on the mailer. On the other hand, it is more expensive and time consuming — requiring the additional step of stuffing the envelopes. All other things being equal, the envelope will usually improve your response.
- *Quality.* Remember image and position. If less than high-quality is selected, a good reason should be given in the piece — for example, "To hold costs down and pass the savings on to you...," "To avoid costly delays in sending this important information to you...," "To help conserve environmental resources...," etc. Remember, whatever the quality level, it should not look like "*junk*" mail.
- *Incentive.* Will an incentive be offered for returning (for example, a free booklet, coffee mug, pen, or free product sample)? As long as the incentive is useful and free, it will boost response.
- *Color.* Color or black & white? While studies show, that all other things being equal, color works better than black & white, black & white can be as or more effective in certain circumstances. With high-tech products, black, white, and various shades of gray (which are the same to the printer as black & white with a screen) can be very effective. It is certainly safer than selecting the "*wrong*" color. And it is much less expensive. Generally, a high-quality black & white piece is much more effective than a low or mediocre-quality color piece. A very popular and effective technique is to use black and white, and shades of gray, with a single color added as an accent. This color is often the color of the product, such as *IBM* blue or *Coca Cola* red.
- *Pages.* How many pages or panels will it have? This depends on the amount of text, pictures and the amount of desired free space. Fewer words and more empty space are usually more effective because most buyers are busy or lazy, and these make the piece easier for them to read.

- *Words.* How many words and how much space? Brevity and simplicity are most effective unless more words help to educate and interest the reader.
- *Pictures.* Will it contain pictures and graphics or just have words? If the product is good looking and the picture or graphic is able to clearly communicate important product benefits, they are well worth including. If not, pictures may only confuse the message.

Mailing List

In addition to having a good mailing piece, the proper mailing list is essential to a successful mailing.

Quality Factors

The quality of the mailing list is determined by a variety of factors including the following:

- *Coverage.* How well does it cover your target market? Often times, it is difficult to know exactly what groups of people fit within your target audience. It may take some experimentation with different lists to find out. If you know your market targets already, you can ask the magazine or mailing list company for a *media ki*t or a profile of the people on their lists. You can than compare this with your profile of your targeted prospects.
- *Targeting Accuracy.* How accurate are the names and addresses? People move, change positions and jobs. In direct marketing parlance, this is called *churn*. On average, a list will have 18% churn each year, 1.5% of the information will change each month. A mailing list is more accurate if it is constantly maintained. As mailers are returned, the incorrect names and addresses should be corrected. Also many lists have genders and titles incorrectly stated. Making mistakes with names and genders is not a good way to begin a business relationship. Remember the purpose of the mailer is to *attract* rather than *alienate* buyers. Therefore, care should be taken to properly maintain and select mailing lists.

Types of Lists

The success of a mailing list is often closely related to the type of list that is rented or purchased. There are three basic types of mailing lists commonly referred to as (1) In-house, (2) Response, and (3) Compiled lists.

- *In House.* In most cases, *in-house lists* are the best. Assuming that you maintain these lists properly, they typically generate the greatest response. The reason is that in-house lists are typically comprised of prospects with whom you have had prior contact. Many of these contacts have already expressed an interest in your products.
- *Response.* After in-house lists, *response lists* usually produce the next best response. They only include those prospects who have purchased products through direct channels before.

Research shows that buyers who have purchased products by direct channels are most likely to purchase through those channels again. When shopping for mailing lists, direct marketers should find out how the lists were compiled. *Standard Rate and Data Service* (SRDS) mailing list directories typically provide information as to the type of list and how the data was compiled. If you are using another source, you should ask them how the list was created, how frequently it is updated, and what was the last update date.

- *Compiled.* Compiled lists are created from publicly-available data such as birth, death, marriage, motor vehicle, and home-purchase records. Because, you have no idea whether or not the people on these lists are interested in buying your products or buying via mail order, they are typically the least effective. However, for certain purposes they can be the most effective. For example, people who have recently-purchased houses may be the most likely candidates for buying home computers or wanting local banking services. Those who have recently had children might be the best candidates for baby monitoring devices or other products for infants. Those who have started new businesses, applied for business licenses, or *filed fictitious* name statements are likely to be good prospects for high-tech office equipment, accounting, and legal services.

Mailing Houses

There are companies, called *mailing houses*, that provide a variety of mailing services. Such services include printing the piece, picking up mailing pieces from other printers, folding, stapling, envelope stuffing, affixing postage and labels, coding, maintaining lists, renting and selling lists, and eliminating duplicates from different lists. Eliminating duplicates, often referred to as *merge purge*, is important if two different lists contain duplicate names. A simple cost effective analysis should be done to determine which, if any, mailing services are best accomplished inside and outside your company. For purposes of control, it is probably best to keep control over the mailing list itself *inside* your company, if possible and if desired.

Ownership of Names on a Mailing List

When you rent a list from a company, the names on that list remain the property of the mailing list company. By contract, you are only allowed to use them for the specific number of times you rent them. To guard against your using names after the rental period expires, mailing list companies include some "dummy" names on every list they rent. If you should send mailings to these names, they will automatically go to a P.O. box or address owned by the mailing list company. The mailing list company will either ask you to pay for the illegal use of the list plus penalties or file a law suit. Because of contract violations and their proof, they will win.

Obtaining ownership and Growing Your In-house List

How then do you obtain ownership of, or rights to, the names on the lists that you rent? The answer is very simple, you make it easy for contacts to respond directly to you or provide an incentive for people on the list to contact you in some way. If they contact you, you obtain the rights to use their name in the future without paying rental fees. By calling you, returning a response card, faxing you, e-mailing you, visiting your office or Web site, or writing you a letter, you obtain ownership of their contact information to use for your business purposes. This is one way to grow your in-house list. Making it easy to respond involves providing multiple response channels as discussed previously. They are more likely to contact you if (1) these response channels are "free"— toll-free numbers, postage-paid response cards, no-cost e-mail responses, or (2) you give them a promotional incentive to respond —entering them in a drawing for a useful prize, free gift, discount, or rebate. Because obtaining ownership of mailing list names will boost your sales, lower future costs, and increase your profits, it is very important to do whatever is feasible to get them to respond. Also, since the average response to a direct mail campaign is only one or two percent, it is important to use a variety of proven techniques to boost response.

Boosting Response

As discussed above, a one percent response to a mailing is considered average. That is, if you send out 100 mailers, you are likely to get one response. Since such a poor response is usually inadequate and very costly, you need to employ techniques that will boost response to much higher levels — allowing you to realize economies of scale and an adequate return-on-investment on your investment in mailing, handling, and printing.

- *More Effective Mailing Piece.* As discussed in a previous section, the key here is to produce a mailing piece that will not be considered "junk" mail. This often involves putting some quality and professionalism into the piece and making the offer and important benefits of the product very clear to the target audience.
- *Better Targeted Mailing List.* The better the mailing list targets those who are most likely to buy your products, the greater the response you will receive. Sending mailers that promote your Macintosh-compatible products to owners of *IBM*-compatible PCs is likely to waste your money and not generate a very good response. Spending a little time to better target your audience, will save significant mailing, printing, and handling costs. These savings can be invested in producing better quality pieces, acquiring additional lists, or employing other response boosting techniques.
- *Repeat mailings.* Various studies agree that repeat mailings boost response significantly — due to (1) the *cumulative* nature of advertising and (2) the increased chance of reaching

prospects when they are ready to buy. The optimal number of repetitions over a year's period is considered to be 6 or 7, or once every two months. The reason for this frequency is that you have no way of knowing when a prospect is ready to buy. Being ready to buy, means their "*buying window*™" is active. For example, let's say you receive mailings from various mobile phone companies who want you to buy phones from them. If you are not ready to buy, your buying window is inactive, and you ignore these mailings. However, as soon as you become interested in buying such a phone, your buying window becomes active, and you pay attention to these mailings. Those companies that sent you mailings once or twice, but who gave up when you didn't respond, will miss out on the opportunity to earn your business. On the other hand, those who faithfully continued to send you mailings every other month have developed somewhat of a relationship with you. Even though their mailings may have annoyed you because you considered them as "junk mail" when your buying window was inactive, you appreciate their persistence when you are ready to buy. After all, who would you rather buy from, a company who gives up after one or two tries or one who is persistent because they believe in their product and have a competent follow-up system? Even if the prospect chooses not to respond to repeat mailings, the repetition serves an important secondary function — to get brand (company and product) names into their minds. That is, as these names become more familiar, they will make future sales easier and future marketing more effective. Prospects are more comfortable buying brands whose names they recognize. Recognition comes with repetition.

- *Inbound telemarketing.* Inbound telemarketing is basically the direct marketer's jargon for a toll-free telephone or fax number. Studies show that toll-free numbers will boost response by 50%. That is, putting a toll-free number in a mailer, direct response ad, Web site, e-mail, or the infomercial will boost a typical response from 1 to 2 percent to 1.5 to 3 percent.

- *Outbound telemarketing.* Outbound telemarketing refers to calling prospects to follow-up on a prior contact, such a mailing that was sent out. Studies show that outbound telemarketing will boost response by 300 to 700%.Thus, by employing outbound telemarketing, an average response of one to two percent can be boosted to from 3 to 14%.

- *Personalized Gifts.* Many companies have found that sending a *personalized gift* — one with the prospective decision maker's name or initials on it, can dramatically boost the response to a mailing. The typical boost given by a personalized gift is 7500% to 8000%! This is not a misprint. Enclosing a personalized gift with a mailing, can boost response 75 to 80 times! This means that an average response of one percent can be boosted to 75% to 80%. Why is this? Firstly, few secretaries will throw away a mailing that is accompanied by a gift. Secondly, the personalized gift distinguishes, or positions, the sender from all other companies that send *me-too* mailers. Thirdly, all other things being equal, decision-makers are more likely to buy from the company that is in the forefront of their minds when they need the products that the company is selling. Of course, the personalized gift should not be used in those industries where gifts to decision-makers are prohibited (i.e. industries that do significant business with the Government). More importantly, the gifts should be of a nominal nature, such as $10 to $20, so that they will not be construed as bribes. They are sent to distinguish your company from your competitors — not to bribe the decision maker. Bribes do nothing but *cheapen* the sender's image, ruin the positioning of the product, and damage the relationship before it has a chance to develop. The most effective gifts have proven to be those that recipients can and will use on a daily basis, such as business card holders, paper weights, clocks, and other office decorations. The strategy is for them to see and use them on a daily basis so they will be continually reminded of you, your company, and your products.

- *Response Compression.* When direct marketers create a direct marketing campaign, they employ a mix of media channels that they think will be most effective. Traditionally, they might place a direct response ad, wait until the response diminishes, send out a direct mail piece, wait until the response dies down, follow-up with outbound telemarketing, do another direct mailing, etc. This process is shown graphically in *Figure 10-1.*

Traditional Direct Marketing Sequence

Outbound telemarketers wait *2 to 3 weeks* after the prospect receives the direct mail piece to place the outbound follow-up call. They do this because an outbound telemarketing call is, on average, 5 to 10 times more expensive than a direct mail piece. They wait for direct mail responses to come so that they don't have to call those who respond by mail — thereby saving the money and duplication of effort to do so.

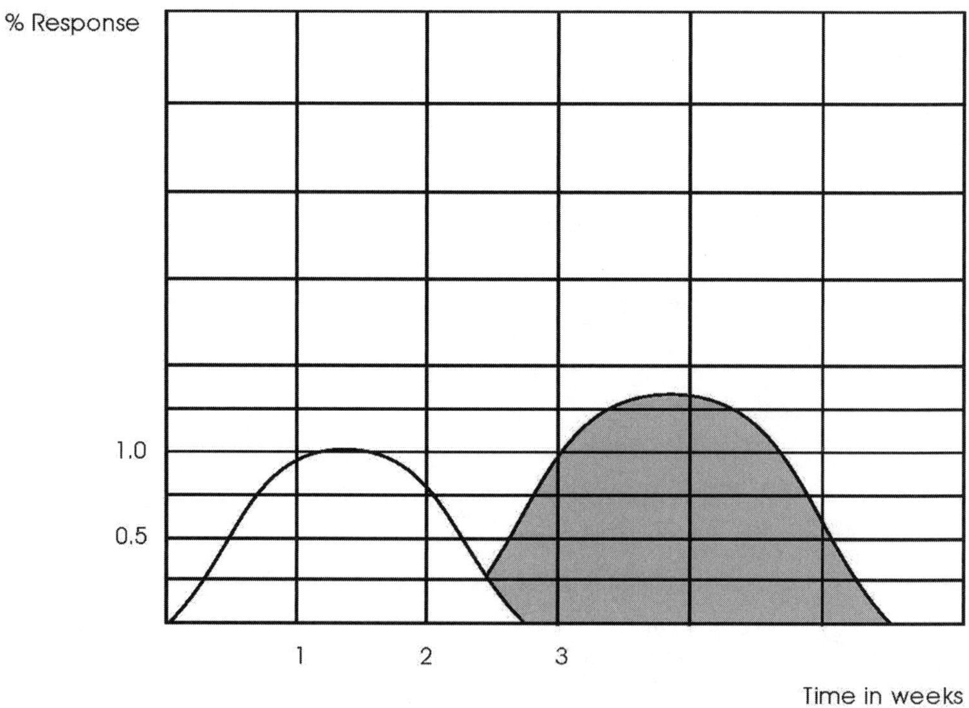

Figure 10-1

In recent years, a new technique, called *response compression*, has proven to be more effective in many cases. The idea of *response compression* is to dramatically shorten the interval between employing one technique and following-up with another. In fact, most *response compression* campaigns will follow-up an initial mailing with outbound telemarketing before the response to the direct mailing dies out. They do the same with the other techniques. By overlapping these techniques, the target audience is exposed to the product and company from multiple sources — one right after the other. Because target audiences see the company and products virtually everywhere, the impact of the campaign is much greater, and the audience responds in greater numbers. A graphical representation of this process is illustrated in *Figure 10-2*.

Response Compression Sequence

Outbound telemarketers place a follow-up call within *3 days* after the prospect receives the direct mail piece. Since traditional responses to direct mail are small — averaging 1 to 2 percent, the duplication of effort and associated increment in cost is small relative to the boost in response which is realized due to the cumulative "impression" which is made on prospects. More specifically, since outbound telemarketing typically produces a response boost of from 300 to 700 per cent, the lift is greater when the response rate is at its peak (say at 1% roughly 3 days after receipt) than when it has already died down to say 0.25% after 2 or 3 weeks. This boost more than compensates for the extra cost for the extra outbound calls.

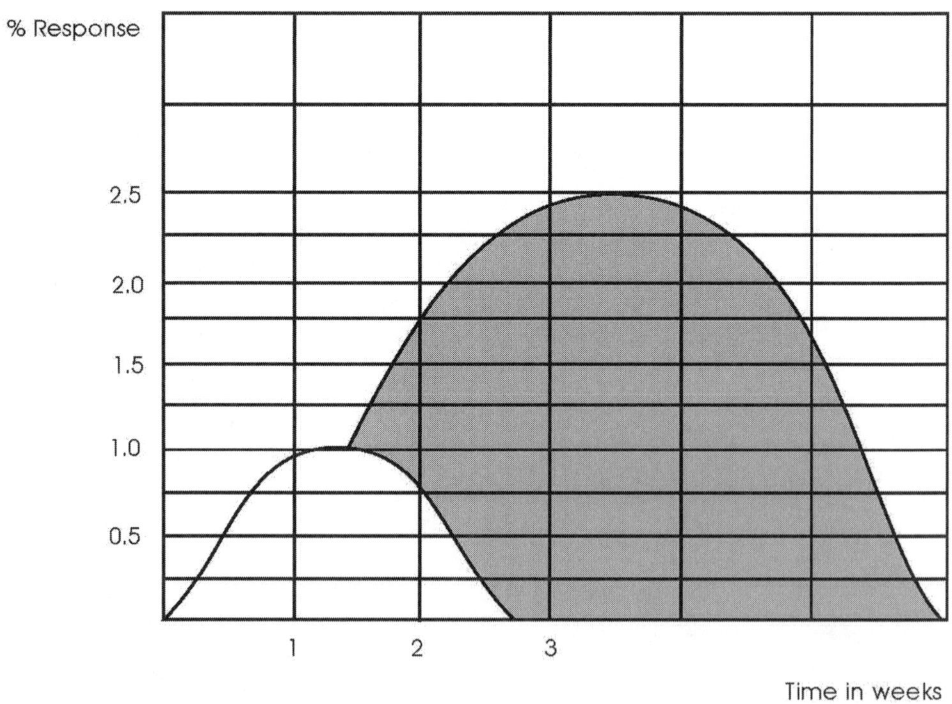

Figure 10-2

- *Personal Mailings.* With word processors, sending personal letters to large numbers of people has become more feasible. Sales people can send such letters to the prospects assigned to them. Personal letters are an excellent way to follow up and develop personal relationships because they are *non-interruptive* and they give the prospects a chance to review them when time is available. Letters are "personal" if they come in a standard envelope with no window, are hand-signed, have the prospect's name and address typed directly on the envelope rather than on a mailing label, are addressed directly to the recipient by name, and have postage stamps rather than postage meter imprints on the envelope.

TELEMARKETING

Direct Mail Advertising has evolved into Direct Marketing largely because of the incorporation of telemarketing into the Direct Marketing mix. There are two basic categories of telemarketing — *Inbound* and *Outbound.*

Inbound Telemarketing

As its name implies, inbound telemarketing involves incoming calls from customers and prospects. Since its introduction in 1967, the *toll-free number* has fueled much of the growth in the direct marketing industry. According to *ATT*, call volume grew from seven million in 1967 to 13 billion by 1993. By putting a toll free number on all media, customers can call the company to order products, ask questions, and provide valuable feedback. By the mid-1990's, roughly *half of all direct marketing orders* came in via inbound phone calls. This percentage has diminished with the increasing use of the Internet channel, but is likely to remain significant for those who don't have Internet access or prefer to use mobile or land phones to order. On average, putting a toll-free number on all mailings, direct response ads, and collateral materials will boost response by 50 percent. It will also boost corporate image and the perception of product quality. According to *Technical Assistance Research Programs* (TARP), a customer service research firm in Washington D.C., 86% of consumers believe toll-free numbers on packages connote quality products.[1]

Prerequisites

In order to insure the success of an inbound telemarketing program, direct marketers need to be sure that they are properly prepared. Some of the more important prerequisites are provided below.

1. *Computer system.* A computer system with an on-line customer database that is quickly and easily-accessible is essential. In addition to having standard *identification data* such as name, address, phone, e-mail, and fax numbers, this data base should provide such information as the following: Order history, purchase preferences, birth date, customer pro-

file characteristics, important notes from previous conversations, and other data that might be important.

2. *Integrated Accounting Software*. In addition to data base information, the computer system should have integrated accounting software so that the telemarketer can check inventory, answer customer questions about the products, and place orders for products or product literature. Once an order is placed, the system should automatically reserve the inventory and process the paperwork and shipping labels to fulfill the order.

3. *Phone system with sufficient phone lines and personnel.* When a toll-free number is provided, call volume can increase dramatically. Direct Marketers should anticipate this and be prepared with a sufficient number of phone lines and personnel to answer them. Software is also available to telemarketing supervisors that tell them how many people are waiting and how long they have been waiting. It also allows calls to be redirected to phone lines and operators who are not busy or have fewer callers waiting. If callers have to wait too long, the benefits provided by toll-free numbers can become liabilities. With input from their customers, Direct Marketers should set guidelines as to the maximum acceptable time callers are to be on hold. Recordings that put a "positive spin" on the wait — "Due to the heavy demand for our products, you may have to wait several minutes to speak with an operator..." and that provide the caller with options — "If you prefer, you may visit our Web site or fax us your questions and orders..." can mitigate any negative effects.

4. *Training.* Telemarketers should be trained how to handle all types of callers — from friendly to hostile. They should also be trained to answer product questions, determine how the caller heard about the company and products, collect valuable marketplace information, and to do *cross-selling* that involves selling additional products on the same call.

5. *Scripting.* Since telemarketers are unlikely to know a company's entire product line, online scripts can help them. Scripts can also help beginning telemarketers during their training period. These scripts, however, should be outlines rather than "canned" presentations. Over-polished insincerity is not the way to promote a positive relationship with callers. If possible the scripting should be provided on-line system so the operator can bring it up on the screen *on-demand.*

6. *Market Information Forms or Screens.* Many callers provide the telemarketer with valuable marketing information when they call. This information might involve complaints, compliments, new product ideas, competition information, or feedback on performance. When this occurs, telemarketers should be provided with a form that facilitates their capturing of this information and forwarding it to marketing decision makers. Unfortunately, too many companies are not aware of the importance of this information, and do nothing to capture it. At *Pillsbury*, the coding of all product packages enables customer service telemarketers, called "respondents," to quickly pinpoint the source of problems and resolve complaints. Respondents simply ask callers for the product code on the package.

They type it into their computer screen, and can tell callers if the product they purchased had been sitting on the shelf too long. If it has, they send the caller coupons for discounts or free products.[2] This ability to tie a problem back to a specific product can also enable manufacturers to spot and correct defects in their manufacturing processes.

Common Uses and Objectives of Inbound Telemarketing

After the prerequisites are in place, direct marketers should establish certain objectives for their inbound telemarketing program. Typical common uses and objectives include the following:

1. *Order Processing.* On average, Direct Marketers take 50% of their orders via inbound telemarketing. The average phone order is roughly 20% larger than mail orders.
2. *Cross-selling.* By reminding inbound callers that your company offers other products for sale, telemarketers can increase the size of orders at the same time they service customer needs. Cross-selling is one of the reasons why phone orders tend to be larger than mail orders.
3. *Customer Service.* Inbound telemarketing is an excellent customer service vehicle. Customers with questions or complaints can get them quickly resolved by placing an inbound call to a toll-free number. Company representatives can answer questions and complaints and turn negative situations into positive ones.
4. *Wait times.* Direct marketers need to establish the maximum acceptable wait times that customers are on hold. The number of phone lines and telemarketing personnel may need to be augmented if wait times become unacceptable. Of course, obtaining software that will automatically reroute calls to less busy operators or supervisors may provide an alternative solution.
5. *Marketplace information.* Everyone who answers the phone should be trained to capture the marketplace information that comes in. Complaint and question calls that go to order-takers should be rerouted to customer service representatives so that they don't interfere with new business.

Techniques for Boosting Inbound Sales

Sophisticated direct marketers employ a variety of techniques to increase sales from their inbound telemarketing program.

1. *Cross-selling.* When customers call to order one product they are reminded of other products that are for sale or are being discounted. This typically increases the size of orders by 20 to 40%.
2. *Credit Cards.* Credit card orders have a tendency to be 35% larger than cash orders.

Therefore the company should consider taking, and perhaps encouraging, credit card orders.

3. *Sales Promotions.* Offering discounts or bonuses if a certain combination or dollar volume of products is ordered can boost sales to higher levels. This should be part of the cross-selling effort.
4. *Pleasant, friendly, and competent operators.* Unfortunately, too many companies don't know the value of good telemarketers. They prefer paying less for telemarketers than investing in well-trained quality operators. The little that they save in compensation, however, is microscopic compared to the business that they lose. As with any other employees, good operators are "worth their weight in gold." They can boost sales tremendously because they are smart and callers like and trust them.
5. *Training.* Training for all direct marketing personnel can increase sales significantly. The more direct marketing personnel know about techniques to sell and service, boost response, and competently process and fill customer orders the more they can increase sales significantly. The same is true for well-trained customer service representatives who know how to efficiently and effectively answer questions and respond to complaints.
6. *Good Marketing Information System.* By collecting, analyzing, reporting, and taking proper action on marketplace information, the company will continue to improve all aspects of its business. These improvements are quickly translated into greater sales.

Outbound Telemarketing

Outbound telemarketing is the direct marketer's name for contacting customers and prospects by calling them on the telephone. It has grown in popularity as the cost of *face-to-face* contacts has increased to prohibitively high levels. According to a *McGraw-Hill* study, the cost of a face-to-face sales contact averaged $252 in 1985. As with most costs, it has grown at least at the rate of inflation since then. In fact, one could make the case that it has grown at a faster rate due to the sharp increase in energy and transportation costs since 1985. Moreover, studies show that it takes an average of five contacts to close a sale. This means that the average cost of selling a product face-to-face at $1,260 or more! On the other hand, outbound telemarketing puts a trained sales representative in direct contact with a prospect at a small fraction of the cost of a personal sales call. That is its main advantage. Its main disadvantage is that it suffers from a bad image. Why does it have a bad image? Its poor image stems from many years of misuse by poorly-trained telemarketers who don't know any better. They continue to use an outdated technique commonly known as "cold calling."

Cold Calling

Cold calls are phone calls made to prospects with whom there has been *no prior contact*. They represent a misuse of outbound telemarketing because they are interruptions from people you don't know asking questions you don't want to answer usually at times you don't want to answer them. Because they are viewed so negatively by most people, they are not a good way to begin a business relationship — especially with professional or high-technology audiences. More importantly, cold calls are really unnecessary because they can be easily replaced by "warm calls."

Warm calls

Warm calls are phone calls made to prospects who have been contacted before. The introductory contact is often made by a personal letter from a sales person. Sales people use these introductory letters as vehicles to introduce themselves, their products and their company. After the introductions, the cover letter establishes the *next step* and explains it as a benefit for the prospect. This next step is often a follow-up phone call to answer any questions the prospect may have. Product literature is often enclosed so the prospect can have a more complete understanding of the product and the company. Unlike the cold call, the introductory letter is not an interruption. The prospect maintains complete control by choosing to read it at his or her convenience. Because the letter establishes the next step as a benefit to the prospect (a follow-up phone call to answer any questions) from a sales person whom the letter has introduced, the subsequent outbound call is not an interruption from a stranger. Furthermore, the sales person does not have to waste the prospect's time making company, product, and personal introductions because the letter with enclosures has already accomplished that.

When used as a follow-up to direct mail efforts, outbound telemarketing can be very effective in boosting response rates by 300 to 700 percent.

Common Uses of Outbound Telemarketing

Because of its flexibility, outbound telemarketing is commonly used for a variety of marketing purposes. Some of the more important ones are listed below.

1. *Provides an immediate and flexible two-way exchange between the prospect and a company representative.* Ads, direct mail pieces, and other promotional vehicles are one-way. That is, they don't allow for a conversation between a company representative and a prospect. Phone conversations allow explanation and clarification of points that the prospect may not have understood from an ad, billboard, or direct mail piece.

2. *Offers an effective way to maintain personal relationships with market targets.* Outbound calls allow sales representatives to talk with customers and prospects on a very personal level.
3. *Boosts the response of a direct mail campaign.* As discussed above, warm calls can boost response by 300 to 700%.
4. *Helps in order processing and creating buying actions.* An order can be clarified and processed on the spot, and a skilled sales person can convince a prospect to take the next step leading to the purchase of the product.
5. *Provides an excellent vehicle for following up on a prospect's interest in your products.* Many prospects that receive direct mail pieces are interested in the products described, but may be preoccupied with other more important matters. The follow-up call provides a convenient way for them to express their interest in the product without taking the time and trouble of calling a toll-free number or returning a response card.
6. *Enables the company to enhance its corporate image.* Companies who follow up their mailings with personal phone calls communicate to the prospect that they are competent, believe in their products, care about the customer, and want to do a good job. This enhances *corporate image.*
7. *Provides a good vehicle for collecting marketplace information.* During phone conversations, prospects give the callers important information. Outbound callers should have *Market Information Forms* or computer screens ready to capture and report this information.
8. *Facilitates identifying key decision makers in a company.* During outbound calls, the prospect that is contacted may or may not be the key decision maker. Outbound telemarketers can use the phone call to identify key decision makers.
9. *Makes another marketing impression.* If nothing else, an outbound call provides another opportunity for a company to imprint its name and the names of its products on the minds of prospects and customers — the more impressions, the more familiarity, and the greater the chance of building relationships and sales.

THE INTERNET AND WORLD WIDE WEB

The *Internet* — more specifically the *World Wide Web* — is rapidly growing in importance as an effective direct marketing channel. Some companies such as *Cisco Systems*, *Dell Computer*, and *Intel* have been selling millions of dollars worth of products each day from their Web sites. Shortly after establishing its business, *Amazon.com* grew to become one of the biggest, if not the biggest, bookstore in the world.

Easy Access

Any prospective buyer who has access to a personal computer and a modem can hook up to an ever-growing network of computers and Web sites from around the world. Each Web site can provide extensive information on a company and its products. If properly designed, a Web site allows the visitor to select just the information in which he/she is interested. When visitors are ready to buy, Web sites allow them to fill in an order form on the screen or point them to other order methods.

Ordering via the Web allows buyers in different time zones to complete orders and send them electronically at any time of the day or night so that sellers can process them as soon as they open for business the next business day. While this is also true of faxed orders, the Internet provides a number of advantages over direct marketing by fax. Examples of these advantages include the following:

- Some buyers may not have fax capabilities.
- Faxes are often held up because the receiving fax machines are busy. Orders sent via the Internet are automatically sent and saved on the recipient's server to be downloaded when convenient.
- Faxes to some parts of the world can be quite costly while orders over the Internet are sent at no additional cost.
- The fax process sometimes degrades document quality to the point where the order is difficult to read whereas orders sent through the Internet typically arrive letter perfect.
- Faxed orders can be held up or lost if the receiving fax machine runs out of paper or is inadvertently turned off at the end of the business day.
- Downloading information from a Web site provides immediate fulfillment of information requests. Quick fulfillment of information requests is only possible if the seller has a faxback service. Even if they do, faxback services tie up the prospect's fax machine and use his paper supply.

Prospects can find you by searching

In addition to these advantages, visitors can stumble upon your site by searching for the types of products you offer through the various search engines available on the Internet. If your Web site makes a good impression, you will be able to convert some of them to customers and enlist others in your sales army.

Like the telephone, communications through the Internet can be both inbound and outbound. Inbound inquiries and orders most often come to the Web site, and outbound responses are sent by e-mail or other traditional outbound methods.

DIRECT RESPONSE ADS

Direct response ads are advertisements that strongly solicit a buying action. That is, they directly ask the reader to order the product. As with all direct media, good direct response ads should provide the reader with multiple channels to respond — a toll-free phone number, order blank/response card, toll-free fax number, e-mail and a mailing address. Direct response ads should follow the guidelines of the *Universal Marketing Structure*™ and properly use the seven building blocks of marketing. While all ads should solicit a buying action, a direct response ad seeks to generate an order directly from the ad. As a secondary objective, direct response ads try to get prospects to return response cards so that they can be added to in-house lists.

While direct response ads often take the form of print ads, they can also be created as billboards, radio ads, Web advertisements, or television commercials. A rapidly growing form of direct response advertising is direct-order links on Web sites and in e-mails.

INFOMERCIALS

Infomercials are long television commercials — usually 15 to 30 minutes in length — that provide in-depth information on the product being marketed. They are designed to combat the number one threat to television advertising — the propensity of viewers to change channels during commercials, commonly known as "channel surfing." Unfortunately, too many of the early infomercials were used by people who have been subsequently indicted for misrepresenting their products. This has tarnished the image of the infomercial medium. Because of this negative image, direct marketers who wish to use the infomercial as a direct marketing tool need to quickly establish the credibility of their infomercial. This can be done if the infomercial is sponsored by a well-respected company, it is endorsed and narrated by a well-known and respected celebrity, and product benefits are stated without exaggerated claims or "cute" gimmicks. To succeed, the infomercial has to be both educational and entertaining. That is, it has to quickly grab the viewer's attention with important product benefits and keep that attention by entertaining the viewer at the same time it goes into more detail about the product's features and benefits. As with any good direct marketing piece, the "close" of the infomercial should solicit a direct buying action by urging viewers to use the response channel of their choice, such as a toll-free phone or fax number, to order the product.

SHOPPING NETWORKS

Home shopping networks have become popular on cable television. They display products for sale at attractive prices providing toll-free numbers and other channels for viewers to order. They are basically the television equivalent of traditional catalogues. While they have not been commonly used to sell high-technology and industrial products, they should not be dismissed without consideration. As with all marketing, the key is to match the product with the audience.

FULFILLMENT

Once an order is generated via one of the direct marketing media channels described above, the next step is to fill the order promptly. This aspect of direct marketing is known as *fulfillment*. Fulfillment is predicated on having good order entry systems, sufficient inventory to fill orders on a timely basis, a well-staffed and competent staff, and efficient and effective order-taking, shipping and delivery systems. Another important ingredient for successful fulfillment is *attitude*. That is, if all the personal involved in the direct marketing activity from the order takers to the fulfillment staff are *screened* and *trained* to have the proper attitude — doing whatever is necessary to quickly and correctly fill the order, the product will be delivered on a timely basis. If the proper attitude is not present, even good systems won't compensate for this deficiency.

While fulfillment usually refers to the products being marketed, it also applies to product literature. Many prospects e-mail or call a toll-free number requesting more information. Unfortunately, too many companies do not view fulfillment of product literature with the same zeal as the fulfillment of product orders. Consequently, many prospects become disillusioned by the slow, or in some cases, complete lack of response to their requests for product literature. Because of the adage, "It doesn't get any better after the sale," many prospects end their relationships with companies when they do **not** respond promptly to requests for product literature. Direct marketers should understand this, and train their personnel to fulfill literature orders with the same speed as product orders. As a general rule, fulfillment is successful if the order or request is filled within a 48-hour period and the customer receives the order within one work week, or five business days.

DIRECT MARKETING TO MAKE PERSONAL SELLING MORE EFFICIENT

Up until this point, direct marketing has been discussed as a separate promotional strategy and distribution channel. It can also be used to improve the efficiency of the company's sales force. Because the costs of selling face-to-face have grown to be prohibitively expensive — over $1,260 per sale as discussed in a previous section, direct marketing techniques can be used to cut down the average number of face-to-face contacts required to close a sale. That is, sales people can employ direct marketing techniques to contact prospects and customers by mail and phone and thereby cut the number of expensive face-to-face calls down to one, two, or, in some cases, zero! *IBM*, *Xerox*, *Dell*, *Hewlett-Packard* and many other companies, large and small, have employed direct marketing techniques with considerable success to improve the efficiency of their sales forces.

Rather than spending all their time visiting prospects and customers, sales people can invest the time and money savings to (1) reach more customers and prospects and (2) boost contact frequencies by calling, writing, or e-mailing them more often. By spending more time in the office, sales people are able to field more inbound phone calls and host more office visits from highly-qualified prospects.

Measuring the actual benefits of employing direct marketing techniques to improve the personal selling efforts is the job of the company's marketing information system. In relation to direct marketing, this system is discussed in the next section.

MARKETING INFORMATION SYSTEM FOR DIRECT MARKETING

As mentioned at the beginning of this chapter, two of the distinguishing characteristics of direct marketing are (1) it uses a database and (2) its results are directly measurable. To build an accurate and up-to-date database and to properly measure the results of direct marketing, a good Marketing Information System is required. While a subsequent chapter of this book will discuss the Marketing Information System in some detail, the elements that specifically relate to direct marketing are more appropriately covered here.

What is measured?

Good marketers make every effort to measure the following:

- What is likely to happen.
- What actually happens.
- Why it happened.
- What is the lifetime value of a customer.
- What should be changed to create a more successful result next time.

Testing to determine what is likely to happen?

Before a direct marketing campaign is put into effect, considerable testing should be done to help insure a successful outcome and to avoid wasting money on the wrong approach.

Many variables are tested, usually one at a time. Some of the most common test variables include the following:

1. *The Offer* (usually presented in the headline of the piece). An offer to a customer can be stated in many different ways. While many marketers believe they know the best way to state an offer, most of them are guessing. The best way to determine which offer will work best in a given situation is to test the different offers. For example, there are many ways to state a special "two for the price of one" promotion — "*Two for the price of one.*" "*Buy*

one, and get the second one free." "Buy one for 99¢... Get the second one for 1¢." "50% off the regular price." "Buy two, and get 50% off." "Half Price on both when you buy two."

2. *Mailer.* Different designs, colors, and words in the mailer can generate different responses. Testing can determine the most successful mailing piece.
3. *Envelope.* If a Solo mailer is used, different envelopes can generate different responses. The size, style (solid or window), design, color, and words written on the envelope may be tested.
4. *Enclosures.* The enclosures inside the envelope can also be tested. The number and types of enclosures as well as the style, color and design of these enclosures can be some of the variables tested.
5. *Mailing List.* Different lists may be tested to determine which one will produce the greatest response before buying or renting the entire lists.

While many other parameters can be tested, the above provides an illustrative list. Rather than discuss other possible variables in detail, it is more important to describe testing procedures.

Common Testing Guidelines

To help insure the accuracy of a test, the following guidelines should be followed:

1. *Test big differences.* The bigger the differences between variables, the more accurate the results. For example, if you are testing color. White vs. Blue will provide a better test than two shades of blue that are very close to each other in the color spectrum.
2. *Test one, or a couple (in the case of grid testing), of things at a time.* When you test one variable, you can be sure that the differences in results are from that one variable. When you test several variables, it is more difficult to be sure what is causing the differences. Also, there may be interactions between the multiple variables.
3. *Numbers.* For each variable or test cell (in the case of Grid Testing explained below), a sample of at least 5,000 names should be tested. The larger the number, the better the level of confidence. The actual sample size you select depends on the response rate and the margin of error you allow, and the level of confidence you desire. Given these parameters, the sample size can be determined using standard statistical tables. The objective is to obtain at least 50 responses per variable or cell. Remember that you can expect an average response of one percent — hence the 5,000 sample. To increase your level of confidence, you can increase the test sample, but you should do so gradually — from 5,000 to say 20,000. You can lower the number if most of the early data converges or agrees.

4. *Test often.* You should test every time you do a mailing or run a direct response ad. Many forego tests because they take time and cost money. However, the time and money is very small compared to what could be lost without proper testing. Therefore, you should test as often as you can.
5. *Budget.* If you want to do it right, you should allocate 10 to 20% of your direct marketing campaign budget to testing.

Common Testing Procedures

When a test is performed on a particular variable or cell, the "winner" becomes the standard against which you will measure all future changes. This standard is called the *Control*. For example, if your most successful mailings are traditionally sent on white stationery, white becomes the Control. In future mailings, if you want to test other colors, you test them against the Control. That is, you will send out at least 5,000 pieces on white stationery and another 5,000 on stationery of the color being tested. If the new color generates a greater response, it becomes the new Control, or the new one to beat.

Grid Testing

A popular method of testing two, or more, variables at once is called Grid Testing. As shown in the table of *Figure 10-3* below, each cell represents the intersection of two variables — Offer and Mailing List.

	Offer 1	Offer 2	TOTAL
Mailing List A	5,000	5,000	10,000
Mailing List B	5,000	5,000	10,000
TOTAL	10,000	10,000	20,000

Figure 10-3

This table shows that each cell (which represents the intersection of "Offer" and "Mailing List") has a sample size of 5,000, and that the four different combinations being tested require a total sample size of 20,000. That's the same number that would result if each of the four variables were tested individually. Therefore, while grid testing tests more than one variable at a time, it provides a sufficient sample size for each cell to provide a statistically significant test — the same sample size if the variables were tested individually.

Measuring what actually happens?

Remember, direct marketers list "measurable results" as one of the distinguishing characteristics of direct marketing. While efforts should be made, using a *marketing information system*, to measure the results of all marketing strategies, direct marketers do perhaps the best job of generating measurable results. Therefore all marketers can learn a lesson in measuring from direct marketers. The first lesson to learn about measuring results is to determine what variables should be measured.

Variables to be measured. While the specific variables to be measured will vary with each situation, most direct marketers would try to measure *responses*, *response rates*, *costs*, *qualified leads*, *average order size*, *sales in units and dollars*, and *numbers required to break-even*. More specifically, the variables to be measured might include the following:

- *Number of responses* — The actual number of responses to a direct mail or outbound telemarketing campaign, or number of "hits" on a Web site.
- *Response rate* — The actual number of responses divided by the total mailed.
- *Cost per response* — The total cost of the campaign divided by the number of responses.
- *Number of qualified leads* — The number of responses who have the interest and ability to buy the product in the current period. Some people may respond to collect information for the future or out of curiosity. They, of course, should be viewed as referral sources and/or future sales prospects.
- *Percentage of qualified leads* — The number of qualified leads divided by the total number of responses.
- *Cost per qualified lead* — The total cost of the campaign divided by the number of qualified leads.
- *Number of buyers* — The actual number who buy the product.
- *Percentage of qualified leads that buy* — The number of buyers divided by the number of qualified leads.
- *Percentage of prospects that buy* — The number of buyers divided by the number of responses.
- *Percentage of total sample that buy* — The number of buyers divided by the number to whom the mailer was sent.
- *Total initial sales in units and $* — The total sales in units and dollars resulting from the campaign.

- *Average Order size in units and $* — The total sales in units and dollars resulting from the campaign divided by the number of buyers.
- *Profit Margin* — The gross profit margin on selling one unit of product. As discussed in the chapter on Pricing Strategies, *Gross Profit Margin* = *(Price - Cost)* ÷ *Price*.
- *Gross Profit Per Order* — Average Order size in $ multiplied by Gross Profit Margin.
- *Number of Sales to Break-even* — The total cost of the campaign divided by the Gross Profit Per Order.
- *Number to be Mailed to Break-even* — [(Number of Sales to Break-even) divided by (1%)] divided by Percentage of responses that buy. For example, if 100 sales are required, on average, to breakeven and the Percentage of responses who buy is 40%, you should mail out 25,000 pieces to breakeven since (100÷0.01)÷0.4 = 25,000.

Measuring Lifetime Value

In addition to measuring what happens and predicting the breakeven quantities, it is important for direct marketers to measure the lifetime value of a customer. Lifetime value is the basis upon which book, record, and CD clubs operate. That is, since they know what the average lifetime value of a customer is, all they have to do to boost sales is boost the number of customers. Because they know the importance of lifetime value, knowledgeable marketers do whatever is necessary to take good care of their customers.

The variables and measurements required to calculate the *lifetime value of a customer* typically include the following:

- *Number of repeat buyers* — The actual number who buy the product more than once via direct channels.
- *Average Number of repeat purchases* — The total number of repeat purchases divided by the actual number who buys the product more than once.
- *Percentage of Repeat Buyers* — The actual number who buy the product more than once divided by the total number of buyers.
- *Average Order size in $* — The total sales in dollars resulting from the campaign divided by the number of buyers.
- *Total Repeat Sales* — Number of repeat buyers multiplied by Average Number of repeat purchases multiplied by Average Order size in dollars.
- *Total Initial Sales in $* — The total sales in units and dollars resulting from the campaign.
- *Lifetime Value* — Total Repeat Sales plus Total Initial Sales in dollars.

- *Lifetime Value of a Customer* — Lifetime Value divided by Number of customers.

Analyzing why it happened?

All marketers should do "post mortems" to analyze the results after each campaign. While Direct Marketers are no exception, they are more much more pragmatic. That is, on each successive campaign, they are focused on beating the *control* from the previous campaign. If they try something new that will beat the *control* mailing package or mailing list, they are happy. Because of this attitude they are willing to experiment. If the experiment does not work during a test, they can always return to the *control* for the main campaign.

Analyzing how to be more successful

Direct marketers use their systematic methodology to be more successful. This methodology is summarized below.

1. Develop systems to measure results.
2. Establish a *control* that is the winning approach to a specific direct marketing problem.
3. Experiment with new approaches all the time.
4. Test these approaches using a statistically valid sample (a sample size of at least 5,000) for each variable tested. The sample size can be smaller when there is converging data.
5. Use the winner of the test as the new *control* for the campaign.
6. Measure the results of the campaign according to the variables described in the above sections on "Measuring What Actually Happens" and "Measuring Lifetime Value."
7. Listen, listen, listen to your customers, accurately record, analyze, and take action on what they say, and take good care of them.

CONCLUSION

Direct Marketing has grown in both scope and importance as the costs of marketing products through traditional distribution channels have skyrocketed. In particular, the cost of face-to-face selling has become prohibitively high for most high-tech and industrial products — rising to over $252 per call, with an average of five calls required to close sales. By combining direct mail, with telemarketing, direct response advertising and other direct channels, many products can be sold directly to the consumer without any face-to-face selling. Those that still require face-to-face sales can also benefit from direct marketing techniques since direct marketing methods can be used to generate leads, boost response, qualify leads, and cut down the number face-to-face calls required to close sales. That is, direct marketing can greatly improve the selling efficiency of the company sales force as well as be used as a separate promotional strategy and distribution channel.

Personal selling is covered in the next chapter as both a promotional strategy and a form of distribution. Since this is a book on marketing rather than personal selling, it is examined from a marketer's perspective.

[1]Carl Qunitanilla and Richard Gibson, "'Do Call Us': More Companies Install 1-800 Phone Lines," *Wall Street Journal*, April 20, 1994, pg. B1.

[2]Richard Gibson, "Pillsbury Telephones Ring with Peeves, Praise," *Wall Street Journal*, April 20, 1994, pg. B1.

TIPS and Exercises

1. Create your own database of prospects if you don't already have one.
2. Identify outside lists (response and compiled lists as appropriate) that match your target audiences.
3. Contact list brokers to get recommendations and pricing.
4. Create effective mailing pieces using the building blocks of marketing and the UMS™.

Chapter 11

DNA of Personal Selling

"Everyone lives by selling something."

Robert Louis Stevenson

As a first step in exploring how marketing should support the sales efforts of a company, it is important for marketers to understand what is meant by the term *Personal Selling*.

What is Personal Selling?

The commonly-accepted definition of Personal Selling is *the process by which you influence another person to make a decision in your favor*. The problem with this definition is that it leaves out most important part of a *market-driven* philosophy — the customer. To correct this problem, our *Universal Sales System*™ definition should be modified to read as follows: *the process by which you influence another person to make a decision in their and your favor*. This incorporates the *both sides must win* philosophy which is the foundation of all business transactions where the customer and the sales person are both better off. It also incorporates the *key mechanism* for achieving success in sales — *developing personal relationships*.

In order to create an effective *personal selling system* that employs this definition and philosophy, we should first understand the prerequisites for successful selling. These prerequisites can be grouped into two main categories — *knowledge prerequisites* and *systems prerequisites*.

KNOWLEDGE PREREQUISITES

A famous English philosopher, named Francis Bacon, is credited with the phrase, "Knowledge is Power." Those with the knowledge have the power to win again and again. They have the tools to make money, and nobody can take these tools away from them. The areas of knowledge that are important for successful sales are provided in the following sections.

Product and Company

Effective sales people should know virtually everything about their product and company including names, models, features, benefits, advantages, performance, prices, company and product history, serviceability, reliability, compatibility, strengths, and weaknesses.

Competition

Although acquiring knowledge about the competition is not as easy as learning about one's own products, an important goal of the sales staff should be to learn as much about key competitors and their products as they know about their own. It is especially important to know the strengths and weaknesses of the competition. The company's Marketing Information

System should collect competitive information and provide it to sales professionals via handy notebooks that they can take with them into the field. For more in-depth competitive information, high-tech marketers should also maintain competitive files and give sales people access to these files. Since sales people have primary contact with the marketplace, their duties should include collecting and inputting critical competitive information into the *Marketing Information System.* Once the data is put into the system, it can be properly shared with all other sales personnel who might benefit from using it.

Customer

Each prospect and customer is different and should be regarded as such. However, successful sales people should know the patterns and profiles that allow them to better understand the needs of prospective buyers. These patterns are often grouped into *Professional, Cultural, Socioeconomic, Personality* and *Adoption to Innovation* tendencies where people in these groups have similar needs and exhibit similar buying behaviors. For example, with regard to *Adoption to Innovation* profiles, the sales person should know that certain subgroups within each target segment are most likely to buy a product during different stages of its *Life Cycle.* When a product is newly introduced, the *Avant Garde,* or *Innovator,* segment of the target audience is likely to buy. As this group accepts the product and sales enter the growth phase, the *Early Adopter* group begins to buy the product. Once the product reaches the maturity stage and becomes more established, the *Early Majority* starts buying. After it has been accepted for a while and begins to decline, the *Late Majority* begins to purchase the product. Once the product is in the decline stage, the group known as the *Laggards* become the most-likely buyers. This process was discussed in *Chapter 5* and graphically illustrated in *Figure 5-3.*

Self confidence

As Socrates is credited with saying, "Know Thyself." In the context of sales, this is particularly important. Successful sales people know their strengths and weaknesses. They use their strengths in sales situations, and work on their weaknesses on their own time — often by attending seminars and taking courses. Most importantly, sales people have to develop *confidence.* Confidence is one of the most important prerequisites for successful selling. When the sales person is not confident, the prospective buyer often interprets this behavior in a negative way. Some think nervousness connotes dishonesty. Others think there is something wrong with the product. Still others believe that the sales person is not competent and therefore unable to take good care of them. A few might feel sorry for the sales person, but most prospects don't buy products because of sorrow or guilt.

Even though sales people should know their weaknesses and tell the truth, they should never reveal them in a sales situation. Admitting or revealing weaknesses communicates negative and confusing messages to prospective buyers who are looking for strengths and benefits — not weaknesses.

How to sell

An area of particular weakness of many sales people is that they have never really learned how to properly sell. Most have learned on the job, and they have picked up many bad habits from their more-experienced mentors. Learning how to properly sell is an ongoing process that requires proper training and ongoing study and practice. Just as professional athletes need to continuously learn and practice their sport, sales people need to continuously learn and practice their profession.

SYSTEMS PREREQUISITES

Complementing their areas of knowledge, successful sales people require the support of certain systems. Systems help them to produce consistently competent results. The most important sales support systems are presented below.

Lead card

All sales people require a system for properly recording and following up on sales leads. The central element to this system is a *lead card*, which can either be a physical card or an image of a lead card on a computer screen — preferably both. An example of a typical lead card is shown in *Figure 9-2* of *Chapter 9* on Promotion. All lead cards should have the following information preprinted on the front of the card: (1) *prospect identification information* such as date of the lead, title, name, position, company name, address, phone number(s), fax number, e-mail address, secretary name, and birth date; (2) *degree of interest* so that all prospects are categorized according to one of three degrees of interest — *hot, medium, or cool;* (3) *product interest* so that the sales person can simply check a box representing the products in which the prospect has expressed an interest, and (4) *lead source* that provides an indication of how the prospect first heard of your product or company. On the back of this lead card, sales people will record the following: (1) the *date of each contact* with the prospect, (2) the *next step* that the prospect and sales person have agreed to take, (3) the *next contact date* upon that the sales person and prospect have agreed to correspond, (4) any *objections* to buying the product that the prospect has identified during the contact, and (5) any other relevant information provided by the prospects such as competitive products that they are considering, additional needs they identify, and key decision makers who will help to make the final purchase decision. The optimal lead card size is 4 x 6 inches (10.16 x 15.24 cm).

Lead Card Filing System

To insure effective follow-up, lead cards need to be properly sorted and filed. The *hot* and *medium* leads should be kept in an *Active* file by next contact date. Each lead should be filed behind a divider tab that corresponds to the day of the month of the next contact date. Each day, the sales person should pull those lead cards behind the divider tab corresponding to that day and should contact those leads as agreed. Cool leads should be filed alphabetically by prospect or company name, in a *Cool, or slower-moving,* file. These cool leads should be contacted at least once every three months, or every other month if possible, by mail or phone. Contact at these regular intervals will insure that prospects are contacted when their *buying window* is active — that is when they are ready to buy. If a computer system is used, leads can be automatically sorted by next contact date. It is recommended, however that a manual card system should be used in conjunction with the computer for one or more of the following reasons:

- Lead cards can be reviewed in places where computer screens are impractical (such as in telephone booths, moving cars, and trade show booths).
- Lead cards can be a back up should the computer malfunction.
- Notes can be taken on lead cards during phone or face-to-face contacts where typing on keyboards might be considered distracting or rude.
- Computers may not be turned on when a prospect relates an important bit of information that needs to be captured quickly.

Once a sale is closed, the lead card should be filed alphabetically in a *Customer* file by customer name. As with *Cool* leads, customers should be contacted at least once every three months by phone or mail. Wooden, plastic, or metal file boxes with divider tabs that accommodate 4 x 6-inch (10.16 x 15.24-centimeter) lead cards can be purchased at stationery and office supply stores.

Hot List

The *Hot List* is used to focus attention and effort on the Hot leads that are likely to close in the current period. To qualify for the *Hot List,* a lead typically should have a 25% or better chance of closing in the current period. While individual sales people use *Hot Lists* to focus on closing their hot leads, sales managers typically use them to *revise sales estimates* in the current period, *help sales people answer objections,* and to *update sales forecasts*. *Figure 11-1* provides an example of an actual *Hot List* used by a company.

Salesperson ______________ **HOT LIST** Date ______________

Contact and/or Firm Name•Address	Decision Maker(s)	Product(s) Proposed	Proposal Date	$Amount Proposal	%Chance Closing *	Expected Value	Objection(s)
Sales Person Sales Forecast This Period							**Amount Over (Under) Quota**
Period Quota or Goal							

Note: This hot list should contain all prospects who have a 25% chance, or better, of closing this period.

Figure 11-1. Hot List

Promotion Effectiveness Report

This report is created and used by marketing to measure the effectiveness of promotional efforts. It summarizes the number of *leads, presentations,* and *sales* generated in the current period by advertising or promotional source. The data for this report comes from the boxes checked in the *lead source* section of each sales person's *lead cards.* Since this report also contains totals for the leads, presentations, and sales generated by each sales person in the current period, it also allows sales managers and individual sales people to calculate their *close ratios.* The *close ratio,* or sales person "batting average," is the percentage of leads or presentations that are converted to sales. Once sales people know their *close ratios,* they know how many leads and presentations they need to achieve their sales goals, or quotas. *Figure 11-2* shows an actual *Promotion Effectiveness Report* used by a company to determine the *effectiveness of promotion strategies* and *close ratios.*

Promotion Effectiveness Form

Name		Sales/Presentations Ratio		Sales/Leads Ratio		Date	

Promotion Type	Specific Source	Leads		Presentations		Sales		Comments
		Tally	Total	Tally	Total	Tally	Total	
E-mail								
Search Engine								
Banner Ad • Link other site								
Referral								
Mailing								
Print Ad								
Virutal Store								
Newsletter								
Trade Show								
Seminar								
Affiliate program								
Speech								
Radio/TV commercial								
Word-of-Mouth								
Walk-in • Web surfer								
Telemarketing								
Other 1								
Other 2								
TOTAL								

Figure 11-2. Promotion Effectiveness Report

Sales Territories

Territories are important sales system elements because they help companies to (1) insure market coverage, (2) achieve overall sales goals, (3) assign sales responsibilities, and (4) provide objective standards, or quotas, against which sales performance can be measured and sales compensation can be determined. Sales territories are usually based on geographical boundaries. However, they may also be set according to product or industry. Therefore, instead of being responsible for sales in say the *Western Region,* a sales person may be responsible for a specific product line — no matter where it is sold — or for all products sold to customers in the bio-medical industry. Marketers typically work with sales managers to create sales territories out of fundamental building blocks. In the United States, geographical sales territories are often formed using one of the following building blocks: zip or postal codes, census tracts, telephone area codes, cities, counties, SMSAs (Standard Metropolitan Statistical Areas), States, time zones, and regions (Northeast, Mid-Atlantic, Southeast, Midwest, Southwest, and Northwest). For international sales, building blocks are often based upon regions, countries, territories defined by language or culture, and continents.

Sales Quotas

Derived from the Marketing Plan, these are the goals sales people must achieve to meet sales objectives. A good sales manager will (1) take the overall sales goals, (2) divide them by the number of sales people, and (3) modify them according to the level of experience, differences in sales territories, historic *close ratios,* and sales person input from each sales person. You may also remember from the discussion of *planning*, that goals are essential elements of the *planning* function of management. Of course, the other essential ingredients of planning are strategies to achieve these goals.

Time and Expense Management

Time and expense management is a critical component to successful personal selling. While most company personnel spend a majority of their time in the office under the watchful eye of a supervisor, many sales people spend a lot of time in the market territory unsupervised. This presents some potential problems for the marketing manager. These include (1) insuring that they are satisfying the needs of their target audience, (2) covering their territory efficiently and effectively, (3) insuring that they are spending their time wisely, and (4) controlling expenses.

Call reports

Call reports are used to insure that the sales person is covering the territory, contacting customers, and following-up on good prospects. They also enable the sales manager to determine if they are calling on sufficient numbers to meet their sales quotas. For inside sales people who don't visit customers in the field, call reports can refer to phone calls, e-mails, or faxes.

Time budgets

Time budgets help to guide sales people on how they should spend their time. They often suggest how much time sales people should spend on the phone, personal visits, demonstrations, letters, travel, sales paperwork, and training. In addition to budgeting time, they guide sales people with numbers such as the number of phone calls, personal visits, leads, demonstrations, and sales they should do each day, week, month, quarter, and year in order to meet their sales quotas.

Expense guidelines and reports

To control travel, lodging and entertainment expenses, sales people should be given pro forma expense guidelines. In addition to providing dollar amounts, these guidelines might include policies on airline travel and hotel stays. For example, they may require sales people to fly tourist class and, if possible, book flights with sufficient lead time to insure the most economical form of travel. They may also require sales people to stay in certain hotels and book rental cars from specific agencies where your company has negotiated a special reduced-price arrangement. At the end of each pay period, sales people should fill out expense reports that detail expenses and attach receipts whenever possible. The conditions under which exceptions to the guidelines are permitted should also be delineated in these guidelines. Giving proper guidance to sales people does them a great service. It facilitates their decision-making and takes the guesswork out of what they should do in given situations. It also reduces the chances of their getting blamed for something that is not their fault.

Sales Notebook

Successful sales people need reference materials to answer questions, quote prices and product options, answer objections, and provide credible proof for their answers. To facilitate their use in the office or the field, these reference materials should be organized into a Sales Notebook. The typical sections of this notebook are likely to include…

1. *Product/Price* section — includes complete descriptions of products, options, accessories, supplies, and other product components with associated prices.
2. *Competition* section — provides important information on the competition to help sales people explain your company's advantages over competitors, and includes articles written by independent third parties that point out the weaknesses of key competitors.

3. *Answers to Frequently-asked Questions* section — includes a company-wide compilation of good consensus answers to common objections.
4. *Credibility* section — contains important *positive* publicity on your company and products along with a company history that lists its accomplishments.
5. *Customer references* section — lists good customers who have agreed to be references for your company and may include customer testimonials and actual examples of customer work produced using your company's products.
6. *Standard Letters* section — contains pre-approved standard letters that have proven effective throughout the various phases of the *Sales Cycle* and that sales people can use to save considerable time when they need to send a letter to a prospect or customer.
7. *Proof* section — contains articles, charts, and other credible data that helps to support answers to prospect objections and questions.

It should be noted that as the sections of this notebook grow, they are likely to involve separate notebooks. Even if that happens, a summary of the best material should be included in a single notebook that sales people can take with them into the field.

Tools

In conjunction with the notebooks and systems, sales people require certain tools that help them to achieve success. Important tools are likely to include the following:

1. *Magic mailbox* that allows the sales person to avoid company mailing inefficiencies and quickly respond to requests. This usually involves finding a mail box outside the office.
2. *Notebook* or *lap-top personal computer* that the sales person can use for lead tracking and follow-up, maintaining mailing lists, creating and modifying standard letters, generating sales quotes, preparing sales paperwork, and faxing, or e-mailing sales paperwork to the factory or home office.
3. *Appointment book* and *calendar* that allows the sales person to schedule up to 8 appointments per day (could be done on the computer).
4. *Pocket calculator* for figuring quotes and sales orders (if not already part of the computer).
5. *Good secretary* or *voice mail system* for distributing calls and taking messages.
6. *Trustworthy pen* for writing quotes or orders, and a backup if it proves untrustworthy.
7. *Quote and proposal forms* to quote a price or write up an order.
8. *Nice briefcase* for transporting any of the above.

While the above list might seem trivial, it is not. There are too many cases of sales people who have lost sales because they have had to interrupt their presentation as a result of not having one or more of the above tools. During such interruptions, anything can happen, and most of it is bad. The negative consequences include the following: (1) Prospects have time to think and become distracted by their busy schedule; (2) Any distractions are likely to result in a reduction of the prospect's *buying temperature* and a lost sale; and (3) If sales people are ill-prepared, prospects are likely to question their competence and their ability to take care of any problems after the sale.

Once these prerequisites are satisfied, it is important for marketers to understand the *Sales Cycle* and the systems and structures required to support *Sales-Cycle* activities.

SALES CYCLE

The *Sales Cycle* provides a framework for understanding the activities required to successfully execute the sales function. The *Sales Cycle,* as graphically illustrated in *Figure 11-3*, includes the following major steps: (1) *Generating* and *categorizing leads,* (2) *Giving presentations,* (3) *Identifying and Answering Objections,* (4) *Closing sales,* and (5) *Post-sale follow-up* activities.

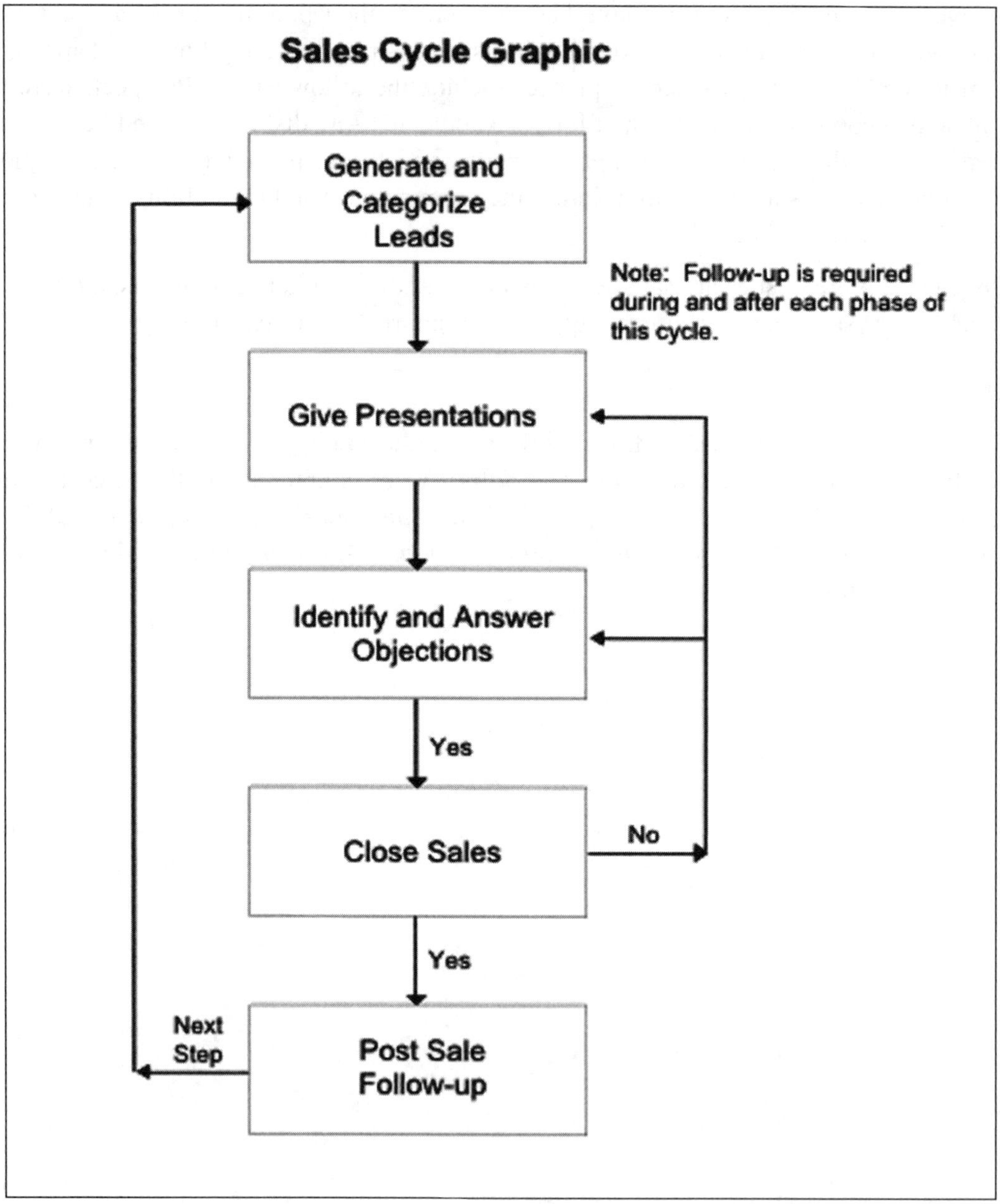

Figure 11-3. Sales Cycle Graphic

The company's marketing rarely provides enough leads for sales people to make their quotas and achieve their earnings potential. Furthermore, the best sales people are good at enlisting others to pass them leads and help them sell. They do this by systematically developing a large network of helpers called their *sales army*. They employ direct marketing techniques, discussed in the previous chapter, to create new sales opportunities. Other good sources of leads can be generated by sending reprints of good ads and publicity to prospects, following-up on abandoned files and leads from sales people who have left the company, and making friends with others in the company who come into contact with good prospects. Once leads are generated, they are categorized as to *hot, medium* or *cool.* Although many believe that leads should be qualified, and cold leads should be discarded, it is not a good idea to discard any leads. There are several reasons for keeping even cool leads including the following: (1) With proper sales techniques, cool leads can be converted to warm or hot leads; (2) Some leads are cool merely because prospects are not ready to buy (their *buying window* is not active), but if you stay in contact, they are more likely to buy from you when they are ready to buy; (3) Even if they don't buy, they can refer others; and (4) Every contact has a name, address, and phone number — precious commodities to a business — especially since companies pay many thousands or even millions of dollars just for the opportunity to make a positive impression on fresh prospects. Also, once a customer and prospect database has been developed, it becomes a valuable commodity that can be sold or rented to other noncompetitive companies.

Giving presentations or demonstrations

Marketers and sales managers should be able to train and guide their sales staffs to give effective presentations. The keys to good presentations are (1) properly *preparing* for the presentation and (2) *controlling* the presentation.

Preparing for the Presentation

Good presentation preparation includes the following:

- Understanding the prospect's business and needs
- Preparing good questions to ask the prospect during the presentation — these questions should identify their needs, competitive products they are considering, how they are filling these needs now, the key decision makers, their budget, time frame for buying
- Making sure the product and equipment used in the presentation work.
- Providing for backup systems just in case they don't work.
- Anticipating the prospect's questions and preparing answers.
- Anticipating and preparing for failures.

Controlling the Presentation

Maintaining control involves the following:

- Asking good questions that clarify the sales person's understanding of the information that has already been collected, or asking these questions for the first time.
- Listening and responding to the answers.
- Communicating everything as benefits to customers that solve their problems or fills their needs identified in the steps above.
- Developing good presentation skills — being prepared, organized, competent, confident, interesting, and responsive.
- Knowing how to handle any objections that might arise.
- Knowing how to handle an argumentative prospect.
- Recognizing and acting upon buying and rejection signals.
- Controlling emotions so that both sides win.

Answering objections

Objections are obstacles to the sale. If the prospect has not bought the product, they have at least one objection. All major objections must be answered before a sale can be made. Before answering them, they need to be identified. This is sometimes difficult because prospects often hide them. Good sales people can uncover them by asking the appropriate probing questions, listening to the answers, and observing the prospect's body language. Objections are best answered with the help of the Sales Notebook discussed above. That is, for the prospect to believe the sales person's statements and answers, credible *proof* needs to be provided by independent third parties. This *proof* comes from articles, surveys, publicity, comparison charts, studies, awards, and other information that is collected and typically stored in the Sales Notebook.

The keys to answering objections

To properly answer objections, sales people should do the following:

1. *Lower the barrier.* Objections are barriers that need to be lowered before sales people can answer or eliminate them. The best way to do that is to empathize with the prospect's pain — by showing understanding as to why they have them.
2. *Identify the real objection.* Before proceeding, it is important to identify the real objection. For example, if the prospect states an objection such as, "It costs too much." The *real* objection is not clear. Does the prospect perceive the price to be high compared with the

price of a competitive product? Is the prospect short of funds? Is the prospect unsure of the quality or value of the product? Is the prospect unaware that the product will pay for itself within a short period of time and save money thereafter? A good sales person will ask some questions to clarify the real objection so that he or she can answer it properly.

3. *Break it down.* Barriers are easier to eliminate if they are first broken down into tangible, answerable components and bite-sized pieces. Tangible components are typically forms of time and money. Bite-sized pieces are created by taking the big obstacle (say a $1,200 price difference) and breaking it down into yearly, monthly, weekly, daily and hourly pieces. Once the big barrier is in small pieces, the sales person can more easily show how the product will save or make more time and money than it will cost — generating a positive return on investment and quick payback.
4. *Answer with confidence.* In all phases of the sales cycle, confidence is very important. It communicates competence and honesty. It makes prospects feel comfortable, and causes them to have trust and confidence in the sales person.
5. *Provide proof to substantiate your answers.* To solidify the trust fostered by the confident answers, proof needs to be provided. The Sales Notebook described above can do this. In fact, when sales people receive objections, they should turn to their notebooks for answers and for proof to support them. If they can't find the proof they need, they should find articles and do other research to obtain the proof they need to substantiate their claims. The best proof is from independent, credible, third party sources.

Get agreement

After providing proof and completing the answer, the sales person should make sure the prospect is satisfied with the answer. If not, more proof or additional answers may be needed.

Closing the sale

After answering a major objection or receiving a *buying signal* are the best times to close a sale. Buying signals can be verbal or nonverbal. Good sales people don't always wait for buying signals. They try to close the sale many times during the sales cycle. They do this by using *trial close* techniques. The *trial close* is based on the sales person's assumption that a sale is possible. The sales person tests the situation by "sprinkling bread on the water and seeing if the prospect bites." A good example of a trial close technique is the *two positive choices close* whereby the sales person gives the prospect two choices — both of which lead to the sale. An example is, "We can deliver on Tuesday or Wednesday, which would you prefer?" If trial closes don't result in a sale, the sales person can identify and answer the new objection per the procedure discussed above. Unlike the trial close, the *standard* close doesn't make assumptions that the sale is made. It gets the prospect's agreement at each point in the sales cycle, summarizes the points of agreement, and asks for the order when all known objections have been answered and the prospect has accepted the answers. The keys to closing the sale are (1) *asking for the order* by posing a closing question, and (2) Doing so with *confidence.* If the sales person exhibits any lack of confidence, the prospect is likely to interpret this as a sign of weakness in the product, company, or sales person. Any such weakness is likely to undermine the sale.

Post-sale follow-up

Sales may become unclosed because of a *"disease"* which many buyers get called *buyer's remorse,* or what consumer behaviorists call post-purchase *cognitive dissonance.* The likelihood of a buyer getting *buyer's remorse* is directly proportional to the *risks* associated with the sale. That is, if the product or service is very expensive or if it requires a commitment to a standard that deviates from the industry norm, the purchase can be perceived as risky. To avoid or mitigate buyers remorse, sales people need to (1) anticipate that it might happen, (2) know what to do if it does, (3) avoid language that tends to scare buyers such as *sign here* or *contract* (both of which point them to their lawyers or cause them to think too much) when completing the sales paperwork, (4) send prospects an *Installation Letter* or *Confirmation Letter*, that reassures them that they have made the right decision and advises them of the next steps, (5) be careful to answer any and all questions in a timely and friendly manner (you don't want to give them the slightest reason to get mad at you or your company), and (6) make sure that others involved in the sale, from the receptionist to the delivery person, do the same. Everyone who has potential contact with customers during this phase should be alerted that buyers may be looking for reasons to change their mind, and cancel the sale. These company personnel should be trained to use extra care in their handling of these buyers. In addition to avoiding buyer's remorse, a secondary objective of this phase is to enlist customers in your *sales army* so they will (1) refer leads, (2) be willing to act as good references, (3) buy from you again, and (4) provide good quotes and testimonials for your ads and other promotional strategies.

BUILDING RELATIONSHIPS

At the end of each step of the *Sales Cycle,* sales people should be sure to (1) *establish the next step* and (2) *get agreement from the prospect* on the next step. Establishing the next step *sets up a test* that the sales person is going to *pass by following-up* with the prospect *as agreed.* The various systems elements described in the previous *Systems Prerequisites* section will help the sales person to properly follow-up and pass the necessary tests. Getting the prospect's agreement on the next step allows the prospect to have *ownership* of the next step. It makes the prospect an *equal partner* in the process (remember the *both sides win* philosophy). When the sales person follows up, the prospect will view this as doing what was already agreed by both parties rather than an interruption or annoyance initiated by one party — the sales person. This mechanism of *setting up the next step* (or test), *getting agreement on the next step,* and *following up as agreed* (or passing the test) is the key mechanism for building solid relationships. If the sales person always follows up as promised and agreed, the prospect is more likely to *trust* the sales person. Buyers know that problems are likely to arise. They want relationships with sales people and companies that will help them to solve those problems. Once *trusted,* sales people are more likely to make the sale, and if they take good care of customers after the sale, a *loyal* relationship usually develops.

In summary, the relationship building process involves the following steps:

1. *During every contact, set up the next step.* This becomes a *test* of the relationship that the sales person will pass.
2. *Get agreement on the next step.* This gives control and part ownership of the next step to the prospect. Having part ownership means they will facilitate rather than block the next step that might be a follow-up phone call or a personal visit.
3. *Perform the next step.* By executing the next step as agreed, the sales person *passes* the test.
4. *Develop trust.* By passing tests repeatedly, the sales person begins to develop a trusting relationship with the prospect.
5. *Sell the product.* This trusting relationship often leads to a sale, and the prospect becomes a customer.
6. *Maintain the relationship.* By staying in contact with, and continuing to take care of, the customer, the sales person maintains a positive relationship.
7. *Develop loyalty.* By continuing to take good care of the customer and pass the tests that arise in the relationship, the trusting relationship grows into a loyal one. Once loyalty is developed, the customer will continue to do business with the sales person, even when competitors offer products with lower prices and highly-desirable features.

Developing loyal relationships with prospective buyers should not be viewed as exclusively belonging to the domain of *professional selling*. It should be incorporated in all of the company's marketing strategies.

SELLING SERVICES AND HIGH-TECH PRODUCTS

While selling high-tech and intangible products follows the same process as discussed in the previous sections, it may require a slightly different approach. The essential difference is that the prospect may need to be *educated* as to what the product is before it can be sold. That is, when selling soap, virtually all prospects know what the product is. Therefore, the sales person does not need to go into a significant explanation in order to sell the product. On the other hand, when selling a highly technical or intangible product, the sales person may need to explain what the product is, what it does, and how it will benefit the prospect before it can be sold. In those cases where the prospect is familiar with the product, the sales person may have to explain some product uses and benefits of which the prospect is unaware. Complementing this educational requirement, selling services and high-tech products often results in the following:

- *Shorter Product Cycles and Longer Sales Cycles.* Selling high-tech products presents a greater challenge because the products, due to continual technological advances, tend to have shorter life cycles. At the same time, because of their greater complexity and need of explanation, they often have longer sales cycles.
- *Greater product knowledge is required of the sales person.* In an effort to shorten sales cycles, sales people need to have the technical knowledge to understand the product and explain it to prospects.
- *Sales people have to be more problem-solving and consulting oriented.* Intangible and high-tech products are often more complex because they solve more complex problems. This requires sales people to be problem solvers and consultants.
- *Training and servicing the customer is necessary after the sale.* Because of their complexity, the successful selling of high-tech products typically requires the company to have training, support, and maintenance personnel to service the product after the sale.

SALESPERSON PROFILE

Successful sales people have certain common characteristics. They typically include the following:

- *Remaining positive.* Whatever happens during the sales process, successful sales people do whatever is necessary to take the *positive* approach.
- *Being Persistent.* Good sales people "never" give up on a prospect.
- *Being honest.* Contrary to popular belief, good sales people are honest with prospects and customers.
- *Selling Benefits.* Throughout the Sales Cycle, successful sales people communicate everything as a *benefit to the customer.*
- *Handling rejection.* The number of closed sales typically represents a small fraction of the number of prospective ones. This means that good sales people need to learn how to handle rejection.
- *Enjoying the challenges of selling.* Successful sales people enjoy the challenges of the selling process. They enjoy the interaction with people, and have fun when a prospect is con-

verted to a customer.

- *Taking personal responsibility.* Successful sales people do not make excuses for losing a sale. They take responsibility, try to determine what they could have done differently, and make the correction at the next available opportunity.
- *Communicating well in at least one way.* Contrary to popular belief, being a "good talker" is not a requirement for a successful sales career. In the absence of verbal skills, successful sales people might write well, have a likable personality, possess charisma, or be masters at the art of body language.
- *Learning from their mistakes.* Everyone makes mistakes. Taking the positive approach, successful sales people learn from them and use them to improve.
- *Learning how to think on their feet.* Prospects often put sales people into difficult situations. The good ones learn to quickly "think on their feet" and to turn these difficulties into advantages. They do whatever they can to turn these negatives into positive benefits for the prospect.
- *Knowing how to recover from mistakes/problems.* Sometimes the difficult situation is not caused by the prospect. It stems from a product breakdown or a mistake made by the sales person. Successful sales people learn to anticipate these and to turn them into positives.
- *Wanting to make a lot of money.* The most successful sales people have a desire to make a lot of money. By their own efforts, they turn this desire into a reality.

The same techniques and fundamentals that lead to success in personal selling also lead to success in other professions, pursuits, and relationships. The reason is that success in all aspects of life requires personal selling skills or incredible luck. As the famous author Robert Louis Stevenson said, "Everyone lives by selling something."

POINTS TO REMEMBER ABOUT SELLING

Marketing's job is to make sales as easy as possible. Irrespective of marketing's assistance, however, sales personnel should learn to be self sufficient in generating leads, giving demonstrations, answering objections, closing sales, and following up after each step — including after the sale is closed. Marketers should understand that all personnel in the company are, in some way or another, sales people. In particular, they might want to train those who have contact with the public in sales techniques. Teaching high-tech sales techniques is perhaps the best approach because it prepares company personnel to educate prospects and sell any type of product. Whatever the approach, the following points are important for company personnel to remember when they are in sales situations:

1. Always tell the truth — the believable truth.

2. Avoid saying the word *"No"* since prospects and customers keep score and misinterpret them.
3. Asks lots of questions to pinpoint what prospects want.
4. Listen, listen, listen to the answers.
5. Be positive at all times.
6. Plant as many seeds as possible — generate leads.
7. Nurture those seeds so they will grow into sales. That is... follow up, follow up, follow up.
8. Remember that successful selling requires developing personal relationships.
9. Identify and answer all real objections.
10. Don't make excuses for losing a sale.
11. Close the sale at the earliest opportunity — after a buying signal or answering a key objection. Use *trial closes* often.
12. Learn to communicate effectively in at least one way.
13. Always try to serve the needs of the prospect/customer.
14. Learn as much as you can about your product, company, competition, customer, and self.
15. Strive to be the best.
16. Learn to enjoy selling.

TO LEARN MORE ABOUT SELLING

1. Hire a consultant to tailor a sales training program for your company.
2. Take a proven *Personal Selling* course.
3. Go to work for a company that is known to provide a good sales training program.
4. Read sales and marketing publications such as, *Sales & Marketing Management*, *Sales and Marketing Strategies & News,* and others published by marketing and sales experts or companies.
5. Read books on sales and marketing — especially those written by people who have been successful in the sales profession.

FINAL COMMENTS

Sales people, along with their service and support counterparts, are the company's *"eyes and ears"* in the marketplace. Therefore, marketers should listen to the information they collect and report very carefully. Whether it is complaints, compliments, information on the competition, new product ideas, or suggestions, this information is invaluable in determining the success or failure of existing marketing strategies and in shaping future strategies. The following Chapter on the *Marketing Information System* will talk about the formal ways this information should be solicited, collected, reported, analyzed and acted upon.

TIPS and Exercises

1. Create a Lead Card and Lead Screen for your sales staff — making sure you have the four key sections of the front (*identification* of the prospect, *product interest, degree of interest,* and *lead source*).
2. Create a Hot List for your Sales Manager to focus on hot leads with your sales people, to help them answer objections, and to forecast sales for the month.
3. Create a Promotion Effectiveness report that ties leads, presentations, and sales back to the lead source originally captured on the Lead Card or Lead Screen. Marketing will use this report to determine the return-on-investments of your various promotional strategies, and Sales Management will use the column totals by sales person to determine their "batting" averages, or sales ratios (sales ÷ presentations and sales ÷ leads).
4. Create a Sales Notebook for sales people to use to more efficiently and effectively sell your products and to train new sales people.
5. Compute batting averages of your sales people, and make sure that each sales person is getting the number of leads and giving the number of presentations they need to meet their sales quotas.

Chapter 12

DNA of the Marketing Information System

"If a tree falls and nobody is around to hear it, does it make a noise?..."

While most companies have enough marketing savvy to recognize the importance of sales and advertising, too few understand the need for a *Marketing Information System*. Because of this lack of understanding, *Marketing Research* and all of the other activities related to the *Marketing Information System* are noticeably absent from the strategic marketing mix of most companies. If research is done, the majority is related to product research, or the *"R"* in *R&D.*

WHAT IS THE MARKETING INFORMATION SYSTEM?

The *Marketing Information System* is a system used to collect, analyze, report, and take action on information that is critically important to the success of the organization. It gives the organization abilities analogous to the senses of the human body — sight, sound, smell, taste, and touch. With a good Marketing Information System, the organization will be able to do the following:

1. *See* opportunities to be exploited and hazards to be avoided.
2. *Hear* customer complaints as a first step in identifying problems and solving them, and *listen* for compliments that can be used in successful marketing programs.
3. *Smell* a "rotten deal" or misinformation from a competitor so it can be avoided, and enjoy the "sweet smell of success" when marketing is working well.
4. Use good *taste* in its marketing programs.
5. *Feel* the "heat" from problems so solutions can be implemented to avoid *getting burned,* and sense when prospects are *hot* so they can be closed.

In other words, the Marketing Information System provides companies with the *radar* and *controls* they need to keep them on the right course toward reaching the goals of the Marketing Plan. Without the MIS, the company's marketing programs are likely to *crash* taking valuable company resources and marketing opportunities with them.

WHAT SHOULD IT DO?

Since it is the organization's "eyes and ears," the *Marketing Information System* has numerous duties to perform. Some of the more important ones are described below.

Collect Market Information

This involves capturing information that is already coming into the organization and conducting research on the needs of the marketplace for information that is not readily available.

Process Information Collected

Once information is collected, it is filtered to separate *signals* from *noise,* summarized into useful categories, and reported to appropriate company decision makers so they can take action. A typical report might be a *Promotion Effectiveness Report* (see *Figure 11-2* in the previous chapter) that lets the *Chief Marketing Officer* know how well the company's various promotional strategies are working and the Sales Manager compute the "batting averages of salespeople. Another report might be the *Hot Lis*t (see *Figure 11-1*) that enables the Sales Manager to forecast sales for the current period and help sales people answer objections.

Analyze Information

After information is collected and processed, the marketing decision makers of the company need to interpret the results. They have to determine if the results represent real and important issues that require prompt attention or unusual environmental factors, outside their control, that are unlikely to reoccur. For example, if a product is not performing well, the reasons may be related to ineffective promotion or distribution rather than the marketplace's rejection of the product. Improper analysis might eliminate a perfectly good product strategy when, in fact, other strategies, misinterpretations, or environmental factors are at fault.

Take Action

Once information is analyzed, an appropriate action should be taken. If the analysis indicates that a strategy is not working, it should be revised as soon as the underlying reasons are determined. However, care must be taken to insure that you understand why the first strategy didn't work so the same mistake is not repeated.

If adjustments to strategies continue to not work, the company has to re-evaluate the workability of its plans and goals. One of the worst mistakes a company can make is to ignore the evidence and plow ahead with original plans and strategies that continue to be ineffective. This will only result in continued losses and cause the wasting of valuable resources. When this happens, it is typically the result of either large executive egos or a faulty *Marketing Information System.*

WHEN IS IT USED?

The *Marketing Information System* should be employed throughout the *Marketing Cycle.* In other words, it should be "on" all the time. A company has to continually collect, analyze, and report marketplace information and take corrective action where and when necessary. If it doesn't, it will be "flying blind" and will have the same probability of success as a pilot who is flying in a storm without visibility or radar. Using another analogy, operating without a good *Marketing Information System* is like turning the wheel of a car in a particular direction without seeing or feeling what the car does in response. While very few people would get on a plane or into a car if they knew that these vehicles have no feedback systems to measure their progress, many operate companies without these systems in place. Perhaps that's one of the reasons why a majority of new businesses fail within their first few years of existence.

WHAT INFORMATION IS COLLECTED?

The *Marketing Information System* should be designed to collect different types of information at various stages of the *marketing cycle.* The types of information that should be collected include those listed below.

- What customers and market targets want.
- Available niches in the marketplace that match up with company strengths.
- Complaints.
- Compliments.
- Competition information.
- New product ideas and new markets for them.
- New technologies that will impact existing products or support new products.
- New markets for existing products.
- Complimentary product opportunities.
- Performance of marketing strategies and the company in general.
- Sales, Costs, and Profits.

In general, any information that can be economically used to benefit your company and publics should be collected.

WHAT ARE TYPICAL SOURCES OF THIS INFORMATION?

Before the above information can be collected, the best sources of information should be identified. Typical sources of marketing information include: transaction documents, accounting systems and reports, other internal forms and reports, various media, market research, industry studies, and reliable word-of-mouth sources. A brief description of each is described below for clarification:

Transaction documents

Transaction documents are simply forms that capture transactions that are input into your accounting system. The most common transaction documents are sales orders and invoices.

Sales Order

The *Sales Order* is the document on which the initial order is originally captured. It is probably the best source of information regarding the performance of sales personnel and the company's marketing strategies. While most sales people are paid commissions based on money that is *invoiced and collected*, the *Sales Order* is often a more accurate indicator of their performance. The reason is that sales lost after the *Sales Order* is written are more often a result of the company's inability to deliver a working product on time than it is a reflection of the performance of the sales person or the company's marketing strategies.

Invoice

The *Invoice* is the document on which the actual items sold and shipped to the customer are listed. It is also the document that is sent to the customer as a bill. The information on the *Invoice* may be different from the original order information on the *Sales Order*. The reasons for this include: customers may change their mind on the exact quantities and items they want; customers may be unable to get financing for the purchase; the company may not be able to ship some of the items and quantities ordered; the product(s) may be leased through a leasing company that changes the *"Bill to"* information from the actual customer to the lease company.

Since the *Invoice* is the *source document* that accurately represents the goods and services that have been actually sold and shipped to the customer, the *Invoice* is used as the basis for sales commissions, historical sales data, and profitability information. Because of its importance, all company personnel who are responsible for recording information on the Invoice should make sure that the data is accurately recorded. Whatever was actually sold and provided to the customer must be recorded on the final invoice.

Internal forms and reports

In most companies, the marketing information required by management is not readily available from source documents such as *Invoices* and *Sales Orders*. In those cases, other subsystems should be put in place to properly capture and report this information. A good example of this is the need to record information on the effectiveness of the company's promotional strategies. While sales information is available from Sales Orders and *Invoices*, information on the promotion sources that prompted these sales are not. Additionally, marketing may want to know how many *leads* and *presentations* were generated by the various different promotion sources. This information does not appear on any of the company's transaction documents.

The solution is to put another system in place. This system needs to capture information *at the source of contact* between the sales person and the prospect. The source of contact is usually at the point of lead generation. Since a *Lead Card* should be filled out for each new lead that is created, the *Lead Card* is the best source document to use for this new system. Sales people should be trained to (1) ask prospects *"where did you first hear about us"* every time they make a new contact and to (2) note down the answer on the *Lead Card, or Lead Screen of a computer system*. To make the sales person's job easier, the Lead Card can have preprinted promotional sources listed so that all a sales person has to do is check the appropriate box or fill in the "Other column" when a new lead is generated (see *Figure 9-2*).

Marketing should create a new form called a *"Promotion Effectiveness Form."* This form should have rows labeled by all of the different sources of promotion for the month vertically down the length of the form, and columns labeled by the words *"Leads", "Presentations (or Demonstrations),"* and *"Sales"* spread horizontally across the top of the page. This form should be distributed to all sales personnel (see *Figure 11-2*).

At the end of the month, sales personnel should go through all their lead cards and note on this form the numbers of new *Leads*, *Appointments*, and *Sales* for the month for each category of promotion. The *Sales Manager* should summarize the results of all the individual sales person's forms into a *Promotion Effectiveness Report* for marketing decision makers. Based on this information, the marketing executives can make future promotional strategies and decisions accordingly.

The above manual system can, of course, be totally automated. Lead cards can be Lead screens on a computer, and the individual reports by sales person and the company-wide summary can be automatically produced. Even so, the information has to be accurately captured and entered into a computer system by sales people who have first-hand knowledge about each lead.

Whether manual or automated, a new system has been put in place to capture the information necessary to measure the success of company promotional efforts. Yes, some effort and resources are required to make this system work, but it is far less expensive than guessing about promotional effectiveness and wasting valuable company resources on ineffective promotional activities and missed sales opportunities. Since cooperation of all sales personnel is essential for this system to work properly, they should be trained on its importance in their training sessions, and their actions in this regard should be closely supervised to insure compliance.

Scanner and Cash Register Input

For retail establishments, scanners tied to cash registers and other devices have proven to be an excellent new source of marketing information. Scanners have the ability to read bar-coded product labels and automatically record sales. These bar codes typically contain valuable information about the product and its price. As shown in *Figure 12-1*, bar codes usually represent a 10-digit number. The first five digits indicate the manufacturer, whose number is assigned by the *Uniform Code Council* in Dayton, Ohio. This council maintains a data base of companies from many different countries. The next five digits are also assigned by the manufacturer and represent the product — including variations for size, color, weight, and/or flavor. Added to the product is another bar code that represents the price and which is usually assigned by the retailer (since the manufacturer is currently prohibited by law in the United States to dictate retail prices). Used in combination with credit, debit, or *frequent-buyer* cards, these scanners allow retailers to collect valuable information on products purchased and the people who have purchased them. This data has proven to be so important that some large retailing chains are charging manufacturers roughly $1 million per year for this information.

Bar Code Example

Figure 12-1

RF Tags

Many predict that RF (radio frequency) tags will replace bar codes in the future. RF tags that are put on a product enable the product to be traced through its life and serve *marketing information system* purposes beyond their use as inventory or security tags to monitor goods leaving a store. As with all new methods, there are some negatives with RF tags. The primary concern is that they will violate the privacy of those who don't want people to know what products they own. If used properly, these tags can give marketers tremendous information on the purchase, use, and useful life of products.

Media

Various media provide good sources of new product ideas, information on the competition, and publicity on your company. Many good ideas are discussed in articles that quote industry leaders about future trends, and most media showcase new products in special "new products" sections. As a result, the marketing department should make sure that it receives subscriptions — most of these are offered free — to all relevant publications that cover the company's industry as well as those that are popular in targeted industries.

General media, such as local newspapers, should also be reviewed regularly since they often contain very useful information relevant to your company and products. They also give the marketing people a good idea of the environmental factors that are influencing purchase decisions in local areas.

Market Research

If the information required is not available from other sources, your company should do some research to collect the information in other ways. Market research can involve library research of secondary sources, the recording of answers to questions posed to market targets in the normal course of business, and formal, statistically valid studies that involve professionally-produced questionnaires, focus groups, and other studies conducted by outside marketing or research firms. Many companies can avoid the time and expense of hiring outside firms if they apply some of their R&D intelligence used in product development to the task of finding and collecting the information they need. The problem is that most do not know what to collect or how to collect it.

Industry Studies

A good source of information about certain industries and their constituent companies are industry studies that have been conducted by respected research organizations such as *Dow Jones*, *Dun and Bradstreet*, and *International Data Corporation*. Industry studies can be purchased on the open market. While some of them can be quite expensive, many are available at no charge from public libraries and stock brokerage houses. They are a good source of information on competition, target industries, and new product ideas.

Word-of-Mouth

One of the best sources of information is so readily available that it is too often overlooked — a company's various publics. Prospects, customers, vendors, and incoming employees are actively engaged in the marketplace. In their travels and investigations, they absorb a lot of good information on new product ideas, competition, new technologies, complaints, compliments, performance, and many other important topics. Unfortunately, most companies don't have a mechanism for capturing this information.

Creating such a mechanism is quite simple. It merely involves designing a form to capture this information. In a previous Chapter, a *Suggestion Form* was introduced as a means for capturing new product information. Perhaps this form can be expanded into a more general form that is called a *Market Information Form* (see *Figure 12-2*) that can be used to collect a wide variety of useful information from the marketplace. The information that should be collected includes the following: *New Product ideas, Competition information, Suggestions for improvement, Performance feedback,* (Sales, costs, and profits), *Marketing strategy feedback* (positioning, product, pricing, distribution, promotion, and corporate image), *Complaints, Compliments, Customer and prospect data,* and *other general marketplace information.* When a customer or prospect provides such useful information, your personnel should be trained to collect it on a *Market Information Form* and to pass it on to the appropriate marketing decision makers. As an added incentive, the collecting and reporting of market information should be one of the criteria upon which personnel are evaluated during their performance and salary reviews. If appropriate, incentives might also be considered — especially for ideas that are actually developed into new products.

No. 419

KALB & ASSOCIATES • Market Information Form

Specializing in High-technology Marketing • Sales • Systems Consulting and Training

INSTRUCTIONS — PLEASE READ FIRST. Continued success of our company requires the on-going assistance of everyone in our organization (the company's "eyes and ears") to provide marketplace information on a timely basis. Whenever you are able to collect such information please complete this form and send it to the marketing department. Bonuses will be awarded to the top submissions, and performance reviews will reflect your efforts. Thank you.

Type of Information — ☐ New product ideas ☐ Competition ☐ Compliment ☐ Complaint ☐ Strategy feedback ☐ Other__________

Source of Information

Name | Date

Position | Phone

Company | Fax

Street | P.O. Box

City | State | Zip

Employee Reporting

Name | Position | Department | Phone Extension

Market Information (Please write on back or attach a separate sheet if necessary.)

The following signature releases the company from any obligations or liabilities associated with using the above information for its marketing or other purposes.

Signature | Title | Date

Form No. K&A 081492 • Last Revision 9/30/92

Please send to Marketing Department when completed.

Figure 12-2

GENERAL SYSTEMS TO CAPTURE INFORMATION

To better understand how a *Marketing Information System* might work, it is useful to look at the systems that are often used in the process.

Forms

The starting point of most systems is the point at which the information is captured. The method of capture is usually some type of *form* —printed on a piece of paper or formatted on a computer screen. The preprinted areas give structure to the form and identify the information that is to be collected. When designing a form, it is useful to look at the information that is to be collected or the reports that are to be generated by the system. The desired output will point to the different boxes and preprinted areas that should be on the form.

Paperwork Flow

The paperwork flow in a company is analogous to the veins and arteries in the human body. It carries the information to the appropriate people and places. It determines *who* gets *what* copy and in *what sequence.* Again, it is useful to work back from the end result to determine the proper journey that the paperwork should follow.

Policies and Procedures

Policies and procedures establish the rules for collecting and processing information — the "what is to be done" and "how and when it is to be done." They also establish the *authorities* and *responsibilities* of each position involved in the process, and govern the paperwork flow. In addition to determining the normal flow, policies and procedures should take care of exceptions to the normal case. Improper planning for exceptions is a serious downfall of many systems.

Control Systems

Control systems need to be established to insure that information is properly captured, policies and procedures are being followed, and the system is working as designed.

Filing and Storage Systems

In many systems, information that is kept is lost in a *"black hole,"* because the system designers did not properly consider the filing and storage part of the system. In a well-designed *Marketing Information System,* all of the information is properly indexed and cross-referenced so it can be easily found. For example, one copy should be stored *alphabetically* by subject, and a second should be kept in a *numerical control* file, with each file having a cross-reference to the other. While some readers may find this discussion outside the bounds of a marketing book, they will change their minds when an important new product idea that has been shelved needs to be quickly retrieved, or when a necessary piece of competitive information is required by a sales manager to close a big deal.

DOCUMENTS ON WHICH INFORMATION IS CAPTURED AND REPORTED

Where should marketing find the information that it needs? The following list indicates the most common sources of information:

Sales Information

Two terms are commonly used when recording orders and sales — bookings and billings.

Bookings

These are found on either *Quotation Forms* or *Sales Orders*. They represent the products that were ordered when the order was originally recorded. They are typically reported on a *Bookings Report* that comes out of the company's accounting system.

Billings

These are found on *Invoices*. They indicate what was actually sold, shipped and billed. Billings are often reported on the company's various sales reports that come out of the accounting system.

New Product Information

New product information can come from inside and outside sources.

Inside Sources

New product ideas created or reported by sales, service or engineering personnel are often captured on a *Suggestion* or *Market Information Form* (see *Figure 12-2*).

Outside Sources

New product ideas from sources outside the company are often found in media articles, advertisements, customer letters, competitive literature, or a *Market Information Form.*

Strategy Performance

The company's marketing strategy performance can come from numerous sources and be captured on a variety of different forms. Examples are provided below for each marketing "building block," or strategy category.

Positioning

Because positioning is less quantitative than the other building blocks, the effectiveness of an organization's positioning strategies is more difficult to measure. Perhaps the best way to measure positioning effectiveness is to do some primary market research. This can be done by asking customers and members of other publics a few simple questions such as, "What business do you think we are in?"; "What is truly unique about our products?"; "What word or phrase first comes to mind when you think of our products?" If you get the answers you want and they are consistent, your strategy is working. If not, it is not working.

Product

The sales performance of various products is captured on the *Invoice* and is usually summarized on a *"Sales by Product"* report. Other useful information comes from customers via sales and service reports. Service reports are particularly important for determining the frequency of different types of failures and for compiling reliability statistics that, if very favorable, can later be used by marketing in various promotional pieces and product literature. *Complaints* and *Compliments* recorded on the *Market Information Form* are also good indicators as to how well product strategies are working.

Pricing

The effectiveness of pricing strategies can be derived from (1) sales and profit reports created from *Invoices,* (2) *Market Information Forms,* reports, and memos from sales and service personnel, (3) letters and phone calls from customers that can be logged on *Market Information Forms*, and (4) *competition reports* and *surveys* that record comparative pricing data from a variety of sources. In many companies, sales personnel are required to report the reasons for lost sales. When price is the reason cited, this should be recorded on a *Market Information Form* and forwarded to the appropriate marketing decision maker.

Distribution

Information on the effectiveness of distribution sources can be captured from *Invoices* (there should be space on the *Invoice* for "Sales Source" or "Sales Person"). In the case of sales to distributors and dealers, they will be recorded on the *Invoices* as customers, and totals will appear on a "Sales by Distributor" or "Sales by Customer" report. Direct sales are likely to be recorded on "Sales by Distribution Channel" or "Sales by Sales Person" reports. Additional information on Distributor performance can be obtained from the "Complaints" and "Compliments" listed on the *Market Information Form* as well as from other sources.

Promotion

As discussed previously, a good place to collect information on the effectiveness of promotional sources are *Lead Cards* (see *Figure 9-2)*. Additional sources are *Quote* forms, response cards from ads and brochures, verbal and written reactions to ads, and publicity on the company. These are eventually recorded and reported on *Promotion Effective Reports* (see *Figure 11-2*).

Corporate Image

Corporate Image strategy performance can be determined from numerous sources. The two primary ones are *Publicity* on the company as reported in the media and the *Complaints* and *Compliments* from market targets as listed on the *Market Information Form.* You can also do the same type of primary research that was conducted to obtain feedback on *Positioning* strategies.

Marketing Information System

While it may seem odd, the marketing information system needs to be utilized to collect information on the performance of itself. It should be designed to be self-policing or self-correcting. That is, if the marketing information is found to collect, analyze and report information accurately and effectively, it will be judged to be an effective and useful tool. If not, its flaws will have to be identified and fixed.

Competition Information

Good sources of competitive information come from sales and service reports, customers, demonstrations of competitive products, industry studies, information collected at trade shows, acquiring or borrowing competitive products, reading articles on the competition in various media. They can be reported on *Market Information Forms* or *memos.* As discussed in *Chapter 11* on *Sales*, marketing should provide sales people with a *Competition Section in their Sales Notebook* that contains information on the competition. Sales people should be encouraged to collect their own information and to share it by sending copies to marketing for review, duplication and distribution to the other sales and marketing personnel.

Credit

Credit policies should come under the jurisdiction of the marketing department. In most organizations, sales pushes for easy credit while accounting pushes for very restrictive credit. The company's actual credit policy should fall somewhere in the middle. Most organizations have found that it is better to have a few bad debts than suffer sales losses because customers are angered by overly-restrictive credit policies. Sources for capturing and reporting credit information typically include the following: *Credit Applications, Credit Reports* which give rejection ratios, *Aged Accounts Receivable Reports,* and the monitoring of customer *complaints* about credit policies from *Market Information Forms* or *memos.*

Exceptions

Many systems fail because they don't provide for exceptions. Personnel should be encouraged to report any exceptions that they feel are noteworthy. Marketing should review these periodically to determine if any of these can serve to improve products or marketing programs. An important source of product exception information is a report that summarizes both dollar and unit information on *returned* and *defective* products.

SYSTEMS TO PROCESS INFORMATION

To be most efficient, the *Marketing Information System* should <u>not</u> attempt to "reinvent the wheel" or create a lot of new systems or unnecessary paperwork. As in the case of finding source documents to collect information, marketing should look for existing systems within the company from which it can draw the information it needs. While this may involve modifying an existing *Invoice* or having a computer system sort and report information in a different way, it does not have to "start from scratch" or create something completely new in most cases.

Accounting System

Perhaps the existing system that is best-suited to process information for your *Marketing Information System* is your company's accounting system. Most companies have them, and much of the macro information needed is already captured in the accounting system. For example, the accounting system can usually produce *Sales, Costs* and *Profits* by any way you want to sort them. Sales by product, distribution channel, sales person, region, customer and retail outlet merely involve sorting the same base of data in different ways. As long as the proper information is captured on the *Sales Order* or *Invoice*, it can be processed by this system.

If properly designed, the accounting system can also produce *sales sensitivity* statistics that show the change in sales prompted by changes in price. In this way, marketing can forecast the effect of discounts and other price variations on sales and profits.

Systems to be Created

As discussed previously, new systems have to be put in place if the required information is not already being captured by existing systems. This is true in the case of promotion effectiveness.

Promotion Effectiveness

While the accounting system provides sales information, it does not have information on the number of leads, demonstrations (or appointments), and promotional sources that produced your sales. As a result, a new system using the *Lead Card* as a source document has to be created. Since this has already been discussed in a previous section, it will not be repeated here.

Competitive Pricing

Although the accounting system can yield information on price sensitivity, it cannot provide the marketing department with the competitive pricing information that it requires because it doesn't have this information. Therefore, competitive pricing data will have to be collected and processed by a new system. This new system can be quickly developed using a database or spreadsheet program on a personal computer. It would involve assigning a marketing analyst to track and input competitive prices and changes in prices, and, if possible, to monitor and input sales responses to these changes. Graphs could even be generated that show the changes in sales that are prompted by price changes.

In some industries where products have become commodities because they are not well-positioned, competitive price changes may have to be met with similar adjustments of your products prices if you are to avoid losing significant market share. The sources of competitive pricing information are usually competitor price lists, news releases, ads, publicity, word-of-mouth and various other market sources. Of course, competitive pricing problems can usually be eliminated by better positioning strategies.

Competition

Pricing is not the only competitive information that should be monitored and collected. All of the competition's other strategies should be closely watched and analyzed. In addition to being a good source of product and promotional ideas, it can provide the basis of important information that should be distributed to the sales force so sales personnel can effectively counter competitive claims and reverse any prospect desires to buy competitive products. Everyone who has contact with the marketplace should be trained to collect *competition* information and to report it on *Market Information Forms.*

Positioning

Positioning is another strategy whose effectiveness is difficult to monitor. It certainly can't be done with internal data alone. To determine the effectiveness of positioning strategies, the company has to look at a variety of data — both qualitative and quantitative. For the quantitative data, sales by *market target segment* needs to be captured on the *Invoice.* If possible, it is useful to compare this with competitor data to determine how well your position is working relative to theirs.

For qualitative information, you have to survey customers and prospects to determine the image they have of your products. As discussed previously, a *key question* to ask your target audience is, "What first comes to mind when you think of this product?" If the data is consistent and the answer you want, your positioning strategy is working.

New Product Development

Most of the ideas that go into a *New Product Development* system come from your *Marketing Information System*. In particular, *Market Information Forms* (see *Figure 12-2*), suggestions that are put into suggestion boxes, and market research provide a wealth of new product ideas for developing new products.

Research Effectiveness

Any good system should have the ability to provide information on how well it is working. At the very least, the effectiveness of your market research activities should be determined. While difficult to quantify, marketing professionals can look at the accuracy of predictions, and analyze those that prove to be inaccurate. When strategies fail to meet their objectives, the systems used to formulate the goals and strategies of your plans should be reevaluated.

REPORTING AND ANALYZING

After collecting and processing marketing information, this information should be reported to decision makers so they can analyze the effectiveness of your company's strategies and make any necessary changes.

The chief marketing executive through immediate subordinates should receive the following types of reports (please note that the reports you need may vary depending on your size, industry, position in the supply chain, organization and style of operation):

Product

1. Sales by Product, Customer, Vendor (if you are a reseller), Region, or Distribution Channel, or other relevant category.
2. Sales and service reports of customer reactions to your products.
3. Service revenues and costs by product.
4. Warranty service by product.
5. Frequency and source of failure by product.
6. Complaints and Compliments on *Market Information Forms.*

Promotion Effectiveness

1. Sales, Presentations, Contacts, and Leads by Promotional or Advertising Source.
2. Name Recognition and product understanding from surveys and focus groups.
3. Corporate Image from surveys and focus groups.
4. Positioning from surveys and focus groups.
5. Complaints and Compliments on *Market Information Forms.*

Pricing

1. Sensitivity, or changes in sales resulting from changes in prices.
2. Competitive pricing by product.
3. Sales and service reports of customer reactions.
4. Customer initiated contact via e-mail, Web site, letters, and phone calls.
5. Complaints and Compliments on *Market Information Forms.*

Distribution

1. Sales by Distribution Channel, Region or Territory, Division, or Sales Person.
2. Complaints and Compliments about distributors on *Market Information Forms.*

Positioning

1. Sales by Industry or product.
2. Market Share reports and measures of *cannibalization* between products.
3. Sales/Service Reports of word-of-mouth reactions.

4. Surveys and focus groups related to name recognition and product image.
5. Complaints (related to confusion between products) and Compliments (usually about clearly-stated unique advantages) on *Market Information Forms*.

Competition

1. Sales and Service Reports.
2. Media Articles.
3. Vendors reports.
4. Industry studies.
5. Customer and prospect word-of-mouth, letters, and e-mails.
6. Trade-show reports and investigations.
7. Competition information reported on *Market Information Forms*.

Credit Reports

1. Percentages of acceptances and rejections.
2. Reasons for Rejections.
3. Rejections as a percentage of total.
4. Aged Accounts Receivable reports.

Marketing Information System

1. Track record of accuracy.
2. Track record of the success of strategies modified because of the system.

Once these reports are read and thoroughly analyzed by the marketing executives and their staffs, the next step is to formulate conclusions and take action.

SYSTEMS FOR TAKING ACTION

The collection, processing, reporting and analyzing of marketing information is very important, but it is basically worthless if there are no mechanisms for taking action. To facilitate taking action, the company should have the following systems in place:

Weekly meetings

Weekly meetings are an important form of communication in a company. They allow decision makers to communicate problems and discuss solutions that cross department lines.

They build a camaraderie and a team spirit. And if properly run, they can serve as an invaluable means of initiating necessary corrective action, rewarding good performance, and correcting bad performance. These meetings should be chaired by one person — usually the senior marketing executive, but the responsibility for chairing the meetings can be rotated depending on the subject matter and availability of management personnel.

The purpose of these meetings should be to (1) communicate new product and competition information, (2) discuss problems, (3) develop solutions, (4) decide on a plan of action to implement solutions, (5) set a time table for executing the plan and following up on the results, and (6) rewarding and punishing good and bad performance.

Periodic Committee Meetings

Weekly meetings are for discussing new matters and finding solutions to short-term problems that arise each week. For more strategic discussions, periodic committee meetings are required. These meetings are for discussing longer-term plans and strategies. Introduction of new products and changes to strategies, plans, and major policies are often the topics of discussion. These meetings typically involve executives at the highest level of the company, with occasional participation by their staffs, accountants, consultants and attorneys.

Follow up

After plans of action have been executed, it is important to follow up by reviewing the following: (1) *action taken,* (2) *results,* and (3) *reasons* why the plan did or did not work.

Staying on track toward Market Plan Goals

While developing and utilizing the *Marketing Information System,* it is important for your system to distinguish between *signal* and *noise,* or what is a *real issue* and what is a *fictitious one* that has been introduced because of a hidden agenda. Successful marketers need to be able to separate the signal from the noise. The main mission of this system is to insure that the company is staying on the proper course toward its marketing goals, and that it is deriving optimum benefit from its investment rather than wasting valuable marketing resources.

Making modifications

To stay on course, it is important to know *when* to make *what* modifications. The plan of actions discussed above refer to modifications to marketing programs. What should be done if these modifications don't work? Assuming there were no serious mistakes in execution of strategies, the company has to look toward revising its strategies. If that doesn't work, it has to consider revising the goals of the plan. If revising goals don't solve the problem, it has to look at making more major revisions including — rethinking the organization's line of business.

Starting with minor adjustments

In short, you typically start with small changes and move towards larger and larger changes if each succeeding step does not work. Every company, no matter how large and successful, goes through this process from time to time. Some companies, go through costly reorganizations every few years. While some say "If it's not broke, don't fix it." Others say "If it's not broke, break it every once in a while." While the changes represented by these reorganizations can be costly, those who advocate periodic change believe that they are much less costly than the alternatives — stagnation or going in the wrong direction. They believe that reorganizations sometimes breathe new life into an organization before it stagnates and gets too "set in going the wrong way."

Responding to an ever-changing marketplace

Many times, modifications are necessary, not because of any strategic mistakes made by the company, but because the marketplace is constantly changing. This *ever-changing* nature of the marketplace, particularly in high-technology and very competitive industries, makes a good *Marketing Information System* all the more necessary. A good system has its "sensors" in all the right places to monitor changes in the marketplace and to report them to the appropriate decision makers in the company. These decision makers, in turn, have the *authority* to make necessary adjustments in response to these changes without fear of political repercussions.

Continual Improvement

The idea is to develop a system that strives for continual improvement — a critical objective in the competitive world. It is so critical in Japan that they have a word for this process — *kaisen*. How do you develop a *Marketing Information System* that works toward continual improvement? This is discussed in the following sections.

DEVELOPING A MARKETING INFORMATION SYSTEM

As already mentioned, good system designers try to avoid "reinventing the wheel." That is, rather than building a system from the ground up, they recognize that most organizations already have systems in place that can collect valuable marketing information. The system that virtually all companies have to measure their performance and keep track of tax obligations is an *accounting system*. Most accounting systems collect sales, cost, and profit information from invoices and other sources. Therefore, the designer of a *Marketing Information System* should start with the accounting system already in place.

To build a marketing information system on top of the foundation already provided by the accounting system, a good system designer is likely to follow the steps listed below.

Audit the existing system

The existing accounting system should be examined for the information that it already collects and produces. As stated above, most accounting systems report sales, cost, and profit information in a variety of different ways — by geographical region, division, product, product line, customer, sales person, and vendor for each reporting period. Some automated systems also have the ability to record the size of a typical purchase and the average number of repeat purchases by customer.

Identify the important information that the existing systems do not collect and report

This step is critical. It typically involves listing all of the types of marketing information which are important to the organization's success but which are not currently being collected and reported. In most organizations this list includes the following:

1. *Effectiveness of various promotion sources.* It is important to measure the effectiveness of specific ads, trade shows, direct mailings, and other promotion sources in producing leads, presentations, and sales. Those that are found to produce a positive *return on investment* can be repeated, and those that do not should be discontinued. Since the promotional source that generated the sale is not often captured on *Invoices* or other accounting system paperwork, separate systems must be developed.

2. *Characteristics of market targets.* The more an organization learns about its target audience, the more efficient and effective it can be in communicating with this audience. The types of information that need to be collected might include: (1) *Psychographics,* or lifestyle characteristics, which the buyers may have in common, (2) *Publications* they read and other media which they consume, (3) Their *age, sex, disposable income, profession, household size* and *location,* and *years of education,* and (4) The products they want to buy. In general, profiles of customers and likely buyers should be developed so that the company can more profitably communicate with, and sell to, them.

3. *Complaints.* It is important to develop systems for recording and responding to complaints in order to identify product problems that need to be fixed, reverse negative word-of-mouth advertising, and improve corporate image.

4. *Compliments.* Compliments are important to collect and report for a variety of reasons. They (1) provide feedback as to what the company is doing correctly, (2) communicate to employees that they are working for a good organization in an effort to reduce turnover,

(3) provide a good source of testimonial quotes that can be used in marketing pieces, and (4) make new hires feel more comfortable about their decision to join the company.

5. *New product ideas.* Many new product ideas come from a company's various publics. Systems need to be put in place to capture, report, and evaluate these ideas.
6. *Competition Information.* Collecting intelligence on the competition is critical for making strategic decisions as well as selling against competitors.
7. *Performance feedback.* Feedback on how well corporate image, positioning, product, price, distribution, promotion, and marketing information system strategies are working is important for continued success.
8. *Technological breakthroughs.* Company personnel need to collect information on new technologies that can be used to make new products and which might obsolete existing ones. Success puts many companies to sleep. Too many ignore new technologies that pose competitive threats to their organizations. Companies that have assumed that products such as consumer rail service, telex machines, slide rules, and typewriters will always be in large demand have been hurt badly by the reality of air travel, fax machines, computers, and word processors.
9. *Publicity.* Collecting and managing publicity on your organization and products is essential for successful marketing. Negative publicity needs to be counteracted to reverse corporate image damage, and positive publicity needs to be capitalized upon in marketing and training programs.

Develop strategies to prompt and measure response

Rather than wait for people to call with *complaints, compliments, new product ideas,* and other critical information about themselves and the competition, you can employ strategies to boost response. Many of these strategies were discussed in previous chapters on *Promotion* and *Direct Marketing.* The objective is to build your database of information on customers, prospects, and other publics. In general, putting *toll-free contact mechanisms* on all ads, promotions, and product packages, providing multiple channels for people to respond (phone, Web page, e-mail, fax, business reply card, and mailing address), and offering promotional incentives will boost response levels. Giving a *unique code* to each contact mechanism will facilitate measurement of the effectiveness of each promotional strategy. For example, business reply cards should have codes that identify the specific media source and date of insertion and *toll-free* numbers should either have extensions that identify the promotion source or trained personnel who ask the question, "May I ask what prompted you to call us?" Remember, every penny invested in collecting timely and accurate information at this stage is likely to save a dollar or more in unnecessary market research, corporate image damage, or lost business from disgruntled customers or misguided strategies.

Fill the information holes with additional systems

Once the critical information that existing systems do not capture is identified, systems should be put in place to collect, analyze, report, and take action on this information. In a sense, building a *marketing information system* is analogous to filling the holes in a security system. You fill all the ones that you know exist until you discover additional ones. Whenever a hole is discovered, it is plugged with another system or add-on.

Do Market Research to plug any remaining holes

After all systems are put in place to capture the information that is already coming to the company and its personnel, any remaining information holes can be plugged with market research. Market Research fits into two main categories — *secondary* and *primary.*

Secondary research. *Secondary research* involves finding research that has been published by others. This secondary research is available on the Internet, in libraries, from media (newspapers, magazines, and broadcast companies), and from research organizations. Many research organizations charge for copies of their research findings whereas others, such as many Internet sources and stock brokerage firms, provide this data to their constituents at no charge. Internet *Search Engines* have become excellent vehicles for finding low-cost secondary research.

Primary research. When secondary research still leaves information holes or when an organization needs to confirm the information collected from secondary sources, *primary research* should be considered. Primary research involves conducting original research by going directly to the source of the information. Primary marketing research typically involves activities such as conducting *focus groups,* designing *questionnaires,* conducting *surveys,* and *monitoring consumer reactions* to company strategies. When surveys or focus groups are conducted, statistics should be employed to determine statistically significant sample sizes.

In the absence of using statistical tables with desired levels of confidence, a sample size of 50 respondents for each variable being tested can be used as a "quick and dirty" rule of thumb. This was discussed in *Chapter 10* on *Direct Marketing.*

For *focus groups,* the sample of 50 or more is typically broken up into separate sessions where 8 to 12 people are asked a series of questions. The objective is to prompt the participants to talk freely about their feelings about the product or the issue being tested. In some cases, the participants are not told the name of the company or product to avoid biasing their responses. An experienced independent focus group moderator, who is not an employee of the company, is used to ask the questions and move the discussion along. Focus groups commonly last for 2 hours. Marketing personnel often view sessions behind a two-way mirror. Sessions are often recorded for accuracy and for playback at a later time. Participants are typically paid an incentive to participate. Participants are recruited by the focus group research organization, a marketing consultant, or the company sponsoring the research.

CONCLUSION

As has been demonstrated, the Marketing Information System is an essential part of a company's marketing efforts. Without it, the company will be "flying blind" and needlessly wasting valuable resources on ineffective marketing strategies when it could be using these resources to make the company grow and prosper. Growing companies make contributions in so many different ways. They provide useful products, create new jobs both inside and outside the company, provide increasing opportunities for employees, and create the wealth for themselves, their vendors and employees, and the communities in which they operate.

TIPS and Exercises

1. Extract macro performance data from your accounting system (sales, costs and expenses, and profits sorted by criteria that important to you such as region, product, distribution channel, sales person, etc.)
2. Create a Market Information Form to extract data on complaints, compliments, new product ideas, competition, and marketing strategy feedback.
3. Use the information collected to improve your performance. Follow up on complaints to turn the negatives into positives and closer relationships. Take the compliments, and after getting the proper permissions, quote them in your marketing communications and sales presentations. Plug the new product ideas into your New Product Development System and Process. Use the competition information to insure that your products are on par with, or exceed the performance of, your competitors. Relay complaints about competitors to sales people so they can use them in their presentations (making sure they do not directly disparage competitors). Use strategy feedback to improve your Corporate Image, Positioning, Product, Price, Distribution, Promotion, and MIS strategies.
4. Extract feedback data from your Hot List and Promotion Effectiveness Report and use that information to improve your marketing communications and sales effectiveness.
5. Fill remaining holes in your data by doing Market Research. Start with secondary research that you can find for free on the Internet (clickz.com, hoovers.com, zapdata.com, and the CIA Factbook). Next use primary research (see the next two points).
6. Use your Web site to collect information on prospects and customers.

7. Create "report cards" that you provide to prospects when you deliver their goods and services. These should have a few critical questions that ask them to rate your performance — allowing them to simply check boxes or circle answers. Filling these out should take no more than a minute or two.
8. Use positive report card data in your marketing communications (for example, "97% of our customers said that we exceeded their expectations for quality, customer service, and on-time performance.").
9. Code and measure everything you can, and take action on strategies that need to be fixed.

Chapter 13

DNA of International Marketing

"The High-tech World has become a Global Village."

INTRODUCTION

After World War II, the United States was the only major industrialized country with its industrial base in tact. Since Europe and Japan were devastated by the war, many businesses in the United States had little or no competition. As a result, U.S. businesses reigned supreme over foreign competitors.

A case for foreign aide

Because of America's leadership position in the Free World, the United States felt obligated to help rebuild Europe and Japan. Government business advisors thought it would be good for the American economy to have a healthy business climate and large consuming markets in Europe, Japan, and other parts of the world. Therefore, the United States invested heavily in rebuilding the countries that were devastated by the war.

Quality products from abroad

Back in the late 50's and early 60's, as a product of American help, Germany began to export *Volkswagen* automobiles to the United States. During the same period, Japan was selling transistor radios and other low-cost products in the United States. While they were not as luxurious, American consumers found *Volkswagens* to be much lower in cost and similar in reliability and quality to American-made cars. On the other hand, early Japanese imports did not enjoy the same quality reputation. In fact, the *made in Japan* label suffered such a poor *corporate image* around the world that the Japanese hired a quality expert from the United States to teach them how to make top-quality products. By the early 70's, Japanese companies had succeeded in turning their "corporate image" around. They started to become known for quality in cameras, electronics, motorcycles, and other product areas. They even began to develop a good reputation for developing quality automobiles.

Foreign products become more desirable

As European and Japanese products continued to develop a good reputation in the United States and other parts of the world, American consumers became more and more interested in purchasing foreign products. In addition to their reputation for quality at a reasonable cost, foreign products tend to occupy an *exotic position* in the minds of status-conscious buyers. As a result of the *imported* label and quality image associated with many foreign products, more and more of them began to pour into the United States to compete with American products. American businesses were no longer the only source of quality products in the world.

In the high-tech arena, quality products now come from England, Finland, Sweden, France, Germany, Holland, Israel, Japan, Korea, India, China, and other countries around the world.

The U.S. becomes a net importer of products

As a result of increased competition from abroad and a corresponding decline in the value perception of certain American products, the United States became a *net importer* of goods in the early 1980's. Being a *net importer* means that Americans buy more from abroad than they sell to foreign buyers.

Of course, with companies such as *Coca Cola*, *McDonald's*, *Apple Computer*, *Boeing*, *Cisco*, *IBM*, *Intel*, *Microsoft*, *Oracle*, auto manufacturers, and the plethora of entertainment and medical products companies, the United States has had a very big impact on the rest of the world in most areas.

Main reasons why the U.S. has become a net importer of goods

The primary reasons why the United States has become a net importer of goods include the following:

- **Inefficiency.** Some U.S. businesses have not been as efficient as foreign competitors in producing and marketing certain key products, such as automobiles.
- **Inability to compete on quality and price.** In many industries, American businesses have not been able to produce products that match the quality and price of those made by foreign competitors. Some have both higher quality standards and, in some cases, lower prices.
- **Ignorance of the world.** Because the United States is bordered by two large oceans and two peaceful neighbors, American business people have remained largely *ignorant* of the rest of the world.
- **Inadequate foreign marketing.** U.S. businesses have not invested sufficient effort to market their products to other countries.
- **Inadequate government assistance.** Historically, the Federal Government has been more of a hindrance than a help in exporting U.S. products abroad. In contrast, many of the governments of foreign competitors continue to provide outstanding export assistance to their companies. Japan's MITI (Ministry of Information Trade and Industry) does an excellent job of assisting Japanese companies to export their products abroad.

In addition to the fact that being a net importer of goods hurts the U.S. economy and erodes America's standard of living over time, there are other compelling reasons why American businesses should do a better job of exporting products overseas. Perhaps the most important reason is that there is an enormous market potential outside the United States.

FOREIGN MARKET POTENTIAL

While the United States has over 294 million people, the potential of mature and newly-emerging markets outside the United States is far greater. This point is illustrated by the market sizes of the major market territories listed below.

1. **EU** (European Union) **countries** — According to figures from Eurostat, the EU's Statistical Office, there were 380.8 million people living in the EU on January 1, 2004.
2. **EFTA (European Free Trade Association) countries** — EFTA member states are Iceland, Liechtenstein, Norway and Switzerland and have a population over 12.6 million people. Former members, Denmark, Finland, Sweden and the United Kingdom have left EFTA to join the EU. EFTA states are finding that in order to participate in the single market they have to abide by rules established by the EU while they play no part in the process of determining the rules.
3. **Japan** — The Japanese market is over 125 million people.
4. **Former Eastern Bloc Countries** — These countries represent a market of over 400 million people.

4\. **China and India** — These newly industrialized countries represent a market of roughly 2.4 billion people with growing consumer and industrial potential.

Adding up the numbers from these groups, the market potential is very exciting — especially when one considers that many of the people in these market areas are in a similar situation to Americans after World War II. That is, they have new-found disposable income, but don't yet have many of the time and money-saving products which are commonplace in the United States.

Additional Markets

The numbers become even more exciting when the other mature and newly-emerging market areas are considered. These are often grouped into blocs and include the following:

Developed countries (DCs) — In addition to the United States, Japan, and the technically-developed countries of Western Europe discussed above, Israel and the English-speaking countries of Canada, Australia, and New Zealand round out the group of industrialized nations known as the Developed Countries.

Newly Industrialized countries (NICs) — The NICs include Brazil, Hong Kong (now united with China), India, Mexico, Singapore, South Korea, Singapore, South Africa, and Taiwan. Thailand is also a strong candidate for this designation. To be considered an NIC, a country must have (1) a middle-income economy with GNP per capita (Gross National Product divided by the population) ranging from $2,000 to $5,000, (2) a heavy concentration of multinational investment, and (3) a significant quantity of high-tech and manufactured goods exports.

Less Developed countries (LDCs) — Most of the remaining countries of Africa, Central and South America, Asia, and the Middle East fall into the LDC category. These LDCs, or "Third World" Countries, typically have many of the following characteristics in common:

1. **GNP per capita income of less than $2,000.**
2. **Unequal distribution of income** — a small group of very wealthy people, a large group of very poor people, and a very small middle class.
3. **A majority of the population earning a livelihood from agricultural labor.**
4. **High population growth** — usually from 2.5 to 4 percent each year.
5. **High rate of illiteracy.**
6. **Significant health problems and malnutrition.**
7. **Political instability.**
8. **Export of a few *primary* products** — usually agricultural products or natural resources.
9. **Inhospitable climate and topography** — rocky soil, jungles, or deserts.
10. **Inadequate infrastructure** — lack of good banking, transportation, communication, and reliable power systems.
11. **Low saving rates** — the majority of people spend most of their earnings on products for consumption.

Based on their GNP per capita figures, many businesses overlook the LDCs as potential markets for their products. This is a mistake — especially since the LDCs spend a large portion of their wealth on consumption, and about 40% of US exports go to LDCs. This potential of doing business with the LDCs adds to the newly-emerging market opportunities in the former Soviet-Bloc countries and the already-established potential in the Developed Countries to form a very exciting opportunity for companies to do business in the international arena.

While some might consider Mainland China and India to be LDC's, these countries of over 2.4 billion people are experiencing exploding economic growth and have already become a manufacturing centers for the many of the world's companies. Because of their size and rapid economic progress, many believe that China and India represents a very exciting markets for those American marketers who learn how to penetrate their gigantic markets.

Benefits of marketing abroad

In addition to the enormous potential for expanding your company's sales and profits, there are many other important reasons for marketing overseas. Some of the most significant ones are presented below.

1. **New markets.** Domestic markets may become saturated or overly competitive. In order to grow, the company may have to move overseas to establish new, faster-growing markets — often in less-competitive environments.
2. **Less competition.** Because many foreign markets have fewer competitors, sales are easier and less subject to discounts.
3. **Investment incentives.** Many foreign governments and agencies will give foreign businesses lucrative incentives such as low tax rates, low-interest loans, low-cost facilities, and even outright donations. They hope that the presence of foreign businesses will boost employment, exports, taxes, and other revenue-generators and economy-builders in the long run.
4. **Lower costs.** Expanding to markets overseas can reduce costs in many ways including (1) *economies of scale* from larger production runs, (2) *lower labor costs* from less expensive labor pools, (3) *lower distribution and freight costs* from proximity to foreign markets, and (4) *avoidance of tariffs* from foreign policies that eliminate tariffs on locally-produced products from foreign-owned companies.
5. **Corporate Image.** Operating in the *international* arena tends to boost the *corporate image* of the business in the eyes of its publics.
6. **Screen-out competitors.** In many foreign countries, the company who gets to a marketplace first will gain a foothold in that market. This will limit the ability of competitors, domestic or foreign, to establish a presence in that market.
7. **Increased product exposure and brand recognition.** As more foreign buyers are exposed to company products, they will tend to ask for such products in their country and in other countries when they travel.
8. **Improved marketing intelligence.** By operating in foreign environments, businesses can learn firsthand what foreign prospects want and need. They can also find new product ideas for their domestic markets.
9. **Exotic image.** Companies operating in foreign markets can benefit from the exotic image associated with doing business on an international scale.
10. **Protect domestic markets.** By gaining a foothold in overseas markets, companies can limit the ability of foreign competitors to gain the resources to build momentum in their domestic markets.

TAPPING THIS POTENTIAL

While it is easy to get excited about the large numbers and the benefits enumerated above, marketers should realize that there is a big gulf between opportunity and success. As with marketing in the domestic arena, bridging this gulf requires a rational and systematic approach. A good place to start this approach is with a model for doing business abroad.

INTERNATIONAL MARKETING MODEL

As we have learned throughout this text, marketing in the domestic arena can be quite a challenge. Doing business in the international arena increases the challenge by at least two orders of magnitude. In addition to doing all that is required to achieve a *domestic* success, marketers operating overseas also have to worry about *foreign* and *pipeline* issues. *Figure 13-1* graphically illustrates this model.

Figure 13-1

Domestic issues refers to those marketing concerns that arise from doing business within the boundaries of one's own country. *Foreign* issues are those that appear when marketing in another country. *Pipeline* issues are those related to moving product and information between domestic and foreign locations on a timely basis. Using this model, we can organize our approach to tapping the foreign market potential described in the previous section. Since we have already covered the important *Domestic* issues for marketing throughout this book, we will concentrate on the *Foreign* and *Pipeline* issues in the following sections.

FOREIGN ISSUES

There are many foreign and pipeline issues that decision makers need to understand before doing business abroad. Perhaps the most important foreign issue is the *cultural differences* between company decision makers and foreign publics.

Cultural Differences

Cultural differences can be a serious barrier to achieving success in foreign markets. There are two main reasons why they can be so troublesome — (1) Even though people in the domestic market may come from many different countries, they are largely *ignorant about other cultures* and (2) many cultural differences are very subtle or even hidden. Examples of cultural differences that have caused problems for businesses include the following:

- **Colors.** Colors have important meanings in other cultures — especially Asian cultures. An American lawn product did not sell in a Southeast Asian country because it was painted green. In that country, green is associated with death from the jungle.
- **Numbers.** While some consider the number 13 unlucky in the U.S., the number 4 in Japan and some other Asian countries is associated with death. Products with four in their name or that come in quantities of four are not likely to sell in Japan.
- **Names.** Names may have a totally different meaning in other languages. Some have even known to be offensive or obscene when viewed in a foreign context. When *Osco Drugs* of Pittsburgh purchased the *Sav-On* drug store chain, they changed the name to *Osco*. When sales at the newly-acquired chain went down, their investigation discovered that *Osco* is an unpleasant word in Spanish that offended many of the company's *Hispanic* customers. After going to the expense of changing all the logos, signs, and stationery to *Osco*, they had to change them back to *Sav-On.* Simple research before the name change could have saved a lot of money, trouble and corporate image damage. One place a company might look is the *International Dictionary of Obscenities,* by Christina Kusnitskaya-Peterson (Berkeley, CA: Berkeley Slavic, 1981).
- **Histories.** In many parts of Europe and the world, Germans are disliked for the part they played in both World Wars. In Muslim countries, many still distrust Europeans because of the Crusades. In some of the Southern and Western parts of the U.S., people are still harboring hatreds from the Civil War. In Belgium, many of the Flemish and French-speaking people have difficulties with each other, and in Canada the same is true of French and English-speaking groups. Knowing and being sensitive to such historic differences is essential to doing business in foreign places.
- **Verbal and nonverbal communication.** In Japan and other parts of Asia, communication is 70% nonverbal. In the U.S. it is 70% verbal.
- **Body language.** In Mediterranean countries, such as Italy and Greece, people frequently talk with their hands. In Northern European countries, people are more stoic and feel uncomfortable when people use their hands to communicate. In Southern Europe, men will walk arm and arm and embrace. In Northern Europe, they avoid physical contact other than shaking hands. The same is true of Japan.
- **Conversational distance.** In warmer climates, people tend to stand much closer together when they talk with each other than do people in colder climates.
- **Conversational volumes.** In Thailand, speaking softly is the rule. In Texas, speaking loudly is the rule.

- **Time frames.** In Japan, business people take much longer to get to know each other before transacting business. In America, business people are in a hurry. They want to make the deal quickly, and move on to the next customer. In cooler climates, people tend to be punctual, whereas they are often late in warmer climates. When someone says I'll meet you at noon, they may mean 2 p.m. or even later.
- **Meals.** In Madrid, Spain, workers take their meals very seriously, and do not like to talk business during lunch. In the U.S., it's just the opposite. In France, many business people stand up while eating lunch. In Spain, they sit down.
- **Language.** Even if the same language is spoken in different countries or in different parts of the same country, the meanings of words can be totally different. To emphasize this point, Churchill once said that "America and England are two countries divided by a common language." For example, in England, *boot* is the word for the trunk of a car. The hood of the car is called a *bonnet.* An elevator is called a *lift,* an apartment is called a *flat,* and a popsicle is called an *ice lolly.*
- **Directional orientations.** In England, Japan and some former English colonies, people drive and walk on the left side of the road while people in the U.S. and in most other countries drive on the right. This directional orientation carries over to the design of products to be sold in countries that have a different orientation from ours. For example, American auto manufacturers want the Japanese to buy more American cars, but they have been reluctant to put the steering wheel on the right to accommodate their driving on the left side of the road.

Doing your homework

The above examples are provided to emphasize the point that understanding cultural differences is critical to success in international marketing. Your personnel should do their *cultural* homework before attempting to do business in a foreign country. In addition to learning about the cultural differences between countries, they should also be aware that people in the same country do not always share the same cultural values. In fact, there can be serious cultural differences within the same country. Such differences may come from *religion*, *language*, *ethnicity*, *history*, *geography*, *politics*, *socioeconomic class*, *wealth*, *family*, *political beliefs*, and numerous other factors. Canada, Belgium, Northern Ireland, and the former country of Yugoslavia are just a few of the many examples of countries that have sharp cultural differences within their borders. While not as serious, most countries have citizens who are divided because of different cultural values.

Employing foreign nationals

In addition to doing your homework, perhaps the best way to avoid problems is to employ, or consult with, people who really understand both cultures — that of the *foreign country* and the domestic country. Perhaps they were born in the foreign country and were educated in the domestic country, or vice versa. Only they understand the important cultural nuances that are critical to successfully marketing to people in the host country. They can properly interpret language inflections, humor, intent, body language, and other verbal and nonverbal signals. They can also understand both sides and determine what each needs to do so that *both sides will win* when they engage in a business transaction.

Thinking outside-in rather than inside-out

The important point is that you should never underestimate the impact of cultural differences on international marketing. Perhaps the worst mistake you can make is to assume that the foreign people with whom you are doing business think as you think, like what you like, act as you act, or want what you want. You should adopt a *marketing-driven* orientation whereby you think from an outside-in rather than an inside-out perspective. In marketing abroad, this becomes even more important because you need to learn the marketplace on a *macro-level* (cultural and historical) as well as on a *micro level* (needs and wants of each sub-segment). In general, if you assume that you are *ignorant* about the foreign culture and have to learn as much as you can about it, you are much more likely to succeed than if you assume that you know enough. Oddly enough, this applies to the domestic market as well. Too many companies have lost business by unknowingly insulting people's sex, religion, race, age, national origin, ethnicity, or subculture.

Once company personnel understand the important cultural differences between the host country and the domestic market, they need to learn about political differences.

Political risks

Politics in other countries can be quite different from politics in the United States or other domestic country. As such, you should be aware of the differences of the countries in which you are doing business.

Political discussions should be avoided

People in other parts of the world take their politics even more seriously than do most Americans. Because they often get so emotionally involved, political discussions or comments should be avoided whenever possible. Otherwise, they could interfere with a good business relationship and good marketing.

Understand the political situation

It is also important to understand the *political stability* of the country in which you are doing business. Unlike the United States, which is one of the most politically stable countries in the world, many other countries suffer from political instability. In certain countries, especially those that are run by a monarchy or a military dictator, coup d'états are a way of life. Moreover, when the government changes overnight, the country's attitude toward foreign business could change just as rapidly. In many cases, businesses in foreign countries have been nationalized or their assets have been confiscated without adequate compensation. To gauge the political stability of the country in which you are thinking of doing business, you can and should check the following:

- **Large international banks and multinational companies.** It is part of their business to do what is called a *Country Risk Assessment, or CRA. Bank Crédit Suisse* has a *CRA Procedure* and *Swiss Bank Corp* has a *Country Risk Monitor.*
- **Lloyds of London and other international insurance companies.** Since their business is based upon risks and probabilities, these companies usually have *CRA* figures on file.
- **Conference Board Publications.** The *Conference Board* is an organization that specializes in providing information to business managers. They are known to have done studies on *CRA.*
- **CIA.** The *Central Intelligence Agency* is known to be a great source of information on foreign countries. Search for the *CIA World Factbook* in your favorite search engine.

Avoid countries that have a history of nationalization

Nationalization refers to the host foreign government's takeover of private property. In the best case, the government reimburses a business for nationalizing its assets. In the worst case, it takes them over without compensation. In most cases, whatever compensation is provided is inadequate, and results in a loss for the company. Therefore, the best course of action is to avoid locating significant facilities or assets in countries that have a history of nationalization for political, economic, or for whatever reasons.

Protecting your assets

Since you know that there is a *rule of business* that the *risks are proportional to the gains*, you may want to do business in a medium or high-risk country. Whether the risks are high or low, you should take certain precautions to protect your assets against political volatility. They should include the following: (1) keep minimal capital in the country (once money is collected in that country, wire transfer it back to your domestic bank or to some other safe place), (2) have contingency plans for quickly moving assets and human resources out of the country in an emergency, and (3) take out insurance — The *MICA*, or *Multilateral Investment Guarantee*

Agency, was set up by the *World Bank* in 1986 to insure businesses against loss from war, riot, and other risks. You should check with *MICA* about their insurance for protecting your assets. If their coverage is inadequate, supplement it with private insurance.

Civil rights

Those who do business in foreign countries should understand that other countries don't offer the "civil rights" protections that they enjoy in the United States. If your domestic country is different from the United States, the same concept applies. That is, you can be sure that the foreign rules and regulations will be different from those with which you are familiar. As such, you should make sure that all of your employees who are doing business in foreign countries know the risks and take precautions to protect themselves. A small handbook that tells them about local laws as well as what to do, and where to go for help in various circumstances can be very helpful. It may also advise them to make friends with the staff of US, or home-country, embassies and consulates, carry pre-approved visas and plane tickets for travel out of the country on short notice, and to avoid walking alone in certain areas.

An example of the difference in civil rights between countries occurred in 1991. A Taiwanese company had an American woman put in jail for two weeks because they claimed that her company owed them money. The fact was that this woman's company in the United States had a running dispute with the Taiwanese company. A line of clothing they had ordered from the Taiwanese company was shipped 3 months late — after the style had already changed for the next season. Because the Taiwanese company had not met the contracted date of shipment and because the American company could not sell the outdated product, they returned the merchandise and didn't pay for it. Rather than arbitrate the dispute in a court of law, the company had her jailed on her next buying trip. If it wasn't for her husband making a big issue of his wife's jailing with the U.S. Government and the media, she might still be in jail without the *due process of law* with which she is familiar in the United States.

Along with the political and cultural issues involved in doing business in a foreign arena, marketing managers should understand the legal issues.

Legal Issues

In addition to the domestic legal issues, doing marketing abroad demands some special legal considerations — especially with regard to copyrights, trademarks, and clearances to use people's names and likenesses in ads and collateral materials.

Establish a relationship with a local foreign law firm

Your company should establish a relationship with a foreign law firm that is well-versed in the business laws of the host country. As always, it is best to establish this relationship early before it is needed. Once established, your company will be able to move forward expeditiously on an emergency legal matter without the pressure of finding and selecting foreign legal counsel at the last minute. In the best of circumstances, you will never have to use this firm. If you do, however, you will be ready.

Jurisdiction and other contract provisions

Having control over the *jurisdiction* of a case can provide an important advantage to a business that is involved in a legal dispute. Without such control, the high costs of domestic litigation can be dwarfed by the additional foreign litigation costs associated with (1) travel time of domestic lawyers and company executives to foreign locations, (2) the retention of a foreign counsel, (3) meeting time between foreign and domestic legal counsels, (4) travel expenses, (5) phone calls and faxes between domestic and foreign locations, and (6) transportation of legal files between domestic and foreign arenas by messenger or some other means. In an effort to control these costs and protect your interests, your business should make every effort to *specify* the following in all of its contracts:

1. **Jurisdiction.** This refers to the country, state, or municipality whose laws should prevail in the event of a dispute.
2. **Language.** The language that should prevail in litigation proceedings should be delineated. By specifying your native language, you can better understand the proceedings. This will help you to avoid misunderstandings from language differences as well as costly translation services.
3. **Court**. By specifying the court wh*ere the dispute is to be heard*, you can avoid the disadvantage of an unfavorable location and you can help to insure the impartiality of the court proceedings.
4. **Patent and trademark protection responsibilities.** In addition to respecting your company's property rights and paying all appropriate fees for use of your property, you need to affix copyright, patent, and trademark notices whenever you use your names and marks in print, and to remind others when they do the same.
5. **Payment method and terms.** The payment *method, terms,* and *currency* should be specified in your contract. Credit sales are very risky in international business. It is much more difficult and expensive to chase those who don't pay around the globe to recover the money they owe. If you are not able to get international customers to prepay their purchases, you should at least require an *irrevocable letter of credit.* With an *irrevocable letter of*

credit, you are guaranteed timely payment from their bank once you provide proof of shipment of what they ordered. Your commercial bank should be able to advise you on the proper procedures for an *irrevocable letter of credit* or to refer you to a bank that can. As discussed previously, if you don't specify the *currency* and *timing* of payment, you could lose money on the currency exchange. That is, the currency could fluctuate *against* your favor between the time the order was placed and it is paid in full.

6. **Binding arbitration.** A binding arbitration clause can save significant litigation fees and expenses. By including such a clause in their contract, both parties agree to be bound by the decision of an independent, third-party arbitrator. Because it can result in the saving of considerable litigation costs, it is a good idea to include an arbitration clause in most contracts. The exception, of course, are those special cases where the company is likely to fare better in a normal court of law. The *International Chamber of Commerce in Paris, the Arbitration Panel* in London, and the *World Bank's International Center for Settlement of Investment Disputes* are just some of the organizations that provide binding arbitration services to companies engaged in international business.

Copyrights, Patents, and Trademarks

According to John Diebold, an industry expert in high technology, American businesses lose between $40 and 60 billion dollars each year because foreign governments fail to properly enforce their *property* rights![2] The United States is not the only country whose businesses suffer from theft. Businesses in many centers around the world have experienced significant losses. To help guard against this enormous loss of revenue, businesses should make sure that they file international copyrights, patents, trademarks and service marks in the major industrialized countries and consuming markets. Additionally, they should make sure that all parties with whom they do business agree, in writing, to recognize and protect these property rights. These precautions will not eliminate all of the theft problems, but should serve to mitigate them.

Enlist the help of foreign governments and international organizations

Before agreeing to locate facilities in foreign countries, marketers should make sure that foreign host governments agree to provide assistance in protecting their property rights, defending them from nuisance law suits, and insuring a "*level playing field*" in the event of litigation initiated by native companies and individuals.

In addition, before doing business in a foreign location, U.S.-owned companies should make sure that they identify the international organizations that can help them to provide legal assistance in the event of litigation or forced nationalization of their assets.

Once these foreign legal issues are addressed, your company needs to focus and the important financial and economic issues that impact their success in a foreign arena.

Financial and economic issues

In addition to *domestic* financial issues, *doing business* abroad involves many other important financial considerations that are of importance to marketers. Many of these are related to the *currency* in which business is transacted and assets are kept.

Hard currency

In order to protect the value of monetary assets, the company should have a policy that requires payment in a *hard currency*. A *hard currency* is one that is easily *convertible* to most other currencies and which business people around the world will readily accept as payment for what is owed them. The commonly recognized hard currencies include the U.S. dollar ($), British pound (£), Japanese Yen (¥), and the European Union Euro (€). If a foreign customer cannot pay in U.S. dollars or some other hard currency, the company should move the payment into a hard currency as soon as it is paid and should figure any exchange fees into the price of the sales agreement. For historical and practical reasons, the U.S. $ was established as a *Keystone currency* at the center of the world's monetary system. This means that most currencies must be first converted to U.S. dollars before being converted again to another currency. The *exchange rates* for converting two non-U.S. currencies are called *cross rates.*

Currency fluctuations and exchange

Because currencies move relative to one another, a company can lose money just by holding monetary assets in a currency which is going down in relation to the others. To optimize the value of assets and to minimize currency fluctuation risk, marketers should coordinate with financial managers to do the following:

Move assets into the strongest currencies. This involves watching currency fluctuations very closely and being prepared to move assets into the stronger currencies by electronic transfer to gain rather than lose money on these fluctuations. To do this, the financial manager needs to watch the *Spot* and the *Forward* currency rates. The *Spot rate* is the exchange rate between currencies for their immediate trade with delivery within two days. The *Forward rate* is the exchange rate between two currencies for delivery in the future (usually in 20, 60, 90, or 180 days). If the *forward* rate is higher than the *spot* rate, the currency will be considered stronger and trade at a *premium*. Conversely, if the *forward rate* is *lower* than the *spot rate,* the currency is considered weaker and will trade at a *discount.* Some countries actually have two spot rates — (1) *Commercial spot rate* for import and export transactions and (2) *Financial spot rate* for all other transactions.

Avoid credit transactions whenever possible. Doing business on credit poses an additional risk in foreign business. While the company is waiting to be paid, the value of the money owed could substantially drop due to currency fluctuations. Another alternative is to contractually tie the actual payment due to the fluctuation of the currency in which it is to be paid.

Negotiate more favorable rates with the bank. The bank makes its money on the difference between *bid* and *asked* prices. The *bid* is lower and is what the bank will pay for a currency. The *asked* is higher and is what you will pay the bank when you buy a currency using another currency. If you do a lot of business with a particular bank, you can sometimes negotiate a more favorable exchange rate.

Avoid currencies that have exchange controls. Exchange controls are host government controls that limit the legal uses of a currency in international commerce. These pose a great risk since they are usually instituted to artificially prop up the value of a weak currency. In the former the Soviet Union, the Soviet government put exchange controls on the *ruble.* These exchange controls have hurt the Russian government's ability to do business internationally.

Balance of Payments imbalances

When a country runs a balance of payments deficit or surplus, it is likely to take market and non-market measures to counteract the imbalance. To counteract a deficit, for example, the *central bank* of the country may devalue the currency, employ restrictive monetary and fiscal policies, or institute currency or trade controls. If significant company assets are in that currency, these assets could lose considerable value. Therefore, if the financial manager expects a devaluation, company assets should be moved out of that currency quickly.

State of the economy and government reactions

A government typically uses *monetary* and *fiscal* policies for a variety of purposes including to… (1) speed up the economy, (2) slow down the economy to quiet inflation, or (3) bring the economy out of a recession.

Monetary Policy. It uses monetary policy to control the amount of money in circulation. It does this by changing the discount rate that the *Federal Reserve* charges to banks for the money they need to operate. Based on this rate, banks change the *prime interest rate* accordingly. The *prime interest rate* is the rate that banks charge their biggest and best customers when they borrow money. This rate, in turn, affects the amount companies must pay to lenders when they borrow money. In general, by lowering the interest rate, businesses will be encouraged to borrow money and expand their businesses. By increasing the interest rate, businesses are less likely to borrow and expand. In the U.S., the money supply is determined by three different measures called *M1, M2,* and *M3. M1* is the most restrictive definition of the money supply and refers to *cash in circulation* plus *money in checking accounts* plus *non-bank travelers checks. M2* is defined as *M1* plus *savings deposits* plus *money market mutual funds. M3* is the broadest definition of the money supply and includes *M2* plus less-liquid (more difficult to convert to cash quickly) accounts such as *certificates of deposit* over $100,000.

Fiscal policy. A government also uses *fiscal policy* to make changes in the economy. Fiscal policy is employed when the government (1) collects money in taxes and (2) spends money to achieve its goals and operate its programs. By spending money for goods and services, the government tends to increase economic activity. Those who receive the money will be able to spend it on the goods and services they need, and they will also pay taxes on their increased income. The taxes go to the government, whereas expenditures for goods and services go to other businesses, which, in turn, pay more taxes and buy goods and services from other businesses.

While *taxes* are a way for the *government to collect money,* they are also a way to *shape the behavior* of businesses and individuals. For example, if the government wants a business to invest in certain areas, it may offer an investment tax credit. If it wants a business to donate money to charities, it will offer a tax deduction for such donations.

Interest Rates

In international business, reference interest rates are typically based on the *U.S. Prime rate* and/or the *London Interbank Office Rate,* or *LIBOR*. In Western Europe, however, as a result of the periodic dominance of the German economy, most interest rates during the '91/'92 recession followed the *German central bank rate* — which has, at times, been considerably higher than the *U.S. Prime rate.* According to the *Wall Street Journal*, "Germany is keeping its base business interest rates at nearly 10% in an effort to offset the inflationary effects of unification. Real rates in Germany are about triple those in the U.S., and many economists expect further increases."[3] This means that financial managers cannot rely on historical patterns alone. They have to stay abreast of current activities in the foreign countries in which the company does business to avoid making the wrong decisions.

Inflation

As economies expand, or heat up, there is a tendency for *inflation* to increase as well. *Inflation* simply refers to *more money chasing fewer goods.* This means that each *dollar, pound, euro,* or *yen* buys fewer goods and services. Inflation is typically caused by (1) increases in the money supply and (2) increased demand for, or shortage of, products. If the currency in which *monetary assets* are kept becomes inflated, the money manager of the business should move these assets to higher-value, or less-inflated, currencies. Since inflation destroys the value of your money (i.e. each *dollar, pound, euro,* or *yen* becomes worth less and less over time), money should be moved to less-inflated currencies or invested to minimize the effect of inflation.

Banking relationship

As in the domestic arena, businesses need to establish a good relationship with a foreign bank. In addition to having a source for foreign capital and a place to safely keep the company's foreign assets, the foreign bank is the one who will (1) transfer money to and from the company's domestic bank, (2) arrange for letters of credit between the company, its customers, and vendors, and (3) provide the company's foreign operations with the support they need while transacting business in the foreign arena. As with lawyers, accountants, ad agencies and other professional firms, the relationship between the business and the bank should be one that is built on trust and loyalty. If it is not, it could fall apart under the strains that are likely to occur in the normal course of doing business. Since building relationships with your companies publics is a critical marketing function, these foreign and financial matters are being covered in this book.

Accounting Practices

Marketers should understand that accounting provides a score-keeping function that is critical to marketing budgets and performance issues related to the marketing information system. Since there are different score-keeping rules in different countries, significant sums of money can be made or lost simply because of the accounting practices used. This can best be illustrated by a failed partnership of *General Motors* and the *Daewoo* group of South Korea as reported in the *Wall Street Journal.* According to *GM* accounting practices, "...*Daewoo* has accumulated losses of $56.3 million since 1986, including a loss of $1.3 million (in fiscal 1991). But *Daewoo Motors* itself says that when its results are stated using Korean accounting methods (which recognize profits from intra-company transactions), it earned about $13.6 million last year."[4]

Relationship between Marketing and Finance

At this juncture, you may be asking yourself why international finance and economic issues are being discussed in a book on the fundamentals of marketing. There are many reasons. Most of these can be explained by the following basic financial equations:

Balance Sheet: **Assets = Liabilities + Owners Equity**
Income Statement: **Profits = Revenues – (Costs+Expenses)**

That is, good marketing will lower costs and increase revenues — both of which raise profits. Profits are either paid out as dividends to shareholders or kept in the business as *Retained Earnings* that increase the value of the company on the Balance Sheet.

Because of the importance of banking, financial, and economic relationships to the health of your foreign business, marketers need to make sure that they consider bankers in their marketing programs. That is, by marketing to banks, foreign government agencies, and other economic institutions as well as to your primary customers, you can lower the cost of capital, taxes, and other fees in that foreign country. Lowering these costs translates to higher profits and greater financial resources to invest in your marketing programs and your business.

Influential Organizations and Groups

Just as a domestic company needs to keep in touch with all of its important publics, an international company needs to do the same. This includes knowing the important organizations and groups that affect the transaction of business in the international arena. Some of the more important organizations include the following:

The World Bank. The world bank is a very important organization in international commerce because it (1) provides loans to finance billions of dollars of purchases from businesses each year, (2) assists financial institutions in *Less Developed Countries* who, in turn, provide sources of capital for companies doing business in or with LDCs, (3) provides a center for arbitration of international business disputes — thereby reducing otherwise exorbitant legal fees, (4) establishes organizations such as MICA to insure investors in foreign countries against loss from war, riots, and other risks, (5) finances projects that provide infrastructure and resources needed for direct investment in foreign countries, and (6) provides excellent information resources about a country or foreign project. The World Bank has an excellent reputation and a triple-A credit rating. It has operated profitably every year since 1947. While it has had some unstable clients, few, if any, have ever defaulted.

International Monetary Fund, or IMF. The IMF works with governments to do the following: (1) promote orderly foreign exchange arrangements between currencies, (2) help insure the convertibility of currencies, and (3) dampen balance of payments disequilibria that can create currency instabilities.

Regional Development Banks. These are regional versions of the World Bank. They primarily function to lend money in LDCs to (1) build infrastructure, (2) support agriculture and industry, and (3) create jobs.

GATT. The General Agreement on Tariffs and Trade were established in 1947. GATT became a de facto international trade organization. Its primary successes have related to lowering tariffs. Since GATT was established, the average tariffs in industrial countries have fallen from 40% to roughly 5%. Tariffs, of course, discourage foreign buyers from buying your products because they are too expensive once tariffs are added to your normal prices.

United Nations. The UN spends $750 million annually, and its member agencies advise member countries on buying products totaling more than $20 billion annually. The *Interagency Procurement Services Unit,* or *IAPSU,* was established in 1985 to match up customers with suppliers. The UN Conference on Trade and Development, has become a forum and advocate for Third World countries, or LDCs.

European Union. Originally called the European Economic Community, the European Union, or EU, is a growing confederation of industrialized European nations headquartered in Brussels Belgium. Some believe the EU is the beginning of the United States of Europe. Others don't believe this will ever happen. Irrespective of who is right, the EU countries are becoming more unified and powerful. As a group, the EU currently represents the largest single import and export market in the world with a *Gross Domestic Product* second only to the United States. *Gross Domestic Product*, or GDP, is the total value of product produced domestically unlike Gross National Product, or GNP, which includes *net factor income*, such as interest and dividends produced abroad. The EU's original base of 12 countries accounted for roughly 20% of world trade, compared with 14% for the U.S. and 9% for Japan. This number will grow considerably as the EU continues to add more countries into its union. The economic objective of the EU is to eliminate all boundaries between member countries so that people, capital and products can move freely within the EU. While some fear that the EU will become a trading bloc, called *Fortress Europe,* that favors dealing with member countries at the expense of outsiders, others recognize the positive benefits that the EU brings to companies around the world. These benefits include the following:

1. **Standards.** Whereas manufacturers formerly had to make many costly versions of their products to meet the varied specifications of different EU countries, the EU is setting common standards that member nations must follow. This means that businesses can make products to one unified standard — thereby making business with EU countries much more economically feasible.
2. **Largest customer.** In 1987, EU countries accounted for 25% of U.S. exports, and they continue to represent the largest customer of American business.
3. **Largest single market.** With over 390 million people in 2004, many of whom are sophisticated consumers, the EU countries currently represent the largest single export market.
4. **Target of large U.S. investment.** Over 40% of U.S. external investment is in EU countries.

5. **Major source of Corporation funds.** EU money and capital markets have become an important source of funds, or capital, for businesses.
6. **Create jobs and income.** EU companies raise money in the U.S. causing over $200 billion in capital swaps each year. These create jobs and income for financial companies.
7. **Represents 20%+ of world trade.** Since the EU does more world trade than either the U.S. or Japan, they are an important player in international business.

Department of Commerce, or DOC. The DOC performs market research and maintains large libraries of information for businesses interested in doing business overseas. Library information is typically available at no charge, databases of information can be accessed for a nominal fee, and reports and surveys can be obtained for a reasonable cost. For any company wanting to do business in the international arena, the DOC is a good place to start. Any information that the DOC does not provide, can then be obtained by foreign consulates, trade offices, and a variety of private import/export and consulting firms.

G-7, or Group of 7. This is the name given to the finance ministers and central bank representatives of the U.S., France, Germany, Japan, the United Kingdom, Canada and Italy who meet periodically to discuss important banking, finance, and economic issues which affect the world economy.

Others. While there are many other important groups and organizations involved in international business, the above list provides you with a good starting list. As you investigate a particular country and industry in greater depth, you will find many other groups and sources of information that can help you. You should add them to the above list.

Standards

As mentioned above, the EU is establishing standard specifications for its products. This will make it far easier and less-costly for marketers to design products to a common standard for export to the EU. Unfortunately, many of the other non-EU countries with which companies do business, may not follow the EU standards. Marketers should be aware of other *standardizing forces* in international business. Two of the most prominent are the *International Electrotechnical Commission (IEC)* and the *International Organization for Standardization (IOS)*. These organizations set the standards and specifications for many products that are sold around the world.

Weights and Measures. International specifications for weights and measures are in the *metric system* not in the *Old English* (feet-inches/pounds-ounces) *system* that is still used in the United States. Standards, of course go beyond weights and measures to include such additional measures as *power* and *quality*. These impact marketing communications as well as product design since specifications listed in marketing communications need to use the "metric language" that the international community understands.

Power and TV. The U.S., Canada, Japan and some other countries use 60-cycle power whereas most countries in Europe, Asia, and other parts of the world use 50-cycle power. These different power standards impact the design of television and other electronic products. Because of the 60-cycle power standard, television in the U.S., Canada and Japan use an *NTSC* 525-scan-line, 60-field, 30 frame-per-second standard. In Europe and other 50-cycle countries, they use a *PAL* 625-scan-line, 50 field, 25 frame-per-second standard. This means that all TV shows filmed or taped in the U.S. have to be converted from the NTSC to the PAL standard before they can be broadcast in Europe and other parts of the world having 50-cycle power. HDTV Standards are still in a state of flux.

Quality. With regard to quality, various measures have been adopted — depending on the product. For defects or traces of impurities, they are often expressed in terms of parts per million. Electronic products are also rated according to *Mean Time Between Failures (MTBF),* and *Mean Time to Repair (MTTR).* While most of these measures are understood and used by different countries, each country may use a different quality standard. Businesses need to learn the standards by which their products will be judged and compared in each foreign country. The move toward ISO 9000, QS 9000, and other international standards will help to insure consistency.

Standard Deviation. In statistics, a standard measure of defect from the norm, or the ideal specimen, is called the *standard deviation* (expressed by the lower case Greek letter sigma). The quality standard of some products may be discussed in terms of the number of standard deviations from the norm that will be tolerated. Increasing international competition is causing companies to adopt a *Total Quality Management (TQM)* approach by which the acceptable deviation from standard is getting smaller and smaller. This means that intensified competition is pushing the quality standard higher and higher. Therefore, companies need to produce better and better products if they want to compete in the international arena, or charge less for lower quality.

Financial Incentives

Foreign governments sometimes offer lucrative financial incentives for businesses from *Developed Countries* to establish operations in their countries. They do this because they believe these incentives are a good investment that is likely to yield an even greater return in the form of jobs, exports, taxes, and the ability to attract other foreign businesses. For example, *Apple computer* and many other manufacturers have located plants in Ireland because of very favorable incentives in addition to the fact that Ireland has a skilled technical labor force.

Avoiding Tariffs and other trade barriers

In addition to providing outright incentives, EU countries offer companies the ability to avoid paying tariffs on goods produced by their EU-based subsidiaries and shipped to other EU countries. *Tariffs* are fees, or *duties,* charged by countries on foreign products that are imported into those countries. By avoiding these tariffs, businesses that sell a lot of products to EU countries can save a lot by establishing a plant in an EU country.

PIPELINE ISSUES

Pipeline issues involve the difficulties related to moving product, money, people, communications, and information between the *domestic* and *foreign arenas* on a timely basis. The longer the *pipeline,* or the distance between the domestic home base and the foreign location, the more difficulties that are likely to arise. The most common sources of problems are described below.

Time-zone differences

Even within the *continental United States,* significant problems are caused because there are three time zones between the West and East Coasts. People on the East Coast are going to lunch when their counterparts on the West Coast are just arriving at work. To overcome these problems, businesses (1) need to be aware of time zone differences, (2) plan ahead, and (3) utilize technology, such as e-mail and faxes, to compensate for these differences.

Freight and insurance expenses

Usually, the longer the pipeline, the greater the freight costs to ship products, brochures, and other items between the home base and the foreign destination. In addition to paying for the transportation, special marine or air freight insurance may be required to insure against loss from the voyage or natural disasters along the way. Of course, product literature can be published on your Web site to save printing and shipping costs.

Special packaging

Because of the longer journeys and rougher voyages, exported products have to be specially packed in a way that the contents are better protected yet allow customs officials to open the packages and inspect their contents.

Delivery times

The longer the pipeline, the longer it takes for transportation to deliver the product to its destination. Long delays between ordering and receiving product can negatively impact your company's competitive position in the foreign marketplace.

Communications

The longer the pipeline, the greater the (1) communication expenses, (2) possibility of communication interference or overloaded channels — exemplified by the common message "all circuits are busy, please try your call again," (3) likelihood of communication difficulties from a variety of sources — especially language problems.

Travel times and expenses

The transaction of business often requires travel to face-to-face meetings and trade shows. The longer the pipeline, the greater the travel times and expenses.

Weather and natural disaster interference

The likelihood of weather and natural disasters interfering with shipments, communications, and travel increases with the length and location of the pipeline.

Jet lag

As the number of time zones increases, so does the jet lag of travelers who must traverse these time zones. Because it affects the ability of travelers to function in a business environment, jet lag often adds *recovery* days (additional time and expense) to a trip. The guideline is *one day of recovery* is required for *every zone, or hour, of time difference.*

Intermediaries

The longer the pipeline, the more likely different organizations will be involved in the transaction. In addition to the buyer and seller, the following additional organizations are likely to be involved in an international transaction:

Banks. In arranging for letters of credit and wire transfers of money, your local bank and the foreign bank representing the foreign buyer or seller are likely to play an important part in processing the transaction.

Department of Commerce. To export some products abroad you need to obtain a license from the Department of Commerce. General licenses are issued for the shipment of unrestricted products to countries that are not being embargoed. Because of embargoes against such countries as Cuba, North Korea, and others, even general-license products have been prohibited from export to them. For the export of high-technology and other products that could be used against the United States, a Special or Restricted License may be required even to friendly countries. The reason for this is that businesses operating in friendly countries have been known to transship these restricted items to prohibited countries.

Foreign Counterpart. There may be foreign counterparts to the *Department of Commerce* in each foreign country. They may or may not get involved in the transaction depending on the product and the country.

Customs officials. Domestic customs officials will be involved in approving your exports and imports as will foreign customs officials for your foreign *buyers and sellers.* They will insist that all paperwork and packaging is in order. In some countries, customs officials have been known to insist on *bribes* in order for them to allow products in the country.

Freight forwarders and export consultants. Freight forwarders and other export specialists are often enlisted to (1) pick up the shipment, (2) prepare the export paperwork, (3) book space with a freight carrier, (4) insure that it passes through customs and is shipped on time, and (5) act as the exporter's *traffic* company.

Freight carrier. Carrying product from the seller to the buyer could involve a number of different freight methods and carriers. On the *domestic* side, the goods are typically picked up by a truck or loaded on to a train that carries them to a warehouse to be stored until they can be shipped or they are taken directly to a dock for loading on to a ship or to an airport for loading onto a plane. In any event, they need to be inspected and cleared for export. The goods are then transported on their journey over the *pipeline* to the *foreign* destination. When they arrive at the *foreign* port (sea or air), they are unloaded and have to clear customs. Once through customs, the goods are loaded on to a truck or train for transport to their destination. If they are put on a train, they may have to be transferred to a truck that will carry them to their final destination. At each juncture, they are handled, inspected, loaded and unloaded. Because of all of this activity, many *things* can happen including breakage, loss, theft, or mixing-up cargo destined for different customers and locations.

Custom house brokers and import consultants. Basically what freight forwarders do for exporters, customhouse brokers do for importers. They (1) bring imported goods through customs, (2) arrange for local transportation once they clear customs, and (3) arrange for transportation from another country if the exporter hasn't already done so.

Because so many people, organizations, and activities may be involved in the transaction, the buyer should understand that the price of the shipment originally quoted by the seller can be quite different from the *fully-landed price.* To avoid being shocked, the buyer should ask the seller to provide the *fully-landed* price in a written quotation.

Paperwork

As one might expect with all the above intermediaries, international business can generate a lot of paperwork. In fact, the average oversees transaction requires 35 documents totaling 360 pages. Depending on the product and volume being shipped, paperwork costs alone account for between 1.4 to 5.7% of the shipment value. These costs should be figured into the company's cost accounting system so they will be properly reflected in pricing systems and profit calculations. Some of the documents included in the document package of an overseas transaction are described below.

1. **Export License.** This provides the authorization for the shipment.
2. **Export Bill of Lading.** Delineates *responsibility for* and *title to* the shipment. This is especially important in the event that the shipment is damaged, lost, or stolen.
3. **Insurance Certificate.** Unlike domestic carriers, international freight carriers typically do not assume responsibility for the merchandise they carry unless the loss is due to their negligence. Therefore, insuring the shipment becomes more necessary.
4. **Sales Agreement.** In addition to the quantity and description of the items purchased, as discussed in the *legal section* above, this should specify, the (1) currency, (2) payment method and terms, (3) patent and trademark protection responsibilities of the buyer, (4) jurisdiction whose laws shall govern any dispute, and (5) a binding arbitration clause.
5. **Commercial Invoice.** This contains all of the information typically included in a domestic invoice plus some or all of the following: (1) origin of the shipment, (2) export packing marks, (3) a clause stating that the goods will not be diverted to another country, (4) the name of the Letter-of-Credit (LC) bank, and (5) Letter-of-Credit numbers. Shipping companies, such as *UPS*, *FedEx*, and *DHL*, can provide you with a proforma sample of the Commercial Invoice that they require.
6. **Consular Invoice.** This is required by some countries in addition to a *Commercial Invoice.* It must be (1) purchased from the local consul, (2) written in the language of the destination country, and (3) *visaed* by the consul.
7. **Certificates of Origin.** These are required by some countries, issued by the local *Chamber of Commerce,* and visaed by the consul. This becomes an even more important issue when buyers want to patronize only certain nation's products and boycott others.
8. **Inspection Certificates.** These are usually required by buyers of foodstuffs and live animals and issued by the *Department of Agriculture.* They may also be required by the buyers of equipment who want the products validated by an independent lab or engineering firm.
9. **Letter of Credit.** If irrevocable, this cannot be canceled by the buyer once the terms and conditions are accepted by the seller. When irrevocable, the seller gets paid once documentation is provided to the foreign buyer's bank that the order has been shipped.

Special Shipment Handling Considerations

Depending on the nature of the pipeline, shipments may require special handling. Examples of such special handling are described below.

1. **Containers.** The type of container used can make a big cost difference to the buyer and the seller. Most containers are large metal boxes similar in shape to a railroad car. They have an 8-foot by 8-foot cross-section and are normally 10, 20, or 40 feet in length. Many sellers will price their shipments according to the number containers required, and many buyers will buy in terms of containers because of freight costs involved — full containers are more cost-effective to ship and handle.
2. **LASH.** An acronym for Lighter Aboard Ship, these ocean-going vessels are designed to carry special barges. These barges, in turn, are loaded in small inland waterways where ocean-going vessels cannot go. In a sense, these barges can be thought of as large containers.
3. **RO-RO.** This is an acronym for Roll-on/Roll-off. These allow vehicles with wheels to be driven on to and off of the vessel.
4. **Demurrage charge.** The *demurrage* charge is an additional charge added to the bill of an exporter or importer for the excess time required to load or unload a vessel — usually the result of inefficient export packaging and handling.
5. **Air Freight.** Unlike ocean-going vessels that can take weeks or months, air freight permits one-day shipment. While it typically costs more for this faster service, there are cost offsets that tend to lower the overall costs of air freight. They include the following: (1) **Insurance** — these costs are typically lower because there is less chance of damage to the shipment, (2) **Packing** — these costs are reduced because air freight does not require the same heavy export packing of ocean-going vessels, (3) **Customs** — there is a saving on *customs charges* because of the lower weight from reduced packing,

   (4) **Replacement costs** — since there is typically less damage with air freight, there is less cause for replacement of damaged items, (5) **Inventory costs** — quicker shipment means less need to store shipments while waiting for less-frequent ocean-vessel departures, (6) **Competitive** — since next day shipment allows companies to better compete with rivals located closer to foreign customers, it lowers competitive costs and tends to increase revenues, and (7) **Customer Satisfaction** — customers always want quicker deliveries after they decide to order so air freight tends to increase customer satisfaction.

Coordination problems

In general, *the longer the pipeline, the more that can go wrong* from any one of the above. Moreover, the longer the pipeline the more difficult the coordination of the many pipeline variables. If you develop an *import/export system* that (1) identifies the critical pipeline variables, (2) coordinates them so that they work together properly, (3) anticipates the problems that are likely to arise, (4) has contingency plans in the event something should go wrong, and (5) solves little problems before they turn into big ones, you'll be able to properly manage the *pipeline* of international business.

International Business Model Summary

Once you truly understand how to integrate and coordinate the three pieces of the international business puzzle — *domestic, foreign* and *pipeline* issues, you should be able to select the alternative methods of marketing abroad which are best suited for your company. Some of the more popular ways of doing business abroad are discussed below.

WAYS OF DOING BUSINESS ABROAD

As improvements in technology continue to shrink the world into a smaller and smaller place — the *global village,* the options for marketing abroad will continue to expand and change. The ones that you select will depend on your business philosophy, your resources, your objectives, and the technology to which you have access. For example, if you don't have the resources and experience to build plants overseas, you may want to be very conservative in your first international venture. Perhaps the most conservative method of doing business abroad is licensing your products or ideas to a foreign company.

Licensing

With licensing, the owner of the product or idea, called the *licenser*, allows the *licensee* to manufacture and market the product in a given *market territory* in exchange for a *license fee*. This *license fee* may be a prepaid lump-sum amount, known as a *fully paid-up license*, or a specific *royalty* on each unit sold. In this way, the licenser can make money oversees without investing abroad.

While licensing can be lucrative, the owner or inventor may have little or no control over how it is manufactured and marketed. This may not be a problem if the licensee is an experienced company with integrity and a good reputation. It can be a big problem, however, if the licensee does anything to ruin the image of the product or the reputation of your company. This problem can be mitigated, if the licenser includes guidelines or contract provisions for (1) manufacturing the product, (2) marketing it to customers, and (3) providing customer service. If these guidelines are not specified and enforced, the *brand image,* or *position,* of the product could be ruined along with the corporate image of the company who owns rights to it.

Even if the licensee does a good job, the domestic licenser is likely to receive little or no feedback from the marketplace about the performance of the product. Without this feedback, the licenser will not be able to make the changes necessary to satisfy the local foreign market. To solve this problem, the licenser could include a provision in the licensing contract requiring the licensee to provide this feedback. Providing *Market Information Forms* to licensees could help to insure that this information is collected in a form that is useful to the domestic licenser. Another option is for the domestic company to become more directly involved in the foreign market by selling its products through foreign agents or distributors.

Foreign distribution

As you may recall from *Chapter 8* on *Distribution,* sales agents, also known as manufacturers representatives, and distributors are common sources of distribution in foreign markets. Agents do *not* take title to (do not buy and resell) the products that they sell. They simply sell them for a client company in exchange for a commission. Distributors, on the other hand, buy the products from the company at a discount from the suggested retail price, and resell them to either retailers or directly to end buyers. The advantage of using foreign agents or distributors is that they know the local foreign language and culture and typically have already-established contacts in the foreign market territory. As with domestic agents and distributors, the disadvantage is that it is difficult to control the way in which they represent your product to their customers. This problem can be solved contractually, and by withholding product if they do not comply. Another potential disadvantage is marketplace feedback. As with licensing, unless you have a well-designed *marketing information system* that collects timely marketplace information from these foreign agents and distributors, you won't get the feedback you need to improve your products and meet the needs of foreign market targets. Again, collecting such feedback should be a contractual requirement. A mechanism, such as providing them with *Market Information Forms* and procedures for completing and forwarding them to the domestic company, should be provided.

Joint Venture

A more involved form of doing business abroad is to set up a *joint venture* with a foreign company, individual, or government who has considerable experience and contacts in doing business in a foreign territory. In a *joint venture,* both parties *share ownership and management* of the joint venture company. Some countries require that their citizens own a minimum fixed percentage of the joint-venture company. In the case of Mexico prior to NAFTA (North American Free Trade Agreement), Mexican nationals had to own at least 51% of the joint venture.

Foreign Sales Branch

Some U.S. companies decide to "go it alone" by opening their own foreign sales branch in a foreign country or territory. Even though such an operation is owned by the domestic parent company, it should employ foreign nationals from that country as an important part of the sales and administrative staff. They know the local territory, culture, and business climate, and they have already-established contacts within their country.

Wholly-owned Foreign Subsidiary

The next step beyond a foreign sales branch, is a *wholly-owned foreign subsidiary*. In such an operation, the domestic company establishes its own manufacturing and marketing presence in a foreign territory. For the reasons given above, it is important to employ foreign nationals to staff these operations — especially in the area of marketing and manufacturing supervision.

Multinational Corporation

A multinational corporation is one that operates internationally and has a headquarters in one country but has large operations and does a significant amount of business in other countries. Some large multinationals have sales revenues that are larger that the economies of many countries.

Selling Direct

With the advent of new communications and transportation technology, it is becoming feasible for companies to sell their products direct to foreign buyers via the Internet, catalogues, direct mail, trade shows, and other direct methods. As sales and operations costs continue to skyrocket and the marketplace becomes more competitive, selling direct will become more cost-effective and more widespread in the international arena.

CONCLUSION

Marketing abroad has many risks and costs associated with it. However, with the newly-emerging world markets hungry for your goods, services, and designs, the potential rewards can far outweigh the risks. In addition to providing new and exciting markets for individual companies, selling your products abroad will help to cure your country's *balance of payments* problems as well as help to right its economy. Since economies with budget deficits tend to be among the largest consuming markets and the largest donors to worthy causes, helping to improve their export sales will help to serve the interests of the entire world.

On this optimistic note, we move on to the final important chapter of this book — *Customer Service.*

[1]Donald A. Ball and William H. McCullogh, Jr., *International Business,* 4th Edition, BPI/Irwin, Homewood, IL, 1990, pg. 32.

[2]John Diebold, *Losing the Future*, ABC Special Report, aired in December of 1988.

[3]Craig Forman and Tim Carrington, "Europe's Economies are Dragging Along Despite Hopes for 1992, *Wall Street Journal,* December 26, 1991, pg A-1.

[4]Damon Darlin and Joseph B. White, "GM Venture in Korea Nears End, Betraying Firm's Fond Hopes," *Wall Street Journal,* January 16, 1992, pg. A-1.

TIPS and Exercises

1. Identify the foreign and pipeline issues you face in each of your foreign markets (use the CIA Factbook and other sources online to collect information on each of your foreign markets).
2. Use trade shows and other opportunities to identify potential foreign distributors and partners who can help you to market your products in other countries. Pick those who have a good and established track record.

Chapter 14

DNA of Customer Service

"Customer satisfaction is the ultimate goal of marketing..."

Because service is so important to the success of any company, it is appropriate that it is the subject of the last chapter of this text.

If it is so important, why isn't in one of the building blocks, or "P's", of marketing? The reason is that it is embodied in all of these building blocks, or it should be. When your company's publics think of your *corporate image* or the *position* of your products, they should be reminded of good service. When they think of your *product,* they should remember the service you provide as part of the product. When they think of *promotion,* they should believe the promise of better service. When they think of *price,* they should be reminded of the service that is included in the price. When they think of a *place* to buy your products, they should think of good service from your distributors. When they see a code on a response coupon, an toll-free number in an ad, or a questionnaire on the back of a warranty card, they should think that you have a *marketing information system* to find out what they want and how to provide them with better service. In *Chapter 6* on *Product,* we did incorporate *customer service* as an integral part of a product when we referred to it as the *peripheral component* of a *complete product.*

WHAT IS SERVICE?

Because the word "service" is used to describe several different business functions and concepts, its usage can be quite confusing. Some of the meanings of service in the context of business are provided below.

Different Meanings of Service

Repair. In some contexts, service refers to repairing a broken product.

Maintenance. Service may also refer to maintaining products to avoid breakdowns.

Product. For companies in service businesses, service refers to their main products.

Customer Service. Service often refers to answering customer questions and taking care of customer problems. Of course, this can also be confusing because, in many contexts, the term "service" refers to taking care of prospects and others who are not yet customers.

Market-driven Definition. In a market-driven company, service should be defined as everything related to taking good care of customers and other publics. Whether your organization sells goods or provides services, customer service should be thought of as an important component of your product mix.

Core and Peripheral Components

To avoid the confusion created by the different meanings above, as explained in *Chapter 6* on the *Product*, it is useful to think of a product as having two main components — a core component and a peripheral component. If a company is in a service business, such as an Internet service provider, its core component is giving customers access to the Internet. Everything else related to taking care of the customer can be thought of as its peripheral component. If a company sells tangible goods, such as computers, its core component is the computer whereas its peripheral component is the service it provides to market targets while they are shopping, during the purchase process, and after they purchase the product. In this context, repair services, maintenance services, and products that are services would all be core components, and customer service would be the peripheral component. The reason this concept of core and peripheral components is useful is that it forces everyone, whether their products are goods or services, to consciously think of the peripheral component — servicing the other needs of customers — as part of every product. Please note that this peripheral component notion fits closely with the market-driven definition of service in Chapter 6 and throughout this book.

CRITICAL FOR HIGH-TECH PRODUCTS

Due to the complexity of technical products, service is particularly important to their success. Customers want a reliable product that won't break down or cause the consumer to get sick or harmed. They want to buy it from a company that can provide them assistance in operating the product whenever they call for help. And if the product should fail, they want a company that will quickly respond to fix or replace it so their business interruption is minimized. *IBM* grew 140 times their size in thirty years in no small part because they understood the importance of servicing customers. The success of many other high-tech organizations can be traced to their market-driven approach and their unswerving devotion to taking good care of their customers.

NEGLECTED BY TOO MANY

Even though it is critically important to the success of most organizations, too many companies neglect service. In his book entitled *Marketing High Technology*, William Davidow says, *"Service is poor in many service industries, abominable in many retail stores, and totally ignored in many technology companies."* The reasons for the poor service reputation of many companies are not related to any malicious intent; they are more related to the fact that companies often concentrate their efforts on the core product rather than servicing customers. Also, they typically don't have the marketing knowhow to understand the importance of marketing and customer service. Too many are inward thinking and don't look to the market for ideas, suggestions, or needs. They have a tendency to be *"company-centric"* and really believe that a good product will sell itself. As they usually discover, products rarely, if ever, sell themselves over a sustained period.

FORCED BY THE COMPETITION

In today's marketplace, the product-driven company-centric approach is *less* likely to work. Even in very sophisticated and specialized high-technology markets, competition has grown to be fierce. In addition to domestic competitors, foreign competitors, who are unknown in the U.S., are entering markets and giving established companies a "run for their money." They are coming from foreign as well as domestic markets around the world. In many cases, they are offering a very similar product for a lower price. In order for domestic companies to compete, they have to become more service oriented as well as do better positioning.

Servicing customers is the one area where it is easier for a company to *position,* or distinguish, itself in a crowded field. Small companies can eliminate any objection to their size by offering excellent service. Customers will return to the company that gives them good service again and again. Moreover, they'll refer their friends and associates by starting a positive word-of-mouth pyramid.

SERVICE GOES FAR BEYOND MAINTENANCE AND REPAIR

In general usage, as discussed above, service refers to much more than repair and maintenance. It refers to the *treatment of the customer during every contact with the company*. The way the receptionist answers the phone, the amount of time the caller is kept on hold while waiting to speak to someone who can help, the speed at which the company can fill a customer's order, the response of the company to a customer problem, the politeness of sales and service personnel — virtually everything about the company's relationship with the customer comes under the aegis of service.

HOW TO DELIVER GOOD SERVICE

The key steps for delivering good service are summarized below.

Make a Reliable Product

The key to good service is a reliable product. Reliable products *do not* tie up customer service lines or overly stress customer service personnel. They avoid situations that anger and frustrate customers such as product breakdowns or long waits, say in bank lines, to speak with a company representative when there is a problem. Product reliability can also be featured in company promotions. The lonely *Maytag repairman* is a useful image that has been driven into the minds of the marketplace to communicate the reliability of the product. The doctor or lawyer that does not make mistakes, the actor that says the right lines, the musician who plays the right notes, the baseball player that makes the right plays are all examples of more reliable core products that are services.

Make a Commitment

The company has to be committed to providing good service. Commitment is established at the highest levels of the company. Unless is has the full support of the Chairman of the Board, the CEO, and the President, the commitment won't hold up under the strains and pressures of daily business operations. For example, the President of *Swissair* once ordered all managers to spend at least one day each month dealing with customers. He states his reason for doing this... "I want everyone, whether they are working in finance or anywhere else, to be aware that ultimately they are working on a product for a customer." During that period, *Swissair* was regularly recognized as one of the best, if not the best, airlines in the world. When *Xerox* won the *Malcolm Baldridge Award* for quality, the compensation of all *Xerox* employees, whether they work in sales or accounting, was based on how well they satisfy their customers — as measured by *Xerox's* customer satisfaction index.

Train and Supervise

Everyone in the company should be trained to deliver the highest levels of service possible. The commitment established at the top has to be translated into actions throughout the company. Managers of the company have to continually follow up to insure that their staffs are complying with the company's service commitment.

Establish the Organization and Resources

Unless the organization and the resources are in place to deliver good service, the commitment will remain an intangible and unreachable goal. Delivery of service starts with the treatment of prospects when they first contact the company. It continues with the taking of an order, the swift filling of that order, delivery, installation, and on-going response to, and support of, the needs of the customer.

Consider Distribution and Logistics

The delivery of service to local and remote areas requires a well though-out distribution and logistics plan. Properly servicing an area that is in close proximity to company headquarters is tough enough. Providing service to remote locations requires a lot more planning and thought.

Provide Quality Control

Customers are the best judges of the quality of service provided to them. Therefore, they should be given the opportunity to rate the company's service after a service call. A person in the marketing department can call customers who have recently received some form of service from the company and ask them if the service has been performed to their satisfaction. The answers should be clearly noted — for example, on a Market Information Form — and reported to both the service manager and a senior marketing executive. If the answers reflect dissatisfaction with the company's service, a technician or marketing representative should be called upon to follow up immediately and solve the problem.

THE BENEFITS OF PROVIDING GOOD SERVICE

Good service isn't always easy, but it's worth the effort. While it may cost more at the time of delivery, it costs much less over the longer run. In fact studies show that it costs *five times* as much to acquire a new customer as it does to service an existing one. Good service creates happy and satisfied customers, who in turn, serve as unpaid sales people and ambassadors for the company. It builds customer loyalty, which, in turn, builds market share and long-term profitability. It avoids unhappy situations, strained relationships, and lots of headaches. It makes employees feel better about themselves and the company for which they work. It saves lots of money — particularly in legal fees. Moreover, it generates lots of money from repeat business and customer referrals.

Increased Profitability

A study reported in the *Harvard Business Review* confirmed the monetary benefits of providing good service. This study showed that "customer retention has a direct and substantial impact on profitability, with the increase in dollar value of repeat customers ranging from 25% to 85%, depending on the industry." The report of this study by Brian S. Morgan and Diane H. Schmalensee, vice presidents of *Opinion Research,* explains that "loyal customers are more profitable because of increased purchases, reduced operating costs, the value of referrals and premium pricing."[1] While the increased purchases and value of referrals have been discussed above, the *reduced operating costs* and *premium pricing* warrant some further explanation.

Operating costs are reduced because of the following:

- *Sales costs are lower* — The time and effort to close an existing customer is substantially less than to close a new prospect. Customers are already comfortable with your company and products.

- *Customer service costs are lower* — Existing customers don't need the training and support required by new customers since they have most likely learned how to use the product on a previous purchase. They also know the procedures of doing business with your company so they don't waste the time of your personnel to traffic phone calls, answer questions, and handle problems.

Higher Prices and Greater Success

Premium pricing is possible because existing customers know your company's service capabilities and are more willing to pay for more expensive models and bundled service and support. Once they understand the added value of your service, they are able and willing to communicate them to referrals. As these referrals learn the tangible *"return on investment"* advantages of your customer service, they will be more willing to pay price premiums for your products. When the *Profit Impact of Market Strategy* program (PIMS) of the *Strategic Planning Institute* in Cambridge, Massachusetts studied 2,600 companies over fifteen years, they found that companies with superior customer service ratings, on average, (1) charge 9 percent more for their products and (2) grow twice as fast as companies with poor customer service ratings. The PIMS studies also found that companies with the highest customer service ratings also lead in other important measures of success including market share, sales, asset turnover, and return on investment.[2]

Because of these "bottom line" benefits of providing good service, everyone in the company should be trained to deliver good service and to go out of his/her way for each customer and prospect. Service should be part of each employee's job description and should be an important point on which employee evaluations and salary reviews are based.

As Robert D. Buzzell, Professor of Marketing at the Harvard Business School, states in the book *Marketing in an Electronic Age*, "...customer satisfaction (is) the ultimate goal of marketing..."[3] Remember this, practice it, and you'll reap the benefits many fold. After all, you are the company to a customer, prospect, or member of your other publics. You can make a big difference. Best of luck.

[1]"The New Appreciation of Service Quality," *Los Angeles Times,* Wednesday, November 1, 1990.

[2]Eric R. Blume, "Customer Service: Giving Companies the Competitive Edge," *Training & Development Journal,* September 1988, pg. 25

[3]Robert D. Buzzell, *Marketing in an Electronic Age*, Harvard Business School Press, Boston, 1985, pg.10.

TIPS and Exercises

1. Do whatever you can to create a customer-focused culture in your company.
2. Make sure your MIS captures customer feedback and allows you to take timely corrective actions to fix problems and avoid negative word-of-mouth pyramids.
3. Train your personnel and tie their performance reviews and compensation to how well they treat your customers and prospects.
4. Make sure everyone understands that your success and profitability is directly tied to the quality of the customer service you provide.

Bibliography

1. Alsop, Ronald and Abrams, Bill (ed.), *The Wall Street Journal On Marketing*, New York: Dow Jones-Irwin, 1986.
2. Buzzell, Robert D. (ed.), *Marketing in an Electronic Age*, Boston: The Harvard Business School Press, 1985.
3. Cateora, Philip R. and Hess, John M., *International Marketing*, Homewood, Illinois: Richard D. Irwin, Inc., 1971.
4. Davidow, William H., *Marketing High Technology: An Insiders View*, New York: The Free Press, 1986.
5. Davidow, William H., "The Ascendency of High-Tech Marketing", *Electronic Business*, May 15, 1988, pp. 130-132.
6. Kalb, Ira S., *High-Tech Marketing: A Practical Approach,* Los Angeles: K&A Press, 1988.
7. Kalb, Ira S., *Fundamentals of High-Technology Marketing: What Marketers Need to Know,* Los Angeles: K&A Press, 1997.
8. Kalb, Ira S., *Selling High-Tech Products and Services,* Los Angeles: K&A Press, 1991.
9. Large, Peter, "The Micro Revolution Revisited", as reported in "Information Overload", *Los Angeles Times Magazine,* January 22, 1989.
10. McCormick, Ernest J., *Human Factors Engineering*, New York: McGraw-Hill, 1964.
11. Nadel, Jack, *Cracking the Global Market*, New York: AMACOM, 1987.
12. Ogilvy, David, *Ogilvy on Advertising*, New York: Vintage Books, 1985.
13. Ries, Al and Trout, Jack, *Positioning: The Battle for Your Mind*, New York: Warner Books, 1986.
14. Ries, Al and Trout, Jack, *The 22 Immutable Laws of Marketing*, New York: Harper Business, 1994.
15. Rodgers, F.G. Buck, *The IBM Way*, New York: Harper and Row, 1886.
16. Sculley, John, *Odyssey Pepsi to Apple*, New York: Harper and Row, 1987.
17. Shanklin, William L. and Ryans Jr., John K., *Marketing High Technology*, New York: Lexington Books, 1984.

18. Toffler, Alvin, *Future Shock*, New York: William Morrow and Company, Inc., 1970.
19. Toffler, Alvin, *The Third Wave*, New York: William Morrow and Company, Inc., 1980.
20. Wentz, Walter B. and Eyrich, Gerald I., *Marketing Theory and Application*, New York: Harcourt, Brace & World, Inc., 1970.

Index

V

W

X

Y

Z

ANOTHER BOOK FROM DNA PRESS THAT YOU MAY ENJOY OR USE AS A GIFT

VISIT US AT WWW.DNAPRESS.COM

THE REAL ESTATE RECIPE: MAKE MILLIONS BY BUYING SMALL APARTMENT PROPERTIES IN YOUR SPARE TIME

Brian K. Friedman

ISBN 0-9748765-9-3

Using step-by-step instructions, sample cases, easy to understand worksheets and real life examples, ***The Real Estate Recipe*** provides the disciplines and analytical tools essential to successful apartment property investing. ***The Real Estate Recipe*** clearly explains:

- Why you should invest in apartment properties;
- Why apartment properties are the safest of all real estate investments;
- How to simply and thoroughly understand real estate investments;
- How to find and buy an apartment property, from the search to the closing table; and
- How to ensure predictable and successful results.

The Real Estate Recipe: Make Millions by Buying Small Apartment Properties in Your Spare Time is a groundbreaking tool for building wealth, engaging in its logic and simplicity.

★ ★ ★

"*The Real Estate Recipe* provides the most detailed framework I have ever seen for pursuing, evaluating, and structuring an apartment building investment. This book includes secrets utilized by seasoned industry professionals with guidelines and illustrations easy to follow for first time investors. *The Real Estate Recipe* is an indispensable resource for experienced apartment owners and anyone looking to get into multifamily ownership as an investment."

Robert D. Falese III, Senior Vice President
General Motors Acceptance Corporation
Commercial Mortgage